# States of Siege

# STATES OF SIEGE
## U.S. Prison Riots, 1971–1986

Bert Useem and Peter Kimball

OXFORD UNIVERSITY PRESS
New York   Oxford

## Oxford University Press

Oxford    New York    Toronto
Delhi    Bombay    Calcutta    Madras    Karachi
Petaling Jaya    Singapore    Hong Kong    Tokyo
Nairobi    Dar es Salaam    Cape Town
Melbourne    Auckland

and associated companies in
Berlin    Ibadan

Copyright © 1991 by Oxford University Press, Inc.

First published in 1989 by Oxford University Press, Inc.,
200 Madison Avenue, New York, New York 10016

Library of Congress Cataloging-in-Publication Data

Useem, Bert. States of siege : U.S. prison riots, 1971–1986/
by Bert Useem and Peter Kimball.
p.    cm.    Bibliography: p.    Includes index.

1. Prison riots—United States—Case studies.
I. Kimball, Peter.    II. Title.
HV9471.U84 1989    365'.641—dc20    88-18792    CIP
ISBN 0-19-505711-2 (Cloth)
ISBN 0-19-507271-5 (Paper)

2  4  6  8  9  7  5  3  1

Printed in the United States of America

# Acknowledgments

This research was made possible by the generous support of the National Science Foundation; the National Institute of Justice (U.S. Department of Justice); and the University of Illinois at Chicago's Research Board, Office of Social Science Research, the Institute for Government Affairs, and Department of Sociology. We greatly appreciate this support and the trust that lay behind it.

Many others were just as essential. Roger and Kathy Morris helped get us started in Santa Fe. Roger shared with us the material he had collected for *The Devil's Butcher Shop*, his book on the riot at the Penitentiary of New Mexico. As we did our own investigation, we came to appreciate the integrity of this work, and the craft of a superb investigative journalist. Also, Helen Gausion, of the New Mexico Department of Corrections, gave freely of her time as we conducted our interviews.

Important in the study of the Joliet riot were the insights and documents provided by Pat MaCannany (Department of Criminal Justice, University of Illinois at Chicago), Janet Musengo (John Howard Association), and Ruthann DeWolfe (Chicago Legal Services Corporation). Robert Buchanan, founder and president of the Correctional Services Group, benefited us with his superb memory of events that had occurred more than a decade earlier, and then gave us an enjoyable tour of Kansas City.

William Kime of the Michigan Department of Corrections kindly assisted our efforts there; we are very grateful to him. One of the authors served briefly as a consultant to the state legislative committee which investigated the 1981 riots and which was chaired by the very able Jeffrey Padden. This experience was important in shaping our agenda. Michael Hodge, formerly of the Attorney General's Office in Michigan, provided a number of documents and an insightful discussion of the post-riot events.

In West Virginia, Warden Jerry Hedrick opened up his penitentiary to us and rose above the call of duty in granting a lengthy interview despite a severe flu. Donald Poffenberger, the court-appointed special master of West Virginia Penitentiary, gave us a foot-deep pile of documents and other assistance. John Price, Governor Arch Moore's press secretary, helped arranged interviews in Charleston and discussed the events freely and intelligently. Paul

Nyden helped us gain access to the computerized archives of the *Charleston Gazette* and *Charleston Daily Mail*.

Back in Chicago, Joseph Peterson and Michael Maltz, as directors of the Center for Research on Law and Justice, provided us office space and an environment in which the project could go forward. David Fogel, a Center Associate, helped us with his extensive contacts around the country. Without his assistance, many of the doors that did open up might have stayed closed.

Most of the effort in this study was in collecting the details of the events under examination. But in collecting these details, we often found it difficult to know beforehand which information would be relevant to the final story. As a result, the first drafts were much too long. Fortunately, we were saved by critical readers who told us to shorten and tighten the entire work. For this, and much other perspicacious advice, we thank Richard Cloward, Frances Fox Piven, Jack Bloom, David Rubinstein, Patty Davies Useem, Natalie Star, Anthony Orum, and Helene Fine.

Finally, we thank our respondents—inmates, correctional officers, prison officials, state officials, and other parties involved in the routine administration of the prisons. We have tried to give back to them as honest and insightful an account as we could muster.

*Chicago, Illinois*                                                     B. U.
*August 1988*                                                          P. K.

# Contents

# 1

# Introduction

Imagine a place with half a million people. Though it has twice the population of Iceland, it is not a country; though it has more inhabitants than Vermont or North Dakota, it is not a state. Though its residents are packed together much more densely than Clevelanders—whom they outnumber—it is not a city.

The residents are forbidden to own weapons; they are punished for peaceful protest. They are mostly destitute, often illiterate. And they are much more heavily policed than the natives of the most oppressive dictatorship.

Yet there are continual revolts. As often as several dozen times a year, the residents of one or another "neighborhood" will briefly drive out the forces of the government. They do so even though they know that the restoration of order is absolutely inevitable. Are they heroes, or lunatics?

The people in question are U.S. citizens; the "place" is the U.S. prison system. The revolts, over 300 since 1970, are commonly known as "prison riots." Under that name, they are deceptively familiar to us. You don't have to be a sociologist to have a theory about prison riots:

> —There's nothing mysterious about prison riots. Many or most prisoners are violent, depraved, or even insane. Naturally they go wild, kill, burn, and loot.
> —There's nothing mysterious about prison riots. Conditions in prison are miserable—overcrowded, dangerous, degrading, and filthy. Everyone knows that people revolt against miserable living conditions.
> —There's nothing mysterious about prison riots. Liberal judges have made it impossible to enforce discipline in prison. Guards are powerless to enforce order.
> —Radical organizations stir up violence.
> —Prisoners are crowded together like rats in a cage. Naturally their frustration builds up and eventually explodes.
> —It's all racial.
> —It's the work of gangs.

—It's the only way the prison inmate has of reaching out to the public. It's a "cry for help."

These are not stupid theories. Every one of them has been seriously defended by scholars or professionals in the corrections field. Every one sounds somewhat plausible. For every theory, you can find a riot that seems to prove it—and several others that seem to refute it. Questions arise, such as:

—If prison riots happen because conditions are bad—or, for that matter, because criminals are violent people—why do they happen in some years and not in others? In some prison systems and not in others? Prison conditions are unpleasant everywhere, and criminals are always known as violent and anti-social. Why aren't there riots everywhere and all the time?

—If prison riots are "cries for help," why do inmates make no demands in some prison riots?

—If rioting inmates are such anti-social people, why are some riots so businesslike and well organized? How can leadership arise which enforces order, protects dissenters, organizes first aid, shares and distributes food, and protects hostages from violent inmates?

Perhaps we should say what the term "prison riot" means in this book. In common usage, we think of "riots" as unorganized, maybe even mindless events. To most people, "riot" is one thing, "protest" something else. Protestors have slogans, political beliefs, grievances; rioters steal, burn, and destroy. "Riot" is a pejorative term; and this is why scholars who saw political content and significance in the urban disorders of the 1960s made a point of calling them "rebellions" or "uprisings," not "riots."

Interestingly, the usage among prisoners can be just the opposite. To them, a "prison riot" is expected to be rather organized and predictable: prisoners with grievances seize hostages and territory, win public attention, and bargain for reform. Such, one inmate told us, is a "real" riot; he went on to claim that the disturbance at his prison wasn't a proper riot at all, being just too anarchic.

We mention these contrasting uses of the term "riot" in order to advise the reader that we do not use either one. For us, a prison riot occurs when the authorities lose control of a significant number of prisoners, in a significant area of the prison, for a significant amount of time. It is just about the only thing the riots in our study have in common.

What prisoners do in that time and space varies *a lot* from riot to riot. Some are mere racial brawls among inmates; in others, inmate leaders consciously promote racial harmony. Others have no leaders at all. Some are good-natured looting sprees; others, the rationally calculated tactics of gangs. Some are highly ideological rebellions; others serve largely as a chance for inmates to steal from each other—or murder each other. Inmates may take guards hostage and torture them—or treat them kindly—or take no hostages at all. In cost, in casualties, in organization, they span the spectrum. Is there any pattern to all this?

We offer case studies of prison riots in five states, representing some portion of the spectrum of variation. This is in no way a "random" or representative sample of prison riots; it is an exploratory study, aimed at looking for new insights and giving old ones a rough test. We selected riots on which we were able to obtain information and which we thought were somehow "noteworthy." All were in men's prisons. There is a certain bias toward "big" riots. Smaller, more quickly subdued riots are common but give less of a chance to see how rioting inmates behave.

Actually, we can impose a certain degree of order on our discussion and comparison of riots by distinguishing five stages in the loss, then re-establishment, of control by the state.[1] First, we distinguish the *pre-riot* stage, the period preceding the riot during which prisoners and the forces of the state develop those material and cognitive resources which will determine the course of the riot event. This is followed by the *initiation*, the action by prisoners which first crosses the line into open rebellion; and the initial response by the state. Assuming the disturbance is not immediately crushed, a stage of *expansion* begins, during which the prisoners most often try to take control of as many human, material, and spatial resources as possible against the resistance or non-resistance of the state.

A more or less stable *state of siege* often follows, during which the prisoners control some territory in the institution, the state assembles its forces and concentrates its options for recapture, and bargaining may (but need not) go on among the state, prisoners, and other parties. The last stage is *termination* or *recapture*. This sparse framework will help to organize the case studies, and we will elaborate more on the characteristics of the different stages in the conclusion.

We believe that from the close study of these incidents in their contexts, some insights emerge—not only about prisons and prisoners, but also about the more general topics of revolt, violence, politics, and even human nature.

In the concluding chapter, we will argue in behalf of a theory with which we propose to predict when and where prison riots are likely. There are several existing schools of theory in sociology which attempt to account for collective action in one context or another, and the reader may want to bear them in mind and mentally test them on the case studies.

"Deprivation" theories argue the common-sense position that riots and protests come in response to bad conditions. Conditions may be objectively bad, or they may be bad in comparison with some frame of reference—how some other group in society is treated, for example. Theories which emphasize the latter point are "relative deprivation" theories.[2]

"Resource mobilization" theorists contend that everyone always can find something to complain about; the key factor enabling groups to take action, in their view, is the availability of material and organizational resources.[3]

"Breakdown" theorists believe that social peace is the product of social mechanisms which channel human desires and actions into "acceptable" paths. These mechanisms range from religion through law to the individual's socialization within the family setting. Riots, suicides, crime, and other disorderly behavior are signs that something has gone haywire with these mechanisms.[4]

"Collective behavior" theorists usually study more chaotic and random phenomena, like fads, rumors, drunken mobs, panic in crowded theaters, and behavior at the scene of disasters. They emphasize the somewhat unpredictable selection of a behavior pattern by a group jostled loose from its familiar routines.[5]

Obviously this is the most cursory possible review of a whole sub-discipline within sociology. We describe the field in more detail in Appendix A, and we encourage interested readers not to stop there but to go on to the sources listed in our notes.

The only important pre-existing sociological theory of prison riots, that of Gresham Sykes, is a classical breakdown theory.[6] Sykes believed that the peaceful prison is (or was earlier in this century) rather personalistic and corrupt. Cliques of inmates run the joint, getting a fat rake-off. They help the administration preserve order so as not to risk losing a good thing. Reform-minded administrators play snake to this Eden. Naively dethroning the inmate cliques, depriving them of their power to reward and punish, they actually take the lid off the kettle. Young punks see their chance to make a name for themselves, and start riots.

This theory has a lot of appeal to sociologists. It is squarely in the tradition of the discipline; its emphasis on the unforeseen dangers of modernization, which breaks up traditional forms of social organization, dates right back to Durkheim and Comte, the founders of modern sociology. This theory has been advanced as an explanation for the New Mexico riot of 1980.[7] We will take up the current adequacy of this theory at the appropriate point.

In writing this book, we received a great deal of help and trust from all sorts of people, from governors to murderers. Correctional officials in Michigan, New Mexico, and West Virginia were remarkably openhanded with us, letting us interview inmates at will, with no assurance of how we would judge them or their systems. Guards were cooperative and communicative, even though university sociologists are sometimes suspected of being the liberal allies of criminals. Inmates told us their stories for hours, most of them with great frankness, even though they had no proof of who we were and their stories often contained evidence against themselves.

We are pretty confident that this book is of use to those interested in prisons and social conflicts. We would like to be as sure that it will improve the lives of all who helped us; but that may be a tall order. Inmates generally have high hopes that if the public finds out "how things really are in here," the majority would demand better prisons. Many guards are equally sure that an informed public would want them given more power and inmates fewer rights. Administrators may read this book as a manual for riot prevention and resolution. In the long run, knowledge improves human life. It's the short run that's troublesome.

# I

# PRISONS AND PRISON RIOTS IN THE 1970s

# 2

# The Historical Context: 1950–1975

Prison riots change with time and place. They are shaped by the political events and issues of the day, the prevailing ideas about imprisonment, and the political struggles in and around prisons. To understand the Attica and Joliet riots, then, we start with a brief disucussion of prisons and their context in the post–World War II years. We divide these years into two periods, which we term "confidence and rehabilitationism" (1950–1965) and "conflict and politicization" (1966–1975).

## Confidence and Rehabilitationism (1950—1965)

In the first decade following the Allied victory, Americans felt confident of their institutions. The economy prospered, and American democracy seemed obviously superior to totalitarian socialism.

The crime rate also gave no reason for alarm. In 1960 sociologist Daniel Bell wrote that "there is probably less crime today in the United States than existed a hundred, or fifty, or even twenty-five years ago, and that today the United States is a more lawful and safe country than popular opinion imagines."[1] Bell's assurances were well founded. The crime rate was low in the 1950s, and declining for some types of crime. The murder rate, for example, fell from 6.9 per 100,000 persons in 1946 to 4.5 per 100,000 in 1962—a one-third decrease.[2]

The prisons, as well, seemed relatively trouble free and inexpensive. In 1950, state and federal penitentiaries held 166,000 prisoners, a decline of 8,000 from a decade earlier.[3] The prison question stirred little passion in public debate. Further, among those concerned with prisons, there was a growing sense that prisons could contribute to the common good in a way they never had before. Prison reformers had long sought to make the "rehabilitation" of inmates the primary goal of imprisonment. Now they were joined by lawmakers and prison officials around the country.[4] Many states passed "indeterminate sentence" laws, which gave their parole boards the authority to tailor the length of an inmate's sentence to the time it would take to "cure" him or her.[5] To underscore its commitment to therapeutic treatment, the American Prison Association in 1954 voted to change its name to the American Correctional Association. The association also counseled its members to redesignate their prisons "correctional institutions" and the punishment blocks in them "adjustment centers."[6]

Two developments, though, threatened the stability in and optimism over prisons. One was a tidal wave of prison riots—40 of them over an 18-month period starting in April 1952. This was more than had occurred in the previous quarter century.[7] Although the disturbances did evoke academic and popular criticism of the prisons—for inmate idleness and poor housing conditions — the criticisms were narrowly drawn in two key respects. First, the riots did not shake the belief in the rehabilitative ideal. Indeed, the disturbances were cited as evidence that more resources had to be put behind the effort.[8]

Second, inmate rioters were viewed not as rational actors making serious demands, but as deranged thugs. One penal expert declared:

> the ringleaders are reckless and unstable men who are not accustomed to weigh the consequences of their actions. . . . The unstable prisoners, of the type generally placed in the vague but convenient category of "psychopaths" and more inelegantly classified in prisons as "screwballs," are the most ready recruits for any riot task force.[9]

Of course, such "screwballs" could have nothing useful to say about prisons or prison riots. Accordingly, when Michigan officials investigated a major riot at the Jackson facility, they interviewed many guards and administrative personnel, and a few inmates who had opposed the riot, but none of the actual riot participants.[10]

Another development which prison officials saw, rightly or wrongly, as destabilizing was the growing number of inmates who identified with the Black Muslim movement. As black inmates grew in number—from 17,200 in 1950 to 28,500 in 1960—mosques in major cities around the country actively recruited them.[11]

Prison officials responded harshly. The 1962 convention of the American Correctional Association passed a resolution denouncing the Muslims as a "race hatred" group unworthy of the special treatment given to bona fide religious groups.[12] Muslim inmates could expect to be denied access to Islamic reading material, visits by their ministers, and the special diets they requested. The warden of a federal prison in Terre Haute, Indiana, gained the notice of his colleagues around the country for having solved the "Muslim problem" which he had faced upon taking office, by breaking up their labor details and isolating them from one another.[13]

Muslim inmates filed hundreds of lawsuits, but with little success.[14] According to the courts' "hands-off" doctrine, inmates experienced a "civil death" upon imprisonment. They could still challenge the fact of their imprisonment, but not the prison conditions, which were left to the discretion of prison officials. In the absence of legal protection, organized dissent by Muslims, or any other group, could not get very far.

In sum, the optimistic spirit of the the 1950s and opening years of the 1960s spilled over to thinking about prisons. It was hoped that new rehabilitationist policies would restore those who could not, through legitimate means, enjoy the fruits of a democratic, prospering society. A wave of prison riots tempered, but did not dispel, this hope.

### Conflict and the Decline of Rehabilitationism (1966–1975)

The 1971 Attica riot had a far more profound effect. In part, this was because of the extensive media coverage given to the riot, including television broadcasts of the negotiations between the inmates and prison authorities. Also, the riot's 43 deaths were (and still are) unsurpassed. More important, however, the riot crystallized doubts about the purposes of imprisonment in America. Three broad forces—a revolution of rising entitlements, fear of public disorder, and a decline in confidence in public institutions—brought these doubts to the fore.

### *Rise of Social Entitlement*

The "revolution of rising entitlements," as Daniel Bell has called it, has not yet run its course.[15] Status groups have not ceased to present to the political and judicial systems their demands for a guarantee of equal treatment, for affirmative action, for benefits they claim that statutes, the Constitution, or the principles of fair play entitle them to. Racial minorities demanded the right to equal education; the poor claimed the right to subsistence and welfare benefits; mental patients claimed the right to treatment; the criminally accused claimed the right to a lawyer, to be informed of his/her rights; and prisoners claimed the full range of citizenship rights previously denied to them.

The federal courts have elevated many of these claims to the level of judicially protected rights. In 1953, the Supreme Court in *Brown v. Board of Education* struck down the "separate but equal" doctrine; in 1966, a federal district judge ruled that patients in mental hospitals have a right to treatment; in three rulings made between 1968 and 1970, the Supreme Court recognized the right of welfare recipients to public assistance.[16]

What the courts have not granted, Congress often has. The Civil Rights Act of 1964, the Age Discrimination in Employment Act, the Rehabilitation Act of 1973, and a host of others are examples. Congress also reordered its spending priorities. In 1960, defense consumed 52 percent of the federal

budget, and social welfare programs, 28 percent. By 1975, these proportions
were more than reversed: defense took 26 percent and social welfare, 54
percent.[17]

In short, the last three decades have brought significant gains to so many
groups on so many fronts that one can hardly think of an example of discrimination or stigma that can be counted on as unchangeable and, hence, legitimate. It is incontestable that the civil rights movement played a major role in
the making of this "revolution." Within the space of ten years (from *Brown* to
the passage of the Civil Rights Act), virtually the entire multifarious panoply
of formal racial segregation, legally mandated or privately enforced, was
outlawed. In winning these victories, the black movement taught militancy to
the rest of society. It became general knowledge that the power of the police,
the mandate of the law, and the moral consensus of the elite may be defied by
a movement convinced of the justice of its cause. Hereafter no government
action would be entitled to unquestioning deference.

The decisions of the Warren Court also created new avenues whereby
convicted prisoners could appeal their convictions, and this drew thousands
into legal activity. Filing motions and writs became a common activity of
inmates, and it was only a short step from challenging convictions to challenging the conditions of imprisonment. Arrested persons became sensitive to
perceived violations of their constitutional rights at every step of the criminal
justice process, and saw legal challenges to decisions by police, judges, and
correctional authorities alike as potentially fruitful. In a decision involving a
raid by Chicago police officers on the home of a black family, the Supreme
Court resurrected a civil rights law passed during Reconstruction as a remedy
for persons deprived of their constitutional rights "under color of law." Inmates quickly learned that nearly any unpleasant act by a prison administrator
or guard could be framed as a violation of due process and challenged as a
"Section 1983" suit.

Further, in the mid-1960s courts, especially federal courts, began to in-
tervene aggressively on behalf of inmates, chipping away and finally demolishing the "hands-off" doctrine. The courts abolished corporal punishment and imposed limitations on the duration and conditions of solitary
confinement. The Muslims won the right to practice their religion. The right
to adequate medical care was established, as was the right to communicate
with lawyers and the courts, and to be free from arbitrary censorship of mail
and publications. Inmates gained the right to express political beliefs and
practice limited forms of political activity. Inmates were also given the right
to procedural due process in parole hearings and disciplinary hearings. In
some areas, the courts held the line and refused to expand the rights of
inmates. But one principle was firmly established: inmates have an unchal-
lengeable right to bring their complaints to the courts and receive a serious
hearing.[18] By 1974, the Supreme Court could state with little shock to anyone: "There is no iron curtain drawn between the Constitution and the
prisons of this country."[19]

## Backlash Against "Disorder"

The 1960s became a decade of political turmoil and social conflict. For those who saw themselves as part of or benefited by the revolution of entitlements, it was an exhilarating time during which important demands and statements were made and many victories won. For those who did *not,* it was a terrible and fearful time. Most of those whites who had enjoyed settled, comfortable lives came to see themselves as attacked or endangered. Of course, some of this was a direct effect of the success of the civil rights movement; one was no longer free to discriminate in who one hired, and blacks might turn up in one's neighborhood or in one's children's school without warning. But the fear went beyond the unpleasantness of integration per se, and even beyond fear of the physical violence that prejudice associates with blacks. It was a physically dangerous public disorder that many whites feared, a phenomenon associated with political strife on the one hand and with random criminal violence on the other. There were several sources for this fear: an apparent disappearance of norms governing public conduct, a real increase in political violence and disorder per se, and an increase in violent crime.

Any sociologist in the tradition of Durkheim believes in the importance of a collective moral standard. Without its stabilizing effect, people go off balance, fall prey to uncontrolled lust and greed, and become dangerous to themselves and others. In the absence of such a standard, external control by the police becomes much more important in the ongoing effort to save society from anarchy.

Many homeowners believe this too; and the 1960s put them on notice that millions of youth no longer shared their moral standard, at least insofar as it proscribed long hair for men, unconventional dress, nudity, recreational sex, consumption of euphoriants and hallucinogens, use of "dirty words" in oral and written speech, and non–Judeo-Christian religion. Furthermore, restrictions on the place, manner, and content of political expression which had taken on the appearance of moral consensus were not respected. Political speech was disrespectful of authority figures, vulgar, and contemptuous toward the flag. As for content, the rise of black power and Black Nationalism, opposition to the Vietnam War, and the resurgence in popularity of socialist and communist doctrines brought into prominence ideas which many had come to believe immoral to disseminate.

This climate of moral and political dissension magnified the perceived danger from the existing level of political disorder. The assassinations of the Kennedy brothers, Martin Luther King, and Malcolm X within a five-year period, and the skepticism that attended the Warren Report, sharpened the picture of the political system as a shaky edifice.

Adding to the threat were the urban riots at mid-decade. In 1964, riots broke out in New York, Chicago, and five other cities. In 1965, a riot in Los Angeles lasted six days, left 34 dead, and resulted in $40 million in property damage. The violence crested in the summer of 1967, when 41 disorders occurred, 8 of which reached major proportions. The two most serious, in Detroit and Newark, left 83 dead and required the National Guard and the army to quell. Major rioting also occurred the following year in response to the assassination of Martin Luther King. In many of these disturbances, rioters engaged in pitched battles with the police, National Guardsmen, and firemen over control of the streets. The targets of the looting, vandalism, and arson were not randomly chosen, but tended to be white-owned stores and other property.[20]

Disorders on campus were also a serious concern, particularly to those baby-boom parents whose children were attending college and might be injured or (worse) recruited.

In 1968, the anti-war movement, the predominantly white youth counter-culture, and important sections of the black movement coalesced for joint action at the Democratic National Convention in Chicago. A member of the *New York Times* staff described the mood of defiance:

> Running through . . . the Chicago streets in that fateful week [were] demonstrators—peaceful and violent, purposeful and confused, inflammatory and jocular, bitter and idealistic—alternatively parading their grievances against flag, country, party and all established doctrines of order and decorum and defying the efforts to contain or disperse them, resorting to petty insult or outrageous taunt of the police but driven also to physical barricading, the throwing of rocks and other dangerous objects, the burning of trash cans and the spreading of foul-smelling chemicals.[21]

The demonstrators were met by a "police riot" —an indiscriminate use of violence against demonstrators, onlookers, newsmen and photographers, and passers-by.

In this same period, the previously low and steady crime rate turned sharply upward. In the last year of the steady rates, 1963, there were 190 violent crimes per 100,000 persons; in 1968 the rate had increased to 298, and by 1971 it stood at 396. By 1972, the murder rate was 9.4 per 100,000, more than double its level of a decade earlier.[22]

Cities, in particular, were becoming increasingly dangerous and unpleasant places to live and work in. In Chicago, homicides increased from 30 to 80 per month between 1965 and 1974. In November 1974, there were 110 homicides, 31 in one weekend.[23] "The litany of urban disorders," Piven and Cloward wrote in 1971, "is by now familiar: rising rates of gang delinquency and other forms of juvenile delinquency, such as school vandalism; spreading drug addiction; an alarming increase in serious crimes, such as armed robbery and burglary."[24] Further, they went on, the objects of attack and violence spread from the black ghetto to the white world and its representatives. Whereas gangs of black youths had fought each other in the 1940s and 1950s, they now began to attack whites on the streets. Teachers working in ghetto schools, welfare caseworkers making home visits in black neighborhoods, and police making arrests on the ghetto streets were increasingly assaulted and harassed.[25]

The rising crime rate and political challenges cut deeply into Americans' feelings of security and sense of order. A February 1968 Gallup poll indicated that, for the first time since scientific polling began in the 1930s, the public rated crime and lawlessness as the most important domestic problem facing the country. A Harris poll, conducted just before the Democratic National Convention, found that 81 percent of the American public believed that law and order had broken down.[26] Perhaps more telling is a 1966 survey of 1,000 Boston homeowners. The purpose of the survey was to find out how big-city residents perceived the "urban crisis." The investigator concluded:

> The "conventional" urban problems—housing, transportation, pollution, urban renewal, and the like—were a major concern of only 18 percent of those questioned, and these were expressed disproportionately by the wealthier, better-educated respondents. Only 9 percent mentioned jobs and employment, even though many of those interviewed had incomes at or even below what is often regarded as the poverty level. *The issue which concerned more respondents than any other was variously stated—crime, violence, rebellious youth, racial tensions, public immorality, delinquency. However stated, the common theme seemed to be a concern for improper behavior in public places.*
>
> For some white respondents this was no doubt a covert way of indicating anti-Negro feelings. But it was not primarily that, for these same forms of impropriety were mentioned more often than other problems by Negro respondents as well. (emphasis in original)[27]

In response to the rising level of disorder, Congress in 1968 established the Law Enforcement Administrative Agency (LEAA), which was to spend over $8 billion to upgrade courts, state and local police, community programs, and prisons.[28]

## Decline in Confidence in Institutions

A third important change was a sharp decline in public confidence in government and other institutions. Opinion polls charted this trend. Beginning 1958, the Survey Research Center of the University of Michigan asked samples of Americans four questions to find out how much they "trust" the national government. From 1958 to 1964, the level of mistrust increased only slightly, an average of 5 percent over the four questions. In the next six years, to 1970, public trust in government plummeted 17 percentage points across the four questions.[29]

Americans' faith in the specific branches of the government and other private institutions followed a similar pattern. The Harris polling firm found that, between 1966 and 1971, the proportion of Americans having a "great deal of confidence" in the people running 17 different institutions declined (on the average) from 48 to 28 percent. For example, the proportion having a great deal of confidence in the leadership of Congress dropped from 42 to 19 percent; of the Supreme Court, from 50 to 23 percent; of the executive branch, from 41 to 23 percent; of education, from 61 to 37 percent; of organized religion, from 41 to 27 percent; and even of medicine, from 72 to 61 percent.[30]

## Effects on Prisons

These three developments—rising entitlements, backlash against disorder, and decline in confidence—created a volatile political environment in and around prisons. Most basic was a breakdown in the consensus over the purposes of imprisonment and the norms that govern their operation. As Allen observes, the rehabilitative ideal can prevail only under certain cultural conditions, including a widespread belief that society's institutions are effective and trustworthy.[31] As this belief began to erode in the late 1960s, the earlier confidence in rehabilitation gave way to pessimism and doubt among some and open hostility among other. Critics on the left charged that rehabilitation works not primarily to help the prisoner overcome his difficulties, but as part of the apparatus of social control and domination.[32] Rehabilitation focuses attention on the convict's psychological deficiencies, it was charged, and ignores the "social" causes of crime.

Further, if one is permitted to believe that the criminal is under the grip of psychic difficulties, then his demands for prison reform can be dismissed as one more manifestation of his imbalance (as with the prison rioters of the 1950s). This of course was anathema to the left, which saw prison rebellions as a constituent element of the broader movement for social change. Finally, the indeterminate sentence came under attack. Not only did it produce inequities in time served for the same crime, but it gave prison authorities another tool to break any inmate resistance. Rebellious inmates could be kept in prison indefinitely for their rebelliousness.

Rehabilitationist policies also drew fire from conservative critics.[33] They charged that rehabilitationism contributed to the skyrocketing rates of crime, insofar as it fostered the coddling of inmates and the early release of dangerous inmates. As the pains (and certainty) of imprisonment went down, it became increasingly "rational" to commit crimes, these critics alleged.

It was in this context of attacks from both left and right that the rehabilitative approach suffered a devastating blow. Researchers discovered, much to their surprise, that inmates who had received treatment were just as likely to return to prison as those who had not. Rehabilitation, apparently, didn't work. This intellectual crisis is commonly associated with an article published by sociologist Robert Martinson in 1974; but the doubts had crystallized at least a half-decade earlier.[34] "By 1970," John Irwin observed, "the opinion of critical criminologists was that nothing that correctional program planners could do would significantly alter rates of recidivism."[35] Some tried to rebut these claims, but none did so with much success.

The decline of the rehabilitative ideal, however, did not mark the end of prison reform efforts; instead they took a different direction with a new ideology, justificatory vocabulary, and policy recommendations. If the image of the inmate under the rehabilitative approach was that of victim, to be helped and perhaps pitied, the new image was that of citizen, with all the rights and dignities of their fellow citizens outside the walls. Among those "rights" were the right to freedom of speech and religion; the right to a certain standard of living, including the right to live in an uncrowded cell, the right to decent food, recreation, and visitation; and the right to be free from punishment without an evidentiary hearing. Perhaps most important, the prisoner, like any citizen, could call upon the court system to protect his or her rights. Finally, in this "progressive" view of imprisonment, inmates are allowed, if not encouraged, to aggregate their interests and express them through formally established groups. This may extend as far as administrative recognition of gangs, inmate councils, and political groups. This "citizenship model" was rooted in the cultural and political swing toward entitlements and reinforced by court decisions described above.

One of the boldest efforts to put the citizenship model into practice occurred at the Washington State Penitentiary at Walla Walla over a four-year period beginning in 1970.[36] Again, there was the symbolic change of terminology: prisoners were no longer "inmates" (as the rehabilitationists had designated them) but "residents." The key reform gave the inmates the right to elect an inmate government that exercised real power. The elected representatives could move freely through the prison to talk to their constituents and could contact the media directly, hold press conferences in the prison, and tour the state to give lectures. The council had control over its own budget and met regularly with the warden, to whom it could propose reforms in all areas of prison life. The reforms granted included inmate representation on disciplinary and classification hearings; liberalization of dress and hair codes; and the right to organize ethnic, hobby, and other special interest groups with few restraints. (The outcome of this experiment is discussed in the conclusion.)

Whereas the rehabilitative ideal had been largely accepted among prison administrators in the 1950s (whether or not in fact they practiced it), prison officials became deeply divided over the citizenship model. Its advocates tended to be younger and politically liberal, to hold advanced academic degrees, and to agree with the ideas underlying the Supreme Court's decisions and the social-justice approach to crime control. The chief architect of the Walla Walla reforms, Dr. William Conte, was a psychiatrist whose background was outside corrections. Those opposed to reform tended to align themselves with a get-tough approach to crime control, to hold conservative political views, to oppose the ideas embodied in many of the Supreme Court decisions, and to have risen through the ranks.

A second major consequence of the changes of the 1960s was an increase in the flow of information, ideas, language, and models of behavior from the prison to the politically active public, and vice versa. A sizeable number of anti-war and civil rights activists, draft resisters, and middle-class drug users were imprisoned in this period. Although often confined in the least punitive prisons for short periods, they did come in contact with more "traditional" prisoners, learned their grievances, and conveyed them to the public after their release.[37]

Advocacy groups for inmates sprang up around the country.[38] In 1969, for example, seven radical Illinois lawyers established the Peoples Law Office (PLO). Living at first on subsistence wages, PLO lawyers provided legal representation to Black Panthers and other leftist groups, then served on the legal defense team at Attica. Later they represented inmates filing class action suits at the federal penitentiary at Marion, Illinois and many of the Illinois state prisons.[39] A second project, Prison Legal Services of Illinois, was started in 1971 by three public interest lawyers. By the mid-1970s, the project employed 7 full-time attorneys and 47 others and "was a potent force in the life of northern Illinois prisons."[40]

Some of the prisoners' rights projects were funded by federal funds channeled through anti-poverty programs; others were sustained by state and local funds; and still others received contributions from private foundations. Counting funds only from the latter, prisoners' rights groups received $200 million in 1969, the first year any such grants were made. By 1975, that figure had risen to almost a billion dollars ($900 million). This was followed by five somewhat leaner years, though still averaging in each year over $600 million in contributions.[41]

Among the first advances made by these prisoners' rights lawyers were constraints on the power of the state to suppress communication with the outside, to punish inmates who filed legal challenges, and to use coercion to stifle dissent. An inmate in Illinois' Stateville prison in the 1950s had been allowed to write one letter a week, and incoming and outgoing mail was censored. He stood to be beaten if he attempted to escape, defied an officer, or complained to the outside.[42] By the end of the 1960s, inmates had relatively free access to the outside world and could convey their grievances with impunity.

Further, some of the leftist political groups of this period argued that prisoners and ex-prisoners should not be shunned but instead should be recruited to the revolutionary cause. Some of these organizations took this very seriously and made a point (as the Muslims did in the 1950s and continued to do) of developing contacts among prisoners and distributing their literature inside the walls. Particularly effective as models for inmates were those black and Latino urban radicals who had themselves been convicted of violent crimes. As inmates identified with these groups, they adopted their vocabulary, their moral standards, and their propensity for rebellious action.

Finally, in the late 1960s and early 1970s, there was a sharp upturn in the incidents of prison riots and other sorts of collective disorders. In 1967 there were 5 prison riots; 15 in 1968; 27 and 37 in 1970 and 1971, respectively; and in 1972 there were 48, more than in any other year in American history. To some, the escalation of conflict in prisons was one more element in the rising tide of disorder that was threatening to overwhelm the forces of stability and order. To others, it seemed that American society was on the brink of some sort of major transformation. The Attica riot was an unmistakable symbol of these possibilities.

# 3

# D Yard Nation—Attica (1971)

In 1929, the nation's first major wave of prison riots hit the prisons of New York State. At Clinton prison, 1,600 inmates rioted, 3 of whom died in the recapture of the institution. At Auburn prison, inmates threw acid in a guard's face and took the keys to the prison arsenal. Before the riot was quelled, six shops were burned, four inmates had escaped, and an assistant warden was killed. In response to these incidents, the state resolved to build the "ultimate prison," escape-proof and riot-proof. The world's most expensive prison to date opened in 1931 in the town of Attica, 275 miles northwest of New York City—as far away as Portland, Maine, or Fredericksburg, Virginia. It was billed as a "paradise for convicts."[1]

But of course Attica turned out to be neither a paradise for convicts nor riot-proof. In September 1971, Attica became the most famous prison in the world, an honor it may still enjoy. It had the most extensively documented and discussed prison riot in history. In addition to book-length accounts by the commissioner of corrections, a leader of the inmates, and two observers who participated in negotiations, there is the report of the McKay Commission.[2] This "citizens' committee," appointed by the Chief Judge of the state's highest court, consisted of nine members with academic and reform credentials, plus a permanent staff of up to 36 attorneys, investigators, and clerical workers, and 60 other attorneys and law students who worked on a volunteer or per diem basis. They interviewed over 1,600 inmates, 400 guards, 270 state police, Commissioner Oswald and 20 other department employees, Governor Rockefeller and his staff, observers, reporters, 100 sheriff's deputies and 200 National Guardsmen. This comes to well over 2,600 interviews. They also had access to photographs, documents, and records. The report of the commission was a 500-page book. It is our chief source of information.

Why, then, do we, who were not there, presume to write about Attica at all? Why do we not simply instruct the reader to read the McKay Commission report and go on to discuss the less well-documented riots? The answer is that the reader *should* read McKay. This chapter cannot substitute for the wealth of information presented there.

But we have an advantage over all the writers we cite. We have had time to think, to compare sources, to generalize. The five books mentioned in note 2 were all written at a time when men were on trial for their lives, when Oswald and Rockefeller faced hostile demonstrations wherever they went. It was a time when anything written or said about Attica was demanded, seized, and disseminated by those to whose point of view it lent support, and reviled by those whose partisan conclusions it undercut. This clamor is not going on as we write.

We have, moreover, a better opportunity to say what Attica "meant," because we can look not just at what led up to it but at what followed. Observers at the time were prone to take features of the Attica rebellion as inevitable consequences of features of the prison, such as harsh conditions or the preponderance of young black inmates. We are in a better position now to point out that the response of young black inmates to harsh conditions varies quite a bit depending on the circumstances of the time and place.

This chapter links the nationwide developments discussed in the previous chapter to the pre-riot situation at Attica. We describe the events that precipitated the riot and show why authorities were unable to stop its expansion. We describe the organization of the state and the organization of the inmates, how each evolved over a four day period of negotiations, and why the riot was terminated by an assault in which 39 died.

## The Prison and Its Prisoners

The heart of the Attica Correctional Facility (see Figure 3–1) was a square formed by four long cell blocks, each housing about 500 inmates. There was no passage between blocks at the corners, but above-ground passageways (called "tunnels" because of their solid, ill-lit construction) ran from the center of each block to a checkpoint in the middle of the square. This latter area was nicknamed "Times Square." The tunnels cut the central recreation space into four yards, each assigned to the block on its right. For example, the yard in the southeast corner of the square, bounded by B Block on the east and D Block on the south, was D Yard. The roofs of the tunnels served as catwalks for patrolling guards.

In 1971 this square was surrounded by 18 subsidiary buildings, connected to each other and to the cell blocks by more "tunnels." The west side of the square was formed by A Block, and to the west of that was the administration building. Beyond B Block, on the east, were the metal shops and power-house. To the north, behind C Block, were the cafeterias, the laundry, the hospital, the disciplinary cell unit (called "HBZ" for Housing Block Z), and a smaller cell block, E Block, assigned to inmates in an experimental rehabilitative program. To the south of D Block were the school and auditorium.

There were three floors of cells to each of the four main blocks. Inmates

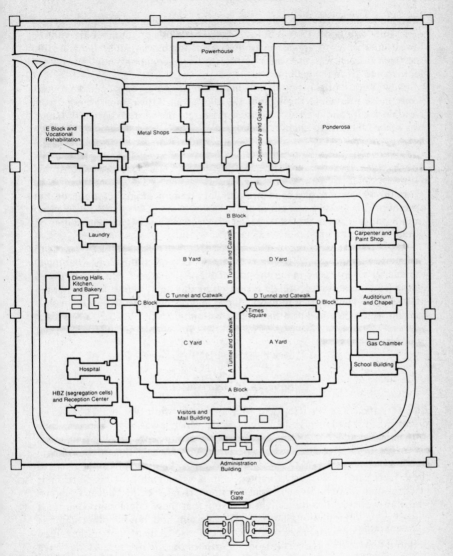

Figure 3–1. Attica Correctional Facility

living in a single row of cells were designated a "company;" there were 4 companies to a floor, 12 to a block. The companies were numbered, with the lowest numbers in A Block. In all but one of the blocks, all an inmate could see from his cell was the wall opposite; inmates commonly used mirrors to look up and down the galleries.[3]

New York's prison population had been growing younger and progressively more non-white throughout the 1960s, but Attica, most remote from New York City and used as a receiving prison for the western part of the state, was one of the last to change. By September 1971, however, the breakdown by race of the 2,243 inmates at Attica was quite similar to that of the population of the system: 54 percent black, 37 percent white, 9 percent Hispanic. Nearly half—43 percent—were from New York City. Sixty-two percent had been convicted of violent crimes; 40 percent were under the age of 30.[4]

In the 1930s there had been an exemplary training program for guards, but after World War II it was eliminated. By the late 1950s guards received no training at all. After that they received a cursory two-week orientation on hiring.[5]

In 1970, the correctional officers negotiated a contract allowing guards to bid on assignments on the basis of seniority. As is often the case, what made the keeper's job easier made the life of the kept harder. Tensions between guards and inmates had already increased by this time, in part because of the influx of non-white urban inmates. Senior guards began to bid on night-shift jobs on which they had as little contact with inmates as possible. Thereafter, the less experienced the guard, the more responsibility he would have for dealing with inmates.[6]

## Sources of Deprivation

Life at Attica was terrible. The McKay Commission devoted 71 pages to discussing how bad it was and all the ways in which it was bad.[7] The cells were cramped, the food was barely edible or nutritious, the medical care was unsatisfactory, the recreation was minimal, the job assignments were boring and unrewarding, and the atmosphere was repressive and degrading. None of these facts can be seriously doubted, and if we devote little space to their elaboration it is not because we consider them trivial. Yet the McKay Commission was probably also quite right in saying that these unpleasant conditions existed at the other major New York State prisons and those in other states as well. To the commission, these aspects did not set Attica apart; rather, they declared that "Attica is every prison."[8] Furthermore, many prisons today have the same problems. Why, then, did the rebellion take place at Attica, and not elsewhere; and in 1971, and not some other time? Probably by "chance," says the report.[9] This might actually be true, but it is our duty to try to do better than that; and, in trying to do better, we look to see whether the pains of imprisonment were especially severe at that time and in that place.

With some exceptions, it is rather hard to contend that conditions at Attica became much worse in the years before the riot; but it is quite clear that the standards by which inmates judged prisons changed dramatically, and that Attica (and many other prisons in the country) failed these new standards.

In more recent years, legal self-help by inmates has come to be viewed by administrators (and federal judges) as a more or less unavoidable nuisance.[10] In the period under consideration, however, such efforts were seen as an unacceptable challenge to the authority of the system. Inmates were subject to harassment for filing lawsuits, especially on behalf of other inmates. Although federal courts and prison administrators would eventually recognize inmates' rights to access to adequate law libraries and other needs for legal self-help, these were often resisted or obstructed by prison administrators in the period under study.

We would expect such legal challenges to be most prevalent in states with a sufficiency of lawyers and civil liberties organizations, and in jurisdictions where state and federal judges were relatively liberal. New York met these criteria. Organizations like the ACLU provided the legal resources to challenge established practice at every point of the criminal justice system; once the legal avenues were opened, thousands of inmates challenged both their convictions and the conditions of their imprisonment. At Attica, legal self-help was "a major occupation for many inmates."[11]

The decisive shift in prisons in many states to a black and Latin majority in the population coincided with the civil rights and black power movements and with radical activism in the Puerto Rican and Chicano communities. It has been observed that white prisoners are mostly isolated and alienated from their communities of origin and identify with a "criminal subculture," if with any group at all. But many young black and Latin prisoners in this period, though they may have committed acts of violence or theft against members of their own community, came to feel a sense of national identification insofar as they confronted racist practices.

One would expect the effect of this conjuncture to be the greater, first, where the practice of racial discrimination was deeper rooted at an institution and, second, where the shift to a black and Latin majority in the population was more rapid. Both factors seem to have operated at Attica. First, formal racial segregation of inmate activities existed at Attica into the 1960s. The McKay Commission found evidence of racial prejudice still in existence among the predominantly white guard force.[12]

The black and Latin inmates had for a long time been a relatively small and powerless minority at Attica. The prison was the remotest in the system, was the last to take the "spill" of black and Latin inmates from New York, and for that reason shifted racially all the more quickly, with the least time for adjustment. "When I first went to Attica [in 1969], the population was a good 80 percent white," said one inmate. "But within a year and a half it had turned over to 85 percent black and Puerto Rican, and whites were in the minority."[13] The real figure was 63 percent, not 85 percent, but the important thing is the perception of rapid change.

Further, radical nationalist and leftist ideas were nowhere stronger at this time in the United States than in the New York area, with the San Francisco Bay Area perhaps a strong second. And in no state system but California's did the Black Panthers and Black Muslims develop as strong a following as in New York. Because Attica was so remote from New York City, and because of its reputation for security, prison administrators tended to send suspected radicals there. As a result, Attica after a while could boast the best concentration of prison revolutionaries and experienced jail and prison rioters east of the Sierras.

Any prisoner whose "political consciousness was raised," through whatever mechanism, immediately found himself in conflict with the prison authorities on a host of issues. Books, magazines, newspapers, and mail were often strictly censored; an inmate might have to go to court for the right to receive, say, a prison reform newsletter.[14] Political organizations were nearly always banned. Prison authorities were hostile to the Black Muslims, sometimes punished inmates for associating with them, and more often forbade them to hold religious services. Not only rebellion but also non-violent protest was punished with segregation, loss of privileges, and additional time. Some of these policies, when taken before the federal courts, were found to be unconstitutional; others were not. These policies had usually existed for many years—or would have existed if there had been occasion for them—but they were not widely seen as a source of deprivation until many prisoners wanted to read political books or attend Islamic services.

Attica exemplified the principle that seemingly arbitrary rules, arbitrarily enforced, can be more frustrating than less lenient but more stable rules. There was one set of rules which applied throughout the New York system, another which was formulated at Attica, and an unknowable number of rules or enforcement standards made up by individual corrections officers. Rulebooks were not being printed at this time, so not even the corrections officers had access to them or knew them with confidence. Some officers printed up an informal guidebook of their own, which said that all inmate requests for permission to do anything should be denied if the officer wasn't sure of the rule.[15]

Actually, much the same situation existed and still exists at many prisons. But Attica added a new wrinkle: in its reorganization of the guards' job assignments in 1970, it abolished assignments of guards to specific companies. This meant that a given company of inmates on a given day could be guarded by any guard in the place, depending on how the mechanics of shift and seniority worked out. By comparison, in the Michigan prisons (ten years later), the "counselor" on a floor might have an arbitrary pattern of enforcement, but at least the inmates would have to learn the patterns of only a limited number of counselors. An inmate at Attica, to avoid being written up, would have to learn what all 400 officers would or would not take as a rule violation. Furthermore, the officers on day shift were now likely to be the least experienced officers with the most arbitrary and variable patterns of enforcement. Of course, this lack of pattern had the added effect of depersonalizing, in the extreme, contact between inmates and guards, and further diminishing the already slim chance that guards would develop any trust or empathy toward individual inmates or vice versa.

## Struggles Over Reform in 1970 and 1971

The years 1970 and 1971 can be looked on as a period during which three forces grappled with the question of reform at Attica and other New York prisons. The forces of liberal reform, embodied in the U.S. courts and in Commissioner of Correctional Services Russell Oswald (appointed January 1, 1971), attempted to enact liberal prison policy, but were hamstrung, on the one hand, by budgetary constraints and, on the other, by the intransigence of the custodial staff. The guards and old-line prison officials constituted a second autonomous force, directed toward the maintenance of traditionalist policy and toward the maximization of their own span of control. The inmates constituted a third force, which throughout this period attempted to test various strategies for exerting power or influence in the prison and to sound out the intentions of the other actors.

The conflict between the liberal and traditionalist forces can be quickly summarized. Court decisions limited the power of prison authorities to punish and limit the rights of inmates. On May 14, 1970, a federal district court struck down the prison's system of internal punishment as denial of due process and limited the right of supervisors to censor inmates' mail.[16] A liberal prison commissioner was appointed. The correctional staff successfully resisted these changes. Armed with a strong sense of group solidarity and with the organizational resources of their labor union, they both mobilized political support for the traditionalist position and invented new forms of suppression of inmate freedoms as old ones were denied to them. For example, ordered to permit inmates to receive newspapers and periodicals, they began to snip out individual articles which they believed inmates should not read. Their determined defense was particularly effective since the state faced a budget crunch which denied the liberal forces the financial resources to implement their policies against this resistance.[17]

This conflict was invisible to inmates. All that could be seen were the statements by the courts and by Oswald that reform ought to be carried out, and the fact that it was not. Oswald made statements to the inmate population at Attica on several occasions in which he asked for time and implied that he was doing his best to overcome the resistance of the custodial staff. However, these statements were couched in polysyllabic and artificially neutral language (e.g., "we are attempting to re-attitudinize all parties")[18] which many inmates must have interpreted as obfuscatory gobbledygook.

There was a reason for this: Oswald, like any prison administrator, shrank from telling the inmates in plain language that on the question of prison reform he was on their side against the guards. To make such a statement would have brought on an internal and external political storm that he probably could not have weathered. Still, it was hard for inmates to see why the commissioner of corrections could not do whatever he wanted with the prison, and easy to conclude that Oswald's reform utterances were all hypocritical jive.

Even inmates who had faith in Oswald's good intentions, but realized that Oswald could reform the prison only at the cost of a difficult struggle against guards and administrators, would not necessarily conclude they should sit tight and wait. Inmates might just as easily reason that direct action was necessary to bring the reform that Oswald could not get on his own. Since it was the officers who were actually defying Oswald's wishes, an apparent inmate "rebellion" could actually be interpreted as grass-roots action to assure the ascendancy of Oswald's own policies and authority! And indeed, in large measure, the riot was to unfold along these lines. Oswald was to accede to nearly every demand for penal reform the inmates would make, much to the dismay, and then fury, of the guards and the prison's superintendent. However, inmates also came to take the position that, because the riot was provoked by the state's failure to effect reform, they should not be punished but should have complete amnesty. The inmates were never able to appreciate the state's commitment to the principle that (at least some of) their actions must be punished, even though taken to obtain changes conceded by the state to be just.

On July 19, 1970, six months before Oswald's appointment, 450 inmates working in the metal shops had taken action on their own: in a sit-down strike, they won a tripling of the wage. (The new wages ranged from $0.25 to $1.10 per day.) Organizers of the peaceful protest were, however, shipped to other prisons.[19] In November 1970, inmates at Auburn prison presented the administration with an instructive show of force: denied permission to celebrate a Black Solidarity Day, they seized control of the yard, disarmed the officers on duty, held a peaceful rally, and then returned control to the administration on a promise of "no reprisals." Despite the promise, inmates identified as leaders were transferred to Attica and confined in HBZ. A federal judge soon ruled that they must be released to the general prison population, to the dismay of the custodial staff.[20]

Other inmates now at Attica had been part of a rebellion at New York City's infamous jail, the "Tombs." Despite assurances of "no reprisals" from New York's Mayor Lindsay, they had been shipped off to Attica in what they saw as a punitive and treacherous move.[21]

In June of 1971, a cell search uncovered evidence that five inmates were attempting to correspond with inmates elsewhere in the state and develop a program of demands. These inmates wrote to Commissioner Oswald on July 2, identifying themselves as the "Attica Liberation Faction." Although the letter was intensely critical of the New York prison system, the substance of its "Manifesto of Demands" was squarely in the liberal-reform tradition. The writers did not challenge their "posture as prisoners," and they emphasized the peaceful and "democratic," or non-rebellious, manner of their presentation. The demands themselves were for legal representation before the Parole Board, improvement in medical care, upkeep of facilities and working condi-

tions, uniform rules, lower commissary prices, and an end to "segregation . . . because of their political beliefs." The McKay Commission summed
up this package as "a strikingly reasonable and civil approach."[22]

Superintendent Mancusi requested the punitive transfer of these inmates
to other prisons, but Oswald denied the request. The five inmates, however,
were unaware of Mancusi's and Oswald's actions. The replies they actually
received from Oswald were vaguely encouraging but non-committal. They
wrote again to Oswald in July and August, charging that Attica officials were
stepping up the harassment and discipline of inmates who were organizing for
prison reform.

While these five inmates were communicating with Oswald, members of
larger inmate organizations were preparing the way for a broader inmate
unity. Inmates in the Black Panther Party apparently took the initiative. Until
that summer, Black Muslims had refused to participate in Panther activities;
now a Muslim inmate leader closely identified with this policy was transferred
from Attica after officers heard that his life was in danger. In mid-August,
guards on the yard witnessed a "ceremony" at which groups of inmates from
the Black Panther Party and the Black Muslims faced each other across a
table, apparently with mediation by Puerto Rican members of the Young
Lords Party. The incident "seemed to confirm their worst fears," that is, of
growing inmate unity.[23]

On August 22, reacting to the news that inmate George Jackson, affiliated
with the Black Panther Party, had been shot and killed by San Quentin prison
guards, black inmates engaged in a solemn act of protest. Up to 700 inmates
wore black armbands, observed silence, and fasted in the mess hall. Two weeks
later, believing that Commissioner Oswald was visiting Attica, 300 inmates
signed up for sick call. Inmates were not disciplined for these actions.[24]

By the first of September, then, inmates at Attica had a considerable
amount of experience with collective action and protest. In contrast with the
other inmates in this study, they had cooperated in the disciplined production
of protest on a large scale. This collective action had been granted a color of
legitimacy by the administration; the peaceful actions had not been punished,
and Commissioner Oswald was engaged in some sort of long-distance dialogue with inmate representatives. Yet nothing had actually changed.

On September 2, Oswald actually visited Attica and began to meet with
inmate leaders. But Oswald's wife was suddenly hospitalized, and he cut the
visit short. A hurriedly taped message was played to inmates after his departure. Again, it contained no concrete concessions, and many inmates reported
feeling frustrated and angry.[25]

## Preliminary Skirmishes

On September 8 and the morning of September 9, a series of incidents took
place which primed the institution for an explosion. At about 3:30 p.m. on
Wednesday, September 8, two inmates were engaged in horseplay on A Yard.

Two correctional officers, apparently interpreting it as a fight, summoned them to talk to the ranking lieutenant on the yard. One of the inmates lost himself in the crowd. The other, Leroy Dewer, a resident of 3 Company in A Block, was ordered by Lieutenant Maroney to return to his cell.

Dewer had previously been told that his next infraction would land him in HBZ. Instead of complying, he turned to go back to the yard. When the lieutenant came after him, Dewer turned and fended him off, striking him two glancing blows. A crowd of inmates immediately collected, shouting encouragement to Dewer. A white inmate named Ray Lamorie, of 5 Company, ran over to join this crowd and shouted something to Lieutenant Maroney. Some guards claimed that he had tried to attack the lieutenant and had shouted obscenities at him, but others said it was someone else who had done that, and the lieutenant could not remember Lamorie's supposed action later. Some in the crowd did yell obscenities, epithets, and threats (e.g., to "burn the place down").

Lieutenant Robert Curtiss now attempted to calm the crowd and persuade Dewer to return to his cell. In this he was not very effective, but many inmates gained the impression that he had promised Dewer that he would not be sent to HBZ. The crowd did not disperse, and eventually the two lieutenants backed off and left the yard. The incident was triply unusual: an inmate had struck an officer, a lieutenant in fact; a crowd had backed him up; and officers had been forced to retreat and to put off the punishment of Dewer.[26]

The matter was put before Deputy Superintendent Vincent immediately. He ordered that Dewer be taken to HBZ after A Block had returned to their cells from the evening meal. Lamorie was also to go to HBZ, but it was impossible to determine afterwards who had ordered this or even who had concluded that he was guilty of an infraction.[27]

At about 5:30 p.m., when 3 Company was locked up, Lt. Maroney and three officers came to Dewer's cell. The inmate refused to leave, the officers went in to bring him out, and a fight ensued. Finally the four officers carried him out of his cell and down the gallery, one at each limb. The other inmates in 3 Company, who had only the sound of the struggle and a moment's glimpse to go by, believed that Dewer had been beaten and mishandled, and that he faced another beating in HBZ. They responded by hurling refuse and insults at the guards as they carried Dewer past.

One floor below, another squad of guards came after Lamorie. Lieutenant Curtiss, who headed the detail, was unable to tell him what he was supposed to have done. While Lamorie walked out without resistance, the response was the same as from 3 Company: epithets and objects flew out of the cells at the officers. A can of soup—allegedly thrown by a Latin inmate, William Ortiz—struck an officer in the head, drawing blood. This was communicated to Vincent and Mancusi, who decided that disciplining Ortiz could wait until the next day.

On the morning of September 9, the correctional officer in charge of 5 Company lined up the inmates to go to breakfast. Ortiz was to be kept in his cell and taken to HBZ later while the others of the company were at chow or on the yard. When they realized that Ortiz was not with them, several inmates declared that they wouldn't leave the gallery either, and started to return to their cells. In the meantime, one of the inmates who was in the line leaving for breakfast reached into the lockbox and manually threw the switch unlocking Ortiz's cell door. (The lockbox was supposed to be relocked before the inmates passed, but "normal practice" was otherwise.) Ortiz and the other inmates hurried to catch up with the rest of the company.

Several points can be made about this series of events. First, encouraged by court actions, inmates in this period were increasingly aware of and assertive of due process safeguards. In this context, inmates believed that their rights had been grossly violated. Inmate Lamorie was ordered to HBZ, but nobody then or since could say who ordered it or what the charge was. Dewer believed he was being sent to HBZ for resisting being sent to HBZ unjustly. Further, inmates thought that Lamorie and Dewer had been (or were being) savagely beaten.[28]

Second, the administrators did not realize how unraveled things had become and did not take the sort of massive action (a lockdown of A Block, for example) which might have forestalled the explosion. In part they were subject to personnel constraints. In fact, they had assigned extra guards to take the companies from A Block to breakfast that morning. In practice, this meant one guard per company (41 men) rather than one for two companies. Such measures showed an awareness of danger, but should have been recognized as completely inadequate to prevent an outbreak of violence if one was in fact threatened. Also, the administration did nothing to dispel the most dire rumors (e.g., the "beating" of the two inmates). Instead, the administrators operated on the "principle" that inmates had no right to know what was happening to Lamorie and Dewer.

Finally, the events of the ninth and tenth broke down into a series of skirmishes in each of which the inmates were at least partially successful through the use of violence, threats, or craft. On the yard, the state had wanted Dewer to go back to his cell; but he hadn't. In A Block, the state had taken two inmates to HBZ; but the inmates had made this difficult and even caused a "casualty." In 5 Company, the guards had put Ortiz on keeplock but inmates had gotten him out; now he was eating breakfast with the rest. They had kept the administration from having things their way, and one can only suppose that it gave inmates—particularly those in 5 Company—a heightened sense of their own efficacy in conflict with the forces of the state.

## Initiation: A Tunnel

While 5 Company was eating breakfast, the top administration became aware that Ortiz was not in his cell, but had been let out of keeplock by inmates.[29] Five Company was scheduled to go to A Yard after breakfast. However, the most important thing now was to lock Ortiz back up. It was decided (by whom is unclear)[30] to return all of 5 Company to their cells and then let everyone except Ortiz out for yard. The reader might think that this was a lot of trouble to separate 1 man from a group of 40 in the middle of a prison. There were two problems, though: first, there was no reserve force of guards to dispatch to perform the operation; second, there was no way to communicate with the officer in charge of 5 Company, now presumably somewhere in transit between the mess hall and A Yard (which they would enter from A Tunnel). Accordingly, Lieutenant Curtiss phoned a guard on duty in A Block, telling him to run and lock the door from A Tunnel to A Yard, and then called Times Square and told the guards there to lock 5 Company into A Tunnel after they had gone through Times Square. Lieutenant Curtiss would explain when he got there.

When Lieutenant Curtiss arrived in A Tunnel, 5 Company was standing there quietly in formation. Two other A Block Companies and the guards in charge of them were also in the tunnel. Lieutenant Curtiss went back alone to explain the situation to 5 Company. According to inmate (and later author) Richard X Clark, who was on the scene, Curtiss communicated his intentions with the words, "Niggers back to your cells."[31] Whether or not he said this, the inmates recognized Curtiss as the man responsible for throwing Lamorie in the "box," and believed he had given lying assurances that nothing would happen to Dewer. "You no good mother," Curtiss heard as he walked past the line of inmates, and he was struck on the side of the head.[32]

A melee broke out in A Tunnel. Quickly all guards in the tunnel were forced to flee. Two were let into Times Square and were safe there for the moment. Lieutenant Curtiss and two others raced back into A Block. Fifteen or 20 inmates, though, were right behind them. In short order they had overpowered all the guards in the block (except those who had postponed capture by barricading themselves in cells), had obtained a set of keys, and were opening all the doors.

About 100 A Block inmates who had gone to early mess were already in A Yard. When they realized what was happening in A Tunnel, some of them independently attacked the guards on duty at the tunnel door with baseball bats. The guards temporarily escaped up onto the catwalk over the tunnel, but the inmates now had their keys and opened the tunnel door. Inmates now controlled A Block, A Tunnel, and A Yard. It was 8:45 a.m.

## Expansion: Times Square and Beyond

For about ten minutes there was relative calm. Inmates regrouping in A Block must have arrived at a rough plan of action—a decision to continue with the offensive rather than to barricade themselves inside A Block—but details of this are unavailable to us.

Although the administration found out quickly that there was trouble in A Block, it was unable to make good use of the time.[33] At Attica, all communication to and from the administration must be conducted via a *single telephone*.[34] To transmit information to the administration one called this phone and hoped the line wasn't busy. The administration could only issue commands to one location at a time, and of course that line could be busy too—guards there might be calling somewhere else trying to find out what was going on.

The only way to sound a general alarm was to blow the steam whistle at the powerhouse, which was at the farthest point from the administration building. When the sergeant on the administration phone finally got through, the only man authorized to blow the whistle was off on an errand, and the assistant who took the call had to go get his okay. The whistle didn't blow until about 9:15. But it made little difference, since the whistle was also blown for escapes and there was no way to indicate that this time it meant something more serious.[35]

A captain who was especially curious or suspicious could send one of his officers out on a scouting mission. This is what the B Block captain did. One of his officers trekked to Times Square to find out what was happening. Officer Quinn, on duty there, told him it was "just a minor disturbance."[36] Later there was no way to correct this misinformation.

To compound the problem of communication, there were no guards "to spare" from any single location. Each guard was tied to a location, a building, a group of prisoners, which he was not supposed to abandon. What was called for was a pre-existing emergency plan for "doubling up" these responsibilities and collecting a mobile force, or even for an orderly evacuation. But there was no such plan. Accordingly, the correctional staff outside the area immediately affected, more or less unaware of what was happening, continued their business as usual and relied on the gates and doors.[37]

Meanwhile, having seized A Block, the inmates could either attack the gates to the administration building, or they could go back down A Tunnel and attack the gate to Times Square. In Times Square would be the keys to the other three tunnels. The other ends of those tunnels could still be sealed off by guards in B, C, and D blocks.

No attempt was ever made on the administration building gates; but, a little after 9:00, about 20 inmates armed with sticks, pipes, and rakes came down A Tunnel and demanded that the officers open the gate. Times Square was still occupied only by Officer Quinn and the two guards who had retreated there from the fight in A Tunnel. No reinforcements had been sent, and Quinn, who by now knew things were serious, could not get administration on the phone (the line was busy). He was keeping all the Times Square gates closed as a precaution. Two officers had arrived from C Tunnel with groups of inmates they were escorting back from the showers, and were surprised to find the gates locked.

Due to the shortage of staff, the gates had not been subject to routine inspection recently.[38] Forty years before, when the prison was built, one of the locking rods of the Times Square A gate had been welded together from two pieces of metal. The weld was bad. The defect had since been buried under layers of paint.

Now 20 inmates began to shake the gate. The ancient weld snapped. The gate broke in. The inmates surged into Times Square, swinging their sticks and pipes, giving Quinn the blow to the head from which he would die in two days. They took the keys and opened the gates to the other three tunnels. The officers in C Tunnel turned to run but were cut off by the inmates they had been guarding. The officers were stripped and were marched back to A Block, carrying the unconscious Quinn. Inmates going the other way constituted themselves as informal assault forces to attack B, C, and D blocks.[39]

Each of those three blocks was supposedly protected by its own gate at the end of its tunnel. In no case did a gate work.

The C Block gate gave the group of 40 to 50 inmates who attacked it less trouble than the Times Square gate had. It held them up "no more than a couple seconds" and then gave way.[40] Inmates opened the B Block gate with a key from Times Square which wasn't supposed to fit that lock; it was speculated that the keys and locks were so worn as to be interchangeable.[41] The D Block gate was open, as the block captain was trying to bring inmates in from D Yard.[42] In each case the outcome was the same. The guards were surprised. Some were overpowered immediately; others locked themselves in cells or offices, only to be taken at the inmates' leisure. Keys were taken; all the doors were opened; a new assault wave poured into the structures beyond.

The details of how the riot struck each area are presented in the other standard sources; we confine ourselves here to some general observations.

The impossibility of communication to, from, or among the separate areas of the prison was fatal to the forces of control. On some occasions it was inmate runners, not custodial sources, who brought the news that a riot was at the doors. Even after the whistle was blown, guards and civilian employees who had time to escape waited indecisively, in one instance locking their own escape route, and were taken prisoner. The facilities continued to prove insecure; Metal Shop 2 was locked from the inside, for example, but a rioter broke the glass window in the door and unlocked it.[43]

Many inmates in the peripheral locations were unsympathetic to the riot and resisted it passively or actively. White inmates in one of the mess halls, presupposing it to be a racial riot, offered to fight the rioters.[44] About 55 inmates in the shop area escaped involvement by hiding in the maintenance building, and a larger number (not all of whom, however, necessarily had assignments in the area) defected from the riot by retreating to a fenced-in field called the "Ponderosa," which could be covered by fire from the guard towers. Of 55 inmates in the school building, almost all chose to leave with the guard and six civilian employees.[45] Inmates in the tailor shop cooperated in concealing the guard in charge; although the building burned, he was rescued through an outside window and was not taken hostage.[46] Inmates working in the garage tried unsuccessfully to protect their civilian foreman, and one 72-year-old black inmate, armed with a lethal iron bar, kept rioters away from the gasoline supply.[47]

Work in the metal shops was considered unpleasant, and the inmates assigned there were mostly black. When rioting inmates pounded on the door, some inmates locked the officer in charge and two civilian employees in a rear office. It appears the idea was both to protect them and to stay out of the riot, since they locked the guard's keys in with him. Some of the inmates in the shop apparently thought better of this, though, and two of them rammed open the shop door from the inside with a fork lift.[48] In Metal Shop 2, some inmates had begun to destroy property before the rioters broke in.

The riot was undertaken primarily by those inmates who had no jobs or were assigned to menial labor. Five Company was a so-called grading company, assigned to intermittent groundskeeping duties like shoveling snow. This was considered undesirable work. Three companies of A Block were made up of new inmates awaiting assignments. Porters and janitors, not assigned to the outbuildings, were on hand to conduct the riot. Inmates who were integrated into the formal job and assignment structure of the prison, particularly those with fixed workstations and small-group job organization, were less rebellious and more likely to act, even at personal risk, to oppose the rioters and to warn or protect guards. (Because the way jobs were assigned, these inmates were more likely to be white and less hostile to begin with.)

By 9:30, or perhaps 9:45, the riot had reached its maximum geographic extent. A decision already had been made, or arrived at by consensus or rumor, by inmates to move to D Yard as a group and bring any hostages who had been taken. Activity in the outer regions was like a series of raids, in which valuables were taken, personnel recruited or conscripted, hostages acquired, buildings set afire, and the locale evacuated.

Efforts by the administration to defend areas of the prison from the riot and, later, to recapture large sections were characterized by lack of central direction and by a rough-and-ready spirit of improvisation and independent initiative. The primitive communication system was in large part responsible for this. Ironically, if guards had shown less initiative and more concern for rules, other critical areas might have fallen to the rioters. For example, guards were supposed to get the administration's approval before using tear gas. The guards on duty at the reception center could not reach the administration, but used a tear gas gun anyway to repel rioting inmates from the mess hall corridors. If they hadn't, the riot might have engulfed the hospital building and the reception center which housed HBZ.[49]

As we shall see, this "pioneer spirit," once developed into a norm among the assemblage of state forces, would later prove disastrous to the organization of the final assault. But for the time being, it was used effectively. Between 10 a.m. and 1 p.m., operations were conducted which retook large parts of the prison. As off-duty correctional officers arrived on the scene, they were issued weapons from the arsenal, including automatic weapons. A squad of these officers operating in the northern sector secured the mess halls, evacuating the inmate crews (which were hostile to the riot). One officer used automatic weapon fire to repel rioters from the corridor south of the mess halls. This was a violation of regulations, and the officers passed the weapon among them so that its user could not be identified by his fingerprints. This squad then secured C and E blocks, both of which were virtually empty by the time they arrived.[50]

A group of correctional officers from Auburn Prison, 90 miles to the east, obtained the keys to enter A Block immediately on their arrival without bothering to wait for orders from anybody. Dashing across the lower tier, they quickly locked the A Tunnel gate, sealing off A Block from the rest of the riot area, and then secured the block. Only about 25 inmates were on hand.[51]

A third squad, this one composed of both correctional officers and state police (who had arrived on the scene about 10 a.m.) under state police command, recaptured the areas east of B Block. They evacuated non-participating inmates from the maintenance building, the Ponderosa, and the powerhouse, the latter group refusing to move until their names were recorded as non-participants. They then secured the buildings on the shop corridor and actually entered B Block. The commander, however, became concerned that their weapons might be taken, and ordered the force to retreat. Unknown to them, three guards were hiding in a toilet shack on B Yard at the time; after inmates reoccupied B Block and B Yard, they were found and taken prisoner. Oswald was later to be wrongly blamed by many of the state's forces for the decision to withdraw and its consequences.

### The Four Days of D Yard Nation—"A Functioning Society"

By 11 a.m., nearly 1,300 inmates were in D Yard. For about an hour, there had been "something bordering on a party atmosphere"—relatively benign but chaotic milling, looting, distribution and consumption of looted materials. There had been little inter-inmate violence thus far. As the hostages were brought into the yard, they were confined to one corner under the supervision and protection of Muslim guards. Forty-five guards and civilians had been taken hostage by then, and five more would be found—three in the B Yard outhouse and two hiding on D Block disguised as inmates. Violence against hostages had been greater for those taken last, particularly those taken in the metal shops area, but once under the protection of the Muslim guards the hostages were relatively safe.

Within the next couple of hours the inmates in D Yard laid the foundations of an inmate countersociety, with a degree of formal organization, articulation of political principles, democratic participation, and law enforcement unprecedented in prison riots.[52]

The process was initiated by a respected inmate "lawyer" who addressed the inmates in D Yard with a bullhorn, "issuing instructions" and calling for volunteers to perform such tasks as obtaining bedding and firewood as well as food from the commissary. A debate then began over what to do with the hostages. While the Muslims favored leaving them in their corner for their protection, others argued for bringing them into a more exposed position as (they believed) insurance against an assault by authorities. It was finally agreed to arrange them in a circle closer to the center of the yard, immediately ringed by the Muslim guards.

Following agreement on this point, a period of "open mike" followed during which inmates addressed the group on various topics. To begin with, speakers declared that it was "not a race riot" and called for brotherhood among black, white, and Latin inmates. Later, speakers declared "rules" to be in effect: there was to be no use of drugs, no fighting, and no sexual activity. Inmates were to stay on D Yard and not go in the blocks.

Volunteers were requested for a "security guard," which was to function as a combination defense force, internal police force, and on-call work gang throughout the uprising. It was estimated that as many as one-quarter of the inmates in D Yard served in the security guard at one time or another. A special effort was made to achieve racial balance in its ranks by recruiting white and Latin inmates. This group broke up fights, put out fires, and built barricades. They eventually evolved a system of colored armbands denoting different shifts, responsibilities, and, as it were, security clearances.

There was also a call for volunteers to assist with injured inmates and hostages, as well as with the medical needs of inmates with chronic conditions. After some debate, Quinn and three other injured guards were taken to the "DMZ" and handed over to the state. (The DMZ was a portion of A Tunnel between A Block and the A Yard door. Located on the direct route from the administration building to D Yard, it became the border checkpoint via which people and information traveled to and from the rebel zone. Inmates named it after the Demilitarized Zone, a slice of formally "neutral" territory between North and South Vietnam prominent in contemporaneous war reportage.) Another necessity was food; one of the first demands made on the state was that they supply food to the D Yard inmates. Eventually sandwiches were prepared in the kitchen twice a day and handed over to the rebel inmates, who held a mess call and distributed them in an orderly fashion. Observers reported that by Friday there was a "functioning, stable society" on D Yard, with "a business section, a residential section, a jail . . . a police station, a food distribution center, and a hospital."[53] A postal system was set up to try to get out mail to the inmates' families.[54]

By early Thursday afternoon a group of seven "spokesmen" had coalesced. They had collected some tables (at which negotiation was intended to take place) and typewriters, had recruited four typists, and were beginning to prepare demands. (The initial list was the "Immediate Demands" in Appendix B.) Beyond that, they would (either as a group or in their individual capacities) serve as a de facto government for the duration of the rebellion. Five were black and two white. Of the five blacks, four had present, past, or indirect affiliation with one or another Muslim group.[55] One of these four was a signer of the Attica Liberation Faction letter. The fifth black leader had no organizational affiliation. One of the two whites had a reputation as a jailhouse lawyer. The other had explicitly "anti-imperialist" politics and had been convicted of planting explosive devices at government targets.[56]

As it evolved over a four-day period, the political order on D Yard had an essentially "democratic" character, though not without the imperfections associated with a society in a state of siege. The riot leaders exhibited concern for democratic forms and, probably, substance. They conducted votes which they lost—for example, on whether to allow the media to take pictures of hostages.[57] They apparently held an election after they came under political criticism.[58] (The fact that they were all re-elected can be taken as a sign either that the election was a sham or that they actually were legitimate leaders.) It was they who protected dissenters against the crowd. They were not corrupt and did not extort wealth or sexual favors. In fact, they attempted to provide good government. When two men were sexually assaulted, they guarded them and investigated the crime.[59]

On the other hand, the consent of the governed was not universal. In addition to those inmates who immediately escaped the riot, quite a few on D Yard had opposed the rebellion from the outset. They stayed on the sidelines, tending to their tents, their possessions, and their own little groups. McKay reports that "many" of the inmates interviewed said they would have escaped D Yard, but were intimidated from doing so by the security guards.[60] Further, D Yard society was harsh toward perceived enemies: 3 of the 32 inmates to die would be killed by inmates after being marked as offenders by the leadership.

In general, however, the leadership was tolerant of varying opinions and of violations of rules. In the later stages there was a resumption of sexual activity and of drug use,[61] but we do not learn of a "purge" of these offenders, even though the Muslims were hostile to both offenses. Political conflict among the leaders never became violent, perhaps because of an unstated ethic that each would be allowed to pursue his own interests.

Specificity of consensus was never a priority. We learn, for example, that most of the leadership did not actively demand transportation out of the country (infra), but that those who did were not dissuaded, while the rest were careful to say that they didn't see the demand as crazy; they saw the minority's point. Lists of demands and of desired observers were developed the same way, with each putting in their favorites and no one being asked to take their favorites out again.[62] The advantage of this was the friendly working relationship and atmosphere of mutual respect which was obtained among representatives of quite a variety of political trends. The disadvantage was that when it was necessary to change a demand or tactic, or adopt a new course of action, it was difficult to do so.

## The Organization of the State

In order to understand fully what happened at Attica and what its "lessons" are, it is necessary to look at the array of forces representing the state of New York which confronted the prisoners, negotiated with them, delivered ultimata to them, and finally recaptured the prison.

The armed forces of the state included about 300 corrections officers employed at the Attica facility and a contingent of corrections officers from Auburn Prison, 100 miles distant. One-fifth of the New York State Police force was on hand, a total of 587 troopers responsible to Major John Monahan, commander of the nearby Batavia post. In addition, nearly 300 "irregulars" were on hand—sheriffs and deputies from nine surrounding counties, plus Genesee County Park Police, each group with its own commander.[63]

This congeries of 1,100 armed men camped in front of the administration building throughout the four days of the uprising. No unified command structure was ever created. During the four days of waiting, assaults on the prison were planned, scrapped, and re-planned, creating an atmosphere of hair-trigger tension. Rumors flew: the hostages had been sodomized, or tortured, or killed; an assault was about to take place. The non-Attica officers, nearly all white, rural men from upstate New York, shared many presuppositions and prejudices about inmates, particularly non-white inmates, and were easily infected by the anger and virtual hysteria of the Attica officers.

The mood voiced among these men was one of unrelieved hatred for the rioting inmates, often taking grossly racist forms. They were outraged that negotiations were taking place. Some openly expressed their loathing for participants in that process, including the observers and Commissioner Oswald himself. The desire to kill or physically punish inmates was openly expressed. It is not certain that every uniformed officer present agreed with these sentiments, but it is certain that these sentiments were voiced to the exclusion of contrasting ones.[64]

At the other end of the organizational chart was New York State Governor Nelson Rockefeller, who would ultimately determine what form the state's action would take. Rockefeller was a political figure of world stature—three years later he would be named vice president—and it is evident that he saw the Attica uprising as not just a prison riot but as a geopolitical event, a "step in an ominous world trend."[65] While he did not prevent Oswald from conducting negotiations with the inmates, he later made it clear that he opposed negotiating with the holders of hostages. To permit an inmate victory at Attica would be treason to the authority and prestige of the United States around the world, from Cuba to Vietnam. Rockefeller's primary loyalty was not to the narrow interests of any group of citizens of New York but to the maintenance of that authority and of the world capitalist/democratic order. In the name of "basic principles" upholding that order, Rockefeller would eventually find it necessary to retake the prison forcibly, whatever the immediate cost.

Caught between Rockefeller's counterrevolutionary determination and the barely repressed hunger for violence of the assembled assault troops, Commissioner Russell Oswald was completely isolated. He bore the responsibility for dealing with the uprising—for the settlement, if there was to be one, for the assault, if one was to be made—and, so far as he knew, no one else in the prison system shared his priorities or had confidence in his strategies. Not even his own deputy supported him.[66]

Supposedly trusted by the governor with full authority to deal with the crisis, Oswald lacked authority in the two most crucial areas. First, he could not delay an assault past the moment, always impending, when Rockefeller would order it. Second, Oswald had no authority over the assault force. They were flagrantly contemptuous and insubordinate. Events would show their defiance of Oswald's every desire and command for restraint. Certainly Oswald made few, if any, attempts to enforce discipline on them; but, then, Oswald was not trained as a battalion commander.

Besides, Oswald did not want to storm the prison. He saw himself as a deeply committed liberal, and an armed assault was so repugnant to him that it must be the responsibility of others, not himself, both morally and practically. He refused to get involved in planning the assault, delegating or ignoring all the crucial tasks. He avoided the hawkish guards and police, preferring instead to associate with his fellow liberals in the observers' committee who were trying to prevent an assault.

Torn between his desire for an impossible peace and his duties in an unthinkable battle, Oswald vacillated, second-guessed himself, begged for understanding, suffered the tortures of the damned, stalled, stalled some more, acted on impulse, and in the end executed no one plan. Instead of pursuing a single negotiating strategy, he pursued three in rapid succession— each lasting about 30 hours, and each discarded at the point when serious conflict arose with inmate leaders. From Thursday through Friday afternoon, he pursued direct negotiations; from Friday night through Saturday night, he accepted observer mediation; from Sunday through Monday morning, he delivered ultimata. Each period will be discussed in turn.

## Direct Negotiation

Oswald arrived at Attica about 2:30 on Thursday afternoon, at a time when the state police commanders believed that they did not yet have enough personnel on hand to retake the rest of the prison. At about the same time, two civilians arrived to offer their services in "mediation." One was Arthur Eve, a black assemblyman from Buffalo, who had in fact been named as a requested observer in the "Immediate Demands." The other was Herman Schwartz, a law professor from the State University of New York at Buffalo, who was active in prisoners' rights litigation and who was known to some of the inmates. Both asked permission to enter D Yard to assess the situation, and Oswald assented. About 3:00 p.m., they were ushered through the tunnels, frisked by inmates in an imitation of the authorities' own security procedure, and admitted to D Yard.[67]

On arriving at the security table, they were given a copy of the "Immediate Demands" (see Appendix B). They included: "complete amnesty," federal intervention, and the "transportation" of inmates to a non-imperialist country. To the "Immediate Demands," inmates added several conditions for the negotiations they wanted to take place. Talks were to take place in D Yard, nowhere else; the discussions were to be broadcast to the entire yard; the spokespeople at the table were not to be considered "leaders," that is, empowered to make decisions over the head of the collectivity. They also wanted Oswald himself to appear in the yard for negotiations.

Schwartz took issue with several of the "Immediate Demands" which, he argued, were impractical, such as passage out of the country and turning Attica over to federal control. Some inmates apparently reacted with hostility to Schwartz's argument. Eve and Schwartz left the yard without incident to report their experiences to Oswald.

Oswald entered the yard at about 4:25, over the objections of his subordinates, accompanied by Schwartz and Eve.[68] Both sides viewed this meeting as essentially a preliminary one to determine the terms for negotiations. They demanded that Oswald return to the yard for further meetings, this time with news media present, and that sharpshooters be taken off the roofs of A and C blocks. Oswald agreed, and also allowed Eve to visit HBZ to determine the condition of Dewer and Lamorie.[69]

The inmates greeted the media representatives, who entered the yard with Oswald, Eve, and Schwartz about 5:45, with an "explosion of rhetoric."[70] Yet inmates presented Oswald with the "Practical Proposals" (see Appendix C), an entirely new and much more moderate set of demands. Despite the negative reaction of some inmates to Schwartz's earlier suggestions, his advice had been taken. Indeed, Schwartz felt the new list didn't go far enough! This action by the inmates was in keeping with the example of the earlier "Manifesto" of the Attica Liberation Faction, whose preamble had blasted the "concentration camps" and whose body had contained a reasonable program.[71] Oswald responded to each of the 15 proposals and stated that he agreed with most of them "in principle."[72]

Apparently, however, the inmates and Oswald had opposite impressions of negotiations at this point. While the inmates must have felt as if progress was being made, Oswald was "deeply depressed" and "despondent."[73] In his view, discussion of the 15 proposals was "completely overshadowed" by the earlier demands for passage out of the country and "complete amnesty."[74] By his later account, the organization of the inmate security force and the character of the "Immediate Demands" convinced him that he was dealing not with a "spontaneous riot against poor prison conditions," but with a carefully planned conspiracy making "revolutionary demands that could not be met."[75] Perhaps this accounts for what Oswald did: he virtually abandoned the negotiating process that had begun as if it were an impossible task.

Having left D Yard at 6:44 p.m., he announced plans to return on Friday morning at 7:00 a.m., instead of making use of the evening hours.[76] He left Deputy Commissioner Dunbar on the yard to discuss the "Practical Proposals." Dunbar made it clear that he was unsympathetic to even the demands that Oswald approved of, and began to debate their merits. Inmates may have interpreted this as a sign that Oswald was not serious in his earlier commitments.[77]

At this time, one of the "inmate lawyers" declared that they wanted a federal injunction against "physical and administrative reprisals" by the administration, and produced a self-drafted complaint by "Inmates of Attica Prison" against "Nelson Rockefeller, Russell Oswald, and Vincent Mancusi," which charged that they had "treated inmates as dogs."[78] Schwartz and Eve, who had accompanied Dunbar onto the yard, began to discuss the matter with inmate Roger Champen. Champen was then allowed to leave D Yard, to go to the superintendent's office to work on the proposed order. The final wording was worked out by Oswald, Schwartz, and Champen together. After Oswald signed the order, Schwartz left that night for Vermont (where there was a judges' conference) to obtain the signature of a federal judge. Champen was returned to D Yard.[79]

Somehow Oswald apparently came to view this injunction as the answer to his prayers, a device to resolve the riot peacefully and speedily without engaging in tedious and doubtful negotiations. Schwartz would return from Vermont and hand him the keys to Attica. When bad weather held up Schwartz's plane, Oswald simply delayed things until he could return and did not show up on D Yard at 7:00 a.m. Friday morning as promised. But inmates were not informed of Schwartz's problems. Further, Oswald and Dunbar had concluded that negotiations were "impractical" on D Yard, and informed inmates at 10:00 a.m. they were to meet in the DMZ. After the inmates refused, Oswald gave in and agreed to enter D Yard one last time. However, by this time suspicion and anger were rife among the inmates.[80]

From the inmates' point of view, there were reasons to believe they were being hustled. For 17 hours, Oswald had not talked with the inmates directly. Many on the yard were unaware that Champen had helped to draft the court order. Oswald hoped that the injunction would convince the inmates to give up the hostages and go back to their cells without further ado; but it was not to be.

Oswald, five observers, and a dozen media people entered the yard at 11:30 a.m. on Friday to discuss the injunction which had been returned by Schwartz earlier in the morning. The injunction read *in toto:*

> Upon the consent of defendants, it is hereby ORDERED that: Defendants, their agents and employees, are enjoined from taking any physical or other administrative reprisals against any inmates participating in the disturbance at the Attica Correctional Facility on September 9, 1971.

Oswald's appearance on the yard with the injunction was not a success. Inmates angrily denounced the injunction as "garbage." They protested that it did not have a seal; it was signed by Oswald and not by Rockefeller; by the time they received it, it was September 10; it was not signed by the black federal judge of their choice. Most important, it did not provide full amnesty—protection from criminal prosecution. Finally one of the spokesmen physically tore it up. Inmates began to cross-examine Oswald, then to revile him. At length, one of the spokesmen proposed to take Oswald hostage. After some chaos, this idea was "resoundingly shouted down."[81] Nevertheless, Oswald left the yard immediately, resolved never to return while inmates controlled it.

On reviewing the events, one is amazed that Oswald had put such hope in this injunction, as if inmates had agreed that this limited amnesty was just what they wanted. An ounce of prevention is worth a pound of cure. An hour more spent on D Yard on Thursday night discussing thoroughly the inmates' demands and making clear what the injunction would and would not do might have saved Professor Schwartz a night's sleep and a hasty flight to Vermont, and might have prevented an emotional letdown, laden with mutual feelings of betrayal, for all the actors.

## Negotiation Through Observers

The effect of the injunction fiasco on the inmates was that their level of distrust for Oswald sharply increased; they announced that no more negotiations would take place until the observers they had requested arrived. The effect on Oswald was that he resolved never to enter D Yard again. The joint result was that the next phase of negotiations took place through a heterogeneous collection of intermediaries.

A total of 33 persons eventually appeared on the scene as observers. Some were individuals named by inmates, some were representatives of groups named by inmates, some were recruited by these persons, some were recruited by the state, and some showed up at the prison on their own.[82] Their politics ranged from the conservative to the revolutionary. The complex interaction among these individuals is described in Wicker and in McKay, but is not the subject of this work and is not (in our view) necessary to detail in order to understand the process which ensued.

The inmates' original plan had been for direct negotiation with the state in D Yard, the process to be "observed" by these respected outsiders. With direct talks now ruled out, the observers would play some other role in some new process. The observers were forced to develop their own conception of what they were supposed to do, with little or no guidance from Oswald. Five roles occurred to at least some from time to time:

1. As couriers, they would deliver the communications of each side to the other, without input of their own. This would imply an actual dialogue between Oswald and the inmates, with the observers channeling the communication impartially.
2. As mediators, they would take a more active role, maneuvering between the opposing sides, facilitating their agreement.
3. As representatives of the inmates, they could negotiate on their behalf, trying to get the best deal possible, perhaps even concluding an agreement with the administration.
4. On the other hand, they might actually function as Oswald's diplomatic representatives to the inmates, helping him manage the situation by translating the solutions he wanted into rhetoric the inmates could accept and then cajoling or maneuvering the inmates into accepting them.
5. Finally, as policy formulators, they could develop solutions of their own and urge both sides to accept them.

As events developed, Oswald came to treat the observers as if they had agreed to the fourth model. The observers were to be a team of experts working for the state, who might, with luck, work a miracle and save the situation. "In Oswald's mind it was *up to them* to arrange a settlement and prevent bloodshed," says Wicker, although this was not clear to the observers at the beginning.[83] But, in fact, as the inmate-state dialogue collapsed, the observers more and more took on the fifth role, trying desperately to come up with new ideas to fend off catastrophe.

The period of negotiations through observers lasted from 5:00 p.m. Friday to midnight Saturday, a period of about 31 hours. There is a lot of data about what all these observers did, what speeches they made, what they argued about, and so on and on, and this data fills many pages in McKay and in the books by Oswald, Tom Wicker, and Herman Badillo. In fact, there is some danger of being led by the quantity of this matter into the mistaken belief that a great deal of negotiation was going on. The truth is otherwise.

While observers then on hand visited the yard between 5:00 and 7:00 p.m. on Friday to introduce themselves, their work did not begin in earnest until 11:30 p.m. Friday, by which time more of their number had come. On this later visit they listened to speeches and declarations and made lists of what was important. Part of this period was disrupted by troop movements on the part of the state which raised fears of an immediate assault. There were also outcries from inmates in (recaptured) C Block, and rumors and complaints that they were being gassed and beaten. Some observers visited C Block and came back with a mostly reassuring report. The observers left the yard about 5:00 a.m., having collected a list of inmate demands (see Appendix D).

Saturday morning, recognizing the importance of the amnesty issue, three of their number visited the local Wyoming County District Attorney Louis James and obtained a statement from him on the question of amnesty and prosecutions (see Appendix E).

From 1:00 to 3:00 p.m. Saturday, the group met and debated what to do with the James statement. Most observers recognized that inmates would regard it as inadequate, but some of them went further—they suggested it not even be shown to the inmates. Others felt that it was their ethical obligation to do so, and this position carried. However, inmates did not receive it until much later.

From 3:00 to 5:00 p.m., the group met with Oswald and obtained from him what became known as the "28 points"—a list of concessions which Oswald was willing to grant, more or less corresponding to the inmates' demands (see Appendix F). As the McKay Commission pointed out, some of these points were vaguely worded and promised little specific. As McKay also pointed out, though, "many of the principles embodied in the 28 points were major advances in penal reform." Oswald also gave ground on amnesty. He would guarantee no administrative reprisals, including segregation of inmates and denial of parole. Oswald also promised that the state would not initiate criminal complaints for the destruction of state property. By the end of the meeting, Oswald and some of the observers were optimistic that the 28 points would settle the situation.

From 5:00 p.m. on, the group discussed how to present the 28 points to the inmates. The flush of optimism quickly wore off, and most came to believe that the inmates would not see this proposal as acceptable. Again the question arose of how and whether to "manage" the proposal. Was the group to recommend to the inmates that they accept the 28 points and surrender the hostages? This viewpoint failed; in the end, they were presented to the inmates without endorsement, but with statements by some observers that they were probably the best that inmates could get.

During this period, word arrived that Officer Quinn had died from the injuries he had received on Thursday. This of course cast a new, chilling light on the amnesty question. New York at the time retained the death penalty for murder only in a limited number of situations, but killing a prison guard was one of them. Surrender under the terms of the 28 points and the James letter might now mean the electric chair for some.

It was not even clear that only those who struck the blows would be prosecuted. Under the felony murder rule then in force in New York, a person who commits a felony is responsible if anyone dies as a result of the felony, whether or not they are present. Unless the James letter could be taken as an abjuration of the felony murder rule, any "organizer" of the riot might face a death sentence. Furthermore, the radio reported that Quinn had been thrown from a window. Since all Attica's windows had bars, even inmates who did not know exactly how Quinn had been hurt had reason to speculate that a frame-up was in the making.

At 9:00 p.m., the observers returned to the yard to deliver the 28 points and the James letter. Some of the observers were physically afraid to stay on the yard for this, and left after Black Panther leader Bobby Seale, who had arrived that evening from California, had given a supportive speech not referring to the negotiated points. Other observers thought an understanding was reached not to present them that night, in the hope that Seale would endorse the points the next day and pull their chestnuts out of the fire. The atmosphere on the yard was quite tense as the 28 points were presented. After the James/Oswald response on amnesty was heard, inmates gave derisive and hostile reactions to the rest of the points. Finally one inmate tore up the piece of paper from which an observer was reading them, and others shouted them down. Most observers left the yard after midnight in a mood of despair, believing the negotiations to have "failed." This attitude was conveyed to Robert Douglass, Governor Rockefeller's representative on the scene, in the early hours of Sunday morning.

All this can actually be summed up quite briefly. The inmates made a proposal (collected Friday night) which the state rejected in part, and the state made a proposal (the 28 points) which the inmates rejected in part. After these two steps, the negotiations were discontinued. Certainly, one can hardly say there had been a very active interchange of views. Furthermore, there was room for further discussion even about the key issue of what crimes would be charged.[84]

The failure of the negotiations came about in part because the stances of Oswald and the inmates were far apart. The inmates believed their violence was justifiable and really the state's responsibility; the state refused to legitimize the inmates' violence, which had brought about Quinn's death. This made an agreement problematic in the best case.

But the divergent readings of the situation by the three "parties" —Oswald, observers, and inmates—created additional obstacles. Half-convinced that the negotiations must be doomed by the inmates' intransigence, Oswald, between his last yard visit on Friday and his meeting with observers on Saturday, devoted no energy to improving their chances. Communication with the inmates might have been enhanced by field telephones or the establishment of a command post at the DMZ, accessible to the inmates. Oswald might have been on hand to debrief the observers whenever they returned from D Yard. Once accepted, the 28 points might have been reproduced and sent in over Oswald's signature. The more contact between the administration and the inmates, the less chance that the inmates would fatally misread the situation. Also, to ease tensions on both sides, Oswald might have camped the assault force a mile down the road rather than in front of the administration building.

The observers faced their own problems. They were deeply divided politically, and arguments among them drained much of their energy. Unable to recommend acceptance of the 28 points themselves, the majority of the observers hoped that Bobby Seale would take this responsibility. When he refused to do so without consulting the Panther headquarters in California, the observers had put a critical decision in the hands of *this* group. Further, when the inmates rejected the 28 points, the observers implicitly accepted the situation as "negotiations having failed" rather than "negotiations being tough." There was some reality to this assessment, but there may have been more room for negotiations even then, though the possibilities were getting slim.

Cut off from negotiations all day Saturday, the inmates fatally misread the situation. They did not realize that, from the point of view of both Oswald and the majority of the observers, Saturday night was *it* and their rejection of the 28 points—presented to them a few minutes before—would be taken as the termination of negotiations. Had they known, they might have been equally firm—or they might have accepted the deal or protested that they needed more time to talk and consider.

Further, the structure of the decision-making process—a large crowd shouting yeas and nays to proposals—made it difficult to compromise. While consensus could be achieved this way, especially in uniting against the administration, a compromise solution could not. For an inmate to urge a compromise in the open meetings on D Yard was to risk losing face or even being branded a traitor. Perhaps *less* (direct) democracy was needed.

## Ultimata

At some time on Sunday morning, Commissioner Oswald concluded that nothing more was to be gained through the strategy of negotiation. Oswald had lost faith in the observers' ability to perform the task he believed they should have undertaken—persuading the inmates to accept a compromise and surrender. "A committee as powerful as this ought to have been able to swing the inmates around," he would charge that evening.[85]

Oswald's conviction was shared by Rockefeller and Douglass. From that moment, the assault was inevitable. Why was it not made immediately? Both because Oswald shrank from ordering it and accepted excuses for postponing it, and because at a critical point Governor Rockefeller acceded to pressure from the observers for a delay. The 24 hours between Sunday and Monday morning were not, however, used by the state in any potentially beneficial way. Instead, they were marked by a series of futile and dithering maneuvers, which were without potential value in re-establishing negotiations, inducing the inmates to surrender, or making the assault more likely to be successful. The chief contacts between the administration and the inmates were two written ultimata, the first delivered at about 2:10 p.m. on Sunday, the second at 7:40 a.m. on Monday (see Appendixes G and H).

When the observers arrived back at the prison early Sunday morning, they found that their role in the situation had been circumscribed; eventually they were told they would not be allowed onto D Yard again. The observers realized with dismay what was coming and spent the day trying to regain some input into the situation by going over Oswald's head. The gravamen of all these efforts was that Governor Rockefeller must come to Attica. To this end the observers conferred with Douglass at 11:00 a.m., and four of them called the Governor at 1:20 p.m. and talked with him for nearly an hour; in the meantime, a message had been delivered in their name to the public of the state (see Appendix I). Most of the observers agreed that this was the key to the situation, and a great deal was written afterward about why Rockefeller didn't come and whether he should have. However, we see no evidence that Rockefeller's belief in the necessity of an armed assault would have been altered by a visit to the scene. While it's conceivable that Rockefeller's presence would have convinced the inmates to surrender, this would have depended upon what Rockefeller said and did once there. But Rockefeller was not Oswald. He was in no mood to appease the inmates.

Oswald had drafted an ultimatum by about 1:00 p.m., after a conversation with Rockefeller (see Appendix G). Oswald insists that this communication was not an ultimatum but a message. We must reject this. The state police were actually poised at their assault stations on Sunday afternoon. The observers had been barred from the yard. Food was not sent in as on previous days. Dunbar's diary records that the Sunday "message" was sent in "with the response due at 3:00 p.m.."[86] Its text is similar to that of Monday's ultimatum. Observers who saw it at 1:20 p.m. took it as an ultimatum (see Appendix H). This is what led four of them to call Governor Rockefeller.

The call lasted about an hour. Rockefeller would not agree to come to Attica, but did promise the callers "more time" and in fact ordered that no assault take place that day. If the purpose was to "giv[e] the inmates an additional day to accept the points,"[87] Rockefeller did not seem to have a plan in mind for putting the day to good use. The governor was convinced there was no more need for the observers.[88]

By the time Rockefeller had made these assurances, Oswald had sent in the ultimatum anyway. An immediate effect of the ultimatum was consternation among the observers, who were compromised with the inmates by Oswald's declaration that the committee had "recommended" the 28 points. The reader will understand that Oswald was amazed that the observers put up a fuss, as he believed he was accurately stating the role of the observers. However, from the inmates' point of view, at least some of the observers were supposed to be "representing" them, that is, trying to get something better than the 28 points from the state—that means, in effect, amnesty. Now the inmates were informed by the state that the observers wanted them to surrender without amnesty.

The observers pleaded with Oswald to be allowed to go in one more time. They had two motives here. First, the inmates had asked for reporters to be sent in to interview the hostages; the observers hoped that these interviews would pressure Rockefeller to come and Oswald to hold off the assault. Second, they wanted to warn the inmates that they were in mortal danger. In sum, they wanted someone—either side—to give in and avert disaster. Such was the fear among many of the observers of how the inmates would react to them after reading the ultimatum, though, that only nine actually went in with the news crew. In their minds, "as they now recall it," says McKay,[89]

another thought was uppermost . . . they had to do something to explain away Oswald's message and win back what they perceived as their lost credibility.

Suspicion of treachery on the part of the observers was rife in the yard when the ultimatum was read. There was debate over whether to let the delegation in at all, and they were warned that they couldn't be promised safe conduct out of the yard.[90]

Several of the observers made speeches of solidarity. McKay argues that what they said falsely raised hopes among inmates that amnesty and transportation could be won. There appears to be something to this. Even without desiring to mislead, speakers were under pressure to make positive and encouraging speeches. Not only did their own passage out of the yard depend on what they said; not only would they have little influence over the inmates unless they made it clear that they were on the inmates' side; but also, they felt betrayed and libeled by Oswald and genuinely wanted to regain the inmates' trust and respect. All of this militated against—and perhaps precluded—clear statements to the inmates about where they stood. Statements that the observers were "more [united] today than we have ever been" and that the commissioner was "frightened now, because we have insisted that the Governor come here"[91] belied the facts that the observers had less power in the situation than ever before, and that the governor had refused to come and was in fact in close touch with Oswald. The observers discussed the legitimacy of the inmates' demands for transportation and amnesty, without at the same time making it clear that the state had no intention of granting these demands, and there were no political forces in play which were likely to change this situation. One observer took advantage of the occasion to warn one of the spokesmen "about the number of men, the guns they had, and [that] they were getting ready to storm the place"; but the spokesman did not pass the word on for fear of creating "panic."[92]

After the speeches came the hostage interviews, during which captive guards pleaded for the governor to come and grant amnesty. Inmates did not expect Rockefeller and Oswald to continue to exercise forbearance on behalf of themselves, but would they risk the lives of their employees? They would, but the inmates were never made clearly aware of this.

On leaving the yard after 6:00 p.m., an observer carried a message to Oswald that the next move was up to him and demanding negotiations in D Yard. This concluded the observers' contact with the inmates. Oswald met with the observers one last time. The observers tried to come up with some fresh idea that would sway Oswald, but it was too late for that. He and Rockefeller were committed to a Monday morning assault.

At 7:40 a.m. Oswald's second ultimatum (Appendix H) was delivered to the inmates at the DMZ. It was read aloud on D Yard; when responses were asked for, only one inmate urged it be accepted, and a member of the negotiating committee felt it necessary to admonish the inmates in the yard not to attack him. Other inmates shouted it down. After this, the hostages were all blindfolded, and eight of them were taken up to the catwalks above A Tunnel, C Tunnel, and Times Square in an attempt to deter the armed assault. Inmate guards held knives to their throats, and one of the hostages was ordered to scream repeatedly, "I don't want to die!" In A Tunnel, a last exchange of shouts took place. An inmate called for Oswald and the observers to come onto D Yard. Dunbar called back that if all the hostages were released Oswald would meet with them. "Negative," called back an inmate.

The theory behind an ultimatum is that a target, if given a clear choice between surrendering and being subjected to violence, will choose the former. For this theory to work, the target must understand the choice posed by the ultimatum, the target must believe the deliverer means it, and the target must be capable of, and disposed to, choosing surrender. Otherwise, an ultimatum is likely to have serious negative consequences: warning the target that an assault is forthcoming, stiffening resistance, or (if the deliverer actually does not act on it) weakening the deliverer's future ability to threaten.

Oswald's ultimata did not clearly spell out the terms of surrender and did not make it clear that an assault with overwhelming force would follow a rejection. The style was sympathetic and polite, rather than simple, direct, and easily comprehensible to uneducated people. That a clearer statement of the intention to assault might have alarmed, warned, or angered the inmates and caused reprisals against the hostages is not a reasonable objection. If one does not want the target to have a clear picture of one's intentions, one should not write ultimata. As it was, the consequences of the second ultimatum were that hostages were taken at knifepoint into the line of fire; a clearer statement could hardly have done worse.

The inmates were confident that the state would not make an assault. This is attributed by McKay to an "air of unreality" afflicting D Yard, and by

Wicker to their trust in the benign nature of the state. Another factor cited by McKay is even more crucial: they (some, anyway) believed that the state must refrain from assaulting them as long as the hostages' lives were at risk. The governor was rumored to be on his way, and extensive media coverage of the observers helped to exaggerate the political resources being swung into action on their behalf. The ultimata said nothing to dispel these beliefs, though they could have. As a result, the ultimata were generally not believed. Of course, the fact that the Sunday ultimatum was not acted on must have prejudiced the credibility of the Monday ultimatum.

## Inmates Under Siege

There is a division of opinion on the subject of the inmates' state of mind as the siege progressed. McKay argues that they were subject to a serious crisis of morale, manifested by witch-hunting. On the other hand, sources from the observers' committee and the inmate leadership pointedly reject this;[93] and McKay declares, in apparent self-contradiction:

> The televised interviews with the hostages and the speeches in D Yard Sunday afternoon undoubtedly contributed to the feeling of power and importance which had been growing among the inmates.

Both sets of perceptions are probably based on fact. We suggest that unity probably did remain high among the spokesmen, the security guard, and "political" inmates who identified with that group.[94] The observers would have dealt with this circle. These inmates did not participate for the most part in the work of the McKay Commission. Furthermore, morale was probably higher when the observers were on the yard (so that's what they saw). Non-participating inmates, not vocal at the time but tapped by McKay's exhaustive interview procedure, probably did become anxious and demoralized as the hours passed without word of negotiations and as rain fell throughout Sunday.

McKay argues that by Sunday the fabric of the D Yard community was falling apart. A doctor reported "psychic or hysterical reactions," including seizures and fits; an inmate medical volunteer reported an increase in stab and slash wounds from fights on Saturday and Sunday nights.[95] (Inmates suffering from such medical problems were released from inmate territory to allow them to use the prison hospital.) Food was held up on Sunday; that evening it rained. Time, and strain, and rain undoubtedly took their toll on the inmates in D Yard. "D Yard Nation was beginning to disintegrate," says Oswald. "Perhaps . . . the other side was even more tired than our own."[96] (Oswald does not draw the obvious conclusion from this, that waiting would have been of advantage to the state.) Yet the situation was not one of "informed" despair; it must have been somewhat akin to "sensory deprivation," in which normally negligible percepts are given disproportionate weight in the absence of more reliable cues. Faced with the need to know where they stood in their conflict with the state, they were given few and inconsistent answers.

As early as Thursday night, the inmate government first decided to act against an internal threat to their social order by locking up Michael Privitiera. He had a reputation for being "unstable and dangerous." On Thursday morning he tried to assault the hostages, threatening to kill them. Later that day,

> he assaulted an inmate with a pipe and was brought before the committee and sent to D Block. Privitiera was permitted to return to the yard, but proceeded almost immediately to assault another inmate. He was again sent to D Block, where he was subsequently beaten and stabbed to death.[97]

On Friday afternoon, two inmates named Kenneth Hess and Barry Schwartz were arrested for treason. Their offense was a conversation with a Buffalo television reporter in which they gave him information about the initial takeover. The reporter was seen to take notes on the conversation, and the rumor started that Hess and Schwartz were naming names. Hess had a reputation as a racist, and Schwartz as an informant. The reporter's notes were confiscated; the two inmates were stripped and taken into D Block. It is not clear if Hess and Schwartz were harmed immediately, but by Monday they were dead, stabbed numerous times, receiving "many more injuries than were required to kill" them—as was the case with Privitiera. Oswald claims that Hess had his throat slit at about 5:30 p.m. on Sunday;[98] perhaps all three inmates were murdered about the same time. That would have been after the breakdown of negotiations and Oswald's first ultimatum.

On Saturday another harsh incident took place. Seven white inmates, generally opposed to the riot and considering escape, were sharing a tent; one of them put a white cloth on a stick on the tent. Apparently the security guard thought this was meant as a "surrender flag," to identify and protect them in case of an assault, and this may have been true; their story that it was meant as a marker to identify the tent was not believed. Their fate was debated among the committee; they were almost taken "upstairs" to D Block, but then they were put under "house arrest," bound and blindfolded, for two hours. They were then told they could save their lives by finishing up a large L-shaped trench in the yard. They dug for hours, subject to verbal abuse from the security guards in charge of their work. When they finished close to evening, their fate was debated again; some "threatened to kill them, charging that they were correction officers in disguise, spying on the inmates."[99] At length they were released but told they would be watched. On Sunday night, four of them were re-arrested and locked up in D Block; and on Monday, two others would be taken up to Times Square, bound and blindfolded, along with the guard hostages. All survived, though.

McKay argues that the killings of Hess, Schwartz, and Privitiera may have had the effect of forcing the committee to hold out for amnesty for self-interested reasons. On the other hand, it is not at all clear that the committee ordered or knew of their deaths. There were other forces out there. McKay reports that a force of inmates separate from the committee controlled B and D blocks.[100] On Sunday afternoon,

> a band of 20 black inmates dressed in clerical vestments and other strange [apparel] taken from the chapel emerged from inside D Block and approached the hostage circle. One of them carried a long spear, another wielded a homemade machete with the word "executioner" painted on its blade, and others had bats, clubs, and gas guns. They . . . announced that they had come to get the hostages. The Muslims lined up shoulder to shoulder, ready to fight to protect the hostages.[101]

After a "tense confrontation," this unknown menacing group backed down. But this same group, or other inmates unanswerable to the committee, may have killed Schwartz, Hess, and Privitiera later that day in D Block.

## Termination: "Preserving a Lawful Society"

It would be a mistake to assume without proof that the armed recapture of Attica Prison was a failure. After all, the prison was recaptured, and the rebellious inmates were "taught a lesson." To many, this was enough to outweigh the defects in execution, and there were plenty of editorials in support of the actions of the state. For many more, the criticism to be made of the assault is not that it killed 39 men but that 10 of those were hostages. For others, the deaths of the inmates themselves were an outcome which should have been avoided. It's a matter of one's priorities. Objective questions are what task the state intended to accomplish, how they went about it, and how well suited their actions were to the accomplishment of that task.

The first question is why the assault was ordered at all. Even if one accepts the view that by Sunday the inmate leadership had shown itself to be unshakably committed to unattainable goals, and that a negotiated settlement was impossible as matters stood, it is not clear that matters would become worse for the state or for the hostages if the impasse were to continue. The deterioration of solidarity on D Yard could have resulted in mass defection. On the other hand, there was reason to believe that with the passage of time the inmates were improving their military position and making recapture progressively more difficult to accomplish. Barricades were constructed across catwalks and tunnels, and rumors flew that Sam Melville, a white radical adept at bomb manufacture, was supervising the construction of bombs and rockets. Apparently, some of the police and guards believed that hostages were being brutalized, though they had no evidence for it.

But, in fact, the reason for the armed assault was political. It was that Oswald and Rockefeller concluded that press coverage of the uprising would give support to revolutionary movements. As Oswald put it:

we were dealing with not just an uprising over prison conditions, over prisoners' grievances, to obtain prison reform. We were dealing with a very sophisticated and determined coalition of revolutionaries who were trying to exploit public sympathy to achieve their political objectives, to trigger a chain reaction undermining authority everywhere.

This obviously was an intolerable situation, not only in terms of the lives of the hostages but also, in a broader view, in terms of preserving a democratic society dedicated to the freedom and security of all citizens.[102]

It was to prevent this exploitation of public sympathy and preserve authority everywhere that the assault was decided upon. The riot must be put down as a public statement, a "decisive reassertion of the state of its sovereignty and power."[103] Rockefeller would write to Oswald after the events:

by your actions, more lives were saved, bloodshed on a far greater scale was averted, the idea of social change through violence and coercion was rejected, and the necessity for preserving a lawful society was upheld.

The importance of upholding these values stemmed from the fact that Attica was front-page news, and that the radical statements made at Attica were obtaining worldwide dissemination. Paradoxically, if the press had not reported the statements of the inmates and the observers, Rockefeller might have found it less urgently necessary to combat their deleterious and corrosive effects on the social order. Much was written after Attica about the effect of intense press coverage on the behavior of riotous inmates, but to our knowledge no one has pointed out its effect on state officials.

As the inmates had frequently threatened to kill the hostages in the event of an armed assault, and, moreover, were apparently capable of doing so before the forces of the state could reach the hostage circle, the decision to forcibly recapture the prison inevitably entailed great risk of life to the hostages, and the likelihood of armed conflict between the inmates and the state. Within these constraints, however, there is no evidence that Rockefeller or Oswald wanted blood spilled; that is to say, they can be presumed to have desired the fewest possible casualties and the smoothest possible operation commensurate with the armed recapture.

### "Not a military organization": Preparing the Assault

The responsibility for the assault was delegated by Oswald, lock, stock, and barrel, to the New York State Police, probably due to his repugnance for the whole business. Hence there was no pre-planning whatever by anyone with the authority to acquire better weaponry and personnel, organize a more complex plan of attack, or arrange for the necessary collateral tasks distinct from firing guns, such as providing medical care, documenting the events, or informing relatives.

The task at hand was a military task, but, as McKay quite justly points out, "the State Police are not a military organization . . . they are not trained to act in concert in complex, coordinated maneuvers."[104] Nor are the officers themselves trained in clandestine or small-unit warfare. There would be no night assaults over the rooftops, then, by men rappelling down ropes into D Yard to free the hostages. Intelligence seems to have been relatively poor, particularly considering that so much of importance was happening in the open in a prison yard. Reports were based on rumor and on casual observation from the windows and roofs of A and C blocks. Their weaponry and technological support were limited. They had no access to troop-carrying helicopters or infrared scopes. Even the tear gas they eventually used was suggested and supplied by the National Guard. They would use shotguns armed with lethal "00" buckshot, and rifle slugs, because they didn't have shot of smaller size in their arsenal. Other troopers had brought their deer rifles from home.

These factors constrained the sort of plan the state police could create and execute. It would have to be a simple plan, a "low-tech" plan. It would be a "one-shot deal," as opposed to an ongoing campaign such as a unit of the armed forces could undertake. When a military unit has an objective under siege, each soldier is on duty 24 hours a day; there is a constant and coordinated effort to tighten the perimeter and to gather intelligence; a maneuver or attack can be ordered and executed with dispatch; hence, it can be deferred until there is the maximum opportunity for success. A product of that quality could not be gotten from this collection of state troopers. The assault would have to be scheduled in advance. The troopers would remain essentially idle and unproductive, gossiping in camp and cleaning their guns, until they were ordered to their assault posts. They would wait until the attack was ordered, and then they would act, essentially, as free agents, loosely grouped together. This is hardly what could be called a "surgical strike," but it is all that could be done with and by the forces on hand.

We should keep in mind that even from the point of view of Rockefeller the problematic feature of the tactical situation was not the recapture of the institution—which could obviously be done at any time—but the rescue of the hostages. Once the hostages were secured the game would be over. When one thinks of the mission at hand not as the recapture of a prison by storm but as the rescue of a group of hostages being held in a known location, one begins to wonder if a small elite force could have gotten better results than Monahan's band of troopers.[105] Perhaps, then, the state should have asked for better trained personnel, intelligence analysts, or even shotgun shells with smaller shot from better equipped forces. However, the question was never considered at the appropriate level. The governor, on Oswald's advice, had the authority to ask for such assistance from the federal government, but not Oswald and certainly not Monahan. By putting the matter in Monahan's hands, Oswald implicitly made the determination that it must be settled by Monahan's means. Monahan might, of course, on considering the matter, have told Oswald that the job could be done better by someone else; but he didn't.

Monahan's plan called for a tear gas drop squarely on D Yard from National Guard helicopters. Troopers would then advance toward Times Square on A and C catwalks and below them in the tunnels—30 on each catwalk and 25 in each tunnel. These forces would be armed with shotguns and handguns. Each catwalk detail would be accompanied by a 10-person detail assigned to barricade removal, carrying bolt cutters, fire extinguishers, and firemen's poles. Following the A catwalk detail would be a hostage rescue detail comprising 25 troopers and two correctional officers. Bringing up the rear on the catwalks was a 15-man reserve. All these people would wear gas masks.

On reaching Times Square, the catwalk parties would fan out to cover D Yard from above with their shotguns, while the rescue party descended with ladders they were carrying and recover the hostages. Meanwhile, the tunnel parties would spread out to secure the other yards and tunnels.

It was thought that the troopers advancing on the catwalks, particularly the barricade removal parties, who were unarmed, might need additional covering fire. For this purpose, four details of troopers armed with high-powered rifles with telescopic sights were posted at the third-floor windows and on the roofs of A and C blocks.

The police expected to encounter fierce resistance from inmates who actually had made hundreds of Molotov cocktails and who might have devised other sorts of booby traps and weaponry. While prepared for inmates using deadly force, however, the troopers were less ready for inmate resistance not involving deadly force. The troopers had been instructed to avoid hand-to-hand combat so as not to risk losing their own weapons to inmates. But this meant that if an inmate threw a rock, or waved a stick, or seemed about to throw a punch at a trooper, the only thing to do was to shoot him with a shotgun (loaded with deadly, as opposed to disabling, pellets).

Commanders were chosen for the various details only on Monday morning. Selection for the details was ad hoc. The detail commanders were briefed ahead of time, and apparently Monahan warned them against unnecessary use of their weapons. But the commanders had little time to brief the men assigned to them, who were strangers to them and with whom they would be virtually unable to communicate during the assault (during which the assault force would be wearing gas masks).

It had been determined by Rockefeller and Oswald that corrections officers (other than the 2 with the rescue party, who were there to identify the hostages) ought not to participate in the recapture of the prison, because of the likelihood of their overreaction. However, the structure of command made it difficult to enforce this order. That Monday morning, Mancusi and Monahan had drafted an agreement that correctional employees would command "in the event of the need for a custodial decision," while Monahan would command "police matters, such as an assault thrust."[106] But while Mancusi apparently did not order corrections officers to participate, neither did he order them to abstain. As the police took their positions, 11 corrections officers, apparently men from Auburn who had no duties and for whom this was their last chance to get into the fight, posted themselves in a window in A

Block, with their personal weapons and a submachine gun they had dug up somewhere. Three equally enterprising Genesee County Park Police found their way to a window in C Block.[107]

This was the situation at 9:00 a.m., when the inmates, responding to Oswald's final ultimatum, brought the eight blindfolded hostages up to the catwalks.

## Execution

At 9:46 a.m. the gas was dropped. Within seconds the rifle squads opened up on the inmates on the catwalks. Oswald portrays this as a race between the inmates' knives and the officers' trigger fingers. McKay says it is not really possible to tell who moved first.[108] Two of the guards being held on the catwalks actually had their throats seriously wounded by inmates' knives—both survived—but both said the shooting started first.

But the rifle fire didn't stop. It extended into a 50-second barrage. It went beyond the "surgical" removal of the "executioners," beyond the task of providing covering fire to protect the barricade removal force from attack. Every inmate on the catwalk—standing, lying, crawling, hiding from the gas—became a target, both for the gunners on the roofs and for the shotguns of the assault forces advancing up the catwalks. Rifle fire killed two of the ten hostages on the catwalks, and nine inmates; five more inmates on the catwalks died from shotgun pellets. When the catwalks were cleared of inmates, the gunners in the blocks began to fire into D Yard itself (about twice the distance). This may have been in an attempt to support the rescue force as it descended into the yard. But this fire killed three inmates and three of the hostages in the Circle.

The assault force on the catwalks met none of the resistance it was prepared for. The inmates were apparently quite incapacitated by the gas. None of Sam Melville's "super weapons" materialized. Melville himself was shot and killed. The rescue force climbed down into D Yard as the assault force lined the catwalks in a covering position. In the yard a Lieutenant Christian was knocked down by an inmate. This is the only act of resistance to the recapture which was described by numerous, reliable witnesses. The assault force on the catwalks responded with their shotguns and apparently continued firing indiscriminately into the yard. But it was not only inmates they hit. The pattern of the "00" buckshot, each pellet of which was capable of inflicting a fatal wound, spread to a width of 2½ feet at 50 yards range (the distance from the catwalks to the hostage circle).[109] Five of the hostages, along with ten of the inmates in D Yard (and one in A Yard) were killed by the shotguns of the assault force. Once in the yard, troopers fired into tents and ditches, picking off targets of opportunity.

At last the shooting stopped. The inmates in D Yard, still suffering from the effects of the gas, were forced through the opposite doors in D Tunnel into A Yard, where they were forced to lie facedown in the mud. Other state police secured B and D blocks.

## "A.A.—After Attica"

The Attica riot per se ended at a little after 10:00 a.m. on Monday, September 13. The period of lawlessness and violence which followed is documented in McKay and in Malcolm Bell's book, *The Turkey Shoot,* and requires no more than a brief summary here.[110]

Oswald and Mancusi had delegated the assault itself to the state police, but had not made provision for other special problems that would arise after the recapture. One such problem was the provision of medical care for the 90-odd wounded inmates and hostages. McKay describes how a National Guard unit and a group of volunteers filled the vacuum of responsibility. Another area left uncovered was the systematic development of reliable information on who was dead and how.

As the dead and wounded were removed from the prison, rumors spread among the state forces about the inmates' supposed acts of murderous brutality. It was not yet known that the dead hostages had been killed by gunfire. The surviving hostages with throat wounds were seen being taken out; the rumor spread that hostages had died with slashed throats. One hostage had sustained a severe gunshot wound in the groin; the word spread that the inmates had emasculated men with knives. This information was released to the press as factual. The corrections officers and state police whose job it was to restore routine heard these inflammatory stories not just as rumor but on the radio news.

As a result, many of them engaged in a day-long frenzy of verbal and physical brutality toward inmates. Inmates were kicked in the head and the privates; wounded inmates were beaten and knocked to the ground; inmates were made to run a gauntlet of guards and beaten the length of it.

Forty-five percent of the inmates who had been in D Yard suffered bruises, lacerations, abrasions, and broken bones.[111]

The ghastly details are fully reported elsewhere,[112] and the self-serving claims by Dunbar and Oswald that this never happened or that they had no idea it was going on are not credible. Oswald probably lacked the authority to stop it, and Dunbar the inclination. (Dunbar had been the chief source for the media's throat-slashing and emasculation stories.)

But that night, autopsies revealed that bullets, not knives, had killed the ten dead hostages. The corrections officers and police who had taken reprisals on the inmates found out the next day that the ten deaths might have been the fault of their own lack of discipline, bad judgment, or poor marksmanship. This unpopular truth is still not universally accepted in the town of Attica,

where a wholly unsubstantiated rumor persists that the physician who per-
formed the autopsy was some sort of left-winger who covered up for the
inmates' crimes.

From that point on, the general lines of the political and legal debate over
Attica were established. On one hand were Rockefeller and Oswald, who
steadfastly maintained that they had done nothing materially wrong and that
the casualties of Attica were no more than you would expect. In arm's-length
alliance with Oswald and Rockefeller were the Attica guards and state police,
in whose interest it was that no one ever find out exactly what happened on
September 13. Accordingly, many of them, abetted by superior officers, destroyed evidence, refused to testify, or fabricated stories to account for the
rounds they had fired.

A special prosecutor was appointed, and charges against the inmates were
vigorously pursued. While inmates were not charged with felony murder
based on the deaths during the assault, three inmate leaders were charged
with felony murder based on the deaths of Hess and Schwartz. Two inmates
were charged with murdering Hess and Schwartz themselves, and two were
charged in the death of Quinn. Three leaders were charged with 34 counts of
kidnapping each. All told, 62 inmates were indicted on a total of 1,289 counts
of criminal activity.[113]

On the other side were the indicted inmates themselves and their defense
committee; liberal analysts, including certain members of the observers' committee; and the McKay Commission itself, which actually took its job of
producing an unbiased and complete report seriously and hence found itself in
necessary opposition to the culpable police and guards and (to some degree)
Oswald.

Scandal broke out in 1975, when a chief assistant to the special Attica
prosecutor went public with charges that his investigation of reprisals and
reckless use of firearms by guards and police was being stifled from above. In
the clamor over his disclosures, a general amnesty was declared. All outstand-
ing indictments of inmates were dropped. Seven inmates who had pleaded
guilty to reduced charges were pardoned by Governor Hugh Carey. The
sentence of John Hill (Dacajaweiah), convicted of killing Quinn, was com-
muted, and he was paroled in March of 1979.[114]

These events were an ironic commentary on the position of the state
during the riot that the state could not interfere with the discretion of County
Prosecutor James, and an amnesty was out of the question.

The seriousness of the effects of Attica are not doubted, but it is harder to
establish what they were. Inmates in prison disturbances for years after that—
and still—have said, "We don't want another Attica." Prison administrators,
in their own way, have said much the same thing. For inmates, the chief lesson
is probably that the state actually will attack, sacrificing hostages, if they are
pushed too far. Inmates have probably been induced to tone down their
demands and to release hostages for a lower price than they would like.
Administrators, in turn, moved (at least for a time) toward a more patient
approach to hostage situations.

But it seems that one of the chief legacies of Attica was an improvement in prison conditions in the New York system. The strongest statement we have found on this subject is in a study of Green Haven Correctional Facility, another upstate New York prison, published in 1978.[115] The author writes in part that

> there have been more changes at New York State's maximum security prisons in the last five years than in the preceding thirty. Most of them were made in 1972, a few months after the Attica riot. Just as in Christianity there is B.C. and A.D., in New York State penology there is B.A. and A.A.—Before Attica and After Attica.[116]

The author goes on to cite improvements in visiting conditions; lessened restrictions on mail; installation of pay phones for inmates' use; less time spent in the cells; establishment of an inmate grievance procedure; a statewide effort to hire black and Puerto Rican guards; and a major expansion of educational programs.[117]

Focusing on Attica itself, Wicker noted many of the same changes. He also cited an improvement in prison food, due to a switch from cost-based to nutrition-based criteria in menu selection. Furthermore, Mancusi—the demand for whose dismissal Oswald had refused to discuss—was dismissed in January of 1972.[118]

One can argue that these changes were not "fundamental" ones, as Wicker does; but they do seem to have been material changes for inmates. Furthermore, these changes might have been due to Oswald's pre-existing desires, or to oversight by the court system. But Sheehan argues that they were intended by the state Department of Corrections to "avoid another uprising by liberalizing prison conditions," and that Attica also encouraged the federal government to make funds available for these measures.[119]

We said above that it should not be assumed without proof that the state's assault was a mistake or a failure. Neither should it be automatically concluded that the inmates' refusal to surrender was foolish, or ill-informed, or crazy. After all, history has made heroes of many bands who refused to surrender and paid with their lives—the Texans at the Alamo, the Jews of Warsaw. The proposition that all such behavior is evidence of mental imbalance will not stand as an empirical one.

Leaving the viewpoint of history aside, there is a real possibility that the decision not to surrender on Monday morning made sense from the mundane standpoint of cost-benefit analysis. To make such a determination, one has to compare the inmates' situation after the assault—which we know—with their situation if they had surrendered immediately. In that case, there would have been much less public attention, no McKay Commission, and no amnesty. The facility would probably have been locked down for a long period, as it actually was, but without public scrutiny. Fewer people may or may not have been charged, but more would probably have been convicted. The hypothetical defense committee probably would have been even less well funded than the actual one. It is far from obvious that the 28 points would have stood up; public and governmental sentiment would likely have opposed the granting of significant concessions to inmates to settle the riot. A great many inmates may have been in prison for years longer, under much worse conditions. There would have been no "post-Attica" impulse for reform.

At the fateful hour, then, the average inmate was wagering about a 1 in 30 chance of death (varying with where he was and what he was doing) and a much greater probability of injury against a very real possibility of earlier release, public attention, and improved conditions in the long run. This is even assuming perfect knowledge on the inmate's part. From the point of view of the inmate, to whom the threat of death or injury is no novelty and to whom the deprivations of prison existence had become severe, this is not obviously a fool's bargain. One question of the rest of this work is why inmates since Attica have not made this choice more often.

# 4

# A Gang in Rebellion—Joliet (1975)

The dissent and violence of the 1960s was without precedent in U.S. history.[1] Assassinations, a half-dozen years of urban riots, protest over the war in Vietnam, and the Attica riot itself had pushed American society, many felt, to the brink of political instability. Writing from the vantage point of an insider, Daniel Moynihan conveys the sense of crisis among the political elite:

> In retrospect, the domestic turbulence of the United States in the late 1960s may come to appear as something less than cataclysmic. But this was not the view of the men then in office. Mayors, governors—presidents—took it as given that things were in a hell of a shape and that something had to be done.[2]

An increase in domestic spending was one response of the "men in office;" another was to develop policies that would try to incorporate into the mainstream those on the margins of society, especially a new generation of inner city blacks. It was such an effort that set the stage for the Joliet riot of April 22, 1975.

The story begins with the rise of politically militant street gangs in the city of Chicago in the mid-1960s.[3] Despite their supposed political conversion, many gang members were convicted of serious crimes and ended up in Illinois' prisons by the end of the decade. Once there, they gained power in the prisons, power which prison authorities did not challenge. A sudden reversal of this policy precipitated the rebellion.

## The Prison and Prisoners

Built in 1860, Joliet is one of the oldest U.S. prison structures still in use. In 1898, a state commission found the conditions in the prison to be horrible. "One is compelled to ask," the commission railed, "what excuse the great

State of Illinois can offer for compelling men . . . [to] eat, rest and sleep in quarters so repellent, so utterly unfit for the purpose that their very existence is a disgrace to the State that permits it."[4] State officials ordered the construction of a new prison to replace the decrepit facilities. Stateville opened 5 miles away in 1919. Both the "replacement" prison and Joliet, though, were still in service in 1975, as they are today.

For three-quarters of a century, Joliet and Stateville were administered as one unit under a single warden. In 1973, the Department of Corrections assigned a warden to each facility. Two years later, Joliet and Stateville operated under separate budgets for the first time.[5]

From the outside Joliet prison looks like a medieval castle. The monumental walls are decorated with a fortress-like facade, and the guard towers appear to be battlements. Inside the walls, there were four living units: East Cellhouse, West Cellhouse, Honor Dormitory, and Segregation (see Figure 4–1). In 1975, the East Cellhouse had no permanent residents but, instead, about 360 recently committed inmates awaiting classification and transfer to another prison. The West Cellhouse housed about 300 maximum security prisoners.[6] Both the East and West cellhouses had four floors. A hallway split the floors into two galleries, each with 38 cells and two showers. The cells were 63 square feet in size, somewhat below the nationally recognized minimum of 70. Most of the cells were equipped with bedsprings and mattresses, though some inmates had to make do with a thin mattress placed over a concrete slab. The only lighting in the cell came from a single bulb in a cavity high on the rear wall of the cell.[7] The East and West cellhouses branched off of the central administration building, located inside the walls on the south side of the prison.

An additional 60 inmates lived in an honor dormitory. Its separate building was once occupied by a shoe factory. A small segregation building, called the Tombs, held another 15. Here each cell had two doors—one barred and the other made of solid steel with a peephole.[8]

The prison had no protective custody unit. Inmates in need of protective custody were transferred to another prison (Sheridan Correctional Facility).

The April 22, 1975 riot was confined to inmates quartered in the West Cellhouse.


## Gangs in the Penitentiary

Located 40 miles southwest of Chicago, Joliet drew (as it does today) the vast majority of its inmates from Chicago. In 1975, 75 percent of the combined Joliet-Stateville population was black, 10 percent Hispanic, and the remainder white.[9]

Gang activity dictated inmate life at almost every turn. Over half of the inmates belonged to one of four Chicago street gangs: the Blackstone Rang-

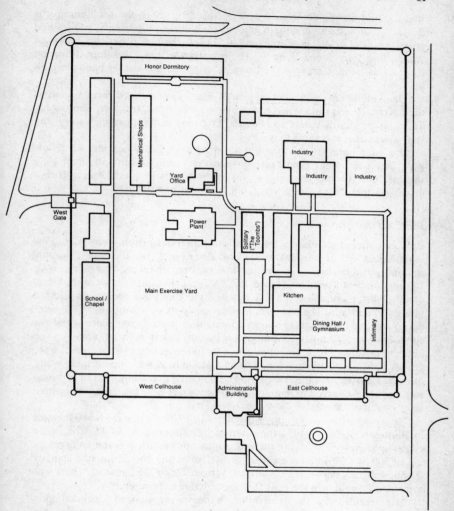

Figure 4–1. Joliet Correctional Center

ers, the Disciples, the Vice Lords, and the Latin Kings. The Latin Kings were a Hispanic gang and the others black.[10]

Prison rules forbade the wearing of gang insignias or names. The warden ordered the "J" in the middle of the the gymnasium floor painted black, so that it could not be associated with a gang color. Still, the prohibition was flouted openly. Gang members greeted each other with esoteric salutes and greetings. The Rangers, for example, raised their clenched fist and said "Stone love" or "Stone thing."[11] The president of the Blackstone Rangers, Eugene Hairston, displayed the Rangers' symbols on a leather band worn on his hand.[12]

Gang members openly defied guards. Each gang claimed certain areas as their territory and threatened to kill anyone who dared trespass. Thoroughly intimidated, guards complied. For the first time in the prison's history, the staff was fearful of coming to work.[13]

If a gang member was brought before a disciplinary hearing, his fellow gang members might congregate outside the hearing room and chant gang slogans. One observer witnessed several instances in which Joliet officials dismissed disciplinary charges to avoid precipitating a riot.[14]

## Inmate Deprivation

By conventional standards, the conditions at Joliet prison were poor. Few inmates had jobs or were involved in any sort of program; the only vocational training was a barbering course. A shoe factory, which once employed over 100 inmates, had been idle since 1972.[15] The living quarters were dark and damp. Plaster crumbled off the walls of the dimly lit, cockroach-infested infirmary, and a burlap sack was used to shade its only window. "One wonders," an outside observer group commented, "what confidence a patient could have in a doctor who would consent to work in such an office."[16] The kitchen facilities, including the stove and refrigeration appliances, were grossly deficient.[17] Inmates complained that the food was of poor quality and often too starchy. An observer group commented that a large vat of of macaroni and cheese served to inmates for dinner "must have been prepared with a small chunk of cheese."[18]

Crowding, though, was not a problem. In 1970, there were 8,600 inmates in Illinois prisons; by 1974 the number had declined to 6,000. The figure edged up slightly in 1975, but the true population explosion (eventually reaching 19,500 by 1986) had not yet set in. At Joliet, the population had actually declined slightly between 1974 and 1975 (from 738 to 725 inmates). There was some double-celling in the East Cellhouse, but not elsewhere.[19]

More realistically, the deprivation an inmate experienced depended upon his membership in a gang. Inmates rejected by the gangs, or who refused to join one, experienced the prison as a nightmare.[20] Some paid protection money to one or more gangs; others were forced to provide sexual favors or run errands. Inmates who refused to accommodate the gangs risked serious injury or even death. White inmates, in the minority and having no gang structure to protect them, were especially vulnerable. An older white inmate stated:

> You used to know what to expect and you could do your time in peace. Now I
> don't know what the hell's going to happen next. I'm more afraid of these

crazy bangers [the most vicious gang members] than I am of the screws [guards].[21]

Almost daily, prison officials received requests from white inmates to transfer to other facilities. Those making the request often claimed they had been been raped or otherwise assaulted. Some of these requests were honored, but most were not.

Prison life for a gang member was vastly better. He was protected from physical assault, as his fellow gang members would retaliate in number. Just as important, James Jacobs found in his study of Stateville and Joliet, were the enhanced status and pride which gang membership brought:

> the organizations [gangs] give to the members a sense of identification, a feeling of belonging, an air of importance. . . . Time and again gang members explained that, whether on the street or in the prison, the gang "allows you to feel like a man"; it is a family with which you can identify.[22]

Further, gangs served as cushion against confinement in segregation or temporary "poverty." Each gang had a welfare fund, or "poor box," to which members were required to contribute cigarettes, coffee, soap, and other commissary items. Kept in a gang member's dresser drawer or an actual box, these items were distributed to members in segregation or in need.[23] Like taxes everywhere, this one was collected through a combination of threats and appeals to loyalty. A memo passed to Blackstone Rangers at Stateville stated:

> For the past month, no Stone has placed anything into the Nation's box (which is for every Stone in need). At present the Box contains twenty-five (25) packs, and none of this comes from any Stone in the Cell House. There have been many Stone's receiving but None giving. "THE EMIR" plainly stated that the Stone's Box was necessary (Mandatory). So therefore it must be kept up, at all time's. As of the above date, all Stone's must pay two packs weekly. There is no reason for any Committee Member to come to you, when you know it's due. "Eusi Outlaw," and JM, are in charge of the box so you can give them to either. Records will be kept of everything coming in, or going out, and everyone shall be kept informed on the progress of all thing's coming in. [Spelling and punctuation as in original.][24]

Further, gang members could trust each other not to inform on one another. A "snitch system" did not and could not operate, since inmates exhibited greater loyalty to the gang than to their own personal interests. Jacobs comments, "While at one time inmates may have endorsed the principle of 'doing your own time,' the gangs endorse the morality of 'doing gang time.' "[25] This loyalty was reinforced by the fear of the violent beating or even death that disloyalty or defection could bring.

## The Blackstone Rangers

The Blackstone Rangers were the largest and most powerful of Joliet's four gangs.[26] It began in 1959, when a dozen boys between the ages of 13 and 14 banded together. They engaged in thievery and robbery and fought with other gangs, especially Disciples, whose territory was an adjoining neighborhood.

About 1965, the Rangers began to break out of this pattern. The leaders mounted an ambitious recruiting campaign, primarily in its own Lawndale neighborhood, but also in other areas in Chicago's South Side black neighborhoods. Membership was expanded both through the recruitment of new individual members and by the affiliation of other, smaller gangs. These smaller gangs, which adopted names such as Apache Rangers, Maniac Rangers, F.B.I Rangers, and Imperial Pimp Rangers, maintained their own organizational structure, leaders, and offices. The confederation became known as the "Blackstone Nation."

At its height, the Nation or Rangers were reputed to have between 2,000 and 8,000 members. For the vast majority, though, membership entailed little more than identification as a Ranger and the wearing of a Ranger patch. Only a core of about 200 members was integrated into the gang structure in the sense that they participated in the gang's day-to-day affairs and knew each other. At meetings open to the full membership, leaders recognized only a fraction of those in attendance, causing them to worry that some might be police informants. To the extent that overall control of the organization did exist, it was vested in Ranger President Eugene "Bull" Hairston, Vice President Jeff Fort, and the "Main 21," a 21-man executive committee.

As their membership grew, the Rangers became involved in a variety of political and community activities. They mobilized efforts to increase voter turnout and elect particular candidates. They set up a luncheonette and formed a singing group which appeared on national television under the Ranger name. When rioting broke out following the assassination of Martin Luther King in 1968, and one other time, the Rangers helped prevent its occurrence in its own neighborhood. A Ranger member explained:

> Our part was to keep the static down, like the looting and burning, because it didn't make sense. Yes, we policed our own neighborhoods. Anyone we saw trying to do this or that, we told them they shouldn't start over here. We had more on our minds than going around tearing up things.[27]

These activities convinced some members of the establishment that the gang might play a positive role in the ghetto. At the local level, Reverend John Fry, a left-leaning minister, offered the Rangers his unreserved support."To be a Ranger was to be really black for the first time," Fry later wrote.[28] He described his initial involvement with the Rangers this way:

> During that summer [of 1966] I encountered a policeman beating a boy on 63rd Street and in anger interposed myself between them, daring the police-

man to beat me before he further abused the child. . . . [From then on], the church would interpose itself between police and Blackstone and dare the police to beat the church up before it continued abusing Blackstone.[29]

Fry's church became the Rangers' headquarters and meeting point. Rank-and-file members hung out on the church's grounds from early morning to late at night, often numbering over 100. General membership meetings were held in the church's auditorium, and the leaders met regularly in Fry's own office.[30]

The federal government was also impressed with the Rangers. In 1967, the Office of Economic Opportunity [OEO] awarded a $927,000 grant for a job-training program to a community organization. The grant specified that Rangers and Disciples were to play key roles in the project, including as recruiters, instructors, and "center chiefs." The immediate goal was to teach skills to school dropouts that would help them get jobs. But there was, as well, a deeper purpose. Referring to the "crisis in our cities," the OEO director explained that

> probably the single most explosive element in that crisis is the problem of jobless-out-of-school and gang youth. . . . Traditional measures by established social and Government institutions apparently have met with little success. . . . A fundamental assumption [of the OEO grant] was that initially it is better to work with the already prominent and undeniably influential gang structure than it is to destroy it. . . . The gang structure would assist in shifting attitudes toward productive and responsible citizenship.[31]

The salaried staff included Ranger President Hairston, Vice President Fort, and several members of the Main 21.

In the same year as the OEO grant, the Rangers received a $50,000 grant from the Kettering Foundation (General Motors money), which was "made on the presumption that self-determination must be identified, treasured, supported, and its fruits honored."[32] W. Clement Stone (head of a large insurance company) loaned the Rangers $60,000 to finance some "short-term business debts," and Charles Merrill, Jr., (son of the founder of Merrill Lynch, Pierce, Fenner and Smith) gave the First Presbyterian Church $60,000 to help support Ranger activities.[33]

Finally, of symbolic importance, Jeff Fort was invited to President Nixon's 1969 inauguration. Although Fort did not attend, two Ranger representatives did. Sociologist Jerome Skolnick, writing for the National Commission on the Causes and Prevention of Violence, summed up the perceived transition of the Rangers: "Youth organizations, like the Blackstone Rangers in Chicago, are becoming more and more capable of mobilizing vast numbers of young people with a view to political or even guerrilla action. . . . The politicization of black youth reflects the growing political interests of youth in general."[34]

Other sectors of the establishment, however, were less convinced of the gang's "politicization." To them, the Rangers were never more than a criminal organization using a thin facade of political rhetoric to capitalize on liberal sentiment. In this judgment, efforts by the government and elites to support the Rangers were not only foolish, but assisted a criminal organization in terrorizing its own community. In June 1968, Senator John L. McClellan held public hearings focusing mainly on the OEO job-training project, but also scrutinizing the roles of the Kettering Foundation and the First Presbyterian Church. Witnesses testified that the training project was a sham, that federal money was being used to bankroll extortion and to traffic in narcotics, and that the First Presbyterian Church was a haven of criminal activities and the locus of a cache of weapons.

Sharing McClellan's view, Mayor Richard Daley set out to destroy the Rangers and the city's other gangs.[35] In 1967, the first citywide police gang unit was established, centralizing a function which had been the responsibility of local district commanders. Within a year, the Gang Intelligence Unit (GIU) expanded from 38 officers to over 200.[36]

One of GIU's targets was the OEO project. According to Irving Spergel, a University of Chicago professor commissioned by the OEO to assess the project, the GIU's harassment of the OEO project played a major role in its demise: "Police Department's lack of commitment to the objectives of the program, its gross failure to understand the complexity of the problem of gang delinquency in the black ghetto, . . . and its punitive law enforcement attitudes and activities made this the community force probably more responsible than any other for directly hindering and, finally, destroying the project."[37]

The legal problems gang members faced, though, went well beyond the demise of the OEO project. Hundreds of gang members were convicted of serious crimes. Ranger President Hairston was convicted of paying three young Ranger members each $2, plus bologna, cheese, and orange juice, to murder a narcotics dealer. The dealer had infringed upon the territory of another narcotics dealer who had been paying protection money to the Rangers. Dozens of other Rangers, including many of those involved in the federal job-training program, were convicted of murdering Disciples or innocent bystanders who either were mistaken for Disciples or caught in a cross fire.[38]

Most were sent to the three maximum-security prisons nearest Chicago—Joliet, Stateville, and Pontiac. Both Hairston and Fort were first imprisoned at Stateville and then transferred to Joliet. By the early 1970s, an estimated 50 to 80 percent of the inmates in these three prisons had either been gang members before their imprisonment or were recruited once there.[39]

Whether or not the Blackstone Rangers were ever a genuinely "political" group, they had acquired skills unavailable to traditional inmates. They had learned a political rhetoric, and how to use it to obtain support among certain elements of the elite. Further, they knew how to run an organization. Both skills would be used behind the bars.

## Administrative Response to Gangs

The influx of gangs into the prisons coincided with a liberalization of the prison administration. From 1936 to 1961, Warden Joseph Ragen ruled

Stateville-Joliet with an iron grip. Strict rules governed every aspect of inmate life. Inmates were not allowed to talk in the dining hall or while marching from one assignment to another, which they did in precise formation. Inmates could speak to guards only in answer to questions. Not even the slightest infraction of the rules went unpunished. Inmates who dared openly challenge the regime—by attempting to escape, defying a direct order from an officer, or organizing collective resistance—could expect a beating by a captain or an inmate helper, and then years in segregation.[40] Ragen's successor, Frank Pate, continued Ragen's management style, though he proved less capable at it.

In the fall of 1969, a recently elected Republican governor, Richard Ogilvie, appointed Peter Bensinger as director of the Department of Corrections. Besinger was 33 years old, educated at Yale, and heir to a famous name in Illinois Republican politics. Formerly an executive of the Brunswick Corporation, he had no background in corrections.[41] Bensinger sought to dismantle the authoritarian system established by Ragen at Stateville-Joliet, and implement a broad set of reforms along the "citizenship" model described in Chapter 2. Censorship of outgoing mail was ended, as was the ban on conversation between inmates and guards. Inmates were given more yard time and allowed for the first time to order *Playboy*. Guards were required to specify charges against an inmate, and the inmate had a right to a hearing within 72 hours of the alleged violation. The disciplinary punishment, when meted out, was to be less severe.

Perhaps most important, Bensinger took the position that the gangs that were filling his prisons should have a voice in their operation. This approach was taken only after long debate, much of it during the monthly meeting of wardens, but in the end it was a "liberal" solution that emerged.

This policy was implemented to the fullest extent at Pontiac Penitentiary, a maximum security facility for young offenders (ages 17 to 25). Warden John Petrelli allowed each gang to live in a separate cell block. He set aside a day for each gang to have a full-membership meeting in the prison's chapel. Inmates could meet with the warden whenever they requested it, and work assignments were based on a principle of representation proportional to gang size.[42]

At the Stateville-Joliet complex, Warden Pate resigned soon after Bensinger's appointment. He considered the new director's reforms unacceptable.[43] Pate's replacement, John Twomey, was young (32) and committed to liberal reforms.

Twomey gave gangs standing and a voice in the operation of the prison in several ways. One was the establishment of an inmate council, called Adult Basic Learning Enterprise (ABLE). Its stated purpose was to "increase communication between inmates and authorities, and thereby improve conditions and help maintain order."[44] An ABLE document described the formation of the organization this way:

An avenue of communications between the inmate population and the Administration, as well as the Department of Corrections was desperately

needed. . . . We emphasized the fact that if heads of the Correctional Department and Administration would sit down with some group of inmates and
hear their recommendations and proposals, and do something about them,
Atticas, and other such similar occurrences would never occur.[45]

ABLE adopted the slogan "Let's do it different from *Attica!*"

From its start, ABLE was dominated by gangs.[46] Membership on the eight-
member executive committee was allocated on a principle of group representation. The Rangers had two representatives, and the Disciples, Vice Lords,
Latin Kings, and Black Panthers each had one. One spot was also given to
independent whites and one to independent blacks.

The executive committee met once a week with the warden and several
other times with assistant wardens and other prison officials. ABLE proposed
various reforms, usually framed in the appropriate rhetoric:

> In the hope of alleviating existing tensions and creating an atmosphere more
> conducive to harmonious relations between residents and officials, Project
> Able proposes the instituting of a nightly T.V. Program. . . . Benefits de-
> rived from such a program would be manifold in number. For not only is T.V.
> a relatively cheap and popular form of entertainment, it has immense educa-
> tional values which are inestimable. . . . Taken as a positive stride toward the
> future, this propose[d] program would make manifest to the public and all
> concern[ed] that Correctional Authorities in this State have indeed rejected
> antiquated concepts of rehabilitation in place of more positive programs
> geared towards allowing residents to retain an active interest in the society
> from whence they came.[47]

The members of ABLE's executive committee were given the right to
move freely throughout the prison. This was done to facilitate the flow of
information between the committee and its constituents. An inmate commented, "These passes assigned real power because it enabled these inmates
to move between divisions and sections of the prison during daylight hours."[48]

A second way that the prison administration recognized gangs was its
response to Beni-Zaken, a supposedly religious organization. ABLE asked
prison officials to recognize the Rangers as a religious organization and give it
the special privileges accorded them. The request stated:

> That Chapel privileges be allwed (*sic*) for inmates whose religious beliefs are
> not presently being conducted. To write and receive mail, literature and
> various correspondence from ministers of their faith. To make Chapel avail-
> able for services conducted under the auspices of Allah's Almighty Black
> Peace Stone Nation, who maintains its own church and conducts religious
> services in the free community.[49]

Although prison officials rejected this demand, the Rangers obtained the
desired results through other means.

In 1968, a group of eight Rangers filed a petition with the Cook County

Recorder's office requesting the recognition of "Beni-Zaken" as a religious organization. The group met the county's simple requirements for incorporation as a religious group: the petitioners completed a form stating that the purpose of Beni-Zaken was religious worship, designated two trustees, and paid a $5 fee.[50] For about two years, Beni-Zaken rented space in a building in Chicago's South Side; after they stopped paying rent, the building was torn down, leaving a vacant lot.

Joliet's policy was to allow an inmate an unlimited number of visits with religious clergymen, which did not count against the three he could have each month. Under this policy, Eugene Hairston spent eight hours a day, three or four days a week, meeting with Ranger members claiming to be Beni-Zaken ministers. When Beni-Zaken ministers first appeared at the prison they were asked to provide certification of their religious status; after that, they were never challenged. These meetings helped Hairston maintain his control over gang operations at Joliet, at the other Illinois prisons, and on the streets.[51] This Hairston did with impunity: his prison record was sufficiently clean that he resided in Joliet's honor dormitory.[52]

A third way authorities extended a measure of official status to the gangs was in the operation of Joliet's Jaycee program. A Jaycee program existed in each of the state's prisons. Their purpose, according to the Department of Corrections' annual report, was to "undertake various projects for character building, leadership training, and community improvement."[53] At Joliet, the chapter sold magazines and greeting cards to inmates, made soft drinks available in the visiting room, and provided a photo service to inmates and visitors. Limited to 50 members, the chapter met twice a month, under the supervision of an advisor appointed by the warden. To join, an inmate had to be nominated by an active member, state why he wanted to join, and attend two meetings. The active members elected an executive committee.

Joliet's gangs vied for influence over the Jaycee program. As the largest and most powerful in the prison, the Rangers had secured control of the program, although in the summer of 1974 they had to fend off a bid by the Disciples. Eugene Hairston held the treasurer's position and was the individual most responsible for maintaining the program under Ranger control.[54]

Finally, Hairston and another Ranger leader were given positions as porters in the East Cellhouse. This was done so that the two could more easily provide authorities with information. If Hairston had difficulty controlling a particular member, this would be passed on to authorities, and the defiant inmate might be sent to segregation. On the other hand, authorities made it clear to Hairston and the other leader that if they did not keep the peace among their members, they would be sent to segregation themselves. Although this would have been against official departmental procedures, it was never necessary.

In sum, it was under the liberal regime of Bensinger and Twomey that gangs gained control of Stateville-Joliet. The extent to which their liberal policies contributed to this control can be debated, though it cannot be doubted that the liberal policies made it easier. Of course, subsequent, more

authoritarian administrators have been no more successful in rooting out the
gangs, and they continue today to dominate Illinois prisons. But the Twomey
regime officially tolerated and legitimated their share of power in the prison,
and the gangs would not recognize future wardens' right to abrogate this
agreement.

## Changes in Prison Policy

The policy of accommodating gangs was abruptly reversed in 1975. The explanation for this lies in the changing currents of Illinois politics. In the fall of
1972, Daniel Walker upset Governor Ogilvie's bid for a second term. This led
Director Bensinger to resign in December. Walker's first nominee to replace
Bensinger was rejected by the Illinois Legislature. Legislative confirmation of
the second nominee, Allyn Sielaff, came almost six months after Bensinger
had resigned.[55]

A former commissioner of corrections in Pennsylvania, Sielaff rejected as
naive Bensinger's citizenship approach. In the preface to the department's
annual report, Sielaff candidly admitted:

> The task, upon my appointment in June of 1973, was made more formidable,
> in that the agency had suffered for six months without leadership as a result of
> the legislature's failure to confirm a Director-designate. . . . Pontiac, over
> the past several years, had gravitated into the control of gang elements.[56]

Sielaff's first priority was to break the gang influence over the prisons, declaring that he planned to reverse the policy of "recognizing gangs." He directed
his wardens to no longer give gang members special privileges. Inmates were
to be transferred to other prisons when this would weaken the gang structure,
and wardens were to devise whatever other policies were needed to "keep the
gang structure off-balance."[57]

The crackdown at Joliet, though, was delayed. In July 1973, Sielaff announced the reorganization plan that would give Joliet and Stateville each its
own warden. This announcement (along with an attractive job offer elsewhere) prompted warden Twomey to tender his resignation.[58] Joliet's first
full-time warden in 75 years, Charles A. Felton, continued the thrust of
Twomey's policies. Felton held a master's degree in social service administration from the University of Chicago and, prior to his appointment at Joliet,
had worked in several states as a probation officer and a caseworker for a
police department. He was black and appeared very young. Upon his appointment, a *Chicago Tribune* editorial mocked: "Certainly a youth of 29 can
expect his age to be a handicap in so difficult and responsible a job as that of a
penitentiary warden. Even a Scoutmaster is in for trouble if he is taken for
one of the boys."[59] Felton did not stay long on the job. In resigning, he
claimed that Department of Correction officials were insensitive to the problems of inmates and that the prison staff refused to implement his reforms.[60]

In December 1974, Director Sielaff appointed Fred Finkbeiner as warden of Joliet prison. Finkbeiner had held a number of positions in corrections, including eight years as chief operational officer at the Cook County Jail.[61] Since most gang members passed through Cook County Jail before their transfer to a state prison, Finkbeiner felt that he was qualified to handle the gang problem at Joliet and implement the director's hard line against gangs. Finkbeiner's first major challenge to the gangs was over the Rangers' control of the Jaycee program.

## The Rebellion

On April 1, 1975 Warden Finkbeiner and several of his assistants met with the inmates on the Jaycees' executive committee, including Hairston. At the meeting, Finkbeiner announced that the business office would audit all of the Jaycees' books, but that the program would continue to operate while the audit was taking place. Hairston strongly objected and stated that he would not cooperate with the audit.

Hairston organized a secret meeting of the Jaycees, attended by 35 of the 50 inmate members. They wrote and signed a petition alleging that Joliet authorities had "totally disregarded the constitution and bylaws and the operating policy for institutional Jaycee chapters." The petition claimed that checks had been issued by prison authorities without the co-signatures by the Jaycee president or treasurer (Hairston), and that the administration had denied the treasurer access to the organization's books. These were said to be violations of Jaycee rules. The petition demanded an investigation of the alleged abuses and that all Jaycees activities be suspended until the investigation was completed. The petition was sent to Director Sielaff and the regional vice president of the Jaycees. Finally, the group declared that all inmates should boycott Jaycee activities until the matter was resolved.[62]

Finkbeiner responded to the inmates' charges in a memorandum to Sielaff on April 15. The warden stated that he had ordered an audit of the Jaycees' books as part of the crackdown against gangs, per Sielaff's mandate. He added:

> It should be further noted that the Petition was initiated and circulated by certain power-seeking members of the Jaycee organization which include resident Eugene Hairston and other residents affiliated with Hairston. My administration has taken a very positive stance in the curtailment of gang-oriented activities and gang influences with this institution, and I am sure that resident Hairston and his associates are feeling the pressure.[63]

Some inmates refused to honor the boycott; three of them were then beaten up. One of those assaulted had allowed his picture to be taken by Jaycee photographer Herbert Catlett. In taking the picture, Catlett was also defying the boycott. Although Catlett was not immediately assaulted, his defiance put him in even greater danger than he had been in previously.

Catlett may have been unique among Joliet prisoners. Described by officials as "a big bruiser of a guy," Catlett had been a member of the Rangers, but then decided to "go straight" and quit the gang. He took a job as a clerk in the prison administration building. For this defection, Eugene Hairston allegedly put a "contract" out on his life. On July 29, 1974, Catlett wrote a note to the assistant warden expressing his fears:

> Today I was told by [inmate name] that I had to continue to be a member of the Black P. Stone nation gang, or transfer, because a *hit* will be put on me. . . .

> I'm not transferring and I'm not going to continue to be a member. I want you to have this information. I also want you to know that Eugene (Bull) Hairston is behind this action.[64]

The first inmate mentioned was known as a Stone member. Then, several days before the April 22, 1975 riot, Catlett told a guard that Hairston intended to kill him. The guard summoned Hairston, who denied it.

Faced with the general problem of gang control and its immediate manifestation in the violence stemming from the Jaycee boycott, Warden Finkbeiner decided to assert his authority. He ordered the transfer of the three inmates identified as most responsible for the boycott violence to the Menard prison downstate. All three were widely known to be Ranger members. One had been one of the two Ranger representatives on the ABLE executive committee; his reputation was that of a highly aggressive inmate who often pressured weaker inmates for sex. Menard, because of its distance from Chicago, was the state's only maximum-security institution not then dominated by gangs.

The three inmates were told about their planned transfer on the morning of April 22. The word quickly spread throughout the prison. At 12:30 p.m., a captain stopped the former ABLE member as he was leaving the dining hall to escort him to the prison's west gate, or back entrance, where a vehicle was waiting to drive him and the two other inmates to Menard. The inmate walked with the captain as far as the exit, but then said, "I'm not going," and turned around and walked back to the West Cellhouse. The rebellion had begun.

Two comments can be made about these events. The transfer of inmates from one prison to another is a routine administrative decision. That Joliet inmates resisted this order probably indicates the extent to which the gang members had grown accustomed to asserting control over the prison's day-to-day affairs.

Further, in retrospect, we can see that Warden Finkbeiner made a tactical error by announcing the transfers early in the morning. This gave inmates plenty of time to mobilize. Had the transfers taken place in the late evening hours—common enough to earn the special term "midnight shipment" —the inmates would not have had a chance to react immediately. Of course, they could have fought the order the next day, but their task then would have been to reverse a *fait accompli*. Perhaps Finkbeiner overestimated the headway he had made in forcing the gangs "off-balance" in the first four months of his appointment.[65]

The correctional officer in charge of the cellhouse, a sergeant, noticed the inmate resisting his transfer enter the cellhouse with five others and then go up a flight of stairs to an upper tier. This was not unusual, but the commotion they then created was. Apparently this was a setup. The officer climbed several flights of stairs to investigate when, suddenly, he was clubbed over the head, opening a large gash. He was then kicked in the ribs, cracking several of them, and the testicles. Meanwhile, other inmates left their posts and were streaming into the cellhouse. All, or nearly all, were Stone members.

The captain who had escorted the inmates to the west gate reported the inmate's defiance to his superior (a major). The two of them went to see Warden Finkbeiner. The warden's immediate reaction was to order the transfer to proceed as scheduled, not realizing that things were quickly getting out of hand in the cellhouse.

By 1:00 p.m. the number of inmates in the cellhouse had grown to about 60 or 70. They chased down and took hostage the other guards stationed in the cellhouse. Some were jostled when taken hostage, but the most serious injury was a broken arm. The sergeant who had been clubbed over the head, though, was bleeding profusely, passing in and out of consciousness and vomiting. He was carried down to the bottom floor and seated in a chair in his office.

Robert Buchanan, the superintendent of the East Cellhouse, was passing by the West Cellhouse door when an inmate on the other side yelled to him: "Tell the warden we've taken over the cellhouse. We are not going to do anything until he agrees to cancel the transfer of the three inmates." Buchanan was young (28 years old), respected by inmates for his athletic prowess (he was a weight lifter and played touch football games on the yard), and knew most of the inmates in his role as director of the reception and classification unit.

Buchanan went to the adminstration building to report to the warden what he had been told. As he was returning, two inmates asked him what had happened. One of them was Herbert Catlett, who was in the administration building because of his job as a clerk. The other was one of the two high-ranking Ranger leaders (not Hairston) assigned as a porter to the East Cellhouse. Apparently he had entered the administration building because he had been aware of the riot plan. The two inmates followed Buchanan back to the cellhouse. Normal security checks would have stopped the two inmates, but they passed freely in the confusion.

Back at the cellhouse door, Buchanan was told by an inmate on the other side that one of the guards had had a heart attack. Buchanan entered the cellhouse to remove the stricken guard, again followed by the two inmates. Catlett's apparent motive was, like Buchanan's, to help carry out the injured guard; the second inmate's was to join the rebellion. Once inside, Buchanan was grabbed by several inmates and taken hostage. Catlett got as far as picking up the injured guard, but then was also taken hostage. The second inmate disappeared into the back of the cellhouse. The next time Buchanan would see the two inmates, Catlett would be dead and the other would be standing over him deciding his fate.

It was now about 45 minutes into the rebellion. Buchanan, along with the other guard hostages, were taken to the top floor of the cellhouse, where they were locked in a storage closet. Also taken hostage were about a dozen white inmates who happened to be in the cellhouse. They were forced to cower in a corner of the top floor; some had their hands tied.

Abandoning the lower floors, the rioters left two guards behind. One was the injured guard; the other was the only black guard in the cellhouse. In interviews, some of the white guards taken hostage speculated that the black guard was in league with the Rangers, though we have no firm evidence on this. The Illinois Department of Corrections, at this time, conducted almost no background checks on the guards they hired. It was widely believed that Stone leaders ordered rank-and-file members on the outside to apply for positions as guards. On the other hand, the reason for his release may have been purely racial. In any case, the black guard and the injured one left the cellhouse. The latter was taken to the prison infirmary and then by ambulance to a hospital.

Two inmates immediately took charge of the riot. One of them was the high ranking Ranger member who had accompanied Buchanan into the cellhouse. The other also held a high position in the gang. (Hairston apparently made no effort, or wasn't in a position, to join the disturbance.) The first task delegated by the leaders was to block the stairwell leading up to the occupied tier. Inmates ripped out the bedsprings from the cells and jammed them down the stairwell.

The hostages in the closet were taken out after about a half an hour. Some had their hands tied. Others were wedged standing upright between the security screen overlooking the tiers and bedsprings tied to the screen. An inmate gave the order: "If they [prison authorities] come through the door, kill them any way you can. Don't show them any mercy because they won't show any mercy to us."[66]

At one point, an inmate jabbed a sharpened serving fork into the neck of the ranking guard taken hostage, a lieutenant. The fork drew blood but did not penetrate deeply. The inmate said, "You're the guy who made me put my cigarette out in the dining room." The lieutenant denied that it had been him. The inmate started to push a little harder, and the flow of blood quickened. One of the two gang leaders then told him to "drop it," and the threatening inmate backed away.

About 90 minutes into the disturbance, Warden Finkbeiner appeared on the exercise yard north of and directly below West Cellhouse's windows. He was visibly furious and in no mood to negotiate. Over a bullhorn, the warden ordered the inmates 75 feet above him to release all of the hostages at once and surrender. He warned them that they were all going to go to the hole after the riot, that they would be prosecuted for rioting, and that they would spend the rest of their lives in prison if a hostage was killed. (Illinois did not have the death penalty at this time.) The threats only seemed to stiffen their resistance and resolve to hold on to the hostages. They chanted back to the warden, "Attica, Attica, Attica," and screamed, "We don't care if we die!"

The two inmate leaders then instructed Superintendent Buchanan to yell to the warden that the inmates had some demands, which he did. Finkbeiner responded with a barrage of tear gas canisters. About half of the over 100 canisters propelled from the yard went through the targeted windows and exploded in the cellhouse. However, the irritating effect of the gas seemed to wear off after about 20 minutes of exposure and did not force an evacuation.

At 3:00 p.m. a group of 15 correctional officers, led by Deputy Warden Ernest Morris, entered the East Cellhouse door and began to march up the stairs to the inmates. The deputy warden carried a pistol, but the remainder of the force was equipped only with batons and shields. When they reached the second tier, an inmate called out that if they came any closer all of the hostages would be killed. They continued to march up the stairs. One of the inmate leaders then told Buchanan, "You tell them to stop. If they come any closer, you're all dead." Buchanan thought that the threat was credible. He pleaded with Morris to stop the assault force. "Ernie," he cried, "if you keep coming, we're dead. Go down to Finkbeiner and tell him that these people have some demands. I don't know what they are yet. But we're going to be dead, and all these other inmates [i.e., white inmates] are going to be dead if he doesn't listen."

Morris responded, "Bob, you know that we can't negotiate, we've got to take back the cellhouse, and the warden made a decision." But on the third tier, the assault force found Catlett dead in a pool of blood with his throat cut. Realizing that the rioters were indeed ready to kill, Morris' squad retreated.

In the meantime, Finkbeiner consulted with Governor Walker, who told him to "open a dialogue with the rioters." Walker dispatched to the prison Al Raby, his aide and a former civil rights leader. Director Sielaff sent as his representative Joseph Feconda, the state's administrator of adult correctional facilities. The two of them flew from Springfield to Joliet. At 4:20 p.m., Finkbeiner entered the seized cellhouse and went to the third floor. Using a bullhorn, Finkbeiner shouted to Buchanan, "Bob, are you all right."

"Yes, we're fine," Buchanan yelled back.

"What do they want?" Finkbeiner asked.

"They want to negotiate."

"Tell them we will negotiate only if they let the hostages go," Finkbeiner responded.

One of the two inmate leaders then gave Buchanan a list of three demands. Buchanan read them to Finkbeiner: the transfer of the three inmates would not take place that day; inmates would not be physically mistreated; a black Chicago TV reporter would be allowed into the prison to cover the riot. Finkbeiner returned to the administration building, where he consulted with Raby and Feconda. Forty-five minutes later, he returned to the cellhouse and announced that he agreed to the demands. Inmates immediately added a fourth demand: that the agreement be taped and played over a Joliet radio station. The warden agreed to this too.

In making these concessions, Finkbeiner was not giving up much. The first demand was only that the three inmates not be transferred *that day*. The pledge not to assault the inmates amounted to no more than a promise to act lawfully.

## Termination

Around 6:00 p.m., Finkbeiner returned to the cellhouse with a statement recorded by himself and Al Raby, which they played to the inmates. A few minutes later, the inmates listened to the same statement over the radio. This apparently satisfied the inmates and convinced them that it was no longer necessary to hold out for the Chicago TV reporter, who was still in transit to Joliet. The inmates began to clear away the bedsprings and other debris they had jammed down the stairwell. About 6:30 p.m., the inmates started to release the hostages one at a time, the injured ones first, holding Buchanan for last. When only Buchanan was left, they told him to lock each inmate in his cell. This, the inmates believed, would minimize the chance of immediate retaliation. Three-quarters of an hour later, Buchanan had secured about half the cells, and then he simply left the cellhouse. The rebellion was over by 7:00 p.m..

Eight of the ten hostages were treated at a hospital, mostly for abrasions, cuts, and tear gas inhalation.

## Aftermath

Damage to the prison was comparatively light, totaling only $5,000. Several hundred windows had to be replaced and the locking systems had to be repaired.[67] In the cleanup, however, guards emptied the cells of their contents, scattering mail, legal papers, pictures, books, and the like. Guitars, stereos, and TV sets were smashed.[68]

In the riot's wake, Director Sielaff told the press: "This [disturbance] was gang inspired. We run the prisons, not gangs. We will not tolerate gangs running the prison."[69] Several days after the riot, the three inmates scheduled to be transferred were transferred. But it is apparent, a decade later, that it is the *gangs* that have prevailed. A 1985 report for the U.S. Department of Justice found Illinois to have the most gang-dominated prisons in the nation.[70]

In the summer of 1986, Joliet Warden James Fairman testified in federal court that gangs held power in Illinois prisons through extortion, violence, and intimidation. His testimony was part of a trial to determine the merits of a civil rights suit filed by the El Rukns, the Rangers' new name. The El Rukns were, again, demanding that the group be given the special privileges reserved for religious groups. They wanted the right to wear special emblems, possess

El Rukn literature, and hold religious services. The federal judge ruled that the El Rukns are indeed a gang and do not merit recognition as a religion.[71]

Also in 1986, four white inmates at Pontiac prison charged in federal court that the Department of Corrections failed to enforce prison regulations against gang activity, and that this violated their Fourteenth Amendment rights to equal protection of the law. Two years later, a court of appeals panel of three judges concluded that 1,800 of the 2,000 inmates belonged to gangs, and their influence was so great they made job assignments and met and negotiated with prison officials, all in violation of the Department's own rules. "No humane society allows its prisons to be run by organized thugs," the opinion delcared. "The punishment for crime does not include terror, rape and murder. Yet the evidence in this case shows that officials at Pontiac tolerate gangs."[72]

In November 1987, Fort, now serving a 13-year prison term on a narcotics conviction in Texas, and four other El Rukn members were convicted of conspiring to blow up government buildings and assassinate U.S. public officials, in exchange for $2.5 million from the Libyan government. The conspiracy was thwarted when federal agents tapped Fort's penitentiary phone and raided the El Rukns' Chicago headquarters, where they found a store of weaponry, including an anti-tank rocket sold to them by FBI agents. The U.S. attorney prosecuting the case called it the first conviction ever of U.S. citizens on terrorism charges.[73] In 1988, Eugene Hairston was shot to death on a Chicago street by his body guard. No longer in the gang's top leadership, Hairston was gunned down, according to police accounts, because he had refused an order from Fort.

# II

# PRISONS AND PRISON
# RIOTS IN THE 1980s

# 5

# The Historical Context: 1976–1986

The social turbulence of the 1960s and early 1970s ended; the crisis in the prisons did not. New issues emerged, and with them new forms of riots. Three changes in American society proved especially important for prisons and the sort of riots that were to occur in them.

## Economic Downturn and Fiscal Crisis

The post-war economic boom, which had sustained real economic growth between 1959 and 1973, abruptly halted around 1974, coinciding with the shock of the oil crisis of 1973–1974. The gross national product grew an average of 4.1 percent between 1960 and 1973; between 1975 and 1981 the rate declined to 2.7 percent. Unemployment increased from 3.5 percent in 1968 to 8.3 percent in 1975. The rate of inflation rose from an average rate of 1.2 percent between 1960 and 1964 to 11 percent in 1974, and then to 13.3 percent in 1979. Beginning with 1973, median household income began a long steady decline, dropping 6 percent by 1984. The average 30-year-old person in 1949 could expect his income to increase by 63 percent by the time he was 40. A 30-year-old in 1973 could expect his income to drop by 1 percent by his fortieth birthday. In short, the economy moved from a period of high growth, low unemployment, and low inflation to one of low growth and high unemployment and inflation.[1]

The demands on the government did not decline in response to the economic downturn and, as a consequence, cities, states, and the national government faced fiscal crises. Some state and local governments bordered on bankruptcy, the federal government slid into long-term deficit spending, and tax revolts broke out in several states. In 1976, California associations representing homeowners, taxpayers, and neighborhoods held hundreds of rallies and protest meetings, demanding tax relief. In June 1978, a referendum sharply lowering the property tax was passed by two thirds of the voters.[2]

## Decline of Social Movements

Many of the movements of the 1960s achieved their goals.[3] The war in Vietnam was ended, and with it the draft. The practice of state-enforced segregation was abolished. Some of the superficial goals of the counterculture were absorbed by the dominant culture, such as changes in hair style and language, but there was no "greening" of America. These victories and defeats, in combination with a declining economy, brought to an end most movement activity.

Further, the American public became increasingly skeptical about the possibility of government reforming society or society reforming government. In 1976, the Democratic Party nominated Jimmy Carter over his liberal rivals, and in 1980 and 1984 the American electorate chose a president with conservative principles.[4]

## Increasing Rates of Incarceration

In the Vietnam era, the number of inmates in state penitentiaries was declining while, at the same time, the crime rate soared. Then, beginning about 1974, public officials began to impose stiffer penalties. Mandatory-sentencing laws were passed in 37 states; the use of parole was reduced in most states and eliminated entirely in seven; and longer sentences were meted out. This caused an explosion in the inmate population. From a 1973 level of 204,000 inmates, the population surged to 420,000 inmates by 1983.[5]

## Effects on Prisons

The increasing number of inmates, in combination with the fiscal problems of state governments, led to severe crowding in prisons. Adding to the difficulties was the soaring cost of prison construction. In 1978, the cost of one new inmate bed ranged from $25,000 to $50,000, depending upon its location and security level. By 1981, the average cost had risen to $72,000.[6]

Many legislatures and electorates refused to pay for prison construction. In 1981, voters in Virginia, Oregon, and New York turned down bond issues for new prisons, and in Michigan voters refused to accept a 0.1 percent increase in their income tax that would have been earmarked for new prison construction. Overall, only four housing units were being constructed for every ten new inmates. The gap had dramatic results:

> In New Jersey prison inmates are sleeping in storage rooms, hallways and lavatories. In Texas prisoners are spilling over into tents and tin sheds. In South Carolina they sleep three at a time in cells not much wider than coffins. In North Carolina's century-old Central Prison some cells are crammed with four inmates and bunks line the walkways in front of the cells. And New York State, in what one observer called "a move with ominous symbolism," lifted a cap on the population of the Attica State Correctional Facility which was placed there in 1971 after a riot that left 43 people dead.[7]

According to a 1979 government study, at least 40 percent of all inmates in state facilities were in housing units that failed to meet the standard for space set by the American Correctional Association. There were, measured by the ACA standards, 119 inmates for every 100 prison spaces.[8]

In the 1960s, the courts abandonded the "hands-off" doctrine, but the complaints they heard were limited to specific practices, such as discrimination against Muslims or mail censorship. In the next decade, courts began to hear class action suits brought by inmates alleging that confinement in a prison, or an entire prison system, as a *whole* violated their Eighth Amendment right to be free from cruel and unusual punishment. The remedy in a successful "conditions suit" often was a plan mandating wide-ranging reform, with precise standards to be met, ranging from the number of hours an inmate had to be out of his cell to the number of shower stalls. If prison officials were seen as recalcitrant, the court might appoint a "monitor" to oversee and enforce its ruling.[9] By 1984, prisons and corrections departments in 35 states were operating under court orders because courts found that the totality of living conditions in them violated the Eighth Amendment.[10]

With the decline of social movements of the 1960s, fewer and fewer prisoners identified with political groups on the outside. Some of the militant rhetoric lingered on, but little else.

The one exception was the Muslims. But, both inside and outside prison, the movement was tame compared to a decade earlier. In 1975, the leadership of the Muslims passed from Elijah Muhammed to his more moderate son, Wallace Muhammad. Wallace Muhammad abandoned the bitterly anti-white theology preached by his father and sought to integrate the movement more fully into the worldwide religion. For their part, prison administrations increasingly recognized the Muslims as a bona fide religion; a number of states, including Illinois, New York, and Michigan, hired Muslim chaplains. Today wardens usually consider the highly disciplined and reverent Muslims model inmates.[11]

The political left had created among the public a sense of concern, if not admiration, for prisoners. They were portrayed as victims of the inequities of society, if not heroic rebels against them. Few share such a view today.

One reason is that many affluent youth who once feared arrest themselves—for wearing their hair long, smoking dope, protesting, or resisting the draft—have homes and children of their own now. Their children have benefited from the decriminalization of pot, the end of the draft, and a greater social tolerance for hair on scalp and face. Both generations fear criminals, not police, and likely will until some period of social repolarization.

The state of mind in the black and Latin communities influences critically the state of mind in most prison systems. While the black community is still far to the left of the white center on many issues, radical and revolutionary sentiment is far, far below its level of 1971. The sentiment that the police are an "occupying army" is almost unheard of now. Complaints from black neighborhoods often demand more police, not fewer.

In part, this is due to the residual gains of the 1960s, such as the hiring of black police officers and the election of black mayors. In part, it may be due to a change in the perception of economic reality. The earlier black movement evolved at a time when most whites, working class or not, were convinced they had it good. Blacks knew they did not and demanded a share of this prosperity. They shared the earlier-noted confidence in the ability of institutions to solve problems, if not in their willingness to do so voluntarily.

Today it is obvious that not even whites enjoy universal prosperity. Also, some black leaders have questioned whether social movement activity can, any longer, advance the interests of blacks. The recent success of Asian-Americans, in the absence of a significant protest movement on their behalf, has tended to reinforce this doubt. Blacks, like everyone else, have become used to having lower expectations of government. If the government really *cannot* eliminate poverty, bad housing, unemployment, or segregated schools —or if the political forces for such results just aren't in the picture—then these unchangeable features of life may come to be seen as *legitimate*. (It is probably true that any revival of the belief that these conditions can be changed by government will have to rest on a stronger foundation than faith in Great Society programs.) And if the social order is legitimate, then criminals really are just criminals.

# 6

# Deadly Conflict—Penitentiary of New Mexico (1980)

There are two riots that every prisoner has heard of. One is Attica. The other was more recent. Prisoners have a hard time placing it exactly; they say it was in Texas, or Mexico, or somewhere in the Southwest. But they know what kind of riot it was: a bloody, deadly thing. They call it "the one where 47 people got killed" or "where they cut everybody's heads off." Their beliefs do the event justice, so far as they go.

It actually took place at the Penitentiary of New Mexico, just outside the state capital of Santa Fe, on February 2 and 3, 1980. Like Attica, the New Mexico riot was widely reported and was the subject of an extensive state investigation. Like Attica, it was feared to be the prototype of the coming trend in prison riots. (As we now know, that belief was wrong in both cases.)

But the New Mexico riot was apparently quite unlike that at Attica. There were no radical organizations to blame, no militant inmate orators, no anti-imperialist demands. There seemed to be only torture and death. It seemed that the inmates there had been simultaneously transformed into beings like Hollywood monsters in their senseless yet deliberate commitment to murder, to mutilation, to shock.

Because that was how it seemed, not only to journalists but to observers on the scene, the features common to other riots have been overlooked. Actually, a dispassionate view of the New Mexico riot belies the popular impression of primordial chaos. It was different from other riots, not because the prisoners were unique in their psychological makeup, but because the situation in which the riot was conceived and executed was different.

Much of this chapter focuses on the ten year period leading up to the riot, during which the prison moved from a relatively well-run organization to one that was out of control. We show how this happened, and the horrible consequences for the inmates.

We also describe how the riot started, and why the state forces were helpless to stop its spread. We detail the actions of inmates in the disturbance, including the brutal attacks of inmates against other inmates and hostages, and show why no inmate organization could, or would, stop them.

There exist two published accounts of the New Mexico riot: a two-volume report produced after an extensive investigation by the state Attorney General's Office, and a well-researched popular account by Santa Fe journalist Roger Morris. We find both accounts to be trustworthy, and we were graciously allowed to use much of the evidence used in their production. In matters of interpretation and causation, our account differs here and there from both.[1]

## An Overcrowded Prison and Its Prisoners

In New Mexico, unlike New York, Illinois, and Michigan, one facility—the Penitentiary of New Mexico (PNM)—housed and still houses the vast majority of all state prisoners. Established in the days of the New Mexico Territory, the prison was originally located in the downtown area of Santa Fe.

In December 1952, inmates at that downtown facility took eight hostages, held them for 20 hours, and demanded the abolition of the prison's underground "dungeon" as punishment. Six months later, inmates held 21 hostages for seven hours, demanding the firing of six guards, better food, no reprisals, and interviews with the press, prison board, and the governor.[2] The state responded by razing the old penitentiary and building a new one a dozen miles south of the city.

Opened in 1956, the new prison's floor plan followed the "telephone pole" model[3] (see Figure 6–1). A two-block-long corridor ran straight from one end of the prison to the other. Forming the crossbars of the pole were 14 units of two-story maximum-security cellblocks and dormitories, a hospital, and an educational unit. Six of these units were designated as the North Wing, and the remainder, the South wing. The two wings were separated by the administrative area, which included a gymnasium, Catholic and Protestant chapels, an inmate store, inmate and staff dining halls, the visiting area, and the control center. Riot control grills were installed at the entrance to each living unit and at various points up and down the main corridor. The grills were designed to reduce staffing needs and, most important, to confine and isolate any disturbance.

In 1972, the penitentiary housed 564 (87 percent) of the state's 682 male inmates; another 87 were housed at the honor farm at Las Lunas, which at that time was organized as a satellite facility of PNM. From 1,196 inmates in the 1960s, PNM's population had fallen steadily, due largely to an updated probation and parole system. As whole blocks at PNM became vacant, they were renovated and transformed into educational, recreational, and therapeu-

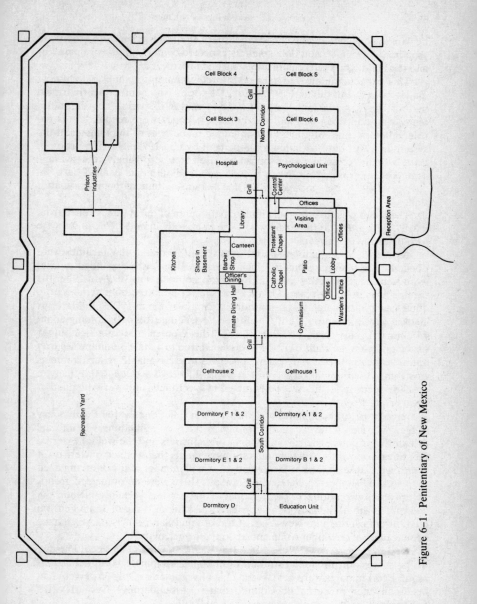

Figure 6–1. Penitentiary of New Mexico

tic wings. Thus the effective residential space at PNM was smaller in the 1970s than in the 1960s. Prison policymakers expected commitments to remain low and the PNM facility to remain adequate and uncrowded.

This expectation proved false. More commitments to the system were made: from 382 in the mid-1970–mid-1971 period, the number nearly tripled in four years, to 962 in the mid-1974 to mid-1975 period. Furthermore, many who had been paroled under the new policy were readmitted as parole violators. First offenders had made up 62 percent of the inmates in the system in 1970, but had fallen to 48 percent by mid-1977. The proportion of third-or-more offenders then began to rise. Not surprisingly, the average sentence also rose. Thus, even though new commitments peaked between 1975 and 1977, the population of the system continued to increase after that.

The result was that the male inmate population of the system swelled from its 1972 low of 682 to the 1,569 who were in custody in mid-1978, an increase of 130 percent in six years.

As the PNM population soared over the 1,000 mark, new facilities were opened. The minimum-security facility at Las Lunas was expanded in size; from housing 87 inmates in 1972, it grew to house 200 in 1979. In 1976, the former boys' school at Sierra Blanca was converted into a minimum-security adult facility; it also grew, until it housed 79 adult men in 1979. On March 1, 1978, a new minimum-security facility was opened at Roswell, holding about 120 inmates. In February/March of 1979, the Women's Division—an annex located outside the walls of PNM—was converted to a male minimum security annex, which housed 54. The new space was made available at such a rate as to stabilize the population of PNM at its 1977 level of about 1,100. Finally, a medium-security facility was constructed at Las Lunas, and was scheduled to open in late 1979.

In contrast to the inmates at Attica or Joliet, the ones at the Penitentiary of New Mexico on the eve of the riot had virtually no affiliations with internal or external groups. The revolutionary consciousness and the web of external identifications with worldwide militant movements that were characteristic of Attica were absent. Except for a relatively small number of prisoners engaged in an ACLU-supported class action lawsuit, there were no organized groups of prisoners promoting reform. Explanations for this certainly include the conservativism of the period, and probably also the distance of Santa Fe from large urban centers like New York, Chicago, and San Francisco, which have been centers of civil-libertarian and prison reform activity.

Criminal gangs of the Illinois variety were also lacking. This could be due to the success of the administration in breaking up inmate groups. Furthermore, PNM inmates were not typically big-city residents. Only 36 percent had been convicted in Bernalillo County, that is, Albuquerque—New Mexico's only city whose 1980 population was over 50,000.

Ethnically based organizations such as the gangs in California and the Black Islamic organizations found in the East did not exist either. Published reports about the presence of the "Mexican Mafia" and the "Aryan Brother-hood" were universally dismissed as hokum by inmates interviewed, although some were willing to admit that a few individual inmates who had done time in California might give allegiance to those groups.

At the time of the riot, Hispanic-surnamed inmates made up 53 percent of the inmate population, white non-Hispanic inmates 37 percent, black inmates 9 percent, and Native Americans 1 percent. While cultural and linguistic bonds caused Hispanic inmates to associate with each other more, mutual identification among Hispanic inmates was low. There was very little open political expression of national unity, though several Hispanic inmates whom we interviewed had photographs of Emiliano Zapata on their walls. The majority of the population of New Mexico is Hispanic. In that state the Hispanic population is not primarily made up of recent arrivals (as in the East, Midwest, and California), but is descended from stable farming communities dating from the 1500s. Many Hispanics in New Mexico make a point of identifying themselves not as "Chicano," "Mexican," or of "La Raza," but as "Spanish," that is, descending from the Spanish colonists. Some observers suggest that this state of affairs has inhibited the spread of a "Latin" conscious-ness of oppression.

Within the prison, Latin consciousness would also not develop in response to a hostile guard force, since the majority of the guards and commanders were also Hispanic. Morris contends that Hispanic inmates were subject to "the worst abuse and brutalization," but few voiced this in either wave of interviews upon which we rely.[4]

Mutual identification among "Anglo" prisoners was also low. Anglo pris-oners interviewed sometimes stated that Hispanic inmates, being in the major-ity, "ran the joint," but in general they did not claim to have been the targets of the sort of racial discrimination, harassment, or hostility that would have led to mutual support among Anglo inmates.

One group that did achieve a measure of intra-group solidarity were the black inmates. A white inmate stated (in 1980):

> Blacks, we've always had kind of a thing with blacks, personal grudges. They protect their own, even the ones that aren't good. If the Chicanos know there's a Chicano that's a snitch, they'll wreck him. But as far as the blacks go, they don't do that. They protect each other. If one of them's a snitch, well too bad, they protect him anyway.[5]

The solidarity achieved among blacks, though, was unrelated to identification with black groups outside of prison.

> *Question:* Do many of the blacks here identify with groups outside of the prison, like Muslims or other groups?
> *Inmate:* No, not really. I wouldn't say that many, if any, blacks in here have anything to do with organizations from the streets.

Another inmate reported that some inmates had identified with the Muslims in the early 1970s, but that in the second half of the decade the Muslim influence had dissipated. This may have been because the proportion of black inmates fell from 14 percent in the early 1970s to 9 percent in 1980, in combination with a diminished presence of Muslims on the streets.

## Disorganization and Deprivation

The system's worst problem was not overcrowding. It was acute disorganization. Beginning about 1975, the state corrections system was subjected to repeated organizational shocks, restructuring, rivalries, and massive turnover at high and low levels of personnel, which ruined the system's internal control, discipline, and general ability to function.

Prior to 1975, the warden of PNM was the most important figure of the system, and was only loosely controlled by the secretary of corrections and his small staff. Both the corrections secretary, Howard Leach, and the PNM warden, Felix Rodriguez, had served throughout the administration of Governor Bruce King. Rodriguez was a veteran of the PNM correctional force whose authority was recognized by guards and inmates alike.

King's term expired at the beginning of 1975. Conflict soon arose between the new governor, Jerry Apodaca, and the top correctional officials left over from the King administration, over the latter's unwillingness to promote a PNM supervisor who had campaigned for Apodaca. Secretary Howard Leach was fired in August, and replaced by Mike Hanrahan. Attorney General Toney Anaya simultaneously began an investigation of charges of corruption at PNM. Reports of drug sales, graft, and large-scale theft of state property were widely circulated. Rodriguez was implicated.

Deputy Warden Herrera was fired on September 22, 1975, and Felix Rodriguez was replaced as PNM warden two days later by Ralph Aaron, a veteran of the federal prison system. To the surprise of many observers, Rodriguez was not fired, but was promoted to a central office position as "director of adult programming," under Hanrahan but over Aaron. Anaya's investigation of corruption was also terminated.[6]

Between 1976 and 1980 the state Department of Corrections experienced three more major reorganizations:

—In May 1977, the central office staff was reorganized and its powers increased. The post of "director of adult institutions" was created, to which Rodriguez was appointed. The wardens of PNM and of the new facilities were to report to the new post.

—In April 1978, the Department of Corrections was reorganized as a division of the Department of Criminal Justice. The new Correctional Division had a director and a deputy director, and a full-fledged corrections bureaucracy was created in Santa Fe.

—In 1979, after Bruce King was returned to the governorship, the corrections bureaucracy again became an independent department. Felix Rodriguez, who had advanced to director of corrections under Criminal Justice Secretary Charles Becknell, became deputy secretary of corrections under Corrections Secretary Becknell.

During this period, three other wardens followed Aaron in quick succession, none with experience at PNM. Aaron was succeeded after nine months by Clyde Malley, whom he had recruited from the federal system as his deputy. Malley resigned in 1978 and was temporarily replaced by Levi Romero as acting warden. In 1979, Jerry Griffin was appointed as PNM warden. He had been an aide to Felix Rodriguez in his Central Office post, and had served for a year as superintendent of the new Roswell minimum-security facility.

When we combined all the successions to the wardenship at PNM, the reorganizations of the corrections bureaucracy, and the various changes of faces therein, we found that the chain of command from governor to PNM warden was changed 12 times between August 1975 and January 1980. The length of this chain varied from two steps (1975) to five steps (1978). A constant feature of this chain was that neither the department secretaries (of Corrections or of Criminal Justice) nor the PNM wardens who were selected either had experience with PNM or commanded much respect from the guards or guard supervisors at PNM. Charles Becknell, a black former professor of Afro-American Studies who served as criminal justice secretary under Apodaca and corrections secretary under King, was particularly short on line support. Furthermore, former warden Felix Rodriguez occupied a intermediary position between the PNM warden and the department secretary from 1977 to 1980, in various posts. Rodriguez was believed to have considerable power in the system during this period, with his location in the chain of command weakening the power of wardens and secretaries alike. This was particularly true after the re-election of Bruce King, who never wavered in his loyalty to Rodriguez.

The command situation within PNM was even worse. Authority over the guards had been fragmented after 1971 as up to six new captain's positions had been created. Each captain acted as if he had the rule-making autonomy of the previous unitary commander. Rules and procedures varied from shift to shift, both for inmates and for guards. Rodriguez had managed to keep a handle on the situation, but his weaker successors lost control completely. Aaron and Malley, who were supported by the guards in their policy of curtailing inmate privileges (infra), were nevertheless unable to compel their subordinates, captains, or line officers to submit to their discipline—for example, to follow security routines. Under Romero and Griffin, who were even weaker, Deputy Warden Robert Montoya virtually assumed control over the day-to-day operation of the prison, and loose control it was.

In short, virtual anarchy reigned in the correctional system. Post-Leach department secretaries were unable to enact policy, lacking authority or legitimacy in the eyes of guards, wardens, or intervening officials. One of these intervening officials was always Rodriguez, who was viewed by many, and possibly by himself, as the real expert on New Mexico prisons. Wardens' desires were virtually ignored by the captains and shift commanders, who believed they could, in a pinch, appeal to their old boss Rodriguez, who was above the wardens organizationally and only 12 miles away geographically. There was nothing to prevent the captains and commanders from maximizing their power through arbitrary treatment of the line officers while minimizing their supervisory effort. The line officers, faced with confusing and arbitrary treatment by their superiors, and also faced with more unpleasant conditions of work as the overcrowding grew serious and guard-inmate hostility worsened, quit their jobs in droves. Yearly turnover more than doubled two years after Rodriguez's departure, and reached an astonishingly high 80 percent in 1978 (see Table 6–1). Paradoxically, this may have made it even more difficult for wardens to control the custodial staff; experienced guards were too valuable to fire.

The shake-ups beginning in 1975 also made life a lot worse for the majority of inmates. The original allegations of corruption had included charges that inmates used community contact programs to bring drugs into the prison, and used programs in which they had positions of responsibility to wield unauthorized power over other inmates or to steal state property. Aaron and Malley made it clear on their arrival from the federal system that, as far as they were concerned, inmates were through running the joint. They abolished many programs at PNM. This was at a time when the prison population was rising rapidly, so even a constant level of programming would have left inmates more idle. The cutbacks dramatically increased the boredom and unpleasantness of prison life. One inmate stated:

TABLE 6-1.   Turnover Rate for Correctional Officers at the Penitentiary of New Mexico, 1972–1982

| | |
|---|---|
| 1970 | 28%* |
| 1971 | 28%* |
| 1972 | 28%* |
| 1973 | 28%* |
| 1974 | 28%* |
| 1975 | 44% |
| 1976 | 44% |
| 1977 | 66% |
| 1978 | 80% |
| 1979 | 76% |
| 1980 | N/A |
| 1981 | 25% |
| 1982 | 21% |

*Estimate—no official figures reported.
Source: G. Larry Mays and William Taggart, "The Impact of Litigation on Changing New Mexico Prison Conditions," Prison Journal (Spring/Summer 1985):45.

When we had Rodriguez everything was running good. . . . Ever since he left we got the rest of them wardens, they all change everything, from better to worse.[7]

Another inmate commented:

When Mr. Rodriguez was here you had programs here. . . . They had people going to college and everything. . . . They give them something to do and it improves their minds and their spirits and everything. . . . We had a good year when they had those programs here.[8]

A third inmate:

*Question:* You've been here for the last five wardens. . . . Give me an idea as to how programs change when the wardens changed.
*Inmate:* They've all gone worse. . . . Straight downhill.
*Question:* No bouncing around?
*Inmate:* No, no bouncing around, just boom, right from ten to zero.[9]

Guards also saw PNM as becoming harsher for inmates with Rodriguez's departure. One commented that "during [Rodriguez's] tenure, there was no escapes. There was no major stabbing, there was no killings, and that's because they [the inmates] had everything they wanted. It was ridiculous, but they did."[10]

We counted the number of times, in a round of interviews conducted shortly after the riot, inmates made favorable or unfavorable comments on the various administrations. As Table 6-2 shows, 160 of the 181 comparisons indicated that conditions were better under Rodriguez. The comparisons are classified by the area of prison life commented upon. In every area, inmates reported that the conditions under Rodriguez were better than under any of the other wardens.

The program structures, which included an inmate council composed of inmates elected from each living unit, had not only provided inmates with activity, variety, and training, but had been useful to the administration in providing an important link between administrators and knowledgeable inmates. Prisoners involved in the programs were motivated, on the one hand, to discourage violence and disorder among inmates and, on the other, to provide the administration with information about potential threats to order in the institution.

These avenues of communication were closed after 1975 with the abolition of the inmate council and curtailment of the inmate programs.[11] In their place, officials began a coercive "snitch" (informant) system. Officials threatened inmates with punishment unless they provided information on other inmates' misbehavior and rewarded those who provided it. The punishments included both direct disciplinary actions and the (false) disclosure to other inmates that a non-cooperative inmate was a "snitch."[12] The rewards for providing informa-

TABLE 6-2.   Comparisons of Prison Conditions Under Various Wardens*

| Condition Mentioned | Prison Better Under: | | | | | | |
|---|---|---|---|---|---|---|---|
| | Baker (1968–1969) | Rodriquez (1970–1975) | Aaron (1975–1976) | Malley (1976–1978) | Romero (1978–1979) | Griffin (1979–1980) | Same Under All |
| Officials/warden fair, competent, or "cares" | — | 21 | — | — | — | 2 | — |
| General conditions | 1 | 20 | — | — | — | — | — |
| Food, mail, TV, case workers, recreation, psych. services, canteen, visitation | — | 17 | — | — | — | 2 | 5 |
| Inmate programs | 1 | 45 | — | — | — | — | — |
| Inmate informants | — | 15 | 1 | — | — | — | — |
| Treatment by guards | — | 18 | — | — | — | — | 2 |
| Discipline, restriction on movement, disciplinary segregation | — | 24 | — | — | — | — | 7 |

*This table is based on the 1980 interviews only. The distribution of responses among the categories in part reflects the questions asked. For example, the inmates were asked to evaluate the programs under each of the wardens since 1970 but were not asked about changes in the quality of the food. Thus, we cannot infer from the table that inmates were more concerned about the inmate programs than, say, the food (although this is probably true). The table does demonstrate that inmates believed that the quality of prison life had declined in virtually every area.
Source: Bert Useem, "Disorganization and the New Mexico Prison Riot of 1980," American Sociological Review, 50, no. 5 (October 1985):682.

tion included desirable housing and work assignments in the prison, favorable reports to the parole board, and transfers to a lower security prison.[13] The snitch system increased the enmity among inmates.

> Inmate: It was getting real bad right before the riot. There was a couple of our friends that we've known for years that had turned snitch. They just got tired of doing time.
> Question: And they wanted to get out?
> Inmate: Yeah, so they just turned snitch in order to get out. It got to a point where we just wouldn't trust nobody.

Another inmate commented:

*Question:* Can you describe to me how the informant system was working six months prior to the riot?

*Inmate:* I'd say it was working real good because there wasn't nobody getting away with nothing. . . . You know somebody's snitching because they have a shakedown and they bust your tattoo gun or your sniff, and there's no way they should bust you, but they bust it every time. There's rats, so there's people sitting around wondering who's snitching.

Inmates who had been imprisoned under Rodriguez clearly perceived the transition:

*Question:* Is the snitch system pretty prevalent?
*Inmate:* Sure.
*Question:* Under Rodriguez? Is that something that's changed?
*Inmate:* When Rodriguez was warden there was no such thing as a protection unit [for "snitches"] and I think it was a whole lot better.

Another inmate stated (in 1980):

*Question:* Are there more [snitches] now than there used to be or are there less?
*Inmate:* Hell, you can't even trust your best friend anymore. . . . They'll snitch on you.
*Question:* When did it start getting to be that bad?
*Inmate:* In about seventy-six.[14]

In addition to eroding solidarity among inmates in general, the snitch system generated strong hostility toward the alleged informants themselves:

*Question:* What do most people think of snitches?
*Inmate:* Bad, very bad.
*Question:* Enough to kill them?
*Inmate:* Yeah. A snitch ain't worth s––t in there.[15]

Another inmate was equally as direct:

*Question:* What do most inmates think of informants?
*Inmate:* I think they should hang them . . . They should pay for their crime.[16]

Finally, in a 1985 interview, an inmate drew a link between the snitch system and the violence during the riot:

It's [the snitch system] a real trashed out system. If that riot would have come down when Rodriguez was warden, I don't think 33 people would have died because I don't think there were 33 snitches in this whole penitentiary. When the riot come down there was about a hundred and some odd down in Cell Block 4 [the protective custody unit], all of them stoned rats.

The snitch system further strained the relationship between guards and inmates. Inmates friendly to a guard would gain a reputation as a snitch.

> You can't get involved with a guard. Another guy is going to put a bad jacket
> on you. You start talking to a guard, there's this guy that don't like you, he's
> going to run and tell his buddy that you snitched off this dude that's just got
> busted and you have nothing to do with it.

Treatment by the guards also worsened, inmates reported, during the
Aaron and Malley administrations. In 1976, inmates staged a non-violent
work strike to protest program cuts and new restrictions on movement. Participants were tear-gassed in their dormitories, stripped, and beaten by a "gauntlet" of guards armed with axe handles. Following the work strike, inmates and
staff reported an increase in verbal and physical abuse of inmates by the
guards. Whether these actions were encouraged or condoned by Malley and
later wardens, or whether the latter were simply unable to control those
elements of the guard force that were most hostile to inmates, the result was
the same from the inmates' point of view.

The overcrowding, the intensely poor management, and the collapse of
programming all contributed to make life at PNM very bad indeed in the late
1970s:

> By the mid-seventies the New Mexico penitentiary was a physical as well as
> psychological horror. Rats and roaches infested the building. Poor ventilation
> made it stifling by summer. Inadequate heating left the cell blocks sickly chill
> in winter. Drinking and waste-water systems were cross-connected, spewing
> sewage into sinks. Food practices were primitive and unsanitary with rodent
> feces openly visible in the kitchen and often in the food. Intestinal diseases
> were pandemic. . . . With exposed and frayed wiring everywhere, successive
> fire marshals' reports warned of potential holocaust. On seeing the pen for
> the first time, a visiting warden thought it "a national disgrace" and "the
> filthiest institution I'd ever seen." There was no full-time doctor for more
> than a year in 1979–1980, and neither a resident dentist nor psychiatrist for a
> population now far over capacity. . . . Inmates were packed into cells until
> many slept on mattresses on the floors, feet pressed against bars, heads
> touching the toilets.[17]

This description, authored by Morris, is supported by our interviews. One
inmate stated:

> It was unlivable before the riot. It was too crowded, the food was bad, the
> goddamned guards talk to you like you're a dog. We're not dogs.

Another inmate described the prison as a place of chronic violence:

> There was one dormitory designed for 45 men, and they had 120 in there. It
> was a jungle after lights out. You couldn't go to the restroom at night without

stepping on someone, and that was all it took for a fight to break out. The guards stayed down in the mess hall, drinking coffee.[18]

A U.S. Justice Department study concluded that the penitentiary was, before the riot, "one of the harshest, most punitive prison environments in the nation."[19]

Not only were conditions at PNM bad, they were illegitimately bad compared to the past, to conditions elsewhere, and to what the law and reason demanded. One indication to inmates that they deserved better was that things had been much better under the Rodriguez administration. As one inmate put it:

> It hadn't been a bed of roses under the Rodriguez clan, but what was to come made it look like it had been.[20]

Furthermore, Rodriguez apparently possessed more power in the penal system than he had in 1975. It would have been natural to hope that at some future time he might return to restore things as they had been, and it is probably no coincidence that it was with Rodriguez—not Warden Griffin or newly appointed Director of Corrections Saenz—that inmates would demand to deal during the riot.

Several inmate interviews indicated that inmates who had done time in other states were particularly critical of conditions at PNM and active in the riot. While it is unknown how many inmates at PNM had actually served time in other state prisons, it is known that only about half of the male prisoners in the New Mexico system in mid-1979 were born in New Mexico.[21]

In many prisons, there is a common belief that bad conditions are due to corruption, nepotism, and incompetence among administrators. In New Mexico, these charges were given weight by legislative and executive investigations. Hardly any actor in the corrections administration escaped the contempt of other actors. Numerous escapes exposed the inability of the prison system to carry out the most basic function of prisons, namely, custody. Warden Malley blamed one such escape on "a complete breakdown of security, established procedures, misinformation, lack of responsible leadership, and general chaos."

A class action lawsuit, *Duran v. Apodaca,* was initiated precisely because the chief plaintiff, committed to PNM for his third term in 1976, found the conditions shocking, compared to what he had been used to.[22] The suit, filed in the U.S. District Court in 1977 and later supported by the American Civil Liberties Union, charged New Mexico with violation of basic constitutional rights and documented this charge with reference to caselaw made by federal judges in other states. The Department of Corrections negotiated a partial consent decree, mandating improvements with respect to correspondence, visitation by attorneys and others, and food services. The department, however, failed to implement most of the provisions in the consent decree. The Attorney General's Report was to comment later that "delays in implementation of new policies frustrated the expectations of the inmates and caused additional mistrust."[23]

Although the organizational changes beginning in 1975 were publicly viewed as an effort to "tighten up" the prison system, in fact they led to a marked decrease in the level of security at PNM, by several paths:

1. Because of the worsened conditions, overcrowding, and violence, prisoners were more motivated to escape.

2. The intelligence provided by the system of informants was not very reliable. In any case, to use intelligence one requires a capable staff. But:

3. The massive turnover of guards produced a predominantly inexperienced, poorly screened, poorly trained, and demoralized guard staff.

4. The shattering of the vertical chain of authority made it impossible for wardens or department officials to convert their concerns for security into actions by the guard staff. The staff were repeatedly observed to flagrantly violate written security procedures such as the closing of riot control grills, and such violations apparently went unpunished.[24]

## Pre-Riot Mobilization: Fall and Winter 1979

The opening of the Las Lunas facility in the fall of 1979 relieved the pressure of overcrowding at PNM almost immediately, and with transfers to that and other facilities the count at PNM fell to 957 in October 1979. The PNM authorities took this opportunity to restore the annex to female occupancy, transferring 34 male inmates to a modular unit within the perimeter fence, and to schedule Cell Block 5, which housed 60 inmates, to be vacated and renovated.

However, after a stabbing incident, transfers to the downstate facilities were halted. New commitments to the state system, arriving at PNM, were not balanced by any outflow to the other locations. As a result, the count at PNM rose by over 20 percent in less than three months. Nevertheless, the PNM administration went ahead with its plans to reduce the space for male inmates. This brought the count at PNM up to 19 percent over the remaining units' design capacity.

Although PNM had resorted to double-celling in previous years, it did not do so in 1979. Therefore, all the increased crowding fell on the dormitory units. These units had a design capacity of either 580 (1977 figures) or 490 (1979 figures), but 753 inmates were housed there on the eve of the riot. Beds filled the floor space of these dormitories the way sardines fill a can. Tiers of double-deck bunk beds lined the walls. Idle inmates would spend their days sitting on these beds in the company of up to 85 other inmates. A single guard would be responsible for two such units.

The Attorney General's Report found crowding to have been a "constant factor" which could not account for the riot.[25] This finding is based on the total population counts for PNM, which were, in fact, higher in the early 1960s and in 1977. But this overlooks the fact that in 1980 the male inmates of PNM were confined in a smaller space than in 1977, due to the renovation of Cell Block 5, and in a much smaller space than in the 1960s, because whole residential blocks that had been in existence at that time were later converted to other uses. When this is taken into account, one finds that PNM was more crowded on the eve of the riot than at any time but one in its history. Furthermore, one should take into account the dynamic effect of the rapid increase in crowding after October 1979, as the total population increased by 200 simultaneously with the shutdown of about 80 units of male housing.

In November 1979, the renovation of Cell Block 5 was begun. This block was a high-security block, very similar in construction to Cell Block 3, the maximum security wing, and Cell Block 4, the protective custody wing. The 60 inmates residing there had been thought in general to be bad security risks, troublemakers, dangerous to other inmates. Now, with Cell Block 5 being vacated, the bulk of these 60 were moved into dormitory housing (rather than, say, to cell blocks 2 and 6); further, most of them were housed together in Dormitory E-2. This group was to become the core of the riot.

A cluster of other incidents capped inmate frustrations. Expectations of an early settlement of the *Duran* suit were dashed in October when the Justice Department mediators were dismissed by Deputy Director Rodriguez. Hundreds were ill after being served rotten turkey for Thanksgiving. Mysterious incidents were reported in which all lights were doused, then rekindled with an armed "goon squad" on hand, apparently by pre-arrangement. These were interpreted as sinister attempts by the administration to provoke disorder so as to be able to use violence on inmates.[26]

On December 9, 11 inmates escaped from PNM. The manner of their escape was indicative of the inadequacy of the penitentiary's security system. While one man engaged the only guard responsible for Cell Block 2 in conversation, ten men cut their way through a window, used knotted sheets to climb, first down to the ground, then over the roof of the penitentiary's central corridor; crossed the lighted yard in full view of the tower; and cut their way through the chain-link fence. The eleventh man leisurely followed the same route an hour and a half later. The sheets had been spotted by a guard on outside patrol, and reported, but no action was taken for hours. It was later learned that individuals involved in the escape had been overheard plotting it over a week earlier.

Despite the manifest incompetence of PNM officials, the only corrections official to be held accountable for the escape was the one most distant from the scene: Corrections Secretary Becknell, whose resignation was quickly accepted by Governor King. Felix Rodriguez took over Becknell's duties, and was expected by many to be appointed to his post. In the event, however, Governor King designated as secretary Adolph Saenz, a friend of his with no corrections experience. Before Saenz could take up his duties, the riot broke out.

While the escape did little to shake up the corrections bureaucracy, its lessons were not lost on inmates. Though 10 of the 11 were recaptured and returned to PNM, the escape nevertheless was an example of successful action which stimulated inmates to think, to imagine, discuss, and plan other actions. In considering what form such action would take, inmates probably kept in mind the work stoppage in 1976. No one wanted to repeat that debacle. As many as a dozen separate plans to seize territory and hostages were heard of by the administration over the next two months. The purported tactics varied: the seizure of a popular disk jockey at a special concert, the taking of female hostages in the psychiatric wing, a takeover in Cell Block 3, collection of arms in E-2, a hostage-taking in the school dorm, and a morning riot at the call for work—all were supposedly on the agenda. One report was that a "white-supremacist group" centered in E-2 would start a riot, but not until spring.

It is difficult to evaluate these plans and determine how real they were, to separate the real plans from the fantasies and the hot air. It is clear in retrospect, though, that in a prison where seemingly everyone is discussing how, where, and when to start a riot and take hostages, eventually someone will try it. It may also be that some of the unusual features of inmate behavior during the New Mexico riot were due to the fact that inmates had had two months to think about what they would do during a riot, and who they would do it to. As early as December 20, one of these reports would state that "one of the primary goals" of an uprising would be to "kill snitches" in Cell Block 4 and in the general population.[27] One black inmate reported:

> Initially, they was saying that they was gonna kill all of the snitches down in four. Later on I heard that it was gonna be a race riot. It was supposed to be kill all of the blacks.

Another black inmate stated:

> I think a lot of us black guys was scared. The word was already out that they, the white and Chicano, rioters was going to take us out.

While it is far from certain that any of the inmates who in fact initiated the riot wanted to injure blacks, this recurrent theme in the pre-riot rumors discouraged blacks from participating in the riot. Black inmates did in fact transfer out of Dormitory E-2 in the period before the riot.

Characteristically, PNM officials reacted to the growing threat of riot not by any actual measures to improve security, but by further reorganizations. The PNM intelligence officer was replaced in mid-January; several PNM departments were instructed to report to Warden Griffin rather than his deputy, Bob Montoya. Griffin also asked staff to review the "riot control plan," but no one could find it. On January 31, an "intelligence sharing" meeting, attended by Rodriguez, Griffin, Montoya, and other corrections, police, and attorney general's representatives, was called by PNM's new intelligence officer. Those present discussed the danger of a takeover and hostage seizure, but did not conclude that any precautions were advisable.

In fact, carelessness in security matters continued to lay the foundations for the rioters' eventual success. Security-threatening situations were reported by subordinates, and dismissed or forgotten by superiors. It was considered whether to continue the practice of storing contractor's tools in Cell Block 5 after a saw taken from there was used in the December escape. The practice was continued. A large, thick but unreinforced glass bay window was installed in the control center, supposedly to improve visibility of the corridors. Uneasy guards and deputies suggested that the breakability of the glass should be tested or that steel bars should be installed to reinforce it. These suggestions were discussed and "tabled."

## The Revolt in E-2

The plan acted upon was hatched during a "hootch" (homemade beer) party in Dormitory E-2 on the evening of February 1. It is indicative of the level of PNM's security that prison inmates could produce and consume illicit alcohol, in a large group, in the middle of an open dormitory. More than half-drunk, they decided on the spur of the moment to attempt a takeover that night.

At 1:30 a.m., three guards, including the shift commander, entered E-2 for a routine inspection. A fourth guard, holding the keys to several south side units, waited outside the E-2 door on a landing. Fifteen fully clothed inmates sprang from their beds and jumped the three guards. Two inmates near the dormitory door (which according to security procedures should have been locked) forced it open and grabbed the guard stationed there. The four guards were stripped, bound, blindfolded, and beaten.

From the moment the planning began, circumstances favored the men overpowering the guards who were entering E-2. The dim lighting (bulbs had been reported broken but not replaced), the crowding of bunk beds, and the overwhelming advantage of numbers had ensured a limited success to the intoxicated men who had decided to act.

If existing security precautions had been taken seriously, the inmate rebels would have ended up with three guard hostages inside the E-2 area, with a locked gate separating them from any keys and with three more locked gates or grills separating them from the glass window of the control center. Their further successes were the result not only of their own decisiveness but of the failure of the custodial staff, despite the imminent danger of riot, to have observed even a single security precaution regarding locks and doors.

At least during the first hours of the uprising, while the inmates from E-2 exercised a measure of leadership, the picture which has come down to us of the New Mexico riot as a "mindless outburst" is belied. Rather, the prison was methodically taken over, wing by wing, block by block. Some units were "recruited;" others were subdued. Precautions were taken against an assault by the state, which was never to come. Terror was used against guard hostages primarily to force them or others to cooperate in unlocking wings and cells, with limited success. Thanks to the utter disorganization of the state, the process of territorial expansion would continue without any serious opposition for five and a quarter hours, until the entire prison was in the inmates' hands.

The initial planners seem to have had a rather ordinary strategy—take hostages, compel negotiations with authorities over demands, bring in news media to tell the public about the conditions. The strategy was, however, ignored by the majority of the PNM inmates, many of whom had their own agendas for personal gratification.

Immediately after the initiation of the riot, several of the E-2 inmates descended to the E-1 level via an unlocked stairwell door, left the E wing through an unlocked riot control grill, entered the F wing through another riot control grill, and ascended through yet another unlocked gate to Dormitory F-2, where they overpowered four more guards. None of the eight guards so far taken hostage had used their radios before capture. If they had, the riot could still have been confined to the south wing.

After the capture of the second group of guards, rioters had possession of all the keys to the south side units. They unlocked the dorms quickly, allowing hundreds of inmates to pour into the south corridor. The control center became aware of the situation about this time, when an unnamed inmate announced on a stolen radio: "We've got the shift commander hostage. There had better be a meeting with the governor, the news media, and Rodriguez."

About this time, two guards left the officers' mess and saw the situation. But the near south corridor grill, which should have prevented inmates from approaching the control center, was also wide open, and the two had no time to close it. They raced behind the near north corridor grill, which was then closed by the two guards on duty in the control center.

Inmates reached the corridor outside the control center a few seconds later, dragging with them a half-naked guard with a belt tied around his neck. Inmates threatened to kill their hostage unless the control center guards opened the gate to the adjoining administrative area. When their demand was refused, they used pipes to beat the hostage into unconsciousness.

Several inmates banged on the control center window with pipes and a fire extinguisher. The recently installed "bullet-proof" pane resisted two blows. The third cracked it. As the manufacturer was later to explain, the glass was meant to resist *bullets;* it was never designed to hold up against angry inmates with metal objects in their hands.

Stunned, the two guards in the control center dashed out the front door of the prison as the triumphant inmates bashed in the remnants of the pane. Having entered the control center, the inmates found riot control gear (tear gas grenades, grenade launchers, batons, and helmets), as well as keys to all the doors to the prison. However, in the excitement keys were removed from the labeled hooks and jumbled together.

At this stage, perhaps 15 minutes after the initiation of the riot, the inmates were in a position to take over the entire institution; over the next five hours, this is what they did.

From the control center, inmates had immediate access to the administration area and the front entrance of the institution. They could also unlock the near north corridor riot grill. The guards from the mess and the north units, who had watched in horror as the control center fell, retreated from there to seek hiding places deeper in the north wing. The inmates had the keys to unlock the cafeteria, the craft shops, the hospital, and the pharmacy. They also had the keys to cell blocks 1, 2, and 3. Cell Block 3 was the prison's punitive detention unit.

Only a few pockets of "resistance" remained. One guard was trapped in the educational wing, which had its own riot control grill. Three guards had retreated into Cell Block 3, to which the E-2 inmates had misplaced the key. One medical technician and seven invalid inmates hid in a closet in the infirmary wing. The 4-Block guard and one other hid in the basement of 5-Block. As he left, he jammed the 4-Block riot control grill shut behind him. This grill could not now be opened using normal means. The prisoners in protective custody were still locked in their cells, and for five hours they would be inaccessible to the rioters. Another group of inmates in Dormitory A-1, an honor unit, declined to join the riot and jammed their own door so that it could not be opened from the outside.

With the front entrance inaccessible, all of these guards and inmates were unable to escape. Exit doors at the ends of the wings existed, but there were no keys in the hands of those trapped in the wings. The keys that tower guards were supposed to have had been mislaid. Rioting inmates had better luck finding the keys to Cell Block 3; soon the guards trapped there were prisoners, and the prisoners residing there were free.

About 3:00 a.m., inmates ransacking the plumbing shop near the cafeteria found an acetylene torch. Inmates proceeded to cut their way into every remaining part of the penitentiary. First the far south grill was penetrated and the guard behind it taken hostage. Then inmates cut their way into 5-Block and obtained two more cutting torches which had been left by contractors doing the remodeling of that unit. At about 7:00 a.m., inmates succeeded in cutting their way through the grill at the entrance to Cell Block 4.

## The Inmate Polity Disintegrates

While inmate organization was strong enough to overcome the infamously poor organization of the correctional force of the State of New Mexico, it was not strong enough to restrain the violent and anarchistic impulses of an influential minority of inmates.

At the beginning, the riot probably had at least the tacit approval of most inmates:

> *Inmate:* When it broke loose, I'd say you'd had a good 90 percent of everybody acting on it. Destroying something, burning something.

Another inmate stated:

> *Inmate:* When it started, everybody I mean everybody was into the idea of
> the riot. Everybody was gung ho behind it. And if the things had turned out a
> lot different from what they did everybody would have stayed with it all the
> way to the end.

Organization among inmates was minuscule; mutual distrust was intense.
There were no "leaders" who could influence the mass of inmates on the basis
of respect for their organizational skills. The plaintiffs in the *Duran* suit
attempted to call a mass meeting in the gym, but it was a failure. There are
several possible reasons for this. First, the prestige of the plaintiffs may have
been low; their suit had not yet yielded any success and they had not participated in the planning of the riot. Second, most inmates did not see such a
meeting as a priority. Their concerns were with the expansion of the riot, the
consumption of drugs or food, self-defense, or the pursuit of personal vendet-
tas. Third, inmates were simply mistrustful:

> There was an order. I heard somebody saying, "Everybody into the gym. We
> got to get together," and I felt that was some kind of a trap for some reason.
> It was just to get in the gym, and, you know, people could get crazy or do
> something.[28]

By default, the E-2 inmates became the only candidates for leadership of
the inmate population. In the initial stages, they organized hostage control
and precautions against an administration assault. For example, one E-2 inmate organized residents of Dormitory B-1 to carry bunks into the corridor
and barricade the far south grill.

> *Inmate:* He was one of the few people that was real hot into getting everyone
> to participate. I saw him going into the F dorms and pushing people around
> and trying to get them to participate and—
> *Question:* Participate in what?
> *Inmate:* Destroying things, I guess. Moving around, getting involved. "Don't
> lie in your bunk. Don't act like you don't care" type of attitude.

As the riot progressed, the E-2 inmates proved inadequate to the task.
First, they had little in the way of the organizational skills necessary to hold
together a diverse body of 1,000 men, or even to see the value of doing this.
Second, most of them were drunk or heavily drugged on and off through
the entire riot. As soon as the pharmacy was taken, they and many other
inmates began to swallow handfuls of barbiturates. Some of them actually
slept through important portions of the uprising; the accounts they have left
suggest that even when awake their mental processes were severely hampered
by drugs and alcohol.
Third, they had no real authority over most inmates. They could give

instructions to people who knew them personally and to people in their immediate presence, but that was the extent of their power.

Fourth, the telephone pole layout of the prison, the difficulty in travel (through holes cut in the grills, e.g.), the smoke in the corridors from the eventual fires, and the hazards (from other inmates) of travel made communication difficult and the exercise of power by a small group nearly impossible.

Fifth, although the E-2 inmates were considered a tough lot, the inmates who were housed in Cell Block 3 were even more feared. The E-2 inmates could not have controlled them even if they had wanted to. Furthermore, some of the Cell Block 3 inmates had intense feelings about what they wanted to do during the riot: to kill and mutilate "snitches" whom they believed had injured them.

> *Inmate:* It's like the people in E-2, like I said, they had a game plan, they had it down what they wanted to do. Then when all these people got out and that all kinda fell apart. These are the gangsters; these dudes were real heavies. They just kinda moved down here and just took over.

The result was that the authority of E-2 inmates never extended very far, particularly after the inmates from Cell Block 3 were released. They did exercise disproportionate control over the process of negotiation, especially on Saturday, and over the movement of the hostages. They also took some actions to prevent or discourage defection by inmates. But the E-2 inmates never made a serious attempt to restrain other inmates who were intent on violence and murder, either because they sympathized with or were indifferent to attacks on "snitches" or because they knew they could do nothing about it. By the end of Saturday, exhausted, ravaged by drugs, betrayed by their own inadequacies, themselves demoralized by the level of bloodletting and murder which had transpired, they had very little power.

The first killings took place in Cell Block 3, soon after the block was under inmate control. In one case, inmates armed with steel pipes gathered in front of the victim's cell. One of the assailants said, "We've got to kill this son-of-a-bitch, man. That's Primie Martinez. We've got to kill him. . . . He snitched on [inmate name]."[29] They beat and then knifed him to death. An eyewitness remembers: "They had him in a corner and they were beating him and beating him and beating him. And he was screaming and screaming and screaming, "No era yo. . . . No lo hice" ("It wasn't me. . . . I didn't do it").[30]

Another unpopular resident of Cell Block 3, seeing what was coming, jammed the door of his cell so successfully that it couldn't be opened for two days after the prison was recaptured. But it did him no good. He was shot in the face through the window of his cell with one of the grenade launchers taken from the control center.

These murders created a model for retribution against "snitches" and enemies. Thereafter it was as if inmates vied with each other to produce imaginative modes of murder and mutilation. Killing one's enemy was not enough; one had to inflict as much pain as possible, and to shock even the victim, before his death, with the grisly way he would die.

In the first murder on Cell Block 4, a group of assailants entered the victim's cell saying, "You son-of-a-bitch, you'll never tell on me again."[31] Begging for his life, the victim was kicked and then bludgeoned to death with a pipe. One of the killers then threw the body over a railing to the basement floor two stories below. Another of the assailants ran to the body to mutilate it further with a shovel.

Another 4-Block resident was heaved over a second-floor railing with a rope tied around his neck. The killers then pulled the body back up to their tier, where they hacked it apart with a knife.[32] Another victim had his eyes gouged out, a screwdriver driven through his head, and his genitals hacked off and stuffed into his mouth. Still another was stabbed to death, and the word "rata" (rat) carved on his forehead.[33] In still another killing, a group of inmates used an acetylene torch to burn through a cell door which had been jammed shut by its occupant. Once inside the cell, assailants used the torch to burn the inmate's head and face and then his groin.[34]

By noon on the first day of the riot, the killings in Cell Block 4 were complete. Only 12 residents of the block were actually killed. The rest were released from their cells, sometimes by personal friends. One group of Cell Block 4 inmates succeeded in obtaining a torch and cutting their way out the exit door in Cell Block 5, escaping the riot.

Violence continued, but in a less "ceremonial" form. Inmates settled old scores in chance encounters with enemies in the smoke- and gas-filled corridors. New feuds were begun. One of the initiators of the riot, who had put on a guard's shirt, was attacked by accident. He thereupon felt an obligation to kill the attacker, though in the end he did not.[35] Inmates heard, sometimes falsely, that their friends had been killed, and set out to avenge them. Some inmates were attacked because it was feared they might inform authorities about other killings.

The violence by inmates against other inmates occurred during the entire course of the riot. The assaults and killing were selective. The primary targets were inmate informants and objects of personal grudges. An inmate stated:

> Most of the people [attacked] were rats or they had jackets. Some of them were killed over little petty beefs. There was a reason behind every one of them. There wasn't helter skelter killing.[36]

Another inmate stated:

> A lot of people think that it was just indiscriminate killing. But, man, it wasn't. There was a whole lot of people sitting up in this joint, given sentences and a whole lot of time [by] rats over there in Cell Block 4.

## Hostages and Negotiations

Most of the 12 guards taken hostage were stripped, bound, blindfolded, in-sulted, and brutally beaten. According to some inmates, a few of the guards were raped by their captors, though the hostages later denied this.[37] In one instance, a guard, bleeding profusely from a beating to the head, was thrown into a cell with a dead inmate. An inmate reported:

> I said, "Is that a guard."
> They said, "Yeah."
> I said, "We got to get him out of there, man. Primie's in there dead."
> The person told me, "It doesn't matter. The guard's going to be dead soon anyway."
> I picked him up, and I said, "Are you a guard?"
> And he said, "I used to be."[38]

A psychiatrist, who treated some of the the guards after the riot, reports that one of his clients was approached by a group of inmates holding the severed head of a black inmate. They warned the guard, "This is what can happen to you. . . . We'll cut you in pieces and throw you out the window."[39] Another hostage reported that an inmate said to him: "First we're going to stab you fifteen times, then we're going to cut your hands off, then we're going to cut your head off."[40]

Inmates killed no hostages for strategic considerations, and perhaps a second reason. Strategically, inmates could use the threat to kill hostages to discourage an armed assault, to strengthen demands for access to news media, and in general to strengthen their bargaining position. Actually killing hostages would have dissipated this advantage and is likely to have brought an immediate assault.

Further, the guards may actually have been less hated by the inmates than the "snitches" were. In other social contexts, the "traitor" arouses more hatred than the overt enemy. For example, in time of war, soldiers and officers of the opposing army are expected to be humanely treated if taken prisoner, while civilians who support the enemy side are frequently executed. The demonstrative means used to kill "snitches" suggest a virtually ritualistic "purging" of traitorous elements, with deliberate cruelty used to dramatize the renunciation of bonds of "fellow-feeling" with the traitor. Guards, on the other hand, however disliked, do what they are expected to do in imprisoning inmates, and do not bear the stigma of treason.

Not all of the guards were abused, and some were treated relatively well and helped to escape.

*Question:* Some of the hostages got messed over pretty bad, and some didn't. Was that mainly a function of different groups holding them, or was it mainly a function of different records of the individual guards?
*Inmate:* I think it was the record of the individual guards. Take for instance

an old man named [guard name]. He was really liked by inmates. He kept his clothes, was fed, wasn't abused, he wasn't beaten on.

This guard was the first hostage to escape the riot. Escorted by sympathetic inmates, he slipped past rioting inmates at about 5:30 a.m. Saturday. In contrast, those guards brutalized were thought to have "deserved" it. Inmates offered to exchange up to three of their hostages for a guard with the worst reputation and Deputy Warden Montoya.

Throughout the riot, guards did manage to escape, were released by inmates or, when severely injured, were carried to the exit by inmates on makeshift stretchers. Three hostages left the riot Saturday morning. Two of these were severely injured, and inmates feared they would die in their custody. The fourth, fifth, and sixth hostages to leave were released by inmates on Saturday night. They were exchanged for interviews of inmates by a television reporter and a radio reporter and for face-to-face conversation with prison authorities. Two of these hostages had to be carried out on a stretcher, and the third had been severely beaten as well. Assisted by sympathetic inmates, three more hostages escaped Sunday morning.

Negotiations had been demanded by the rioters at the very beginning. However, for the first 12 hours their state was chaotic. Inmates in different parts of the prison used as many as eight captured walkie-talkies to make demands on the administration. The transmissions were often garbled or confused; often, more than one inmate tried to talk at once, and some of the demands were contradictory.[41]

The "negotiators" appear to have had no special status among inmates. Instead, they were whoever wanted to and was able to grab hold of a walkie-talkie. An E-2 inmate reported that he found it "enjoyable to give [Deputy Warden] Montoya a piece of my mind." Inmates used various code names, such as "Chopper one," but as one inmate stated, "I don't think nobody really knew exactly who Chopper one was." Other inmates speculated that several inmates had used the code name, but no one was sure. The transmission included requests for medical help, threats to kill the hostages if authorities tried to retake the prison, and demands related to prison reform. The latter included the firing of the deputy warden, access to the media so inmates could voice their complaints about poor food, crowding, inadequate recreation, and mismanagement, and a conversation with the governor and Deputy Secretary of Corrections Rodriguez.[42]

Face-to-face meetings between inmate negotiators and administration representatives began at about 9:00 a.m. and at first mostly involved E-2 inmates. By Saturday afternoon, about 12 hours after the riot had begun, a small, more stable group of inmates became involved in the negotiations; by the next morning they had virtually taken control of inmate representation. The group was led by an inmate, who had been a co-author of an ACLU-sponsored class action suit against the prison. He was considered a jailhouse lawyer and had some higher education.[43] Also in this group of negotiators were two other Hispanic inmate leaders who often had acted as spokesmen for inmate grievances. This group formulated a set of relatively coherent demands. They included "reduce overcrowding," "comply with all court orders," "no charges to be filed against inmates," and "due process in classification procedures."

This negotiating group exercised little influence over other inmates or the course of the riot. Most inmates were either unaware of the group during the riot or did not trust them.

> *Question:* During the riot, did you know that the negotiation was going on?
> *Inmate:* I didn't until the last. I heard it on the news. And they said that they were talking for all the inmates. They weren't talking for me. It's bunch of bull.

Another inmate:

> *Question:* If [the negotiators] had made a settlement with the administration, could they have stopped the riot right there?
> *Inmate:* No, hell no. I mean they were out there negotiating, but I don't think they really knew what the f––k was happening in here.

Another inmate stated that the negotiators made it

> *seem* like that at any time they could come back in here and change the events of what was going on. That wasn't true. None of those guys could have come back here and said, "Give me this guy [a hostage] and give me this guy." And take'em out there and turn them over to [prison authorities]. Because if they [had], they would have got killed right there on the spot.

In a clear minority were the inmates who considered the negotiators as legitimate spokesmen. One in this group told us, "Those that did negotiate, they knew what could happen to them for being in front of the camera, for being the spokesmen. They were really braving it out, and I give them a lot of credit."

Even so, inmates opposed to the negotiations were so disunited that they could not and did not prevent the negotiators from releasing some of the hostages. The negotiators handed over to authorities 6 of the 12 hostages for health reasons or in exchange for access to media.[44]

Inmates left much of the prison in ruins, though the targets of destruction were selective. Areas not significantly damaged included the inmate library, the Catholic chapel, and the hobby shop. One of the first areas to be destroyed was the psychological clinic. Inmates smashed the clinic's furniture and ransacked the files, and then set the unit on fire.[45] Many inmates hated its director, who, they believed, passed information obtained in therapy sessions to prison authorities and the parole board. Other areas gutted by fire included the control center, the gymnasium, the caseworkers' offices, and administrative offices. In the cell blocks, inmates ripped out the plumbing and destroyed the wall fixtures and fuse boxes.[46]

Many inmates took large doses of drugs during the riot. Some injected morphine with syringes taken from the pharmacy; others dumped large quantities of pills into boxes, which they distributed to their friends.[47] One inmate explained his decision to overdose ("OD") this way:

> I can't even really explain to you what it [the riot] was like because I can't find the words, how to put it. I see a lot of shit going on. Walking by F-1 there were four bodies stacked up in the corridor. . . . I took a bunch of pills, started shooting up a lot of valium because I wanted to OD. I just wanted to erase everything that was going on and I didn't want to see what was going on.

Three identifiable groups refused to participate in the riot. One was the residents of Dormitory E-1. E-1 was the prison's second protective custody unit, although its residents were thought to require a lower degree of protective security than the Cell Block 4 inmates. Soon after the riot started, the E-1 inmates barricaded the entrance to their dormitory. A small group of inmates actively participating in the riot tried to persuade the E-1 residents to join them. When this failed, the rioting inmates lobbed tear gas grenades into the dorm and started fires in front of the entrance. This too failed, as the E-1 inmates were able to fan the gas and smoke back into the corridor, dispersing the rioters. Later an inmate friendly to one of the E-1 residents passed him a wrench, which was then used to knock out a window. All the E-1 inmates climbed though the window and surrendered to authorities.[48]

Most of the residents in Cell Block 1, the honor unit for inmates with the cleanest prison records, also chose not to participate. The privileges and amenities accorded to honor block residents were substantial, especially in the context of an otherwise highly depriving environment. Somehow these inmates obtained the keys to the grill leading into their dormitory and locked themselves in. No serious effort was made to break into this dormitory, though several inmates threatened to burn open the gate.[49]

Black inmates, the third group, organized their escape from the riot soon after it began. Their initial meeting point was Cell Block 2, the housing unit of about one-half of their number. Once together, several groups volunteered to go into the other parts of the prison to rescue black inmates who they thought might be stranded and in danger.

> We felt that we would be deserting them if we ran off and left them. So we set out in groups, like 10 or 15 of us, to find these people. We would meet back at a certain time.

These rescue forces met some resistance, especially in Cell Block 4. A black inmate describes how he was able to pry another black inmate away from would be assassins.

> They said, "We gonna kill this nigger here." I told 'em, "Say, ya can't kill him. You kill your own, we gonna kill our own." This was the method I used to get him out.

Virtually all of the blacks left the prison en masse Saturday about noon.

Inmates defected from the riot throughout the 36 hours. By 5:15 p.m. Saturday, 350 inmates had fled the riot. By 8:00 a.m. Sunday, this figure had risen to 800. There were about 100 inmates still in the penitentiary when officials retook it Sunday afternoon.[50]

Some inmates stationed themselves near the various exits to prevent defections. One inmate went from exit to exit sealing them closed with an acetylene torch. These efforts, however, were uncoordinated and ineffective.

Authorities confined surrendering inmates to the exercise yard for the duration of the riot. These inmates were able, however, to move freely between the yard and the prison through a kitchen entrance. Inmates would return to the institution to collect food or just to see what was going on.[51]

On Sunday afternoon, a large group of Chicanos began to threaten a dozen black inmates on the yard. This conflict apparently arose over food which black inmates had foraged from the kitchen. Yelling "kill the blacks," the Chicanos chased the blacks around the yard, eventually cornering them against the fence. A National Guard commander ordered 20 of his men to "lock and load" their rifles and aim them at the onrushing Chicanos. The commander gave the Chicano group five minutes to leave or be fired upon. They retreated at the last moment.[52]

## End of Riot

The strategy pursued by corrections officials throughout the riot was a passive one. Plans to retake the institution were discussed, then abandoned. Little effort was made to actively promote a negotiated settlement. For example, one of the initial demands made by inmates was for access to news media. This was eventually granted late Saturday night, nearly 24 hours after it was first raised. It is fair to say that the riot ended after 36 hours primarily because of massive defections from the riot and because of exhaustion, low morale, and disorganization among those who had been most active, and not because of administration action.

Two hours before the riot ended, in exchange for the release of a hostage, the administration allowed a TV camera and crew into the prison to record the negotiators' statements. The three negotiators complained about the placing of inmates in segregation permanently, the quality of psychological services, and the absence of programs for inmates. They also sought reassurances that retaliation would not be taken against rioting inmates.[53]

A settlement was reached in a final round of negotiations between the inmate spokesmen and Rodriguez. Prison officials agreed that there would be no retaliation against the rioters and that the riot negotiators would be transferred out of state immediately. In return, the inmate negotiators released the remaining two hostages.[54] The state police entered the prison without encountering resistance.

## Aftermath

The riot was directly responsible for significant improvements in living conditions in the New Mexico prison system, including the elimination of overcrowding, suppression of guard brutality, increased programming, less reliance on "snitches" for information, and fewer restrictions on personal property.[55] One inmate stated:

> At that time [before the riot], they wasn't giving up anything. I mean it was a real f--ked up place to be. You know it's still a real f--ked up place to be. But at least a guy can live here with relative safety, and you get fairly decent food and clean linen, showers and exercise. . . . I have been in better joints than this, but the improvement now compared to before 1980 was—man—it's 1,000 percent better. Now they have pay jobs, and there is industrial jobs where your can work a day and get a day cut off your sentence. There's different pay jobs, but before the riot none of that. Probably 75 percent of the population was on idle. No one worked.

Speaking in 1985, a 1980 riot participant observed that he probably would not participate in another riot, because of the improved conditions:

> Myself, I wouldn't feel near as good about participating in another one because there have been some things that have gotten better. They've gotten off my case and they've gotten off a lot of people's cases, for the most part. . . . It's never going to be enjoyable but it's livable. Now, that that [harassment] is not happening, well you feel a little better about yourself. You do your time, you know you got "x" number of years to do. You gonna do it the best way you can and hopefully get out in one piece. And I think you stand a better chance of that now than you did before.

Another inmate reported that the riot had caused groups outside of the prison to take an interest in the welfare of the inmates, which he and other inmates "appreciate a lot." Prior to the riot, he added, "we had nothing coming from the public; nothing at all from the public." Finally, an inmate stated:

> [The riot] was all about trying to get as much as we could, as quick as we could from the police. . . . It's a shame that we had to fight to get [the improvements], but that's basically what it was about—to get rid of the man's snitch system. I mean these people that ran the joint did exactly what they wanted and if you did not like it they would beat your f--kin' ass and put you in the hole. All that's changed now.

As further evidence that the riot contributed to the improvements in the penitentiary, the Department of Corrections secretary, interviewed on the fifth anniversary of the riot, stated that the 1980 riot had motivated him to try to improve the prison.[56] He said that, in his opinion, the riot was the product of inmate idleness, crowding, and understaffing, and that he was seeking to remedy these problems. Calling the snitch system "disgusting and immoral," he stated that it had been banned. He felt that these changes would decrease the possibility of another riot.[57]

These changes did not come cheaply. In 1985, New Mexico spent more per inmate than did any other state in the country except Alaska. The state's per inmate cost was $22,699, as compared to the nationwide average of $14,591. In 1979, New Mexico had ranked in the bottom fifth of states in allocation per inmate.[58]

For most of the hostages, the trauma of 36 hours of terror was devastating. A psychiatrist who treated 9 of the 12 guard hostages reports that during the riot most experienced extreme feelings of fear and imagined the horrible ways that inmates would kill them and how their dead bodies would be discovered after the riot. Years later, some were still unable to hold a steady job.[59]

# 7

# Guards and Inmates in Conflict—
# Michigan Prisons (1981)

If ever a state walked into a riot situation with its eyes wide open, choosing at each decision point the policy publicly identified as the more likely to bring on riots, Michigan was that state. Informed that the three prisons housing the toughest offenders in the state were unacceptably decrepit, the electorate chose not to replace them; moreover, they mandated that more and more prisoners be packed into the existing facilities. Corrections professionals warned for years that this must lead to disaster.

But when the riots came, erupting one after another like a string of fire-crackers in the last days of May 1981, they did not come as one might expect—as the spontaneous reaction of inmates, aggrieved by overcrowded and unsanitary accommodations. No, the catalyst was a mutiny by the guards themselves, an organized takeover of the State Prison of Southern Michigan (SPSM), the largest prison in the western world.

While the riots cost the state $5 million in property damage and over $4 million in indirect costs,[1] they were mild compared to the others described here. There were no hostages, no deaths, and relatively few injuries. As a result, they were never subjected to the same sort of in-depth investigation as the riots at Attica and Santa Fe. It is true that two commissions were established to look into them—one by the governor and one by the state legislature (the Padden Commission)—but they had neither the budget, the staff, nor the sense of urgency evidenced in the other two book-length reports, and produced nowhere near as detailed an account of the riot events. Our account here relies heavily on our own interviews at the riot scenes and draws from other published sources as well.[2]

The story is rather complicated. For one thing, we are dealing with a string of five riots at three prisons over a five-day period. Furthermore, the background to the riots was rather complex. During the five-year period before the riots, the Michigan prison system and its policies, ranging from guard staffing levels to inmate discipline to new prison construction, were the subject of intense public debate. Courts made decisions, the state legislature passed bills, the governor proposed measures, the public voted in two separate referenda, and actors within the prison system made public accusations and counter-accusations. By 1981, both guards and inmates were frustrated, angry, and primed to revolt.

## The Interests of Inmates

During the late 1970s, top prison officials found themselves fighting a two-front war with other policymakers. On the one hand, they continually battled for the funds to relieve the unhealthy and overcrowded conditions in the system by building new prisons and demolishing the old ones. On the other, politicians responsive to, or capitalizing on, public fears of crime proposed measure after measure to send more prisoners to jail, keep them there longer, and deny corrections administrators the power to let them out. Besides worsening the overcrowding problem, such moves seemed likely to promote disorder in the system. But the Department of Corrections lost on both fronts.

### Money and Beds

In 1973, the Michigan prison system had housed 7,683 men. By 1978, the number was well over 14,000. As early as 1977, the shortage of beds was described as "at crisis point"—and it got worse.[3]

By 1980, 40 prisoners a day were arriving at the system's reception center at the State Prison of Southern Michigan. "Thus begins the daily game of musical beds," editorialized the *Detroit News*. "When 40 new people walk in the door, 40 others must be moved somewhere."[4]

The Department of Corrections was unable to build enough new prisons to keep up with the supply of inmates. The new men's facilities that opened in the years 1976 to 1980 came, first, from building where prisons already existed and, second, from acquiring and remodeling institutional facilities in rural areas with depressed economies. Instances of the first were the Northside medium-security complex built at SPSM and the Riverside facility built in the town of Ionia (already home to two prisons). Examples of the second were the Kinross facility, converted from the abandoned Kincheloe Air Force Base near Sault Ste. Marie, and the Michigan Dunes facility, converted from a seminary in the southwestern part of the state. In addition, residence homes and halfway houses were acquired which by 1979 housed over 1,500 men.

What the department really wanted to do, however, was to build or convert large facilities in or near Detroit. Here it was stymied. Its attempts to purchase and convert to prison use a department store warehouse, a child development center, and the former Women's House of Corrections were blocked by community and political pressure.

In 1979, Governor William Milliken proposed to appropriate $400 million toward a plan which would eventually produce 21 new prisons. If it were not passed, Corrections Director Perry Johnson testified prophetically,

> Either the courts will find that the conditions generally caused by this prob-
> lem amount to unconstitutional treatment of prisoners and order a reduc-
> tion of commitments or early release of prisoners, or the prisoners them-
> selves will rebel against these conditions, resulting in disastrous institutional
> disturbances.[5]

But hard times in the auto industry had cut deeply into the state's tax base, and the construction plan disappeared in the legislature.

The effects of this crisis of money and beds were most serious at the state's two largest maximum-security prisons.

In 1981, about 40 percent of Michigan's male inmates—5,600—were housed at SPSM, located north of the city of Jackson. This depression-era experiment in monumental prison construction had long set a standard in the corrections field for excessive size and unmanageability. Corrections policy-makers had long hoped either to close it or divide it up into five or six smaller prisons. But now the state had no beds for the one or funds to spare for the other. In 1979, 200 inmates were "housed" on bunk beds in the stairwells, with no privacy, no place to keep their valuables, and no shelter from the "ever-burning overhead lights." Another 300 were trapped in the Reception and Guidance Center (RGC) under virtual lockdown conditions. Inmates "normally" spend a month in RGC while the department determines their security classification and where they are to serve their sentence. In practice, however, inmates might spend months there.[6]

The situation was worse, if possible, at the Michigan Reformatory (MR) in Ionia, the "oldest and most decrepit prison facility in Michigan." Built in the 1870s as an insane asylum, by 1980 it housed up to 1,500 inmates in space meant for 1,183. Supposedly intended for inmates under 23, the crunch had forced inmates from 15 to over 30 into the cramped and unsanitary quarters. One hundred eighty beds had been placed in the recreation areas, and the only indoor recreation was now an unhealthy basement beneath the kitchen. "Sewage, leaking from rusted-out pipes, drips down five stories and collects in a stagnant pool in the basement," wrote a reporter in 1979. "The 19th-century sewage system has wooden lines which frequently collapse, forming foul sub-terranean pools. The steam heating system also frequently breaks down. Wa-ter freezes in the toilet bowls in winter."[7]

The state had been trying to close MR as early as 1973. In 1977, the state auditor general condemned the facility as "substandard in every way." "Can you imagine a young guy looking at a ten-year stretch coming to a place like this?" asked MR Warden Dale Foltz in 1979. Replacing MR was the top priority of the proposed construction plan of 1979. Republican Governor Milliken was even more emphatic on a tour in October, 1980: "This institution is outworn, outdated, and ought to be literally razed to the ground."[8]

Milliken's tour was part of a new solution to the problem of funds: a task force of the state legislature on prison overcrowding had proposed that new funds for prison construction come from an increase in the state income tax from 4.6 to 4.7 percent. This measure was placed on the November 1980 ballot as Proposal E. Though the measure was supported by the media, the governor, and most corrections officials, the voters were cool to the idea of even this modest tax increase. Milliken's Ionia tour, intended to drum up support for the measure, was destined to have little effect.

## Passage of Proposal B

The crime rate actually fell in Michigan during the late 1970s, but public pressure had brought about more intensive prosecution, less plea bargaining, and stiffer sentences. For example, in 1976, a law was passed providing for an additional mandatory, non-parolable two-year sentence for anyone convicted of a crime in which a gun was used. This would rise to five years for a second conviction, and ten years for a third. Later, corrections officials claimed that just as great a proportion of criminals used guns after its passage as before.[9]

In the public debate over these measures, corrections officials often came out sounding like defenders of criminals. But in their view, such measures not only threatened to increase the population pressures in the system, but also were intended to take away from judges, prison administrators, and parole officials the power to treat inmates on an individual basis.

An inmate in the Michigan system had chances to significantly shorten his sentence by maintaining a clean prison record. If he avoided "tickets" (write-ups for rule violations), he accrued "good time" at the rate of ten days per month, which were subtracted from both his minimum and maximum sentences. That meant that he was eligible for earlier consideration by the parole board. Once his case came before the board, his behavior in prison would be a factor in the board's decision.

A prisoner sentenced by a judge to serve from 10 to 20 years, by impressing both the prison administration and the parole board with his good behavior, might go home in roughly 7 years and 7 months. Some inmates could earn "special good time" and come before the parole board even sooner. As in many states, these incentives were important in maintaining internal order.

One long-time critic of the state's "lenient" parole policies was L. Brooks Patterson, the Oakland County prosecutor. Throughout the time period we consider, he was the best-publicized county prosecutor in Michigan. Patterson started public life as the attorney for anti-busing forces in the city of Pontiac. Elected in 1973, he exemplified the law-and-order sentiments of the middle-class residents of his suburban county, many of whom had fled from Detroit either because it was unsafe or because of its growing black majority. Enjoying good press, Patterson became known as the "scourge of gamblers and welfare cheats."[10] Patterson was also a quite ambitious man.

In the early hours of Tuesday, December 7, 1976, three people executed an armed raid on Pontiac General Hospital. Their purpose was to rescue from police custody a patient named Benny Lee Clay, who had been wounded in a shootout with police the previous day after a busted liquor store holdup. While another woman waited with the car, Janice Love and Melvin Scott entered the hospital and, at 5:20 a.m., burst into Clay's room and disarmed the officer on duty.

The officer's relief walked in just at the wrong time. Scott put five bullets in him; but the dying officer drew from the floor and wounded Scott fatally. All the other participants were captured less than an hour later.[11]

Patterson's response to this dramatic incident came later that day. He announced that both Clay and Scott were parolees who, credited with "good time," had been released before the completion of their minimum sentences. Furthermore, Patterson was going to "drop everything" to organize "a statewide team of 4,000 persons" to put a referendum on the 1978 ballot repealing the "good time" provision.[12]

The press swung enthusiastically into line behind Patterson's petition drive. "A policeman is dead because two people were on parole—and shouldn't have been," declared a *Detroit News* editorial.[13] A *News* columnist printed the stories of eight grisly murders of men, women, and children in Oakland County—all, according to Patterson, committed by men paroled before serving their minimum sentences. "Patterson's office has already been flooded by telephone calls . . . letters and cards from some 1,500 persons" wishing to support the referendum campaign, wrote the columnist. Another *News* writer called on the public to "join the army. The pay is low, but the rewards are great." By the middle of January 1977, Patterson claimed to have 2,500 volunteers in his "army," and he had a backlog of 40 speaking engagements around the state.[14] The referendum campaign gave Patterson statewide recognition; and in January 1978, Patterson announced his candidacy for the U.S. Senate.

He lost the bid, but his referendum did better. Placed on the ballot as Proposal B, it won media endorsement and was passed in November 1978 by a three-to-one margin of the Michigan electorate. It provided that anyone convicted of certain violent crimes must serve at least the minimum sentence imposed by the trial judge.

DOC officials objected to Proposal B not only because it would worsen the overcrowding, but also because it would eliminate their power to deny "good time" as punishment for assaults, gambling, smuggling, drug abuse, and other violations of the prison order. Some tools remained to them: the authorities could impose short-term segregation and could grant or deny transfers to better housing, transfers to better prisons, more lucrative job assignments, and admission to desirable programs. The latter items were more or less available as rewards depending on how available money and beds were. But prospects were good on neither score.

However, DOC officials felt it necessary to respond to public criticism of the parole system. In January 1978, the DOC produced the results of a five-year study intended to help the parole board predict which inmates might commit violent crimes if paroled. They claimed to have identified "risk factors" which would improve the parole board's record: mostly rather common-sense stuff, including a violent criminal record, juvenile arrests, and "major misconducts" in prison. These findings came to be used by the parole board in making their decisions.[15]

Inmates were angry about both the passage of Proposal B and the new parole guidelines. It should be pointed out that, under a state court ruling, inmates imprisoned before the passage of the referendum continued to accrue "good time" for the remainder of their sentences. So the only inmates directly affected were those sentenced after the law came into force; and one could argue that they had no reasonable cause to complain, since they could have avoided its effects by not committing crimes.

But, reasonable or not, many inmates convicted and sentenced after 1978 considered themselves to be victims of injustice, as their punishment was greater than if Proposal B had not been passed. Others not directly affected took it as a symbolic outrage—an expression of irrational hostility by the Michigan public, exploited with crass calculation by an ambitious politician. In developing these views, both groups could lean on declarations from corrections professionals that Proposal B actually was a counterproductive measure.

Many inmates were more directly threatened by the new parole policies. According to the ideology, or rhetoric, of rehabilitation, it is possible for "criminals" to transform themselves into "non-criminals," and thereafter they have the right to re-enter society. If one believes this—as inmates often do, at least when it is in their interest —then it is a criminal's present nature, not his or her past crimes, that should guide whether or not to grant a parole.

But in fact it was the inmate's pre-prison record which dominated the new parole guidelines. Inmates with records of violent crime as juveniles, now years in the past, found to their frustration that they were treated as bad parole risks regardless of how "rehabilitated" they believed they had become in prison.

## The Ferency Lawsuit

Before the referendum ballot on Proposal E, the state's prison plans were overtaken by the resolution of a prisoner's rights lawsuit. Zolton Ferency, a lawyer well known in Michigan as a campaigner for liberal causes, had filed the suit in 1976, claiming that conditions in the overcrowded state prisons constituted "cruel and unusual punishment." A procedural logjam broke in 1980, and settlement talks among Ferency, the attorney general's office, the DOC, and the Ingham County Circuit Court occupied most of the year.

The order handed down on October 27, 1980, compelled the state to reduce its prison population to 13,013 by January 1 and to cap it at that level. Prisoners must be released on completion of their minimum sentence unless a majority of the parole board agreed they were a menace to the public safety; and parolees could not be returned for technical violations.[16]

The decision muddled even further the status of Proposal E. Some corrections figures who were critical of what they saw as a trend to unnecessary imprisonment, such as Leonard Esquina, the system's ombudsman, had previously argued that new prisons should not be built until the criteria for confinement had been reviewed. Ferency, even more strongly of this temper, announced that the court order had sounded "the death knell" for Proposal E, and tried unsuccessfully to have it stricken from the ballot. In any case, the Michigan electorate overwhelmingly rejected Proposal E—probably not because they favored alternative punishments, but rather to save the money. Disappointed, Director Johnson predicted that Michigan Reformatory would "remain in use at least through the next decade."[17]

To keep the prison population below the court-mandated level, the legislature quickly passed a bill authorizing the governor to declare an "overcrowding emergency." This would make hundreds of prisoners eligible for parole 90 days before the expiration of their minimum sentences. On March 19, 1981, the Department of Corrections asked the governor to implement the early release procedure.

At this point, however, the Oakland County prosecutor dealt himself into the state corrections policy game again, filing suit to challenge the constitutionality of the early-release law. An uncharitable view of this would be that Patterson was again putting his name before the public in view of another upcoming election. (In fact, Patterson filed to run for governor four months later.) Whatever his motives, Patterson's suit held up the early parole of 1,000 prisoners for two months. Finally, the state supreme court having ruled the law constitutional, Governor Milliken signed the early-release order on May 20, 1981.

Conditions were bad in the Michigan prison system long before 1981. In fact, the maximum crowding at SPSM, MR, and Marquette Branch Prison occurred in 1977, before the opening of Riverside, Kinross, and Michigan Dunes, and the acquisition of the community facilities; by 1981, their populations had been steadily, though slowly, declining for over three years. What was new was that state officials one after another *publicly agreed* that conditions were intolerable and unjust and that the laws under which inmates were confined were unwise. By 1981, many were subject to the "no-good-time" rule of Proposal B, and many (especially in the maximum security prisons) were subject to the gun law of 1976. The prisoners knew that prison administrators had thought these measures unwise and hasty; and in the case of Proposal B, they felt they had been sacrificed to Patterson's ambition.

Inmates at Michigan Reformatory must have felt particularly outraged about their living conditions. It is one thing when inmates gripe among themselves about crowded, unhealthy conditions. It is another thing when the Department of Corrections itself has been begging for the chance to close the prison for seven years, and when the governor of the state declares that it should be razed flat. The same applied to SPSM, universally condemned in the corrections profession as too old and too big.

Again, under normal circumstances it may be tolerable to live in a bunk in a gymnasium. But after a judge has ruled it unconstitutional, one expects the situation to improve immediately as a matter of *right*. When this right was frustrated by Prosecutor Patterson for two months, inmates were outraged. The issue was closely followed by inmate newspapers at SPSM and MR; the *Hill Top News* (MR) editorialized, under the headline "Come on Brooks . . . once is enough!":

> ONCE AGAIN the residents of the Michigan Penal system are caught in the middle . . . do we dare count on the law? Do we dare count on anything?[18]

## The Interests of Guards

However, it was prison guards, not inmates, who organized and carried out the act of rebellion which touched off the 1981 riots. Guards at SPSM, like inmates at MR and elsewhere in the system, felt bitter, frustrated, victimized, and "caught in the middle." They believed their own bosses were in league with inmates and liberals against them to the degree that their own lives were jeopardized. The spiral of interaction among guards, inmates, and administration at SPSM is reminiscent of the series of events at Attica; but it led guards, not inmates, to take over the prison—at least at first.

The tone for the newly organized Michigan Corrections Organization's actions was set by its first job action, which took place not in Jackson but at Marquette.

Marquette Branch Prison sets the standard for remoteness. Its red stone battlements hug the wind-swept southern shore of Lake Superior, a few miles from the National Ski Hall of Fame in Negaunee. Hemingway fished the trout streams to the east and west. By car, it is as far north and west of Detroit as Washington, D.C., is south and east. In consequence, visits were infrequent. Inmates were allowed one phone call per month. A prison official told a journalist in 1979, "We are the bottom of the barrel of 15,000 inmates in Michigan."[19] The inmates on F Block, Marquette's "hole," or segregation unit, were at the bottom of the bottom. The tensions in such a unit—the harshest unit in the state's harshest prison—can be unbelievably intense.

In August 1979, some residents of F Block reportedly engaged in a "five-day waste-throwing spree," collecting their own urine and excrement in paper cups and hurling it through the bars at passing guards. Such actions are not unknown, and indeed a similar incident in Block 10 at Walpole (the "bottom of the barrel" in Massachusetts) had precipitated a guards' strike there four months before.[20] At Marquette, Warden Theodore Koehler acted to take away the offenders' "good time." However, a Marquette judge ruled that under existing regulations Koehler had no power to do that. Infuriated, the Marquette guards voted 83–1 to strike.[21]

In June of that year, corrections workers in the state of Michigan had voted in a union representation election. Of the 2,362 employees in the unit, about two-thirds voted; of that number, barely over half voted to be represented by the Michigan Corrections Organization (MCO), affiliated with the

Service Employees International Union (SEIU). Only 50 voted for "no union."[22]

Significantly, Koehler did not condemn the strike vote, and told the press that "the administration and the guards are on the same track." MCO locals at other institutions voted to go out in support of the Marquette guards. However, the threatened systemwide guards' strike did not transpire. Six days after the initial vote, Governor Milliken signed emergency orders granting Koehler the power to revoke "good time." The MCO had its first victory—an expansion of the wardens' power to punish inmates.[23]

## Guards in Ferment at SPSM: Discipline

At Jackson, the largest MCO bargaining unit, the administration and the guards were on different tracks. Serious conflict developed over issues of inmate discipline and guard safety.

In its 1974 decision in *Wolff v. McDonnell,* the U.S. Supreme Court ruled that a prison had to give an inmate charged with breaking a prison rule a fair hearing before he or she could be punished. In the Court's interpretation, a fair hearing required that a guilty finding be supported by a preponderance of the evidence; that an officer's word had to be treated as an accusation, not a finding; that inmates must have 24 hours' written notice of the charges before the hearing; and that inmates must be allowed to call witnesses and present documentary evidence. The state must provide accused inmates with assistance in their defense if they were illiterate or the issues were complex, and the hearing officer must be impartial.[24]

As one might expect, prison administrators were not enthusiastic about implementing the *Wolff* decision. Compliance on paper often fell short in practice and in spirit.

In 1979, Michigan moved in the direction of full compliance with *Wolff* with the passage of Public Act 140 (PA 140). This act established a Lansing-based hearings division, with the responsibility for conducting all the major misconduct hearings in each of the state's prisons. Attorneys would be hired as hearing officers.[25] An inmate grievance procedure for non-disciplinary matters was also created, and a DOC ombudsman's office established to oversee it.

SPSM Warden Charles E. Anderson resented PA 140 and *Wolff,* believing they infringed on the necessary authority of corrections personnel. Anderson was a 21-year veteran of the deparment, having worked his way up from the ranks to his appointment as warden in 1977. Anderson pursued a "calculated policy" of loose discipline, condoned gambling, and tolerated "mayors," or clique leaders, with recognized "turf" in the prison; and his tenure was marred by scandals such as the ombudsman's exposure of a ring of inmate trusties extorting sexual favors from new inmates. But he identified closely with the guards, and they, in turn, tended to see him as fair and security-minded.[26]

Anderson and his staff complained openly about the intrusion by "outsiders" into the operation of SPSM and called for the return of the old days when prison personnel conducted the hearings themselves. They were also less than cooperative with the new hearings division. Marjorie VanOchten, appointed in 1979 as chief hearings administrator, reported that SPSM officials made rude, hostile comments to her, challenged her competence, and complained that she failed to realize that "they had an institution to run."[27]

In June 1980, Anderson was replaced by Barry Mintzes, 38, with a Ph.D. in clinical psychology. Mintzes had started with the department as a staff psychologist at SPSM, but was quickly promoted to administrative aide to DOC Director Johnson. In 1978, Mintzes became warden of the newly opened Kinross medium-security facility, making him the state's youngest warden.[28]

Mintzes took steps to ensure that the new hearing procedures worked at Kinross. He required his staff to review each ticket not upheld by a hearing officer, to find out what had been done incorrectly, and to remedy any problem. These efforts paid off in a lower dismissal rate than at other prisons in the state.[29]

At Jackson, Mintzes received little support from his subordinates. Even though he took action to eliminate the "mayor" system and transfer "hoods" to other prisons, guards and upper-level prison officials distrusted Mintzes' supposed sympathies with inmates and would not be reconciled to PA 140.[30]

In April 1980, Deputy Warden Elton Scott sent a memo to Warden Mintzes describing the conclusions of a "task force" on violence at SPSM, which included two deputy wardens, three captains, all resident unit managers, and a number of other upper-echelon SPSM administrators. They concluded that

> due process is a major cause of violence being perpetrated in this facility. Most people indicated that there were no sanctions and the residents know it. The supervisors indicated that the staff feels that there is nothing they can do to the residents and feel they are frustrated.
>
> The task force felt Lansing should let the institutional people run the institution and not the Lansing people, whom [sic] for the most part, have not worked in an institution. Times have changed and the Policy Directives and Operational Procedures do not apply.
>
> The task force felt that the violence really started and could be correlated with the inception of the Hearings Division.

An SPSM guard expressed a similar sentiment in a note to us:

> The young female lawyer [i.e., VanOchten] has never worked in a prison and has no idea what it is like to put in 8 hours a day in a housing unit with over 100 convicted felons.
>
> Several years ago, any major misconduct occurring in the dining room . . . meant automatic immediate segregation time and everyone knew it. Several months ago I saw an inmate pick up a metal food tray and assault another inmate who was working on the serving line. The resident was only given 5 days in segregation and put back in general population. Two days later the

same inmate cut another inmate with a piece of glass requiring 88 stitches in the face under the eye. Last month an officer suffered broken ribs, another tore lingaments [*sic*] in the wrist, and several more had cuts and bruises breaking up a fight. The officers were off work longer than the inmates spent in detention.

While guards throughout the system were discontented with *Wolff,* at SPSM top officials actively encouraged and legitimated these complaints.[31] Not bothering to master the workings of the system they and their superiors found so ridiculous, guards at SPSM wrote tickets so poorly that a high percentage of them were dismissed. In 1979, 33 percent of the SPSM inmates cited for misconduct were found not guilty, compared to 8 percent of the inmates charged at Marquette, and a systemwide average of 17 percent. Guards and administrators at SPSM took the high dismissal rate as further evidence that the hearing officers were biased toward inmates and the procedure was unworkable.[32]

Whatever the cause, a breakdown in discipline was observed by both guards and inmates. Fred Parks, executive director of the MCO, commented that

> MCO has long been a strong advocate of safe and secure prison concept. This "security first" philosophy seems to fly head on with the present Department of Corrections philosophy of "prisoner appeasement." . . . We now have inmates who *know* little or nothing will happened to them when they defy orders or violate rules. . . . It is not uncommon for an inmate, knowing the officer has little recourse, to tell an officer to "f‒‒k off" or give him "the finger" and continue on his way in direct defiance of simple instruction.[33] (emphasis in original)

An inmate reported,

> *Inmate:* It used to be if the guard and the inmate would bump shoulders, the inmate had a ticket coming. Now, they say it's the officer's word against the inmate's word.
> *Question:* Does this mean that more tickets are getting dismissed?
> *Inmate:* No, but they're different types of tickets. Ten years ago, of a hundred tickets, they'd be for fighting, horseplay, and insolence. [Now] unless you get in the officer's face and start swinging, they don't go out of their way to write you a ticket.

Guards in the whole system overwhelmingly distrusted the DOC in Lansing; but at SPSM—as distinct from MR and Marquette—they viewed their own warden as an incompetent and a traitor, a man with too much power. The SPSM guards came to believe that they had no friends in the system; both Mintzes and Johnson were their enemies, and their actions were interpreted as callous and reckless disregard of prison discipline and the guards' safety.

## SPSM—The Prison and Prisoners

The sprawling facility which Warden Barry Mintzes inherited in 1980 occupied 57 acres "inside the walls" and an additional 4,000 acres in the Trusty Division outside the walls. SPSM was divided into a maximum-security Central Complex (3,100 inmates), a medium-security Northside Complex (1,000 inmates), and a minimum security Trusty Division (1,500 inmates) (see Figure 7–1). Barriers prevented inmates from passing freely from one complex to the next. In the construction of Northside, two cell blocks which had been part of

Figure 7–1. State Prison of Southern Michigan

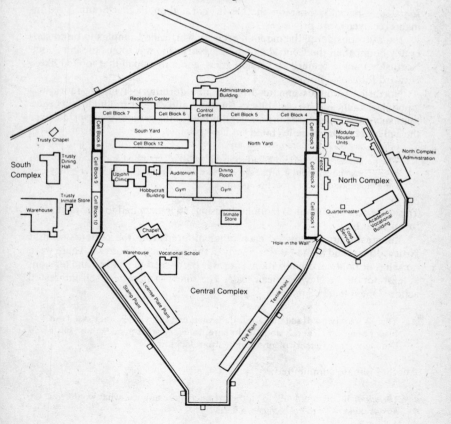

the Central Complex and which were physically attached to Central's Block 3 had their south entrances sealed off and new entrances opened onto Northside's yard. A gate linking the Central and Northside complexes was known as the "hole in the wall." This was used by Northside residents to go to work at the centrally located prison industries.

The Central Complex was further divided into a "North Yard" (blocks 3, 4, and 5) and a "South Yard" (blocks 6, 7, 8, 11 and 12). The more violent and less well adjusted inmates were assigned to North Yard blocks. Most residents perceived the North Yard blocks as the prison's most dangerous. One inmate commented:

> They use blocks 3 and 4 as a dumping ground. If you come out of the hole [punishment], and they feel you have a lot of hostility, they dump you in those blocks. Most of your killings are in 3 and 4.

Inmates, especially those on the North Yard, thought that South Yard inmates received more privileges.

Inmates considered the medium-security Northside Complex to be considerably better than the Central Complex. "Northside was top of the line," one Northside inmate remarked. "It had grass, and a mess hall that looked like a Howard Johnsons, flowers."

Northside Complex inmates lived in nine dormitory-style, pre-fabricated "modular" units and two cell blocks (blocks 1 and 2). The modular units were relatively new, bright, clean, air-conditioned, and generally preferred over the cell blocks. One inmate stated:

> The people in blocks 1 and 2 had to live in cells, all cramped and uncomfortable. These new modular homes [were] like army barracks only newer—they were clean, had no cockroaches, no mice.

To secure an assignment to modular housing, an inmate had to stay ticket free for six months.

Inmates' attitudes toward each other differed from the patterns seen at Attica, Joliet, and Santa Fe—primarily in the very lack of pattern. There were no gangs or political organizations; nor was there seething hatred and tension, at least not on the New Mexican scale. The rule was atomized, self-interested action. One inmate stated

> There's a lot [who'd] sell out, for little favors, extra privileges, they'd sell out for a phone call. There's no unity in here. In every other pen, Jackson has a bad name; they're leery of guys coming from Jackson.

Another inmate commented:

> *Question:* If you could talk to all the prisoners here at once, what would you advise them to do to get changes in here?

*Inmate:* I couldn't advise these guys to do s––t. I wouldn't last three minutes. We are not dealing with people who could get together. I don't think you could get 20 together. I doubt if you could get 15 together in here.

By 1981, there were no gangs at SPSM and few inmates belonged to solidaristic organizations. However, a substantial number of blacks belonged to several Muslim sects, including the Moorish Science Temple, American Muslim Temple, and Orthodox Sunni Muslims. The latter group, for example, met two nights a week and claimed over 50 members. Adherents would associate together on the yard and on work assignments.

Another small group of inmates made up the Prisoner Progress Association (PPA). Formed in the early 1970s, the PPA filed class action suits on behalf of inmates and assisted inmates in filing individual suits. At its height during the mid-1970s, the PPA established regular contact with liberal political figures and organizations in the state, including Zolton Ferency and the American Friends Service Committee. One inmate described the PPA's activities.

The main thing was to provide legal support for whoever needed help on their own rights, mental rights and so on. Also we did a visitation suit, where the visitors were being f––ed over—a guy's daughter couldn't sit on his lap— they'd have to wait two hours in the front, and when they got in, they could only visit one hour.

By 1981, most inmates were either unaware of the organization's existence or contemptuous of it. According to a current member of the PPA, the organization fell from favor because "egotistical prisoners" had misused the group's funds.

This general disorganization is more like New Mexico than like Attica. An important difference, however, was the Michigan DOC's policy that snitches "should not be 'fostered.' "[34] Inmates confirmed that "officers say, 'Don't snitch,' " and some even *complained* that the guards did not act on the information given to them by inmates.

[If you tell] a guard, say, "This guy is going to stab me," he'll say, "What are you telling me for?" They have turned their backs.

Hence, "snitches" did not generate the enmity that was evident in New Mexico. Neither did inmates have the same degree of hatred for the guards and administration. Of course, it is somewhat risky to attempt to compare degrees of hate on the basis of interviews. Still, the average inmate at Jackson talked about the guards in relatively evenhanded terms. One stated:

These guards here, all they care about is coming in, putting in eight hours, making a living.
*Question:* Are there guards who dislike and harass you?
*Inmate:* Not out here. Not toward me they don't.

Another inmate stated:

> I get along with the majority of the officers, but some hate blacks, some are racist, some are homosexuals.

One reason for the absence of strong hatred toward prison authorities is that many inmates felt they benefited from the prison's educational and vocational programs. One inmate stated:

> One thing about Jackson is that it had good vocation. I have the skills of optics as the result of being in Jackson. They teach [inmates] how to make prescription glasses. You can take trades, like how to become a dental technician, [or] small-engine repairman. You [can] receive up to a bachelor degree in psychology, business, sociology. They have computer programs—up-to-date programs.

A small minority of inmates, though, did express untempered hostility:

> Some [guards] are so sadistic. I think they go home after work and kick the cat or dog [that's the kind of people they are].

On living conditions in general, another inmate declared:

> This place is not worth the spit I would spit from my mouth. It is not worth two dead flies. I wish the feds would tear it down. It's a real trip. You wake up, and there are pigeons flying in—roaches, bugs, little insects.
> *Question:* Pigeons?
> *Inmate:* They *live* in the block. Bats. You can go to the infirmary, and come back blind and crippled.

Beginning in the 1960s, in response to complaints by the custodial staff that civilian counselors were obstructing their work, the administration began to train guards in counseling. In the early 1970s, the civilian counselors were dismissed and guards trained as counselors were attached to the residential units. Inmates we interviewed were mistrustful of the guards-turned-counselors, believed them to be unsympathetic, and were unwilling to trust them with their problems. One inmate wrote:

> The counselors here do more of a guard's job than one of a counselor. Counselors shakedown residents, walk in the blocks taking down wire that men use for TV reception, sit at the guards' desks, etc.[35]

Warden Mintzes, however, was generally popular among inmates and accurately perceived as believing in due process. One inmate declared:

> Barry Mintzes was the best thing that happened to Jackson, a psychologist, who understood human nature, talked to people—but the guards think might makes right, and give no credence to [him].

## Guards in Ferment at SPSM: Staffing and Safety

In response to the fiscal crisis, the state legislature reduced the DOC's funding for the 1980 fiscal year by $7.7 million.[36] The cutback resulted in the elimination of 69 staff positions statewide and a sharp reduction in the overtime work available to guards. For fiscal year 1981, the state legislature cut the previous year's budget by an additional $2.9 million, eliminating 125 more positions, 27 of them at SPSM.

To curtail overtime costs, some shifts were operated below the officially designated "critical level" —the minimum number of guards required to operate the prison safely with normal activities. Guards complained bitterly to the union. The following plea from a Northside shift representative illustrates the distrust guards felt for Lansing by this point:

> Is it the department's intention to get an officer hurt thru neglect, or do they want a Riot for a lever to increase prison funds from our legislators?[37]

On March 2, 1981, Mintzes sent a memo to shift commanders instructing them to staff all shifts to the critical level. The memo did not satisfy the MCO, which distrusted what they saw as equivocal phrasing. More basically, the MCO wanted staffing brought up to "normal level," not left at critical level. In a memo to MCO chapters, MCO Executive Director Fred Parks later urged local leaders to push the issue of normal staffing with the press, emphasizing that critical level was an expedient which could be resorted to on emergencies but was unsafe for the ongoing operation of a prison.[38]

On March 11, 1981, MCO's Jackson chapter staged an "informational picket" in front of the prison. Their leaflet blasted the administration and the hearings procedure:

> Staffing is at a critical low. . . . With the Warden having full knowledge of the potential dangers and the guard's insecure feelings while on the job, we do not understand why there is such a problem increasing the custody staff at S.P.S.M.
> The resident disciplineary [sic] process presently being used is ineffective, as it in many ways rewards residents who break institutional rules and regulations and laws, by not punishing them.[39]

On April 22, after a guard at Michigan Reformatory was assaulted, Fred Parks wrote Perry Johnson protesting the "prolifacy of weapons" among inmates and demanding shakedowns for weapons at institutions around the state. Johnson sent Parks a conciliatory response, more or less agreeing to the shakedowns on terms to be worked out at the individual institutions.[40]

The shakedown at the SPSM Central Complex was set for May 20. Deputy Warden Scott sent a memo to supervisory officers on May 14, setting forth procedures for the shakedown, in which he repeated the MCO's claim that there had been "a rash of stabbings." This phrase was used by the MCO after the riot to demonstrate a serious decline in guard safety. However, DOC statistics presented to the Padden Commission showed yearly assault figures to be constant from 1979 to 1981. There actually had been a rash of 22 assaults in February, but the totals were much lower in March and April.[41]

The May 20 shakedown at SPSM Central uncovered only six weapons. The warden characterized the shakedown as the most thorough in the institution's history. Guards dismissed the search as a farce. After the riot, the MCO claimed that Scott's May 14 memo had gotten into the hands of the inmates and forewarned them. They also protested the fact that civilian employees, like school employees and factory foremen, had been brought in on the search. The MCO claimed these civilians were unable to spot where inmates hid weapons; one guard, said the MCO, had found four knives in an area already searched by civilians. Finally, the fact that only six weapons were found "contradict[ed] the generally accepted fact that 50% to 60% of the inmates are armed with some type of weapon" and proved that the search was ineffective.[42]

These statements have to be taken with a lot of salt, since they were made after the riot, when there was a pressing need to demonstrate that the May 20 search had failed. Furthermore, union members often provide dubious reasons why untrained people cannot possibly do their jobs competently and only genuine union members (at overtime) can do the work.

However, the Jackson guards clearly believed that SPSM was full of weapons, and that any search recovering only six could not have been a good search. This depends on what is taken as a "weapon." Inmates had access to many things that could be *used* as weapons. Jars can be broken and the shards used as knives; chairs can be broken up into clubs. However, the MCO was hard put to come up with evidence that the prisoners actually had many fabricated weapons hidden away for ready use.

By this time, however, fear had become a unifying ideology for guards. They would only get more staff hired if they managed to convince the public and policymakers that their lives were in imminent danger.

Actually, the staffing situation had significantly improved; whereas in November 1980, about 25 percent of the shifts at SPSM were being operated below critical, this had fallen to 4 percent by April, 1981. However, the MCO took these instances as violations of the understanding reached in March. Four days before the shakedown, on May 16, MCO leaders met to discuss the staffing issue; attending was Gerald Fryt, a guard at SPSM Central Complex who was head of the Jackson chapter and president of the MCO. The conference developed a tough resolution on staffing to be submitted to the local chapters for approval, which concluded that

> The members, officers, and chapters of MCO will uniformly and collectively do whatever is deemed necessary to protect the health, safety, and well-being of the membership.[43]

The conferees apparently discussed the possible forms this uniform and collective action could take. A memo from Parks, dated May 21, summarizing the discussion, advised local leaders:

Tell them not to worry about the legalities—Central's handling that with the attorneys. The one thing we CANNOT do is a regular, at the gate, sign-carrying strike. . . . Your membership may have other possible ideas. Anything that fits your institution is okay.[44]

The memo suggested having members arrive late for their shifts, or even having them arrive *early* in order to dramatize that double staffing was necessary to make the institution safe. Those actions would be legal, said Parks, as they did not cause "harm to the workplace."

On the evening of May 20, hours after the shakedown, the Jackson guards met to vote on and approve the resolution on staffing. Many were angry and suspicious about the apparent failure of the shakedown. As added fuel to the flame, Governor Milliken had signed the emergency release order (seen as a victory for inmates) that very day.

In this emotional atmosphere, it was proposed that the guards organize their *own* shakedown. This would dramatize the desperate conditions guards faced, and if guards successfully uncovered a store of weapons that Mintzes' shakedown had missed, it would demonstrate the warden's incompetence. It would neither be an "at the gate, sign-carrying strike" nor "harm the workplace." Fryt later claimed to have opposed the idea, but two guard sources told the Padden Commission that such an action was tentatively planned for June.[45]

At about 6:45 p.m. the next evening, a violent incident broke out on Block 4, which guards saw as proof of the desperate situation they were in. At that hour inmates were out of their cells, on their way to yard and to other assignments. One of the guards on duty was very unpopular with inmates, reportedly because he closed down inmate "stores." (Inmates bought supplies from the canteen for re-sale to other inmates at a high markup.) Ten months before, a 22-pound mop wringer had been dropped on his head from three tiers up. The DOC ombudsman had recommended that he be transferred out of Block 4, but this advice had not been followed, and he had just returned from injury leave.

Shortly beforehand, this guard had instructed an inmate with a reputation for being mentally disturbed to dispose of a "contraband" padlock. (Inmates were permitted to possess padlocks to secure their doors when they were outside their cells.) The inmate returned to his cell in a state of rage, tied a shoestring to the offending padlock, and broke his broom in half, creating a sort of homemade spear. He then approached the unpopular guard and a second guard, who were working at the unit desk signing passes. Pulling the broken stick out from under his jacket, he stabbed the second guard in the chest. When the second guard grabbed at the broom handle, the resident swung his padlock wildly on the string, hitting both guards repeatedly in the head. The guards tried to restrain the inmate, and the unpopular guard went to the floor wrestling with him.

A crowd of inmates gathered as additional guards arrived. Some inmates helped subdue the assailant. Others shouted threats at the guards and threw jars at the unpopular guard. One hit him. The guards ordered the inmates to lock up in their cells; inmates resisted this order, claiming they had done nothing to be locked up for.[46]

Order was restored without physical confrontation or further injury. The guards were taken by ambulance to a local emergency room, treated, and released. However, guards saw the attack as the last straw. They took it as proof that the previous day's shakedown had failed, apparently choosing not to believe that the inmate had produced these weapons on the spot.

Fryt was out of town that evening. When he returned home, he found 25 angry and frantic phone calls on his answering machine. It was a "spontaneous employee reaction," he claimed. Fryt spent more time on the phone that night. When he arrived for work in the early hours of Friday morning (Fryt worked the 6 a.m. to 2 p.m. shift), he was "deluged by people in the parking lot." Once inside, guards scheduled for the second shift started calling on his office phone.[47]

The rank and file were hot to act. They wanted to implement their own shakedown now, that day, and not wait till June. Fryt initially tried to cool them down (as he told it later), but they would have none of it. Finally, Fryt agreed to *ask* the administration to authorize them to conduct the shakedown. What he had planned if they refused him became a matter of dispute.

## The Guard Takeover

Friday, May 22, was a state holiday, the beginning of Memorial Day weekend. Prison officials had the day off. Deputy Warden Scott, however, stopped by SPSM at about 9:15 a.m. anyway to see what the climate was following the previous day's attack.

Fryt and two union stewards had been pressuring the captain in charge to authorize the shakedown, but he said he didn't have the authority and refused. Scott also refused. Fryt then said that the guards would do it themselves. This may have been either a prediction or a threat. The deputy warden warned Fryt that an unauthorized lockdown would constitute "gross insubordination" and would be illegal. (The MCO denied Scott said this.) At this point, Deputy Warden Scott asked one of the MCO officials, "Is MCO taking over?" According to Scott, the union official told him that this was indeed the case, and that the administration no longer controlled the prison.[48]

As these conversations were taking place, on-duty MCO guards telephoned off-duty members to ask them to assist with the shakedown. When they arrived, however, the off-duty officers were refused entrance into the prison.

At 9:45 a.m. the bugle blew, indicating to the over 3,000 inmates in the Central Complex that the morning recreation period was over and that they should return to their cells. About 200 inmates remained on the yard; a few of them were stragglers but most were allowed to stay on the yard because of their assignments (e.g., kitchen crew, yard, gym, and store details).

Around 10:00 a.m. several MCO leaders went to each of the Central

Complex's blocks to inform the guards on duty that a shakedown would begin shortly, and not to release the inmates for lunch at 11:00 a.m. as was normally done. A sergeant loyal to the administration called each block to tell the guards to disregard the MCO's instruction and to proceed as usual for lunch. Most guards either refused to answer their phone or pretended not to understand the sergeant due to a bad connection. Meanwhile, guards on duty at the gate where visitors arrived closed off the entrance and refused orders to open it. Guards on duty in Block 8 (an honor block, whose cells were kept open during the day) ordered residents into their cells and locked them in.

About 10:15 a.m., Warden Mintzes arrived at the prison and, like Scott, ordered the MCO officials to halt the lockdown. They again refused. Mintzes asked MCO President Fryt if the union had taken charge of the administration of the prison. He replied, "I guess you can say that."

## The Inmate Response at SPSM

The MCO controlled SPSM's Central Complex for about two hours. The circumstances under which they lost it were hotly debated later; but lose it they did.

Rumors quickly spread among inmates that the guards planned to lock down the prison for the entire three-day Memorial Day weekend. Such long weekends are traditionally periods of extra free time, recreation, and visits. Not only would there be a loss of these privileges, but some inmates believed the guards intended to starve them the whole weekend. Inmates assigned to the kitchen crew heard news reports of the guards' actions on their portable radios, including the fact that the lockdown was in violation of Mintzes' orders.

Shortly before noon, a group of inmates from the yard entered Block 3. There are two stories about what happened. According to the guards involved, there was a big crowd of inmates, between 80 and 150. They swarmed over the defenseless guards and took their keys.

The second story was supported by most inmates on the scene and given credence by DOC officials. In this story, only five or six inmates from the group who had remained on the yard came in and asked the guards stationed there why the inmates had not been let out for lunch. Under no duress, one of the guards handed over his keys to the inmates. One inmate eyewitness claimed that the guard "took the keys and said, 'If you want them out, you all let them out and you guys have a good time.'" Another inmate reported hearing a guard say, "Take the son of a bitch," as he handed over his keys.[49]

When this story came out, the *Detroit News* gave nine inmate witnesses polygraph tests. Seven inmates who said the guards gave up the keys voluntarily passed; the two who backed up the guards' story failed. At first impression, it may seem utterly incredible that prison guards would do such a thing, polygraph or no polygraph. But it may indeed have happened that way under those highly unusual circumstances.

First, even if the inmates from the yard did not exert physical force or make threats, they may have been rude, loud, and abusive. We have no direct evidence, but we doubt that prison inmates discussed the unauthorized lockdown and denial of meals in a meek and polite manner.

Second, the guards must have been under tremendous stress. They were engaged in insubordinate action, risking their jobs. They were very frustrated and angry men; possibly one of the inmates said just the right or the wrong thing.

Third, the guards were furious with the administration. They wanted to see Mintzes and the DOC punished. Industrial sabotage, sometimes a feature of bitter labor-management disputes, has also been reported in prison settings.[50] The SPSM guards had the same motive for letting out prisoners that striking newspaper workers have for destroying printing presses.

Fourth, a fatalistic mind-set may have arisen among the guards which saw a riot as the *natural result* of the administration's policies. The administration was seen as treasonous; it favored inmates, but sent guards to face injury and death. Guards tried to maintain security, but Mintzes and Johnson wanted prisoners to have total freedom and total power. Guards wanted to suppress rebelliousness, but the department rewarded rebelliousness. Mintzes believed prisoners should "have a good time;" why not let him have his way? A childish and intemperate reaction, perhaps, but a child is inside us all and comes to the surface when we feel as powerless and aggrieved as children.

However it happened, inmates got the keys, and the two guards stationed in Block 3 fled through a nearby door leading to Block 4. Inmates began unlocking the cells; then one discovered a key to the box enclosing the block's "break levers" (large wrenches that unlock an entire tier of cells at one time). All inmates on Block 3 were free in minutes.

Some of the inmates set fires in the counselors' offices, a storage room, a guards' bathroom, and a guards' desk. An inmate wrote later of this desk:

> Some of the guards who sat there were exceptionally decent men . . . but one in particular . . . was an exceptionally sadistic martinet with the kind of unenlightened, combative attitude toward prisoners that you might expect from an uneducated thug. . . . Every time I heard an inmate mention that burned-up officer's desk, they spoke that particular officer's name as if the sorry, charred remnant of furniture somehow contained the officer's soul.[51]

At the same time, a group of inmates entered Block 4, adjoining. They overpowered the guards stationed there, seized their keys, and unlocked the Block 4 inmates. A group of inmates then headed for Block 5, the segregation unit. Around 12:30 p.m. the inmates succeeded in breaking in the entrance of Block 5. Another group of inmates, wielding bats, pipes, and other weapons, began beating on the door to Block 8.

After the riot started, the guards closed ranks with the administration. The first two rifle squads assembled were sent to blocks 5 and 8 where, threatening to shoot, they forced rioting inmates to retreat. Gun squads were also deployed around the perimeter of the prison, and then in each of the other blocks not seized by inmates. These actions limited participation in the riot to the inmates from blocks 3 and 4 and the 200 inmates who had remained on the yard after the 9:45 bugle. Guards were also stationed on the roofs overseeing the yard, some of whom videotaped the activities on the yard.

By 12:30 p.m., smoke filled blocks 3 and 4, forcing out the inmates still there. At 1:10 p.m., a gun squad secured the two blocks, making sure no inmate was trapped inside.

The inmates on the yard, nearly 1,000, roamed about, looted the inmate store and a soft-drink stand, and set on fire the paint shop and the staff dining hall. As the afternoon wore on, inmates talked, played cards and basketball, wandered peacefully about, and traded and consumed items from the store. One inmate described the atmosphere this way: "When they broke into the [store], they got clothes and food—it was a field day. People were taking their clothes off, putting on new ones—walking around eating big sandwiches." Another inmate reported:

> Even the guys that were nice and model inmates participated because the store was open and the store is where everything is at that you want in a penitentiary as far as luxury. Because they had TVs, and they had trunks and clothes and, you know, they had all the food, and the money was in there also. Stamps and stuff like that. So everyone went in there and got what they wanted.

Muslim inmates abstained from looting, however, gathering instead in the prison chapel.

Relations between inmates and guards on the yard were not hostile, and in fact the guards appeared to have been infected by the mood of the inmates. One inmate reported that guards were "halfway cool about it" and accepted looted cigarettes from inmates. Another inmate recalls:

> Well, the guards were saying go ahead and loot. It was a carnival atmosphere. The guards were eating ice cream that the inmates went in and got. The guards announced there would be no prosecution for that.

And finally, one inmate remembered,

> In 30 minutes you could get all you could carry. Then you'd trade for what you wanted—yell "I've got two cans of peaches! I want fruit cocktail!" The guards didn't say a word, they were quiet and meek.

Inmates took no hostages, and violence among inmates was isolated. An inmate recalled:

> There was one incident—there were two at most. It was a guy who was supposed to be snitching. He got busted a couple of times with a pipe, but he

walked away under his own steam. During the disturbance was the only time there was real unity. People eating together, the things they got from the store, they brought them to the middle of the yard so guys could eat them—there were ten guys cooking in the kitchen, cooking for everybody, pork and beans and bread and stuff.

No leadership group emerged and inmates made no demands for prison reform. One inmate reported that "during the riot, Deputy [Warden] Scott wanted somebody to bring up front a list of grievances. Nobody had one."

After the fires forced the evacuation of blocks 3 and 4, inmates occupied no buildings and their activities could be observed from the towers and roofs. Since (in Deputy Warden Scott's words) "it was known that inmates were not harming each other and vandalism had subsided after the early stages, a decision was made by the Warden not to forcibly remove prisoners from the yard."[52] Still, as a precaution, 150 state troopers were assembled outside the prison, in the event that force was necessary, and the National Guard was asked to provide auxiliary lighting in case the riot extended into the evening.

At 7:45 p.m, the deputy warden ordered unarmed guards to replace the gun squads in blocks 3 and 4. At 8:00 p.m., the yard siren was blown and Warden Mintzes broadcast a conciliatory message over the public address system:

> Attention all inmates, this is Warden Mintzes. We are aware of all that took place today. At this time we are only interested in restoring order. We want to permit you all to return to your housing units so that we can get you fed and start getting operations back to normal. We are not interested in reprisals. We simply want to blow the yard in and gradually begin to restore order. If you will all cooperate, we can accomplish this in an orderly fashion. . . . Let's work together to get order restored and rebuild what has been destroyed.[53]

One inmate, when asked how the yard was cleared, said:

> They told the guys that they could take the food and stuff from the store, clothing and things, and go back in the blocks, and they told they would feed us. And also [it was evening and] there were mosquitoes on the yard that big [indicates a length of several inches], and that helped convince us.

Another inmate explained:

> They let it die down, guys got tired. They'd stole what there was to steal, destroyed what there was to destroy.

## Northside Complex Riot I—May 22, 1981

Inmates of the Northside Medium Security Complex at SPSM first became aware of the riot in the Central Complex when, around noon, they saw smoke rising from the complex and officers waving visitors back in the parking lot.

Soon a crowd of Northside inmates lined the fence that divides the two complexes. A group of Central Complex inmates yelled through the fence to their Northside counterparts, urging them to start their own.

At 12:15, the emergency siren sounded, signaling inmates to lock up immediately. However, the guards, instead of ushering the inmates back to their cells, simply left the complex, apparently to aid in controlling the situation in Central Complex. The MCO later claimed that management had given them the "unusual" order to abandon their posts; a DOC official stated that they had asked to leave their posts and were given permission.[54]

In any event, the Northside inmates found themselves suddenly in control of their complex, having done nothing to take it. Since Northside was sealed off from the Central Complex, there were in effect two riots going on at the same time, each requiring its own response by prison authorities.

Many inmates reported that their first reaction was confusion:

> It was chaotic. I seen police [i.e., guards] (laughter) running out. No one assaulted or threatened the guards as they left. People were grabbing weapons—knives, pipes, everything. So I picked me up a club because I didn't know what they [the other inmates] were thinking. Don't nobody. Everybody was paranoid; people milling around.

Inmates armed themselves mainly for self-protection rather than for aggression against guards or other inmates. As in the Central Complex, the next thing was to loot the stores and kitchen. "Everyone took part in it," said one inmate, "because it wasn't really a riot"—that is, an organized action—"it was more of a looting spree. It wasn't never a riot because they had chances to get hostages, and hold them, and hurt them, but they didn't." Inmates grilled steaks and divided up cases of cigarettes.

Two modular units were set on fire; one was a regular housing unit and the other was being prepared for use as an office. Inmates also vandalized the school building, including the audio-visual equipment in it, and looted the inmate store. There were a few fights, but little racial antagonism.

Reporters and camera crews collected along the double chain-link fence separating the Northside yard from the main highway. Some inmates shouted out to the reporters, urging them to write that the "guards had started it" and that black and white inmates had not attacked each other.[55] Others chanted, "Give us back our good time," and denounced L. Brooks Patterson.[56]

Late in the afternoon, a group of about 12 inmates with personal influence and/or legal experience got together to formulate a set of demands, apparently on the principle that it would be a shame to waste the occasion. The group asked to meet with Warden Mintzes. Mintzes responded that he would not discuss inmate grievances until all inmates had returned to their living units, but agreed to a meeting the following morning.

Around 9:00 p.m., the warden announced over the public address system that the inmates in the Central Complex had returned to their cells; this apparently had a settling effect on the inmates on the yard. Inmates returned to their living quarters without incident.

## Northside Complex Riot II—May 26, 1981

Tension remained high at SPSM over the weekend. Outside the prison, the MCO and prison officials publicly exchanged accusations, each blaming the other side for Friday's riots. (The riot at Michigan Reformatory, which took place that same evening, is described below.) "Inmate Uprising at Jackson, Corrections Head Blames Guards" was the banner headline in Saturday's *Detroit Free Press*. Perry Johnson denounced the MCO's action as an "illegal strike" and said he empathized with the inmates' frustrated response.

Inmates were locked down the next day (Saturday, May 23), and many reported abusive retaliation by the guards. One stated:

> During the lockdown there was lot of things [the guards] did that prompted guys to want to do something. They'd come in your house, handcuff you to the end of the gallery, and throw your stuff out on the base [that is, they would throw it over the railing and let it crash on the floor of the lowest tier]. They'd say, "That's not your number" [engraved on the item], or "It's contraband." A lot of stuff I bought through the store, they threw away—guys' typewriters, TVs. I guess they called that getting revenge.

Another remarked:

> They locked us down, and fed us poorly. They had been feeding us through putting food on a plate and pushing it through the bars. The bars were about that wide [indicates a distance of about one-half inch]. It was atrocious, man. It wasn't sanitary. A lot of people were angry about it. We made noise in the block. Some of us busted jars; some guys threw stuff on the gallery.

Also on Saturday, Warden Mintzes met as promised with the Northside inmates who had approached him during the Friday riot. The "Group of Thirteen," as they had come to be known, complained to the warden about handling of inmate mail, medical treatment, and processing of inmate grievances. Also on their agenda was "amnesty" for inmates who participated in Friday's riot. The inmates' position was that since the guards had "started" the riot, inmates should not be punished for it. Mintzes refused to discuss "total blanket amnesty," which the Group, in one member's words, took as a "sign of defiance."

The Group left with the firm impression that Mintzes had agreed to meet with them on Tuesday. One of the Group indicated that Deputy Warden Willie Cason had told them this, but it later turned out that Mintzes wasn't party to this understanding. This turned out later to be an important point, but we do not have firm information on it.

Many inmates were mistrustful of the Group of Thirteen, believing they were out for themselves or even "stool pigeons." But as inmates discussed the riot over the weekend, their solidarity increased and plans for action were developed. "Between Friday and Tuesday, we was all trying to figure out what had happened," reported one inmate. "Rumors [were] going around that we would have to materialize that we was unified, and maybe retaliate in another form." Another inmate recalled:

> Word got back that they weren't going to give up anything, that it was going to get worse. Barry Mintzes' attitude was he washed his hands of it. It came to be a thing where the general feeling, the attitude, was like a sense of solidarity, like a chance for us to change the structure. It was an attitude of general frustration. They [the negotiating committee] came back and said, "They ain't giving us nothing, and the state police are on 24-hour alert." That's when guys started organizing in small groups—"You get the kitchen, you get the modules, you get the blocks." It was get them before they get us.
> *Question:* Was it actually that organized—dividing up the blocks, the modules, and so on?
> *Inmate:* Yes, but I don't think it called for a hell of a lot of organizing ability.

On Sunday, the warden ordered the end of the lockdown and a return to normal activities. There was nothing normal, though, in the situation. Sunday night, a small fire was started in storage room on the Northside; the following Monday, a small group of Central Complex inmates looted what remained of the inmate store. Rumors circulated that the modular units of Northside would be burned down at noon on Tuesday; even the Monday, May 25, *Detroit News* reported them, having been phoned about them by an inmate.[57] Warden Mintzes later claimed not to have heard these rumors, but everyone else in the prison apparently did.

At 7:00 a.m. Tuesday morning, a group of inmates wielding clubs collected near the "hole in the wall" to prevent inmates from going to work assignments in the Central Complex. As educational and medical employees arrived, they were told that a riot would occur that day and that they should leave by noon.[58] During the 8:30 a.m. exercise period, many inmates armed themselves and began to discuss what should be done. Three positions emerged.

The Group of Thirteen and their supporters were opposed to a second disturbance. This group pinned its hopes on negotiations with the administration, which were scheduled to begin at 11:00 a.m. that morning with (as they understood it) the warden and a representative of Director Johnson. "With the pressure rising now on the yard," recalled one member of the Group of Thirteen, "we tried to hold a constructive meeting of our own in the school building before the meeting with Warden Mintzes." They discussed the demands they would try to win, still including amnesty. They then circulated around the yard, "telling the guys to hold off until we could speak with the warden."

A second group of inmates, mostly those who lived in the modules, feared that a riot would destroy their personal property, cause them to lose their privileged housing assignment, and result in a long lockdown. "This is my home and I don't want it burned down," said one modular resident. "About a hundred" inmates were talking about organizing to protect the modules and prevent a second disturbance, estimated another inmate, "but it never got done."

The inmates actively organizing the riot were mostly residents of the cell blocks. Many inmates perceived them as "hotheads"—younger inmates who were less adjusted to the institution and its discipline. This group distrusted the Group of Thirteen and was scornful of the anti-riot inmates as "profiteers" and "connivers."

As noon approached, the balance of power shifted in favor of burning the modules. The riot organizers agreed to give the residents of the modules time to remove their personal property; in return, at least some of those residents agreed not to interfere with the riot. "Why should we fight each other about something that belongs to the state?" said one. "Let's move our stuff out, then they can do what they want."

Warden Mintzes and Johnson's representatives did not appear at 11:00. One of the Group recalled,

> So some of the guys said, "They're playing games with us." Many of us began talking to residents to buy time. I was trying to keep a lid on things, but the guys wouldn't wait no more. It's nothing you can do. You can't beat them up. They have knives and pipes and all that, what you gonna do?

Lunch was served at 11:00 a.m. without incident, but rumors were flying:

> A guy working in the chow line said they would burn modules at 12 if the warden wasn't back with a package deal. . . . The noon chow was ran without any problem, but about 12:10 p.m. all hell started breaking loose.

A group of about 12 to 15 inmates gathered near the quartermaster (see Figure 7–1) with flammable materials. They announced that inmates should wear white armbands if they were "neutral" and would neither join the riot nor attempt to prevent it.

It seems to us that by this point inmates had accomplished a great deal in the way of open mobilization without any interference from the guards or administration. Things had gone beyond the stage of rumor five hours before, when Northsiders had stayed away from their assignments en masse—out of solidarity, intimidation, or desire to be on hand to save their possessions. Every inmate in the complex apparently knew what was being planned by whom; meetings were held; strategy was debated; and throughout the whole morning the administrative structure remained utterly passive.

A reasonable explanation for this never appeared in the press or the official investigations. Our best guess, though, is that the Northside administration believed that the guards reporting these phenomena were crying wolf. From their point of view, the guards had caused the earlier riots by their alarmist and insubordinate plans for a lockdown. The guards were still determined to get that lockdown, but the administration merely wanted to return to normal operation. We suspect, then, that guards bringing tales up front about the inmates' alarming activities were disbelieved. If so, it was a mistake.

The riot organizers set on fire the quartermaster and then moved into

Block 1 and Block 2, wielding knives and clubs. They chased six guards through the blocks until, finally, the guards made their way into a caged catwalk that connected the two cell blocks. The guards slammed the gate closed and locked it. The inmates tried to pry it open, but couldn't. They they then set mattresses on fire in an attempt to smoke the guards out. This too failed. The guards broke waterlines and used their wetted shirts as gas masks. (The guards remained there for an hour, until they were rescued by a gun squad.)

Around 12:20 a.m., the group of active rioters, augmented by reinforcements from the blocks, approached the modules. A crowd of modular residents assembled, ready to defend them. But the truce discussed earlier was brought into effect. After the residents were allowed to remove their property, all but two of the units were set on fire. About the same time, fires were started in the food services building, the academic building, and the gym. By 1:30 most of Northside Complex that could burn was ablaze. Two exceptions stood out: a lens-grinding shop (which many inmates felt was beneficial to inmates) and the library.

Inmates roamed the yard for the next seven hours. Absent was the good-humored, festive atmosphere of the riot four days earlier. The mood, wrote a newspaper reporter, was

> tense and angry, as inmates sat in the yard, many of them with cardboard boxes filled with their personal possessions. . . . Where they had bounced basketballs and swigged soda in the prison yard on Friday, they brandished two-by-fours, shovels, and lengths of pipe on Tuesday.[59]

Some inmates climbed the chain-link fence in an apparent escape try, but were turned back by shots from a guard tower.

Shortly after the riot began, the warden, who had been conferring with officials in Lansing, arrived at the prison and had the Group of Thirteen called up to meet with him.

As soon as the riot began, Central Complex was locked down. Around 3:00, fire equipment from three departments arrived at the prison. Gun squads were assigned to each fire engine, but by then many of the buildings were nearly destroyed. Gun squads were also assigned to the two blocks and to the roof of the administration building. Reinforcements were obtained from the Jackson Police Department and the Michigan State Police.

Plans were made to retake the Northside Complex by force. About 8:00 p.m., 100 armed correctional officers entered the yard and formed a line at one end of the yard. Other officers used the state police public address system to order inmates to move into the two cell blocks. At this point, some of those inmates who lived in the blocks asked if they could return to their own cells. They were given permission to do so, and it was announced that inmates from the modules could double- or triple-cell inmates of their choice. Inmates dropped their weapons and moved into the blocks without further coercion.[60]

## Michigan Reformatory Riot—May 22, 1981

During the first disturbance at SPSM, mobile crews from TV stations in Jackson had filmed the smoke rising from the fires in the cell blocks, the burning modulars, and the inmates crowded against the chain-link fence surrounding Northside. These pictures were broadcast at 5:00 p.m. on every TV station in Michigan, including the Lansing stations received by inmates in Ionia. Before the yards at Jackson had been cleared, the yard at Michigan Reformatory had exploded.

### The Prison and Prisoners

Ionia is about 60 miles northwest of Jackson. This town of about 6,000 inhabitants contains three major state correctional facilities: Michigan Training Unit (a minimum-security youth facility), Riverside (a medical facility), and Michigan Reformatory (a maximum security facility for "young" offenders). In 1981, of MR's 1,325 inmates, 64 percent were black, 34 percent were white, and 1 percent were "Mexican-American."[61]

Most of MR's inmates lived in two huge cell blocks—I-Block and J-Block (see Figure 7–2). These wings have five floors, each with two tiers, or "rocks," one on each side. Where the two blocks meet at a right angle, there are doors on each floor which, if they were not usually kept locked, would permit passage between the blocks.

At the other end of the central yard from J-Block, the prison's control center is housed in a rotunda from which wings branch in six directions. These wings include the administration area, the infirmary, and other residential units, including a dormitory housing about 230 "trusty" inmates.

Most MR inmates who made the comparison declared that MR was the worst prison in Michigan. More than the dilapidated condition of the institution, inmates objected to the presence of vermin in the cells and in the meals. Inmates who had worked in the kitchen complained:

> There were rats in the toaster. The food sits for weeks. The pans sit out on the dock, and they get all full of maggots, and they rinse them out with a hose.

One inmate, who had served as a "representative" of his tier to the warden's offices, reported:

> I brought up requests as far as store merchandise, headphone equipment, rock changes, what things they might let us have, and to date they haven't approved none of this. I feel this administration wants the institution to stay as tight as possible. This institution has been considered the tightest joint in Michigan, as far as freedom is concerned.

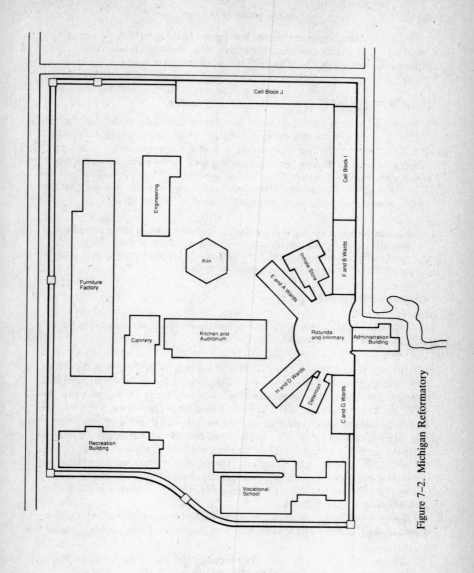

Figure 7–2. Michigan Reformatory

He and others we interviewed, having never done time at Marquette or Jackson, believed that inmates were better off in the latter prisons due to their supposedly better conditions and organization among inmates.

## Inmates and Guards

A lopsided majority of the inmates we interviewed charged the correctional staff with gross abuses of authority, such as verbal abuse, physical brutality, administrative retaliation for pursuing grievance procedures, filing false charges or reports, racism, and demanding food items from inmates for personal consumption. Inmates disagreed as to whether "most" or "a few" guards were guilty of such practices. There was general agreement, though, that the situation was often intensely frustrating. One white inmate stated:

> I wouldn't treat a dog like they treat us. The officers come in with a harassing attitude, a young punk attitude, they're disrespectful to everybody. I'd say 10 percent of the guards really care, but they can't help you because their peers, which are the majority, have a dogmatic attitude.

Another white inmate stated:

> The staff breaks and bends the rules as fast as any inmate. If a guy goes to the hole, he has his food and other stuff be taken.

Another cause to which inmates attributed the guards' hostility was the difference in background between the guards and the inmates—particularly black inmates, but also white urban inmates. "Most of them are rednecks to the max," said one white inmate. "They've never been out of Ionia in their life except to Lansing or Grand Rapids." Other inmates boasted of their travels and experience with urban life, and scorned the small-town guards as provincials. Inmates also complained—as inmates in every small-town prison probably complain—that guards' "brothers, fathers, uncles, cousins" all worked for the Department of Corrections, and that this enabled guards to orchestrate informal campaigns of retribution against inmates whom they wanted to punish for behavior they disliked.

Shared hostility for all, most, or some of the correctional staff and resentment of their abuses was one of the few forces for unity among inmates:

> When an officer comes by and says something smart, and I say, "Look, bitch, I don't want to hear it," and he says he's writing me a ticket, everyone on the rock feels an animosity. This is about the only unity you'll find, staff against inmates.

Otherwise, as in the other Michigan prisons, the general level of mutual solidarity among inmates was low:

If I'm in the control center, and a guy came running in with cuts all over him, it wouldn't mean nothing. Not because I have no feeling for life. But it would be none of my business. That may seem cold and s––tty, but in this environment no one else gives a damn about you but you.

One force for inmate individualism seems to have been inequality of wealth among inmates. Inmates working in the most desirable jobs in the prison's furniture factory could earn hundreds of dollars. However, the furniture produced in the factory was sold to state government departments. The state budget cuts caused the state to purchase less furniture, causing layoffs inside the walls.[62]

Most other jobs paid much less than a dollar a day, and many inmates were without job assignments. These latter had to depend on the generosity of relatives and friends; some, of course, were much more fortunate than others. Two inmates made these comments:

*Inmate:* If you have no money to buy things, you're in tough luck. The state-issue soap burns up your skin. Toothpaste, they don't issue it. If you're in general population and have no money, you don't get [anything] unless your friends give it to you. There's a guy in J-Block, his people don't look out for him, his mother and father don't visit. I give him toothpaste, let him wear my clothes.

*Inmate:* About 35, 40 percent don't have nothing. If you got no money at all, they give you nothing but the blues [i.e., official-issue blue overalls]—no T-shirts, no underwear. They give you grey socks, you have to wear them for one week.

The situation was exacerbated by a system of venture capitalism among inmates. Many inmates made a business of purchasing goods at the store and then selling them to inmates on credit at double the purchase price. Conflicts inevitably arose over the debts (which reportedly compounded at 100 percent interest every two weeks). An inmate described the situation:

A lot get in fights and disturbances—say I get stuff from you on credit. How am I going to get it up with no job, no money. There are some people on my rock who get no visitors. Them are the people that loot. They want to know what it is to have clothes and cosmetics . . . if they only have a bar of soap and the state blues.

With the exception of an Islamic temple in nearby Grand Rapids, which the authorities permitted to organize activities in the prison, no organization held the inmates' allegiance. Inmates generally depicted the population as unorganized—and unorganizable:

These young people don't know how to organize, to sit down in the yard and say, we want to talk to the warden. These young ones are too wild.

PRISONS AND PRISON RIOTS IN THE 1980S

While inmates cited the presence of informal gang activity and criminal enterprise at MR to a greater extent than at the two other Michigan prisons studied, no one ascribed to it a very important role. "Gangs" appeared to be relatively informal groups of men from the same city or neighborhood—nothing like the powerful formal organizations active then and now in the Illinois prison system.

In summary, although dissatisfaction with prison conditions, particularly with abuses of authority by the staff and with the food, were near universal before the riot, these attitudes had not taken organized form.

The absence of organization notwithstanding, one inmate declared to us that a group of inmates actually planned two weeks in advance to riot on May 22, and that their action coincided with the Jackson riot by sheer coincidence:

> I was right around the individuals who really sparked it. Really one individual started it, how he did this, he was really extroverted, letting people know how they were being f--ked around, said "Y'all can't accept all this bulls--t," he had geeked them up, and as he went along it built up like a ball in snow. [These were] guys with a lot of time to do. A couple came from other institutions, and they saw how we were treated here, and they couldn't accept it.

All this may have been true, but the talk may have gone nowhere without the example of the Jackson riot. No other inmate we interviewed claimed to have heard of riot plans or rumors, in contrast with the pre-riot situation at New Mexico.

## The Michigan Reformatory Riot

An inmate reports the common reaction at MR to the news of the Jackson riot:

> People were already stirred up because of how this institution was run. When they heard about the riots [at Jackson] it stirred them up even more. People looked around and said, "We're tired of this s--t."

At 7:00 p.m., inmates of J-Block were released for their evening recreation. Some inmates recall increased tension from both guards and the 500 inmates on the yard.

> Before we came out, they put extra guards on the roof, extra police, we were late coming out, and we could see, they're waiting, wanting us to riot—so they said let's give them what they're waiting for. People were saying, "Let's riot, let's riot." You could see the tension, people started grouping up. It was not a usual day with basketball.

Shortly after 8:00 p.m., a fight broke out at a group of picnic tables near the entrance to J-Block, when a black inmate apparently struck a white inmate in the head. Many inmates told us that this was part of a plan by a group of black inmates to draw officers into a fight. A white inmate declared:

> The blacks were attacking the whites, but it was not so much a racial thing as just to get the police there. Then, when the police came, the attackers turned on them and fought.

Other inmates declared vehemently that the incident was spontaneous.

> There were a white guy and a black guy in a fight, and the officers set the riot off. Four or five officers rushed up and grabbed them—in this institution, when they see a fight, they rush up, choke your neck, grab you—200 were watching them do this.

A guard stationed in a tower overlooking the yard fired a blank shot to break up the fight; when this failed, he shot several rounds of live ammunition. This gave enough cover for the guards to flee the yard for the control center and for the door to J-Block.

"Within four or five minutes," Warden Foltz later commented, "the prison went from normalcy to pandemonium."[63] The siren was sounded for the 500 inmates to return to J-Block, and about a third of them complied—mostly those who had already been waiting near the door before the fight started, so as to be the first ones back to their cells. Guards on the tiers immediately began to lock up those inmates who returned to their cells.

Simultaneously, however, inmates entering J-Block fresh from the melee on the yard overpowered two guards, held them briefly, and obtained their keys to both J- and I-blocks. One guard was injured seriously enough to require hospitalization. No attempt was made to hold these guards as hostages. Inmates used the keys to release the rest of the prisoners in J-Block, who spilled back onto the yard; a large group entered I-Block and began to release inmates housed there. Inmates on the upper tiers of I-Block broke through the connecting doors into the upper tiers of J, destroying whatever would break and setting fire to whatever would burn. All guards on the yard and in I- and J-blocks retreated to the control center.

Warden Foltz acted quickly to implement the DOC's riot contingency plan. Ten minutes after the disturbance began, a gun squad was sent to the rotunda area to protect the control center. A few minutes after getting there, the riot squad observed about 75 inmates breaking into the infirmary, which abuts the rotunda area. The gun squad forced this group to retreat, probably saving not only the infirmary but the control center as well. In addition, the gun squads allowed officials to bring groups of inmates who wanted to leave the riot through a gate into the rotunda, and to house them temporarily in the honor blocks.

By about 8:20, Warden Foltz had called for assistance from the nearby Riverside Correctional Facility, Michigan Training Unit, and the Michigan State Police. These forces began to arrive at 8:30 p.m.

Twenty minutes into the riot, inmates controlled much of the prison, including the two main cell blocks, the furniture factory, and the food services building. To be more precise, these areas were out of the control of the administration, and inmates moved freely in these areas. Inmates did not try to "fortify" these areas or patrol them. They had armed themselves with makeshift weapons, mostly for personal defense. The riot lasted six hours, not because of any defensive strategy by inmates, but because the forces of the state were waiting for the best conditions for an offensive.

Organization among inmates throughout the riot was virtually nil. While some few inmates apparently made futile attempts to develop demands, these attempts went unnoticed by the inmate population and by the administration. For the duration of the riot, inmates' activity took essentially three forms: anarchic destruction of prison property; mostly anarchic conflict among inmates over wealth, sex, grudges, and (to a debatable extent) race; and attempts by uninvolved inmates to obtain food, avoid fire and smoke, avoid violence, and (if possible) enjoy the experience.

During the riot at SPSM's Central Complex, inmates had been on the yard, their actions observable by officials. In contrast, at MR inmates roamed in and out of the several buildings they controlled; besides, it was night. This gave a greater opportunity for crime and violence.

Immediately following the expulsion of the guards, groups of inmates set fire to the counselors' offices in both blocks and moved through the blocks smashing windows and plumbing. Most inmates moved out of I- and J-blocks to escape the smoke. In addition to the blocks, inmates set fires in the chapel, the two-story school building, and the food services building, and an attempt was made to set a guard tower afire. Many were unhappy with the widespread destruction, but none were willing to fight about it.

> I heard that the guy who burned the kitchen down, a guy told him, "We got to go in there and eat," but he said, "F--k those motherf--kers, they been dogging us. Let's just tear [this place] up."

Some inmates looted other inmates' cells, stealing and destroying property:

> People were going in the rooms, taking TVs, radios, clothes and everything, money, food, what they cook up with. Guys in the rock were calling out names, acting like police. A guy say, "Break [a cell number]," and another would break the door [i.e., open it manually] and they'd go in the cell, and take what they wanted out of the room.

But some "rocks" were guarded by organized patrols:

> Inside of our rock they looted a bit. We put a desk in the doorway and said, "There's not going to be any looting here." What we did was, we held a big party. We were getting high on dope and spud juice [alcoholic liquid brewed from anything fermentable].

The food services building was broken into and food distributed freely:

> There was a food line. Eight or nine guys would go in the kitchen and bring out food and cereal. Two or three were in the kitchen making hamburgers, and they brought out boxes of cereal, crates of milk, boxes of cheese and crackers, 5-gallon containers of coffee.

But while many ate and conversed on the yard, in other areas groups of prisoners committed multiple rapes. Over 30 inmates later claimed to have been sexually assaulted during the riot. One inmate, after being repeatedly raped, reportedly had a metal object shoved into his rectum.

The number of inmates injured by other inmates rose to over 60, but only a few of the injuries were serious.

Some inmates who were injured by other inmates then received medical assistance from a spontaneously organized first-aid team:

> *Question:* After you got hurt, what happened?
> *Inmate:* Two Muslim brothers escorted me up across the yard to where they had first aid.
> *Question:* What kind of first aid was there?
> *Inmate:* Inmates had broken into the laundry and gotten out towels and blankets, and went in the kitchen and got some ice, so they could give a little first aid.

Inmates disagreed over the degree of racial character of the riot. While some white prisoners said afterwards that there was not much racial violence and that they were not afraid of black inmates, others stated that "the whole thing was racial" and that they had gone to great lengths to defend themselves from black inmates. One group of white inmates climbed onto the roof of an auxiliary building out of fear of attack by black inmates:

> *Inmate:* We [a group of whites] got on [the roof of] the cannery. There were only two ways to get up. And the guys up there were all white, and they let us up. They had the two entrances guarded. There were about 125 of us on the cannery when the state troopers came in.
> *Question:* What was this group of blacks doing?
> *Inmate:* They were trying to grab some of the white guys and pull them off the roof and force them to have sex. Some blacks in the yard had pool balls and they were throwing them at us.

Other white inmates, though, denied that the riot was "racial." These white inmates seemed to have been around longer and were less subject to attack due to the personal relationships they had established, or the respect they had earned. One white inmate of seven years' residence reported:

> I was standing where I lock [i.e., my cell] on I-Block, fourth floor. And they were hitting the door [i.e., from J-Block], and I thought I was going to get an

ass-whipping. [But when they broke in] I knew the [black] guy in the front of the group, and I smiled at him. And they were busting windows with a long stick. And I pulled out windows and busted them with them to join in for my own preservation.

The white inmate quoted earlier who spent the riot hiding on the cannery roof had been transferred to Ionia one month before the riot after a suicide attempt at a minimum-security institution.

In short, it appears that some more seasoned inmates had developed a sense of low-level identification with each other across racial lines and did not see each other as enemies or targets.

More experienced inmates were also more likely to see the riot as a potential appeal to the outside world, or a means to get "better living conditions." They tended to characterize the Jackson riot as a rational protest, imputing to it more of a sense of purpose than was really there, and to feel as if the Ionia riot may have been a "failure" by comparison:

The whole thing was really nothing. The people at Jackson were fighting for something—they were tired of harassment by the police. Here, they just went nuts.

Some inmates read the Bible in groups, played basketball, lifted weights; others armed themselves with sticks and prepared to resist the police reoccupation. Islamic inmates were cited by both black and white inmates as abstaining from violence in an organized way during the riot.

Because inmates were dispersed throughout the institution, retaking the prison was difficult and slow, lasting over four hours. At 10:40 p.m., gun squads of guards and state police entered the prison and began to sweep outlying areas, which had mostly been vacated by inmates by this time. Just before 11:00 p.m., the first floor of the furniture factory was swept and secured. Fifteen minutes later, a platoon ordered the group of white inmates off the roof of cannery, but they refused to go back on the yard. Finally the police agreed to lock them inside the cannery.

At 11:45, gun squads swept and secured the section of the school area that had not burnt to the ground; between midnight and 12:30, the recreation basement, chapel, and maintenance building were secured. By that time, only about 150 inmates were still on the yard; the rest had returned to their own cells. The inmates on the yard had lit fires and obtained blankets; many were eating or engaged in other peaceful activities. "The violentness decreased over time, like a watch running down."

At 1:15 a.m., inmates on the yard were ordered over the yard loudspeaker to return to their cells; most complied. A few who approached the advancing police line—"about thirty or forty of the main instigators"—were met by tear gas. Squads of guards with state police protection entered J-Block and secured it tier by tier, locking inmates in the nearest available cells. By 1:25 a.m., J-Block was secured, followed by I-Block at 1:50 a.m.; and finally, at

3:00 a.m., the group of inmates who had been secured in the cannery were moved to J-Block.[64]

Warden Foltz and his subordinates were generally praised for their response to the riot. State Representative Paul Henry, who was present in the control room that evening, declared that he was "deeply impressed with the professionalism and sophistication" displayed by Foltz and the state police commander on the scene.[65]

However, some inmates we interviewed stated that they either knew of or had seen widespread physical brutality on the part of guards against inmates suspected of being involved in the riot. Inmates also reported massive destruction of inmates' property by guards after the riot. We have no independent evidence of these charges.

Inmates reported their conditions of confinement to be much worse since the riot: assignments fewer, yard time sharply restricted. Inmates who did not participate in the riot were critical of the administration's seeming disinterest in distinguishing between participants and non-participants. The inmate who was on the cannery said:

> [After we were locked in the cannery] we got a paper and pencil and wrote a note, with our locks [cell numbers] and numbers; we said we had nothing to do with the riot, we got on the cannery to stay out of it. And still, when they locked us up, they treated us like we did something. They fed us bologna sandwiches once a day, they said it was twice, it was not true; they were unsanitary, not wrapped; there were no showers for about two weeks; if your plumbing was stuck up, that was too bad, you had to live with it.

Most inmates believed that any effect of the riot on public perceptions was negative; some attributed this to a "cover-up" by Foltz and the media and to reports that the riot was racial. Inmates were aware of post-riot prosecutions, and a representative evaluation was "Yeah, they got the main ones, and they got a few that didn't have anything to do with it." The only improvement that some inmates contended had taken place since the riot was in the food.

## Marquette Branch Prison—The Prison and Prisoners

At about the time that the May 26 riot at SPSM was ending, inmates at Marquette Branch Prison began Michigan's fifth riot in as many days.

In 1981, the prison housed about 1,000 inmates. Of this total, 650 lived in seven maximum security cell blocks, 250 resided in a trusty division, and 90 were in the Michigan Intensive Program Center (MIPC) (see Figure 7–3). The latter was a special "behavior-modification" treatment center for inmates with "extreme adjustment problems." The riot was confined to the maximum-security unit.

Most Marquette inmates believed that their conditions were far worse than the conditions in other prisons, including SPSM. One salient difference

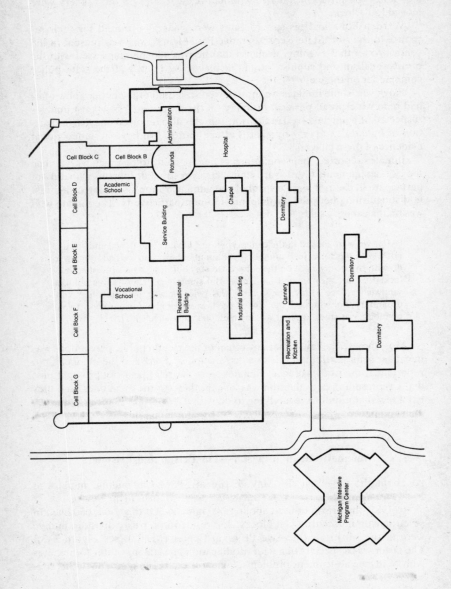

was Marquette's strict discipline and unsparing use of lockdowns. One inmate stated:

> Marquette will lock you up longer than any institution I've ever known. Jackson, you might stay locked up six or seven months. Marquette will leave you locked up in F-Block [disciplinary unit] for years. You see, they don't give a f––k. Excuse the expression, but they don't.

Another inmate responded:

> *Question:* Does [this prison] violate constitutional rights?
> *Inmate:* F-Block is indefensible. They put you in a small cell, they don't allow you nothing but a toothbrush this [indicates two inches] long. You ask them for [toilet] paper, and they give you a little strip. There's a concrete toilet bowl, and the cold gets in your bones. It hurts, because when you're idle, then you begin to think, and then it begins to hurt. You get the attitude, "You've took everything but my life, why not take that too?" I've been in the hole and I've been close to that attitude—"Just shoot me, I don't give a f––k."

Another source of deprivation was the the prison's remote location, which many inmates viewed as a deliberate attempt to break their spirit.

> Marquette is an illegal disciplinary prison because they use this prison to break family ties. I've lost all contact with my family. And it hurts me and it hurts a lot of other prisoners here. Because most of the black population here, family's on welfare. They can't afford an 800 mile visit to come here, to have to get a hotel.

Most inmates reported that they received few outside visitors.

> *Question:* Do you get any visits?
> *Inmate:* This [i.e., the interview] is the first visit I've had since 1976.
> *Question:* Do you feel as if you have a good sense of what it's like on the outside?
> *Inmate:* No. I've lost touch with society. I've lost touch personally with individuals; I'm behind the times. I haven't talked to a female in so long it's pathetic, in eight years.

Most inmates also felt that the shortage and poor quality of prison programs violated their "rights," including the "right" to rehabilitation.

> *Question:* Why did the vocational school get burned?
> *Inmate:* The cons get 25 cents, 50 cents an hour. It was limited as far as the machinery and the number of people; and it was so out of date, like the welding instruments. And the person they had running it was a real idiot. A

---

Figure 7–3 (left). State House of Corrections and Branch Prison (Marquette Branch Prison)

person with no understanding [a racist]. There was nothing for a person to learn there that would be valid on the street. There was no equipment, no instruments, that you could learn nothing on, and it was hazardous.

Many inmates complained about the absence of a gym.

Now I can't even come out for yard, because it's getting winter time and they don't have a gym. Most of the older inmates sit in their cells and deteriorate in the winter time 'cause they can't stand the colder weather. They don't send 'em downstate where there's a gym, where they can exercise.

Another inmate commented, "Imagine 240 people out in the snow with one basketball, nothing to do but walk." Finally, one inmate stated:

This place is like a dungeon. It is so cold and bleak. You have to have a strong constitution to survive. Guys hang themselves here.

As at SPSM, there was little sense of prisonwide loyalty among inmates. Few inmates identified with groups in or outside of the prison, including gangs. One said:

They lock a guy down three or four years, man, and won't think nothing of it. And that could be the reason there ain't no gangs. Guys say, "Damn, if you get in a gang, man, and they found out about it, they going to lock you up two or three years." You don't want to be in the hole two or three years.

Islamic inmates, though, displayed group loyalty and were in principle moderate. A member of the Moorish Science Temple (MST) stated:

[Other inmates] respect us. We're for peace, not destruction. We adhere to the tenets of Islam. We are not about encouraging people to act out irrationally. We like to go through the courts. We like to sit down man to man.

Another MST inmate stated:

Question: If you could talk to all the inmates in here at once, what would you suggest they do to get changes?
Inmate: Write their legislators.
Question: You think that's effective?
Inmate: I believe so. Flood the world with letters of complaint. The only changes that be made are through the politicians.

Allegations of guard racism were frequent. Black inmates claimed they were punished more harshly for infractions than whites. One added:

Some of the guards try to treat you like a human man, but that's a very very very few. And make sure you underline "very." Some of the guards are human, but most of them are monsters.

## Food Cutback, Protest, and Riot Rumors

The week before the first riot at SPSM, Marquette officials, to cut costs, ordered a reduction in the food portions. Inmates were furious:

> They started giving out milk in little-bitty bowls. It wasn't a regular bowl we were getting. They started cutting down on bread. Right now we get two slices of bread. We were getting four. From the milk to the bread, they started cutting all the rations down and talking about they didn't have no money to buy no food.

Inmates protested by boycotting the cafeteria. "Word was passed out that said no one was to go the mess hall, period. Everyone stayed away, except a few knuckleheads."

After three or four days of this, prison officials restored the portions served; but they also imposed a partial lockdown for several days. Inmates were allowed outside visitors and religious services, but were prohibited from participating in their usual daytime activities.

The boycott increased unity among inmates. "It was kind of a feeling of accomplishment," said one. "There's nothing like unity to cheer you up."

## Marquette Branch Riot—May 26, 1981

Several days after the food protest, rumors began to circulate that a riot would take place. Then came the riots at SPSM and MR. In response, Marquette officials locked down the prison for the holiday weekend. Angered inmates charged they were being punished for the acts of others.

As inmates were released from their lockdown on Monday, rumors again began to circulate that inmates would riot, probably on Wednesday. Events at SPSM intervened again. In response to the second riot on the SPSM's Northside, DOC Director Johnson immediately ordered prisons statewide to take added security precautions. Marquette officials took a number of steps visible to inmates, including the cancellation of a baseball game with an outside team and an increase in the number of guards patrolling the yard. Many inmates reported that they feared another lockdown, perhaps a longer one.

> You could feel the attitudes and the tensions change, so they locked us back up again. Then they let us out, and Jackson jumped again. And we knew once we went back in our cells we wouldn't come out for a while. And there's a lot of guys who have no tobacco, no coffee, no T.V.

Another inmate remembered, "It had been on the news about the [second] riot at Jackson, and guys were tensed up. Everybody wanted to see, man, what's going to occur up here."

About 8:10 p.m. on Tuesday, just after an intramural basketball game, a fight broke out between an inmate and a guard. There were several versions of the fight's cause. The administration said that a tower guard had spotted the inmate with a weapon and told the yard guard about it.[66] The story we got from most inmates, though, including eyewitnesses, was that two other inmates playing basketball started to fight or engage in horseplay. The officer on the yard grabbed one of the inmates, but the other escaped into a crowd of inmates. The officer chased the second inmate, but mistakenly seized the wrong man, a popular resident. One eyewitness reported:

> [Inmate name] never gets involved in anything much. He's been up here in Marquette for about six going on seven years. And the guys respect him because he does his own time, doesn't mess with anyone.

The guard in question was reportedly "the most disliked staff member we have run across in our interviews," according to a Padden Commision interviewer.[67]

The inmate resisted the officer, and the two began to wrestle on the ground; the inmate bit the guard in the face, fracturing his cheekbone. A second inmate, his nephew, joined the fight. A half-dozen guards rushed to the scene. One inmate reported,

> [The guards] swooped down on these two inmates. And in breaking the inmates up, they was abusing. They was punching and twisting their arms and putting handcuffs on one of 'em so tight his wrist started bleeding. A couple of inmates on the side just screamed, "No, no, leave him alone!" And they just kept on.

More inmates joined the fight, which turned into a wild brawl. Some inmates tried to pull the uncle and the nephew free from the pile. Others beat up three of the guards. At length the officers were ordered by bullhorn to retreat to the control center. A guard in a gun tower fired two warning shots above the heads of the inmates, forcing them to back off.

> After they left the yard, everybody was saying, "Well, they done pressed this thing and took it this far, and now we're going to go head on."

Some inmates firmly rejected the notion that the riots at SPSM and Ionia helped bring on their own riot. From their point of view, the conditions and events at Marquette were enough to account for the riot in themselves. To really believe that, one needs a great deal of faith in coincidence. Perhaps these inmates felt the need to insist that their riot had had a purpose of its own—something more than "just" a mechanical response to someone else's riot. Other inmates drew the connection:

> *Question:* What was different that night?
> *Inmate:* Because of the incidents leading up to it. There was a little strike up here, where the inmates had refused to eat. Everyone was pretty much fired up. Then you had the riots in Jackson and Ionia. And they said, "We've been treated as bad—why not here?" They figured, it can't get worser—let's do or die.

Another put all the events together, from an inmate point of view:

> *Question:* Why was it different that day, that it turned into a riot?
> *Inmate:* It was like waking up from a dream—we could really tear the place down. We'd heard about Jackson. And the guy [inmate name], he was a well-liked convict, a warm guy, not a f--k-up, keeps to himself, does his own time, likable. And the pigs happened to make a bad mistake. Too much had happened outside the wall for any con to get f--ked with that night. And 40 pigs on one man—beating him, stomping, restraining him, and then kicking him.

An emergency whistle signaled inmates to return to their cells. A portion of those on the yard obeyed, leaving about 200 to 300 inmates on the yard. But the guards in the cell blocks felt immediately threatened, and retreated to the control center, giving control of the blocks to inmates. Since all blocks were on the yard for the exercise period, nearly the entire population in the maximum-security blocks had the opportunity to join the riot. The major exception was the inmates in the detention block, who had a separate exercise yard and were locked in when the riot started.

More inmates than at the other two Michigan prisons seemed to have positive memories of the riot. One inmate claimed "a good hundred" were involved in setting fires. "Everyone I knew who was involved in the riot had been in the hole," said another.

Inmates looted the inmate store and vandalized and set fires in the vocational school and the industries building. One inmate reported his course of action.

> *Inmate:* When I saw what was happening, I was happy. I wanted to tear up things too. But I didn't want to get caught. So I went somewhere I couldn't be seen and set a fire.
> *Question:* What sort of things were people doing while they had control of the yard?
> *Inmate:* Some were by the walls, or by the blocks; some were walking around; some were burning the school or the factory. Three-quarters were just hanging around.

One rioter described his experience this way:

> I never experienced [a riot] before, because the riot in Detroit happened in '67. I was in the army then, so I had never been in a riot before. And it was a thrill man. (Laughs.) It was like being free. You do what you want without nobody saying like go this way and don't do that. You had everything you wanted in the institution, man.

Another commented:

> Everybody was respected who took part in the riot. Because it was, I guess you would say it was the noble thing to do. It wasn't right for the riot to

happen and you stand out there and not do some looting, you know, or scream or run up and down the yard, you know, and say we're free.

At 9:10, about 30 minutes after the riot began, four squads of 11 guards each left the control center and entered one end of the exercise yard. Wearing gas masks, riot vests, and carrying 12-gauge shotguns, the riot squads fired several warning shots at the ground immediately in front of the inmates, forcing them to retreat to a wall on the opposite side of the yard. One inmate was wounded in the leg by a ricocheting bullet. Over the next two hours, the two groups remained at more or less of a standoff, with inmates massed on one side of the yard and armed guards on the other.[68]

One guard had become trapped in a block, but was able to radio his location to prison officials. A gun squad was sent to rescue him, but before it arrived, several inmates escorted the trapped guard to safety. Several inmates later said they regretted this. An inmate, who was facing criminal charges for his role in the riot, commented:

> *Question:* Why did guys escort [guard's name] out?
> *Inmate:* That was the cats who was trying to save their paroles, and ass-kissing informers. Real punk motherf--kers. They helped the enemy. Why the motherf--kers didn't move on 'em is a real mystery to me.

Another inmate stated:

> They had [guard's name], but they let him go. It surprised me he walked out alive. He treated me like a piece of s--t.

A number of inmates assaulted or raped other inmates, and some inmates had property stolen from their cells. One inmate reported that his

> rap partner [had] his house burned, because he loaned a book to a guard. They threw in a balled [wad of] toilet paper that was set afire.

These acts, however, were isolated. Only 14 inmates were treated for injuries after the riot, and just one inmate was injured seriously. The latter was an inmate who had been sexually assaulted and stabbed in the neck. The rest had bruises, lacerations, and other minor injuries.

Fire trucks were unable to enter the prison until 9:30, when prison guards and state troopers escorted them in. About 9:20, officials used the public address system to order the inmates on the yard to move into G-Block. Most inmates complied, but by 10:00 p.m. about 100 inmates remained on the yard. Some of them wanted to continue the riot; others thought G-Block was a dangerous place:

> There was no officers in the blocks. G-Block was wide open. You had 100 to 150 guys in G-Block, just running around the block. Guys have enemies for various different reasons, you know, refused to go to the block.

Another block enjoyed another sort of freedom during the riot:

> On C-Block we locked the guards out, and they locked us in. So we were very sociable. We played music, had conversations. There was no conflict or confrontation. Then, later on, the guards came to the door, kicking at it, yelling to let them in, so we let them in and we all went to our cells.

No inmates attempted to formulate demands and no leadership group emerged. According to one inmate, pre-riot inmate leaders "mostly stayed out of the way. The leaders didn't encourage or discourage." Racial conflict did not develop.

At 11:00 p.m., the riot squad moved on the 100 inmates remaining on the yard. They fired warning shots in the air and then laid down a volley on the ground between themselves and the inmates. The inmates were then herded into G-Block. Each inmate was shaken down for weapons, handcuffed, and taken to his own housing unit. The prison was secured by 11:30 p.m.

## Aftermath

The stage of "aftermath" consists largely of the allocation of blame. Here the MCO was the obvious target, especially after the *Detroit News* broke the charge that the Block 3 guards had turned over their keys voluntarily.

On June 15, Perry Johnson announced that Gerald Fryt and another local officer were being fired, and 14 other correctional officers, including the 2 from Block 3, were suspended. The MCO threatened a statewide guards' strike. However, on June 26, Fred Parks and Perry Johnson signed an agreement which ended the strike threat. Thirty vacancies were filled at SPSM, and it was agreed that the DOC and MCO would jointly review the discipline policy.

Also, on June 15, Perry Johnson fired the deputy warden of the Northside Complex and demoted the assistant deputy warden and the commander of the morning shift. They "had information on May 25," said Johnson, about plans for the disturbance, and neither acted on them nor informed the warden.[69]

Perhaps the Michigan riots were too easy to explain. The first SPSM riot was brought on by the MCO. MR rioted because Jackson rioted. The May 26 Northside riot happened because certain officials were incompetent. Johnson originally claimed that "Marquette was clearly a planned, calculated disturbance by some really tough, hard-core, maximum-security prisoners."[70] In support of this, Marquette officials originally claimed that the fires had been started with incendiary devices prepared in advance. Later, however, the investigators for the Padden Commission found no evidence for this. That left the department with the fallback explanation: Marquette rioted because of all the other riots.[71] To us this is a little thin. A riot in one prison does not automatically bring on a wave of riots in other facilities in the state. Attica didn't. Joliet didn't. We suspect that the turmoil in the entire state system had something to do with it.

160       PRISONS AND PRISON RIOTS IN THE 1980S

On the other hand, a newspaper poll reported on June 1 found that the public in Michigan thought "lax discipline" was to blame. Fifty-three percent of their sample of Michigan residents agreed that was "a real reason" why inmates rioted, compared with only 32 percent who blamed the guards. (Eighty-three percent cited overcrowding as a reason.)[72]

The universal belief among inmates we interviewed was that the guards had been the victors. A year after the riot inmates had fewer privileges, less yard time, and were locked in their cells more. Some believed that the guards had provoked the riots at all three institutions on purpose, in order to justify tighter security measures. Others believed in a conspiracy to provoke inmates to riot and then make graft off the contracts to rebuild. Inmates at Marquette—not so much elsewhere—believed that the riot had been a unifying experience and were more likely to see it as a justified rebellion. One inmate who had faced charges after the riot said it would have been morally wrong for him to plead guilty to a lesser charge, and that he was obliged to show courage, having been named as a "leader."

Shortly after the riot, the U.S. Department of Justice filed suit against the State of Michigan, charging that the conditions at SPSM, MR, and Marquette were unconstitutionally bad. The suit was settled in 1984 with a consent decree, which required the state to provide for better sanitation, medical services, and access to courts and lawyers.

The Padden Commission produced a set of recommendations, targeting for reform staff racism and the grievance procedure as well as other problems. However, there has not been enough money in the DOC budget, or enough interest on the part of the state legislature, to implement them in a systematic way.

Gerald Fryt took his bid for reinstatement to arbitration but lost. The arbitrator's opinion declared that the wave of riots had taken place because of Fryt's individual action. Barry Mintzes was replaced at SPSM by Dale Foltz. Michigan Reformatory is still open. The Michigan prisons are still full to capacity, and the Emergency Powers Act has been invoked repeatedly. Violent disturbances, small riots, and deadly assaults on inmates and guards have been recurrent features of the system since 1981.

Commissioner Oswald talks to the inmate negotiating committee on the second day of the Attica Riot. (AP/Wide World Photos.)

On the catwalks at Times Square area, Attica inmates hold blindfolded hostages at knife-point, minutes before the police assault to retake the prison. (AP/Wide World Photos.)

Ransacked dormitory shortly after end of the riot at the Penitentiary of New Mexico. (Dennis Dahl.)

The control center at the Penitentiary of New Mexico seen through the recently installed "bullet proof" glass. (Dennis Dahl.)

Start of the second riot at the North Complex of the State Prison of Southern Michigan, with the Central Complex and Trusty Division in the background. (Jackson City Patriot.)

Minutes later, two modules are burned to the ground (on right) and others are afire, while authorities observe events from the roof of a cellblock (far right). (Jackson City Patriot.)

Governor Arch Moore escorts a prison guard to an awaiting ambulance as the siege of the West Virginia Penitentiary comes to an end. (Kenny Kemp.)

Governor Moore then meets with inmate negotiators to discuss grievances. Here inmate leader Alvin Gregory and Governor Moore shake hands at the start of the meeting. (AP/Wide World Photos.)

# 8

# Routine Riot—West Virginia Penitentiary (1986)

The riot which began at the West Virginia Penitentiary at Moundsville on New Year's Day, 1986, comes closest of our cases to being a "routine" large prison riot, if there is such a thing. Absent here are the bloody debacles of Attica and New Mexico, the domineering gangs of Joliet, and the rebellious guards of Michigan. This is a story of prisoners conducting a riot, and negotiators resolving it, in a competent, businesslike fashion. Yet—or therefore?—its results have apparently been disastrous for the inmate participants, and the unusual circumstances which brought on the riot have not yet been resolved.[1]

To account for the occurrence and form of this riot, we have to begin with some economic and cultural features of West Virginia itself which set it apart from the other 49 states.

## West Virginia Exceptionalism: Economics and Crime

West Virginia rises and falls with the coal industry. After the turn of the century, and particularly since World War II, consumers of coal for purposes ranging from locomotive fuel to home heating switched to oil and natural gas. And ever since the Great Depression, West Virginia has been a virtual synonym for the grinding poverty of Appalachia.

The 1973 oil embargo reversed the trend; coal was immune to OPEC threats and plentiful. In consequence, the 1970s were an unusual period of economic growth and relative prosperity for West Virginia. At the start of the decade, the state's per capita income was 22 percent below the national average, but by its end the gap had narrowed to 14 percent. Employment in these ten years rose from just over a half million to 716,000.[2] John Denver's lyrics "Almost heaven, West Virginia" became the state's semi-official slogan.

But about 1980 the boom turned back to bust. Slowed economic growth lowered the demand for energy, an oil "glut" replaced the energy "crisis" in public perceptions, and foreign-produced coal beat out higher-priced American coal in the international market. In West Virginia, 25 to 30 percent of the coal industry jobs were lost. The collapse of the U.S. steel industry not only eliminated a market for coal and coke, but cost West Virginia 40 percent of the jobs in its other major industry.

The state lacked the economic diversification that might buffer these losses and an educated labor force that might attract high-technology industry. By 1983, the number of state residents employed was back down to 664,000, and unemployment jumped to 21 percent, the highest rate in the country. West Virginia's per capita income declined by 13.1 percent between 1980 and 1984; only Wyoming and Oregon did worse.

As the plummeting economy cut sharply into state revenues, a surprising state court decision placed new demands on the state treasury. In May 1982, Circuit Judge Arthur Recht ruled that the state's school system failed to provide the "thorough and efficient" education that the state's constitution guaranteed.[3] He also found that the method used to finance the schools, which relied heavily on county taxes to supplement state funds, discriminated against poorer counties. Recht ordered a new tax system to pay for the schools and set down specific educational standards which had to be met, including foreign language instruction in elementary schools and art and humanities courses in high school. He characterized his decision as "no less than a call to the Legislature to completely reconstruct the entire system of education in West Virginia."[4] The cost of this controversial "reconstruction" was estimated as high as $1.5 billion.

In response to the fiscal crisis, the state legislature cut spending and raised taxes. This, though, contributed to the state's poor climate for business, rated the worst in the country in 1982. Still first in joblessness, the state by 1985 owed millions of dollars to the federal government for help in keeping the state's unemployment fund solvent. And then, in November 1985, floods caused $550 million in damage in 29 counties.[5]

There was one bright spot: crime, the costs associated with its control, and the proportion of state residents imprisoned were all lower in West Virginia than in any other state. The statistics are striking. In 1985, West Virginia had 2,252 "index" crimes per 100,000 residents, far below the national average of 5,206.[6] The other prisons we have considered were in states with crime rates more than double that of West Virginia (Michigan, 6,556; New Mexico, 6,243; New York, 5,577; Illinois, 5,304).[7]

Fighting crime was cheaper too. Only 3.2 percent of state and local funds in 1983 were spent on "criminal justice activities"—the lowest proportion in the country and just over half the national average of 6.2 percent.[8] Even so, a high proportion of the index crimes committed in the state were "solved or cleared."[9] Ninety-three percent of the murders in West Virginia were cleared, compared with 53 percent in Michigan; and 72 percent of the rapes, compared with 44 percent in Illinois.[10]

Eighty-one of every 100,000 West Virginia residents were in prison, the third fewest in the country and far below the rates in New York (182 per 100,0000), Michigan (159 per 100,000), Illinois (146 per 100,000), and New Mexico (137 per 100,000).[11] And West Virginia was also third from the bottom in expenditures per inmate—$6,298 in 1982, less than 40 percent of the national average.[12] (By 1985, West Virginia's per inmate expenditure had risen to $8,275, but this was still far below the national average of $14,591.) Not surprisingly, West Virginia's prisons and jails took less of state and local funds than in any other state—only .7 percent, compared to 2.9 in New Mexico, 2.0 in New York, and a national average of 1.7.[13]

Crime was low, criminals were mostly caught, punishment was cheap, and the public hostility and fear felt toward criminals in Michigan, for example, was largely absent. Apparently as a result, inmates benefited—until recently—by a comparatively mellow relationship with guards and administration and lax conditions of imprisonment. This is further detailed below.

## The Penitentiary and Its Transformation

The West Virginia Penitentiary at Moundsville in the state's northern panhandle has served as the state's only maximum-security prison for over a century. In the 1860s, huge blocks of sandstone were shipped down the Ohio River and assembled into an imposing outer wall 25 feet high and 4 feet thick at the base.[14] Its six guard towers gave it the look of a medieval castle, much like Joliet.

The main structures that now stand inside the walls were built in 1908 and 1929. The hub is an administration and services area, which includes a dining hall, infirmary, library, visiting room, administrative offices, and gymnasium (see Figure 8–1). Extending in a line in either direction are the living quarters, North Hall and South Hall.

On January 1, 1986, the penitentiary held 741 inmates, 65 above the officially rated capacity of 696. Eighty percent (614) of them were white and the rest were black. The majority of inmates, about 70 percent, lived in two cell blocks in South Hall—New Wall and P & R. These and the other cell blocks consisted of four floors of cells. At the far end of South Hall was the punitive segregation unit, commonly known as "Max," which held 35 inmates. In the smaller North Hall were the Old Mens Colony (OMC), which housed the aged and infirm, and a separate protective custody block, the two top tiers of which were unoccupied and under renovation.

Near the north end of South Hall was a booth built of bricks and iron bars known as the "captain's office," housing the shift commander and his communication equipment. It was designed to be a secure command post during a riot. Nearby was the glassed-in "cage." An officer stationed there controlled the main grills leading from the South Hall corridor to the prison entrance, and was equipped with firearms with which he could cover the corridor through gun ports.

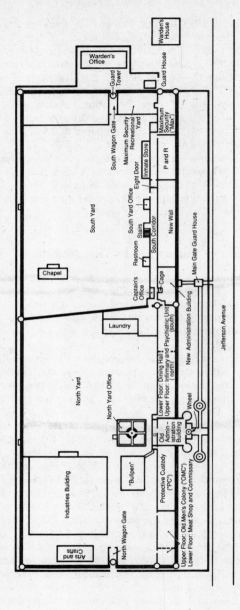

Figure 8–1. West Virginia Penitentiary

Just outside the walls were the warden's home and a small building of administrative offices, including the warden's. After the 1980 New Mexico riot, all arms (except in the cage), ammunition, tear gas, and other security equipment were moved to these offices.

By all accounts, the West Virginia Penitentiary before 1979 was minimally oppressive. The rules were loosely enforced. One inmate remembered (in a 1986 interview):

> the man, he came here, put in his time and went home. That's all he did. The rules and regulations, it was like they weren't enforced. This was a cons' prison. If you had to do time, this was the place to do it, here in Moundsville.

Another inmate recalls the relaxed rules for property and dress:

> you could have blue jeans, suits, any type of clothing and jewelry. We were allowed stereos and colored TVs, fans, and electrical appliances galore in our cells. We were allowed to have mustaches and beards and to grow hair at any length.

A newspaper feature on the prison described one inmate who wedged into his cell $7,000 in electronics equipment, including four tape recorders, a television, a turntable, an amplifier, and four huge speakers, leaving him barely enough space to turn around.[15]

Moundsville was also a "con's prison" in that the locks on most of the cell doors did not work. This not only allowed inmates to roam freely, but it made lockdowns nearly impossible: the prison did not have the manpower necessary to secure every cell with a chain and padlock. (In 1978, there were only 237 employees for an inmate population of 670.) A consulting firm hired to survey the conditions at the prison concluded that the penitentiary "was less secure than Reiley's Motel in [neighboring] Glen Dale."[16]

Further, the pains of imprisonment were lessened by ample leisure activities, relaxed visitation rules, and release time. In the prison's basement, or "Sugar Shack," inmates could play pinball, ping-pong, and pool; a music room provided space for inmates to play instruments or just listen.[17] Open-house parties were held annually on Halloween, near Christmas Day, and on the Fourth of July. These events drew large crowds. One picnic was described this way:

> All the makings of a traditional family picnic were there—fried chicken, checkered table cloths, and even bees to swat. Noisily children frolicked on the grass and tossed frisbees while their parents danced to rock music or watched exhibition boxing matches.[18]

The prison's boxing team and football team (the "Moundsville Cougars") competed both inside and outside the prison. One Moundsville resident remembers, "Some of the best prize fights . . . [and] football games in the world were held behind those walls." He added, "You could take your children there on a Sunday afternoon and mingle with the convicts—let me say inmates—and they were the deadliest killers in the United States."[19] Visitors were permitted to attend religious services with the inmates. According to some accounts, fornication and oral sex were common in the pews.[20]

Inmates were given furloughs to attend special events outside the prisons, such as a Jaycee convention. This opportunity was extended even to inmates sentenced to life with no chance of parole.

The penitentiary was a con's prison in one final respect: it was easy to escape from. The banner year was 1973, when 35 walked out. Between 1970 and 1979, 238 inmates escaped, an average of 3.7 percent of the population each year—this from the state's only maximum security prison. Of course, the escape rate from the state's other prisons was even higher. In 1974, 437 escaped, representing 32.5 percent of the state's prisoners.[21]

This phase of the prison's history ended abruptly in November 1979. Inmates tricked a guard in the cage into opening its door. Then they produced a gun and ordered the guard to open the security grills leading out the prison. For a few minutes the prison stood wide open, and the largest prison break in U.S. history could have taken place. As it developed, only the 15 inmates planning the escape made their way through the grills and into the small guardhouse in front of the prison. There they demanded a car from the two guards on duty. Told none was available, they shoved one of the guards onto the highway in front of the prison, forcing an approaching car to stop.

In it were a 23-year-old off-duty state trooper and his wife. The inmates forced the two out of their car and climbed in. Before the inmates could speed away, the trooper drew a gun from his ankle holster and fired into the car, killing the driver. An inmate shot back, hitting the trooper in the chest. He died a few minutes later in his wife's arms.

The escape and murder sent shock waves through West Virginia. Demands for reform came from many quarters, including the governor's office. Two weeks after the break, with three of the escapees still free, Governor Jay Rockefeller issued an emergency order declaring that the conditions at the penitentiary posed "an imminent threat of a disaster of major proportions to the safety and welfare of the inhabitants of this State."[22] The governor ordered the commissioner of corrections and the superintendent of the state police to develop a master plan—the "Joint Operation" —to reassert control over the penitentiary.

On November 21, 1979, 100 state troopers filed into the prison carrying nightsticks and gas masks. Within several minutes, they had chained and padlocked every inmate in his cell. Over the next ten days, as the state police stayed on duty, the sheets that many inmates had draped on their cell doors were torn down, inmates were given military-style haircuts, all "non-essential" property was removed from cells, and visiting privileges were temporarily suspended.

The Department of Corrections issued a new set of restrictive rules. Inmates were required to wear prison-issued khaki uniforms and could no longer have beards, mustaches, or hair longer than 3 inches or over the ears or shirt collar. The amount of property an inmate could have in his cell was cut back sharply. The Sugar Shack and gymnasium were closed. All trips outside the prison were terminated. New cell locks were installed, and a security fence was built around the prison.

In interviews conducted seven years later, many inmates claimed that the state police beat inmates with riot sticks, denied them medical treatment, and awakened inmates in the middle of the night. One inmate stated:

> The state police came in and just brutally intimidated us. They singled out for beatings inmates that sort of had it coming, if you accept that. And the other inmates, they just made it known that each minute was a potential for beating, if you even thought of getting out of line.

Inmates sued prison officials and state police in federal court, but none of the charges were upheld. Still, the supposed brutality of the state police became part of the folklore of the prison.

The state police left the prison on December 7, 1979. To continue the clampdown, Governor Rockefeller hired Donald Bordenkircher as warden. Upon taking office, Bordenkircher told the press that he saw his mandate as to "tighten the place up so much, it squeaks."[23]

Bordenkircher's personality was suited to the task. Tough-talking, often profane, he was considered a stern, though fair, disciplinarian toward both inmates and guards. He had no qualms about firing corrupt guards. Soon after taking office, he told a local reporter, "We had officers stealing license plates. We've got officers involved in drugs. We fired them. I've got others still involved in it. I know I do. I can't prove it yet but I will. Nothing thrills me more than to bust a dirty cop."[24] To keep guards on their toes, he would snatch an inmate, bring him to his office, and time how long it would take for the disappearance to be reported. He commented in a 1986 interview, "I can assure you no one ever called me nice, whether staff or inmate. But I really believe in my heart that every inmate knew where he was at and so did every staff member. I never talked forked-tongue bull-s--t."

Bordenkircher often locked down the entire prison, even for relatively minor infractions by just a few. The inmates charged with the infraction could expect to spend many months, if not years, in segregation. "I have never been in so many lockdowns until this Bordenkircher came in," one inmate commented. "I'm talking about the whole population." Another inmate reported:

> I never liked Bordenkircher, due to his egotistical mania. But he knew what he was doing when he was running this institution. He had everything in place; he had discipline; the guards' morale was up; and if they did something wrong, he'd get on their asses the same he would us. But we walked the line.

The new warden's most controversial policy was his tough stance toward hostage-taking. He told inmates, his staff, and the press that if a hostage was taken,

> a select team, of which I will be a member, will go to the area where the hostages and their takers are. I'll respectfully request one time that the hostages be released. There will be no debate. If they do not comply with my request, then we'll execute the hostage-taker on the spot.[25]

In addition to tight discipline, the prison "squeaked" in a second way. Never in the prison's 114 year history had there been a year without at least one escape; in 1980, 1981, and 1982 there were none.

Yet Bordenkircher was hamstrung by an inadequate budget and antiquated facilities. Three times in 1981 he was forced to lock down the prison, not because of disciplinary problems, but because there were too few guards to operate it safely.[26] The warden pleaded to the state legislature for additional funds, but without success. In July 1981, Bordenkircher voiced his complaints to a state legislative committee that was touring the prison:

> We have not had an increase in personnel in five years. We asked for 37 new correctional officers; a dietician and five cooks; and four medical personnel for this new budget year. We received *zero!* There isn't a toilet or sink that doesn't leak. . . . If it's 100 degrees outside it's 116 degrees in the cell areas, and in the winter it's as cold as hell.[27]

A member of the legislative committee observed: "The institution is in a deplorable condition. It's a little cleaner, more orderly since Donald Bordenkircher has been here. But you can't put silk stockings on a hog."[28]

Gresham Sykes, it will be recalled, argued that riots happen when authorities tighten up controls to regain power which had fallen into the hands of prisoners. This is what the Joint Operation and Bordenkircher had done, yet the prison was disturbance free. Other conditions had to be met.


## Prison Litigation

Beginning in the mid-1970s, the West Virginia Department of Corrections found itself increasingly in court defending itself against inmate suits. By 1981, this litigation cost the state an estimated $500,000—this to defend a department of corrections whose entire operating budget was only $12.3 million.[29]

In February 1982, 36 petitions consolidated under the name *Crain v. Bordenkircher* came to trial before Judge Arthur Recht, who, remember, had ordered sweeping changes in the state's school system a few months earlier. After a personal visit to the penitentiary and a two week trial, Judge Recht ruled that the penitentiary violated the Eighth Amendment of the U.S. Constitution (prohibiting "cruel and unusual punishment"), as well as the West Virginia constitution and statutes.[30]

First, he ruled, the physical conditions of the penitentiary and its services inflicted "wanton" and "unnecessary" pain on the inmates. Among the deficiencies cited were:

—the entire prison was infested with roaches, lice, fleas, maggots, rats, and mice;

—the prison's ancient plumbing leaked and backed up, causing toilet waste to flow into the living areas and up into the sinks;

—a gagging stench from sewer gas and sewage pervaded the entire penitentiary;

—an antiquated heating and ventilating system produced unbearably hot temperatures in the summer and cold temperatures in the winter;

—broken windows were often left unrepaired, allowing pigeons and sparrows to roost in the tiers and dirty the living quarters with their droppings;

—the food was often poorly prepared, served cold, contaminated with insects, hair, and other inedible material, served on dirty trays, and insufficient to meet the "minimum nutritional basic necessities of life";

—water leaked into an antiquated wiring system, causing frequent shortouts and posing a serious fire hazard;

—inadequate lighting in the cells made reading extremely difficult in the evenings;

—recreational facilities were inadequate;

—inmates were given the responsibility to clean their cells and dining area, but were not provided with the most rudimentary cleaning supplies and equipment.

The two most serious deficiencies were the tiny cells and the medical care. Each cell measured 5 feet by 7 feet, 60 percent of which was taken up by a sink, toilet, and bed. This floor space was less than half that recommended by the American Correctional Association. The health, dental, and psychological services, Recht declared, fell below "contemporary standards of decency" and were "grossly inadequate." "Dental care," the judge wrote, "is either non-existent, or delayed to such an extent to be considered non-existent."[31]

Further, it was established that these conditions fell far below contemporary penal standards. At the trial, Michael Lane, director of the Illinois Department of Corrections, testified that the penitentiary had "the most dismal overall conditions that I have even seen in a facility anywhere." Michael Mahoney, head of a respected Chicago-based prison reform organization, concluded: "I would describe [the conditions] as grossly inadequate, substantially below minimum constitutional standards. And I would have to personally describe the West Virginia Penitentiary as the worst correctional maximum security facility I've ever visited." Even Warden Bordenkircher could not come to the prison's defense, testifying, "I have always said do not spend a nickel on that old one hundred and fifteen year old facility. It is a waste of our money."[32]

The second ground on which the penitentiary was found to be unlawful turned on an issue of state law. In 1981, the state supreme court had ruled in *Cooper v. Gwinn* that prison inmates in West Virginia had a *right* to "rehabilitation."[33]

Federal courts do not recognize this right. They have held that the U.S. Constitution requires only that inmates receive the "basic necessities of life," like "reasonably adequate food, clothing, shelter, sanitation, medical care, and personal safety."[34] But the *Cooper* ruling was based on a *state* statute, interpreted by the court to mean that "the Legislature requires rehabilitation to be the primary goal of the West Virginia corrections system." This right could not be interfered with by the executive branch. The governor and state legislature were required to give priority in the budget to this entitlement before addressing other "societal luxuries."[35]

Applying the *Cooper* precedent, there was little doubt that the penitentiary failed to provide the requisite "rehabilitation." Not only were the conditions self-evident, but Judge Recht could rely on a report issued just six months earlier by a legislative committee which stipulated: "Due to the lack of upkeep and neglect, the Penitentiary is not only difficult to operate and keep secure but is an impossible environment to even attempt the rehabilitation of inmates."

Judge Recht ordered the Department of Corrections to submit, within 180 days, a compliance plan that would bring the penitentiary up to constitutional and statutory standards and which must conform to the standards for rehabilitation established by the American Correctional Association. The lack of public funds would not be accepted as an excuse for denying inmates their constitutional and statutory rights.[36] The Department of Corrections did not appeal the order.

Judge Recht resigned from the bench in the fall of 1983; his replacement, Judge John Bronson, was considered less sympathetic to inmate concerns than Recht. On September 1, 1984, Judge Bronson approved the plan which the Department of Corrections submitted over the objections of the inmates' attorneys. He did, however, honor the inmates' request to appoint a "special master" to monitor compliance with the court-mandated reforms. Bronson chose Donald Poffenberger, a professor of criminal justice, and required him to file quarterly reports on his findings.

In the space of a few years, the state government had been instructed by West Virginia judges, on the basis of West Virginia law and the Constitution, to restructure both its school and its prison systems, and had been clearly warned that financial difficulties were not a legal excuse for failure. Did policymakers in that law-abiding state take these orders seriously, reasoning that all, from the meanest of citizens to the governor's chair, must respect the power of the courts? No. Resistance to Recht's school decision continued unabated into the third year after the decision was made. In January 1985, State Senator Ralph Williams, chairman of the Education Committee, commented: "Certainly, the Recht [school] decision won't be implemented in my lifetime and probably not in this century. And it shouldn't be. Everybody knows what it was. A few people on the Supreme Court ran around and got somebody to write something they wanted."[37] In November 1984, voters overwhelmingly rejected a referendum measure to eliminate the system of school financing that Recht found objectionable.

If voters and the state legislators balked in response to Recht's order to improve the schools, they were even more steadfast in their refusal to shoulder the cost of prison reform. The chairman of the House Judiciary Committee, Joseph Albright, praised Recht "for putting the problem [of prison reform] on the agenda," but added that given the state's other needs, "I would be unable to predict when we'd have the money to do anything about it."[38]

The Department of Corrections requested $19.2 million over five years to rebuild the penitentiary. The 1984 and 1985 legislatures provided $3 million, plus a small increment to hire a few extra teachers and nurses. An editorial in the paper serving Moundsville reflected the sentiment in the legislature:

> Major renovation at Moundsville just isn't going to happen. Not this year, or next, or the year after. To do what the courts have ordered at the penitentiary would cost about $19 million. If our Legislature is confronted with choosing whether to spend $19 million at Moundsville or flood relief—as it will be—how will it vote? If the choice is between $19 million for jails or new schools which will get the money? If a decision must be made whether to fund teacher pay increases or install a new heating system for the penitentiary, which will be funded? The answers are obvious. . . . For, West Virginia is poor. There are many other places where our tax dollars are needed more than Moundsville.[39]

The failure to achieve the reform mandated by Recht is reflected in the quarterly reports issued by Special Master Poffenberger. The message of the first quarterly report, covering the period October 1984 to January 1985, was that the Department of Corrections had worked hard to improve conditions but that many problems remained. Poffenberger noted, for example, that improvements had been made in the steam heating system, but none in the ventilation system. An outdoor lighting system had been installed, but inmates still did not have adequate cleaning supplies.[40] Asked about the report by a newspaper reporter, Poffenberger commented, "The Department of Corrections has indeed made a real tangible effort in terms of making physical improvements."[41] In contrast, Poffenberger's report covering the period of July 9, 1985, to October 9, 1985, was critical and pessimistic:

> No one can find the money in the Department of Correction's budget to finance fulfillment of their Plan of Compliance. Like a jilted bride, the Court is confronted by a litany of unkept promises. . . . Departmental officials spend budgeted sums as they become available, but it is not enough.[42]

Poffenberger's assessment was echoed by the newly appointed commissioner of corrections, A. V. Dodrill. Testifying at a state legislative committee, Dodrill candidly admitted: "We are not complying [with Recht's decision]. We are actually in contempt of court. We don't have the money to comply with court orders."[43] By the end of 1985, fewer than 10 percent of the court-ordered changes had been made.

Failure to meet legal standards of imprisonment was not the only problem. In a report filed at the end of 1985, Poffenberger observed that the prison's system of security appeared to be faltering. The biggest problem was a short-age of officers. He cited a September 9, 1985, "incident report" filed by a correctional officer:

> This date . . . a total of sixteen officers [were] not at the institution out of thirty-six scheduled leaving a total of twenty officers to fill a minimum thirty-three positions needed to safely run this institution.[44]

To implement the Recht decision fully, the penitentiary must be replaced, a measure which the state had been considering for at least a decade; but, as in Michigan, the project did not command sufficient political support. In West Virginia, there was yet an additional impediment to the construction of a new prison. Long before the Gramm-Rudman spirit caught hold in Washington, West Virginia had written into its constitution and statutes provisions designed to prevent deficit spending. One of them prohibited the state from entering long-term contracts that pledged the credit of the state. Thus, the bondholders for any state project had to assume the risk that the state might break its contract at any time. In short, even if the state legislature was committed to building a new prison (and it wasn't), serious obstacles to financing its construction had to be overcome.

### Deprivation and Inmate Groups

Despite all this, inmates of the West Virginia Penitentiary found that their conditions compared favorably with those in other prisons in several important respects. Inmates felt relatively secure from assaults by other inmates, in striking contrast to, for example, New Mexico. One inmate, who had been imprisoned in a number of states, observed:

> This prison has been a very peaceful prison, oddly enough. How and why that came about I don't know other than that you just get into a trend of non-violence and this is a habit. In many prisons you have this utterly barbaric inmate code that if you and I disagree, one of us has got to kill each other. This has not been the case here. You and I can go out in on the yard, and you can hit me in the mouth, and I can walk off and that will be the end of it.

Another compared the penitentiary to Attica, where he had been imprisoned from 1974 to 1983:

> *Question:* How would you compare this place to Attica?
> *Inmate:* No comparison, really. The inmates are more serious there—tougher than down here. The inmates up there, in Attica, it's like they don't take nothing the way inmates do down here. Up there, you have to fight. You kill me or I'll kill you. They don't take no s--t, period. From no one, guards or inmates.

We asked another inmate:

> *Question:* Is there much tough-guy hustling?
> *Inmate:* No, I don't see it very much. I have seen it a few times, but not very much.

Judge Recht found that, despite the prison's other shortcomings:

> A semblance of inmate security has been achieved by the current administration. Inmates are exposed to some risk of physical and sexual assault primarily due to the configuration and overall inadequate conditions at the Penitentiary, as well as the lack of trained correctional officers. However, there is no constant threat of violence or of sexual assault.[45]

In addition, inmates reported that although the penitentiary was not the cons' prison it had been before 1979, it was still considerably less regimented than prisons elsewhere. The inmate who had been at Attica made this comparison:

> Far as roaming around in this prison, tier to tier, freedom to move around within the prison, you got a lot of freedom here. . . . Attica is very strict. You move from a tap of a stick. You stop from a tap of a stick. They go out in groups, like military style. No smoking in mess hall; no talking; you got to get permission to get up out of your seat in the mess hall. Solitary confinement here is easy compared to the one up there. Here, you get TVs, radios; your blankets, mattresses. Up there, the mattress is on a block of cement; it's [the toilet] a hole in the floor.

Another inmate commented:

> General inmate population as a rule had the run of the yard, run of the hall, run of the housing units. You could pretty much go and come [as you want]. I can [still] go from here [interview room] right now, and walk out on the yard, back in, and over to industry [building], to OMC and back. I can't go to PC or to Max, but pretty well anywhere else I can go. Although they had some signs [restricting movement], they didn't enforce them.

Further, some inmates stated that they preferred the penitentiary to the state's medium-security prison at Huttonsville. At Huttonsville, all inmates were housed in dormitories. Although the cells at Moundsville were cramped, many inmates preferred the security and privacy they provided over dormitory living. Most inmates had their own radio and television, and the penitentiary provided cable service, making the cells' size more tolerable.

Finally, although difficult to gauge, guard hostility toward inmates and inmate hostility toward guards appears to have been substantially below what it is in many prisons. A penal expert from Massachusetts testified at the 1982 trial, "There was a general attitude of respect. The inmates referred to the staff in the way you would expect a prisoner to refer to authority. The officers seemed confident in themselves—in the exchanges [between inmates and prison officials]. There was no insolence or bad feelings on either side."[46] One inmate told us:

> In many prisons there are a lot of guard to inmate and inmate to guard type problems. There has never been that here. The guards have never been that abusive. It's an occasional thing.

Further, black inmates did not perceive the guards as racist, as had been the case especially at Attica. A black inmate commented:

> *Question:* Are any of the guards racist?
> *Inmate:* I never seen none of them come out with no racist slurs or nothing towards me. I get along with all of them. To my knowledge, I ain't never heard none of them shout no racist slurs.

Neither were there many complaints from blacks of racist treatment by white inmates. Another black inmate responded:

> *Question:* Was there racial tension in the penitentiary before the riot?
> *Inmate:* No, I don't think there was. Maybe someone is having a bad day, but that was the extent of it.

Few inmates identified with political or other civic groups. There were no black organizations or gangs; one inmate reported:

> We tried to get the Muslims back in the late 1970s. But it was a joke. Nobody in here knew what they were talking about. They faded out.

Another inmate observed:

> There is no militant black leaders in the sense of the guy who gets up and orate. You just don't have that motivation. [Inmate name] is a strong leader. Blacks look up to him to protect their interests. But he's no leader in the sense that he's going to fight for black pride. It just doesn't happen in West Virginia.

Two groups were exceptions. About 25 born-again Christians met once or twice a week to discuss religious matters. The other group was a penitentiary chapter of the Avengers motorcycle gang.

The Avengers have chapters in West Virginia, Pennsylvania, and other neighboring states. The prison's chapter was started by Danny Lehman, who in 1981 had been imprisoned for life for the murder of a member of a rival motorcycle gang.[47] In 1982, seven more Avengers were imprisoned. This group recruited other inmates, mostly from the maximum-security unit, all of them white. At the time of the riot, the Avengers had about 20 to 25 inmate members.

Small in stature, Lehman had a forceful personality. He was also a bit of a philosopher and a talented painter. He painted on the infirmary walls murals of farmlands and forests, about which he commented:

> What I'm into is motorcycles and medieval times, the old barbarians and their women. I did the farm scenes because they wouldn't let me do crossbones or any naked women. I would enjoy living in medieval society. Now, there's too many people in the world. It's moving too fast. There's no honor left, no chivalry left in the world. You have to have honor to have respect.[48]

In July 1984, Lehman had gone on a hunger strike to protest beatings by guards of three Avengers. He claimed the guards "beat everyone because of me," sparing him because of a medical condition (phlebitis in his legs).[49]

Although no one denied that the Avengers were a "gang," least of all its members, it was unlike the gangs that dominated Illinois' prisons. The Avengers did not make it a practice to intimidate and extort non-gang members. Warden Bordenkircher told the press that the Avengers operated a protection racket within the prison; this was universally disputed. A white inmate who, as a born-again Christian, would not have belonged to the Avengers, nevertheless commented:

> They are inmates just like we are. They are not tough, rank. They are not bullies. They just get together and talk about the good times they had. No danger, no threat.

Another inmate observed that the Avengers are

> take-no-bull-s--t inmates. Strong-willed, but they didn't rob, steal, or rape. They mind their own business. They didn't tread on anyone. I didn't join the group but I respected that group, for what they are about and what they stand for.

A black inmate observed:

> *Question:* What do you think of the Avengers?
> *Inmate:* By being a large group, a lot of people felt intimidated, man. But I know for a fact these guys don't run around terrorizing the institution. They wanted a brotherhood. They helped each other. But, hell, I know the vast majority of them. I never had no trouble with them.

## Appointments of Wardens Holland and Hedrick

In September 1983, Bordenkircher resigned to run for sheriff of the county in which the penitentiary is located. He won. Manford Holland, his 34-year-old deputy warden, was appointed to take his place. Groomed by Bordenkircher, Holland pledged to continue the policies established by his mentor: "I think the groundwork Bordenkircher has laid is right in tune with my philosophy. I don't see any major changes I would want to make, not operational or personnel-wise."[50] Although Holland was a black in a predominantly white prison, and confined to a wheelchair, he gained the respect of most inmates. One inmate stated:

> Holland would come in the tiers a lot. He was in a wheelchair, but he managed to get in this institution and talk to inmates honestly. Talk face to face. He was honest about it. He was not two-faced.

Holland's tenure was short. In 1985, Jay Rockefeller won a seat in the U.S. Senate, and Arch Moore, who had preceded him in the state house, regained the governorship. In September 1985, Moore's new commissioner of corrections, A. V. Dodrill, promoted Holland to a post in the central office in Charleston and named Jerry Hedrick, then warden at the Huttonsville medium-security prison, to replace him.

Hedrick had served as a deputy warden to Bordenkircher before moving to Huttonsville in 1984. Although overshadowed by Bordenkircher, Hedrick had developed a reputation among the Moundsville inmates as a stern disciplinarian:

> Seventy-five percent of the guys in here knew Hedrick when he was under Bordenkircher's administration as a deputy warden. They knew the only thing he knew was punishment—disciplinary, disciplinary punishment.

Hedrick himself commented: "I was not wanted back by the inmate population, due the fact that I am an authoritarian. I consider myself a strong disciplinarian. I was not welcomed back with open arms."

The inmates' fears were soon confirmed. Inmates claimed that Hedrick imposed four additional hardships in his first months on the job. (Hedrick denies that any of his policy changes imposed new hardships: "I never took anything away. I came in here with an open mind, to provide more programs.") By inmate accounts, Hedrick

—imposed stricter rules governing visitation. Inmates could have "contact" visits only with members of their family. Others must use the "non-contact" visiting room, where the inmate and visitor talked over an intercom system, viewed each other through a plexiglass shield, and sat on uncomfortable stools.

—prohibited inmates from receiving packages from ex-inmates or the families of ex-inmates. For many inmates, this was their sole source of commodities from outside the prison.

—required inmates in Max to follow a humiliating procedure whenever they were taken out of their cell. The inmate had to put his nose against the back wall before the door was opened. Then, in the presence of at least two guards, he had to walk backwards out of his cell with his hands in the air.

—ordered a cutback in the amount of property inmates would be permitted in their cells. Inmates would be limited to three books, two magazine subscriptions, and fewer items of clothing. Hedrick gave inmates until January 5 to dispose of their "excess" property; after that, officials would enter cells to remove it themselves.

In the post-riot interviews, inmates' memories differed on some of these points. Some inmates, for example, stated that the more restrictive visitation policy had been put in place before Warden Hedrick had arrived. Still, there was a common perception that Warden Hedrick would make life in the penitentiary tougher.

One change ordered by Hedrick, though, did not go into effect. Traditionally, inmates were given extended visiting privileges the first weekend after Christmas. Hedrick changed this to Christmas Day. Many inmates anticipated that their family and friends would be unable or unwilling to visit them on that day. The inmates appealed to the commissioner, who reversed Hedrick's decision.

All of these changes or attempted changes angered inmates, but it was the property cutback they resented most. It reminded many of the harsh deprivations imposed by the Joint Operation. One inmate commented that "everyone was of the opinion that he was going to leave us with next to nothing, much like after '79."

Unpleasant as it was, inmates may have seen the 1979 crackdown as an understandable response to the mass escape and murder and to the lax conditions. While they may grumble, prisoners generally take it as competence, not malice, when the authorities insist that cells have locks on them that work. That's what they would do if they were wardens, after all. Furthermore, Bordenkircher's measures had been directed against crooked and incompetent guards as much as against inmates, which may have also taken the edge off.

But, in inmates' eyes, there was no obvious excuse for this new stringent agenda. Had Bordenkircher and Holland been so "lax" themselves that the screw must be tightened another turn? Even Dodrill had agreed that Hedrick had "gone too far" with his Christmas visit rule—so inmates reasoned.

Most glaringly, their lives were about to be made harder just when the state courts had ruled they must be made easier.

We thought we are going to have improvements and it was just the reverse. We get a warden who starts taking privileges away. He's coming down real hard. There was obviously no perceivable progress under the prison condition case, which told us in '83 that conditions in the penitentiary were cruel and unusual punishment. Inmates said, "Just wait and things will change." Well, wait and things will change is a viable message in June 1983. It starts wearing a little thin in June of '84. By June of '85—"I thought you said that we are going to have change."

The January 5 deadline gave inmates time to brood about the unfairness of the property cutback. They knew, or sensed, that after January 5 Hedrick's style of management would be all the more difficult to challenge. Something must be done before that date, but what? There grew a mood of readiness.

In developing a common spirit of rebelliousness against Hedrick, inmates were aided by the fact that—as they saw it—the guards judged Hedrick as unworthy of respect, unlike his predecessors.

> *Question:* What do you think the guards think of Hedrick?
> *Inmate:* I don't think they give him his due respect. Because he doesn't project enough to them.
> *Question:* Do most of the inmates know that the guards don't like Hedrick?
> *Inmate:* Oh yeah. Because they give them their opinion.

Another inmate stated:

> *Question:* What do you think the guards think about Hedrick?
> *Inmate:* They don't like him no more than what we do.

Some guards admitted as much to us. One stated:

> Hedrick has a very poor relationship with the officers. A majority of them would like to see him go.
> *Question:* Does Hedrick have a tough-guy image?
> *Guard:* To me he's a wimp. To me he has a tough-guy *image*. Bordenkircher was this [actually tough].

Another guard stated:

> Bordenkircher is the kind of guy that stands behind what he tells you. Where Hedrick is the kind of guy who backs off from what he appears to be.

## Initiation

Beginning late November and continuing into December, rumors flew that some sort of mass resistance to Hedrick would take place before January 5. One group of four inmates plotted a takeover. As one inmate privy to these plans explained, this group wanted a "constructive" riot, not like the blood-bath of New Mexico they had heard about. It was not this group, though, that initiated the riot, and when it did happen on January 1, it came as a surprise to them.[51]

On the morning of January 1, 1986, one officer filed an "incident report," stating, "While making a routine tour of New Wall I was informed by [inmate name] that [inmate names] plan to take over the prison on this day." Informed of this, the deputy warden in charge concluded that no special precautions were necessary.

That New Year's Day, 16 officers on the 3:00 p.m to 11:00 p.m. shift called in sick. This was predictable, as a similar rate of "illness" seemed to happen every New Year's Day. Several guards from the day shift agreed to stay over, but the 31-man shift was still below the critical level—the minimum number of guards required to operate the prison safely.

Security procedure dictates a lockdown whenever the critical level is breached, but this was not done. Shift Commander Glasscock, unaware of the morning's incident report, juggled the available personnel. Two of the positions left vacant were especially important to the security of the prison. The officer stationed in the cage was temporarily reassigned to the front gate; and Captain Glasscock left his post in the captain's office to help serve the evening meal in the dining room. One of the guards taken hostage later remarked, "You are really understaffed when your shift commander has to pass out forks and spoons. Why should your shift commander be taken? Who is in charge then?"

Usually, only two or three tiers of a block would eat in the dining room at one time. This New Year's, though, inmates were packed into the mess hall en masse, so they could go back to their cells and watch the bowl games. At 5:30 p.m., about five minutes after the New Wall residents were seated for dinner, 20 inmates armed with knives burst through the door. An Avenger (not its president) led the group, but most were unaffiliated with the gang; most, but not all, were white. Captain Glasscock immediately sent out a "1033" (distress call) over his walkie-talkie. But within seconds, he, five other guards, and a food service worker were tackled and slammed to the floor. Inmates put knives to their throats and handcuffed them with their own handcuffs. The Avenger leader stood in the middle of the dining room and yelled to the other inmates, "Leave the f--king food alone—we've taken the penitentiary—let's go." The inmates told the hostages that they would not be hurt, but they must not say anything or look around.[52]

The group initiating the riot then picked their hostages off the floor, and forced them into the south corridor, with Captain Glasscock and another guard shoved to the front. They immediately confronted another guard, who had run down the hall after hearing the 1033. For a moment, the guard thought he might escape through the grill operated by the guard in the cage—but, of course, there was no one in the cage. This officer, near retirement, offered little resistance. Another guard soon arrived at the same area, tried to fight the inmates, but was outnumbered and easily overcome.

Meanwhile, a female nurse, who had been dispensing medication through a caged window into the dining hall, dashed upstairs and warned two guards in the infirmary and psychiatric unit that a takeover had begun. The three of them, along with several inmates who had fled from the dining room, escaped onto the North Yard and safety.

Just as the dining room was being taken, or nearly so, a group of five inmates entered P & R; their arms were crossed as if concealing something. The guard working the bottom tier was already worried; the inmates appeared tense to him, and one had asked to be locked in his cell. The guard was about to go to the second tier to confer with his colleague, when another inmate asked to be locked in his cell. Just as he inserted his key to do this, two inmates piled into him, pinning him against the wall. One stuck a knife against the guard's throat, telling him, "Don't f--k up." The other ripped off the guard's shirt, saying, "Man, we are going to get these f--king clothes off you. We are gonna dress you up with a little khaki clothes [inmates' clothes]. We'll cut your hair and we are going to treat you son-of-a bitches like you treat us." The other three inmates went up to the second tier, then the third, to subdue the two remaining guards in the block. The three guards were thrown into a cell on the second tier and forced to lie facedown in a spread-eagle position.

The five guards in maximum security were alerted by Captain Glasscock's 1033. Responding, two of them headed up the South Hall corridor toward the dining hall. They passed the entrance of P & R, not realizing that at that moment P & R was also being taken. Just as they passed the "eight door" (see Figure 8–1), a security grill, the two Max guards saw Captain Glasscock and a second hostage being shoved down the hall. "Get the hell out of here!" the captain shouted. As the two fled back toward Max, one stopped to try to secure the eight door. But its dead-bolt lock required a key which, since the eight door was routinely kept open, the guard did not have. As he was trying to fasten it with his handcuffs, the inmates grabbed him through the barred door, shoved it open, and pinned him against the wall. Though a strong man, he was outnumbered and overpowered.

As the other guard sprinted back toward Max, inmates poured out of P & R into the hallway. Three of them tried to grab him, but he stiff-armed them away. The three guards still in Max let him in, with seconds to spare, then slammed and locked the door.

The three guards in New Wall had by now heard of the disturbance, but before they could do anything, inmates stormed into the unit, captured them, and took them to P & R. They were roughed up and threatened along the way, but not seriously assaulted.

Of the South Hall units, only Max belonged to the state. If this unit could be held, the prison's most dangerous residents would be kept out of the riot. It would also give officials direct access to South Hall; and firearms at the door of Max would pin down inmate movement in South Hall at least as far as the eight door.

But the inmates worked too quickly. Breaking into the basement, they found a sledgehammer in storage. Lugged upstairs, the hammer was then used to pound the wall that separated Max from South Hall. Hearing this, the three guards inside the unit assumed that the inmates would eventually work their way in, but that the solid concrete wall would hold for a while. They assumed wrong. The wall was constructed not of concrete but of cinder blocks covered with a facade of plaster. It began to disintegrate quickly. "As soon as we saw the cement cracking," one guard later said, "we knew we had to get out."[53]

The three guards dashed out onto the empty Max exercise yard. It was enclosed by a 12-foot chain-link fence and a separate 15-foot sheet-metal wall, both topped by rolled barbed wire. Before leaving the block, the guards had called the control center to ask that a door leading out of the yard be opened, giving the three an easy escape. The key could not be found. (One of the post-riot reforms was to put this key in the guardhouse immediately adjacent to the yard.)

Along part of the perimeter of the yard ran the catwalk of Tower Six. The three trapped guards shouted up to the tower guard to throw them blankets to help them get over the wire—or to throw them weapons (against prison policy)—or to at least cover the yard with his own gun and protect them until help came. But the tower guard froze under the pressure and refused to leave his tower or assist in any way.

Meanwhile, the rioting inmates realized that the lock on the Max door was even flimsier than the flimsy walls. Several blows with the sledgehammer snapped it off. Once inside the block, the rioting inmates had little trouble opening the cells. A hard yank on most of the doors activated their automatic opening system. Some had to be knocked off their hinges, but this did not take long either. Other inmates worked on the door leading to the exercise yard, which had been locked by the fleeing guards. It gave way in about 15 minutes. The guards, though, had steeled themselves to climb over the barbed wire unaided, and got over the fence just in time.

Other inmates seized the law library on the first floor and the infirmary and records office on the second floor. North Hall was not taken. It could have been reached through a door from the dining room, but it was locked and no one tried to break it down. Apparently, taking the Old Men's Colony and protective custody unit were not a priority.

## Formation of A Negotiating Committee

The inmates who initiated the riot were not prepared to take charge of it. A group of about 30 inmates met in the law library to discuss what was to be done. Some had been involved in the takeover, but many had not. The four inmates who had planned a "constructive" riot, but had not been involved in the initial takeover, now came to take a central role. Two problems grabbed the immediate attention of the assembled group: who should contact the authorities and what to do with the hostages. Danny Lehman, the Avengers' president, was quickly agreed upon as best suited for the task of negotiating with authorities and presenting the demands to the media. Lehman then asked Alvin Gregory, a black inmate, if he would be willing to serve as negotiator with him.

Gregory was respected as an articulate spokesman for inmate interests. He had worked in the law library for several years, assisting inmates with their court cases. He also helped inmates prepare for disciplinary hearings. According to Gregory's account:

> Danny asked me if I would go up with him. I said, "Cool." And when Danny asked if anybody had any problem with that, everybody said no. I said yes. It was that simple.

The assembled inmates then decided to form a committee to formulate a set of demands for prison reform. A black inmate described how he and others were chosen to serve on the committee:

> Reason I and [inmate name] ended up on it was due to the fact that we was working on the *Crain* case, so we knew what's really happening out there, what really needs to be taken care of. And we gotta have some blacks and we gotta have some whites, cause that's mostly what the penitentiary's made of. So they had three blacks, me, [inmate name], and [inmate name], and nine whites.
> *Question:* Why were [inmate name] and [inmate name] picked?
> *Inmate:* Cause these guys had influence not only on blacks but they had influence on whites as well. And they had big time [i.e., long sentences to serve]. Ain't nobody sitting at that table had small time.

Throughout the riot, the law library was to remain the center of inmate discussion and planning. One inmate recalled:

> The law library was basically a command post. We had a telephone there and it was well lighted. We had coffee and general conversation occurred there. The typing up of the demands occurred there.

To deter an assault, inmate leaders ordered the hostages moved in groups of two to four into each of the three captured housing units. Inmates were assigned to guard the hostages and told to "execute the guards if the place is stormed." One hostage later reported:

> We were told, a couple of 'em [inmates] came to me and said, "If the mother f——king greens [state police] come in, you're dead." That's an exact quote, and I had no reason whatsoever to doubt that.

Inmates used the walkie-talkie radios seized in the takeover to coordinate the movement of the hostages.

## Administrative Response and First Meeting

Reached at home, Warden Hedrick immediately went to the guardhouse at the front gate. Within minutes, he was joined by Sheriff Bordenkircher, who had brought with him 18 of his deputies. Also showing up were 10 to 15 state police and some on- and off-duty correctional officers.

Bordenkircher believed the prison must be retaken immediately. "Well, Jake, here's what I think," he urged Hedrick. "Look at the sergeant and tell him, 'Sarge, follow me.' Here is a brand new bullhorn that I brought in from my office. You take the lead. You are the warden and let's take this penitentiary back. In about 20 minutes you are going to have your joint back."

"I can't do that," responded Hedrick, but Bordenkircher was insistent:

"Do it, do it now. They are not organized. We are now into this 45 minutes. Just take the bullhorn, you go in there like daddy, we will be right behind you, and we will take the god-damned joint back." Hedrick rejected Bordenkircher's advice. In Hedrick's words:

> I don't know how many times he [Bordenkircher] urged me on. Finally, I said, "No." I chose—and it was a very difficult decision—not to do that. I did not appreciate being urged, and to keep on being urged to assault.

Hedrick based his decision on a number of considerations. He did not know where the hostages were. If an assault force had to search for the hostages, inmates would have plenty of time to injure or kill them if they wanted. Further, he was receiving reports that the inmates were barricading the entrances with filing cabinets, office furniture, and other debris, and jamming gates closed. Opening these gates would have been a slow process, perhaps requiring torches or explosives which he didn't have just then.

And a last consideration, Captain Glasscock had called Hedrick at the gate and told him that the hostages were not being harmed, but that they faced near certain death if the penitentiary was rushed. The captain pleaded with him not to assault. Hedrick later commented:

> I've got a lot of faith in Pat Glasscock's judgment. I chose at that particular time to hold off, maintain communication, let my people talk to their spokesman, to actually get a feel.

David Fromhart, director of arts and crafts, was the penitentiary's designated negotiator. He had attended a weekend seminar on hostage negotiations several years earlier—not much training, in his own view. However, he had a good rapport with inmates. Now at the front gate, David Fromhart asked his brother Jeff, an inmate counselor, to come along. Carrying a walkie-talkie, Dave and Jeff Fromhart entered North Hall through the Wheel, an ancient rotating device once used as the prison's main entrance. The Fromharts did not know if the inmates controlled this part of the penitentiary. They didn't. Cautiously working their way through the North Hall units, they reported back that PC and OMC had not been taken; armed guards were sent in to secure those areas. Working their way south, the brothers heard a banging on the door leading from the dining hall, and inmates demanding to be let through. They were not sure if these inmates were trying to break through to take control of North Hall or trying to escape from the riot. They decided not to open the door to find out.

The inmates pounding on the door were born-again Christians trying to escape the riot. The group's leader later reported:

> Whichever way they moved the hostages, our goal was to go in the opposite direction. I gathered the other Christian brothers and told them, "There is only one safe spot in this joint. If the man do come in shooting, he ain't going to come into OMC." So we moved in that direction.

The group had gone through the dining room, and were stopped there by the door that the Fromhart brothers refused to open.

> The door was locked. We stayed there waiting to see whether we can get through to OMC. As we were waiting, I think of another brother who is down in South Hall. He is a Christian and I got concerned about him. Another guy and I went back there to get this man. . . . [After returning], we yelled, "Let us out. We ain't got no part."

Meanwhile, Lehman had called the guardhouse to begin negotiations with the state. "The place is taken over, I didn't do it, but that don't matter. We have 17 hostages," Lehman told Paul Kirby, chief of medical services, who had picked up the call. Lehman agreed to talk with the Fromharts but demanded that Dr. Norman Wood, the penitentiary's staff physician for 20 years, and Kirby himself also participate. Kirby, who had allowed Lehman to paint the murals on the infirmary walls, had Lehman's confidence: "He's administration, I realized that; we don't have a friendship. But he's one I could trust."

The Fromharts were radioed to let Lehman and Gregory out the very door they had been worried about. They were relieved to find the band of Christians behind it. The group remained in OMC throughout the riot. One of this group, who before his recent conversion had had a reputation as one of the most violent and defiant inmates in the penitentiary, commented: "In retrospect it was the greatest thing I ever did in my life. I perhaps never did more than one or two things right in my life. And those two are accepting Christ in my life, then continuing to walk in Christ, January 1, 1986. Those were the two greatest decisions I ever made."

The two Fromhart brothers, now joined by Dr. Wood and Paul Kirby, met with Lehman and Gregory in an attorney-client room near the Wheel. Jeff Fromhart describes the brief meeting this way:

> Initially, they [the inmate negotiators] were very formal. We shook hands, sat down. We did not really get into negotiations. We wanted to find out the medical conditions of the hostages. We were trying to get information. Of course, they were too.

Lehman and Gregory told the four administration negotiators that hostages had been placed in housing units with inmates they could trust, and that those inmates would see to it that hostages were not harmed. The two inmates added that they could not ensure the safety of the inmates, for which they were sorry, but warned against an assault. Finally, they said that they believed a negotiated settlement was possible and that demands for prison reform would be forthcoming.

Lehman and Gregory returned to the law library to to discuss with the inmate committee what sort of demands to make. According to Lehman:

The first thing they [the members of the committee] told me is they don't want state troopers in here. And they wanted Hedrick out. They wanted a new warden.

These demands were incorporated in a hastily typed list of 15 "major grievances" (see Appendix J).

While these negotiations were taking place, inmates were making good use of the penitentiary's phones. Many called relatives and friends around the state and country; others contacted the media. One inmate called Cable News Network in Washington, D.C., told the network of the riot, and then put Captain Glasscock on the phone. "The inmates do not wish to be violent," Glasscock was reported as saying. "They wish to negotiate with the Governor of West Virginia, Arch Moore. The inmates do not wish to escape but to negotiate serious problems. The inmates do not wish to harm anyone and everyone is safe." CNN sent its mobile unit—a semi-truck with a satellite dish—to Moundsville.[54]

Though Governor Moore was on vacation in Florida, he could be expected to become directly involved in the negotiations, for several reasons. Over a long public life as a Republican in an overwhelmingly Democratic state, Governor Moore had developed a "hands-on" style of administration. And he was from Glen Dale, a town adjacent to Moundsville, and knew the prison and many of its people. During his six terms in Congress, Moore had received mail from the penitentiary and followed its affairs closely.

In 1973, during Moore's first term as governor, there had been an earlier riot at the penitentiary—a "spontaneous" rebellion for better living conditions, by press accounts. Inmates took five hostages and seized control of South Hall. The governor's administrative assistant negotiated a settlement with the prisoners, agreeing to 20 of the inmates' 22 demands for improved conditions. The guards were released shortly after Moore arrived at the penitentiary to give his official approval to the negotiated demands. As the guards walked out of the penitentiary, Moore warmly greeted them.[55]

As soon as he heard of the 1986 riot, Moore decided to follow the 1973 strategy. In his words, "I laid down the same ground rules [as 1973]: my presence in exchange for broad based discussion. Uninhibited discussion in exchange for the hostages and the return of the facility." Moore instructed Commissioner Dodrill and State Police Superintendent Fred Donohoe to go to Moundsville themselves. Colonel Donohoe, in turn, ordered 100 armed state police to Moundsville and arranged for them to be supplied with tear gas, gas masks, other riot gear, and motel accommodations.

Brought to Moundsville in the state police helicopter, Dodrill, Donohoe, and John Price (the governor's press secretary) met Hedrick that evening at 10:30 in the state police barracks near the penitentiary. Discussing the situation calmly, they agreed not to assault the prison unless the condition of the hostages worsened.

To better coordinate their work, Commissioner Dodrill and Superintendent Donohoe rented a motel room together. Throughout the riot, they remained at each other's side, allowing each to overhear the other's phone calls and orders. They also stayed in continual contact with the governor, who had come home secretly hours after the riot began.

## Inmate Relations and Hostage Treatment

Relations among inmates remained relatively civil throughout the riot. One inmate observed:

> There was a great deal of camaraderie between inmates. There was a great deal of sharing. Outside of the three killings [infra], I don't know of another incident that involved hostility between inmates. There were no fights that I was personally aware of. The taking of the goods from the prison store was another amazing feat. Once the loot had been secured, they brought it up and took it to various units and shared everything that was there. People wasn't grabbing and hoarding and fighting over it. I ate a lot of cake, and pop, and candy, and I fried ham and pork chops and eggs and things like that. Many others would cook and bring it out to other prisoners. I mean it was basically well run.

At first, some of the black inmates feared the riot would turn against them. One black inmate recalled:

> We didn't know what was happening, so all of the blacks got together up in the J.C. office on the third floor. We armed ourselves with sticks and different things.
> *Question:* You thought it was racial?
> *Inmate:* Yes, because we didn't know. After a while the two spokesmen came in and said it was not a racial thing. It was against the administration. So then we were more at ease.

Gregory, by his account, told Lehman:

> "Look here, man, everybody's getting paranoid. Everyone thinks a race riot is about to jump off. Get your people and tell them its a bunch a s−−t. I'll get mine and tell them, and we can get on with it." That's what we did.

Although Lehman and other Avengers played a central role in the disturbance, they did not use intimidation or force to control it. Lehman relied on other Avengers to ensure the hostages' safety and carry out other tasks of the moment, but his authority in the situation came from popular consensus, not the power of the organization.

Soon after the takeover, the inmates in the law library began to debate what to do with the hostages. In the words of one inmate:

Within a few hours of the riot, people were discussing the fate of the guards. What are we going to do with them? Initially there was some talk of just killing 'em to make a statement, to make a point. No inmate was in favor of abusing them, simply beating them. No inmate said, "Let's give them a good ass kick. Let's take them and torture them and not kill them." . . . Finally, the inmates seemed all towards non-violence as far as killing was concerned. We could say, "Look, we had your asses. We could show you what could be done, and it could be done again. You'd better straighten your f——king act up. You'd better get this prison in shipshape."

Indeed, no hostage was killed or injured, except in the initial takeover. (In the takeover, one guard sustained a broken nose; another aggravated his chronically strained back; and another received an abrasion on the face.) After that, the hostages were treated well. One hostage reported:

> Our life wasn't too bad. I was in there for two days. The bunks in the cells they put us in, all they had was steel. Towards the morning someone brought us a mattress. Oh, it made a big difference.

Another hostage told a newspaper reporter, "They called us punks, but that's all. Otherwise they treated us very well."[56] Another hostage remembered, "Once they had me where they wanted me, they treated me like a king. They fed me, they asked me if I was warm enough."[57] Still, some hostages had harrowing experiences. One reported:

> After they got us in the cell they left us alone for a few minutes and then an inmate came in and ripped my blindfold off. He was acting crazy and wild. He was carrying a homemade shank about 12 inches long, sharpened to a point. He kept passing it from his left hand to his right hand, making crazy statements that he was the one who was going to kill us. Every once in a while he would put the shank to my neck and then to the other officer's necks. He would run it from side to side and from ear to ear like he was going to slit our throats. About this time, [inmate name] [the Avenger who led the takeover in the mess hall] appeared on the scene. He assured us that we were not going to be harmed. . . .
> At one time inmate Alvin Gregory gave me Tylenol for the pain in my back. Inmate Danny Lehman came down and checked me with a stethoscope. . . . Alvin Gregory came in and asked if there was anything he could do. I [told] him that somebody got my watch and I'd like to have my watch back. A short time later, somebody came in and put a watch in my hand.[58]

Several hours into the riot, inmates ordered the hostages to state over a walkie-talkie their name, rank, and that they were "all right." A hostage explained:

> [Inmate name] would come in with that radio and would say, "Give them you name, tell them where you at, tell them you're all right." What he expected

you to say was "West Virginia Penitentiary." When you said, "P & R, P side, cell nineteen" (laughter), there was a plunk on the head.

During the second day, the inmate leaders arranged to have the hostages talk briefly to their families over the phone from the law library. The inmates told the hostages that "it would be a good thing" if they would urge their family members to contact the press and tell them that they would not be hurt as long as the prison was not stormed. This was done by several of the hostages' families.

A crowd of reporters and camera crews from local and national media assembled in front of the penitentiary. To many of the local residents, they were an annoyance; to others, a windfall. Reporters and other media people were desperate for phone lines and other facilities. The Associated Press paid one homeowner $50 for the exclusive use of his telephone. NBC paid a resident for the use of his entire house, including its telephones, bathroom, and electric outlet.[59] Some reporters hired taxicabs to park in front of the penitentiary, which became their base.

For the administration negotiators, the media were a serious problem. According to Kirby:

> People were on the street that didn't know what was going on, telling stories to the media. Then it immediately went on the news. Where every inmate in the joint had a tube, they were seeing it, and they were either becoming infuriated because they were telling a lie, or they would laugh because they had pulled one off on the system. I had to respond to what went over the news, and I couldn't keep up with every channel.

One local television station reported that inmates were being incinerated in the kitchen oven. (In fact, prison records were being burned.) Two national television networks reported that "as many as" ten inmates "might" be dead.[60] Inmates speculated that the false stories had been aired to justify an assault.

The four administration negotiators, however, had one advantage: they had arrived at the prison in denim jackets and other casual clothing and could blend in with onlookers or pass between the prison and the warden's office without attracting the reporters' attention.

The four knew that the guard taken hostage at eight door was probably the most hated in the prison and in the greatest danger. They told Lehman and Gregory that that hostage might die if he did not receive medication for high blood pressure. As Kirby later explained, the negotiating group

> manufactured the health problems to be even worse than they were, to the inmates. We actually tested the inmates to see how vulnerable they were to being scared of losing an officer. We played up the illness to the point where he could die on them.

A heated debate broke out among the inmates. As recalled by one inmate:

[Hostage name], he had been treating inmates so bad while he was working in maximum security that some guys didn't feel that it was right to let him go. So I said, "Man, I can understand where you all are coming from, but you don't want to have this kind of murder on your hands." So they debated and they talked. And I said, "Hell, you keep talking he's going to be dead." So finally they agreed to let him go.

The hostage was released at 11:45 p.m. out the South Wagon Gate. (The South and North wagon gates are vehicular entrances into the South and North yards, respectively.) Taken in an ambulance to a local hospital, he was treated but not admitted.

From the administration's point of view, the release of the first hostage constituted a major step. "Once that happened," Kirby later commented, "we knew—we were not controlling those people, they had all the aces—we knew they would listen to what we were saying."

The next concession the administration negotiators sought was the return of the kitchen and the infirmary. Soon after the riot began, some inmates had broken into the infirmary and swallowed whatever little medication was there. Kirby had kept little on hand, with just such an event in mind. The infirmary was not otherwise ransacked nor was the expensive dental and medical equipment disturbed. Around midnight, the inmates agreed to return the infirmary (but not the kitchen) to the control of the authorities. An inmate trusty, who lived full-time in the infirmary and was opposed to the riot, reported:

> The word came [from the inmate leaders] that all those who did not live there [the infirmary] should leave. And they left quite orderly. I was impressed by the concern from some of the other inmates, because I kept getting the word that they [the rioting inmates] were not to bother anyone up there [in the infirmary]. . . . We made sure that those inmates were provided with their daily medication, made sure that the diabetics received their insulin shots.

About 2:00 a.m., inmate leaders discovered the body of Kent Slie. The 38-year-old inmate had been serving a life sentence for kidnapping and murder. "He was an informer," one inmate commented, "but that he was an informer is not the real reason that he got killed. It's cause he and this other dude, they had problems before. The dude already told him if anything ever jumps off, and I can get out of maximum security, you'll be the first one I kill." Lehman arranged with the administration negotiators to turn over the body at the South Wagon Gate. The autopsy report showed no evidence of torture or mutilation.

In the early morning hours, the members of the negotiating committee returned to their cells for rest. Lehman and Gregory stayed up all night in contact with the four administration negotiators. Kirby later reflected, "I told myself, 'I got more stamina than they got. I can stay here longer than they can.' I was hoping to beat them on that end of it, that they would wear down."

Inmates were up early on the second day. A second hostage, who had been roughed up during the takeover, began to complain of sharp pains in his back and neck. An inmate told the hostage to quit "lying" when he reported over the radio to authorities that his condition was satisfactory. In the next transmission, the guard stated, "My name is [guard's name]. I think I got some hurt ribs, my arms hurt, but other than that, I'm okay."[61] At 5:40 a.m., the hostage was taken from P & R to the law library, where he was examined by two inmates with medical backgrounds. They concluded that the hostage should be released, and Kirby was called to arrange it. Blindfolded, the hostage was taken to the South Wagon Gate in a wheelchair and then transported to a hospital in an ambulance. Like the first hostage, the second one was treated but not admitted.

The last hostage released for health reasons was Captain Glasscock. He had complained of symptoms associated with high blood pressure, which the inmates judged serious enough to to warrant his release. Captain Glasscock was turned over to the administration negotiators at the South Wagon Gate at 12:45 p.m. When asked if any other hostages could be released for health reasons, the inmates responded that the next one would come out when they saw the governor.

## Accord Signed

By the morning of the second day, the inmates' principal demand had become firm: a face-to-face meeting with the governor to discuss their concerns. "We felt the governor's the only person that would listen and could get something done," recalled an inmate on the negotiation committee. Informed (falsely) that the governor was out of the state, the inmates said they would "just sit on this thing until the governor gets back."

The governor had flown into Pittsburgh on the evening of the first and had secretly been rushed to his home in Glen Dale by the West Virginia State Police. His presence was concealed from the inmates and the press, for reasons explained by the governor's press secretary, John Price:

> The inmates demanded that the governor appear. But in negotiations you make them pay for every last little thing. We didn't want to bring him right up. So there was a time he was actually in the vicinity but just hadn't surfaced. . . . Instead of demanding this or demanding that, we focused their energies on demanding the governor, whom we could easily produce.

Price let Kirby know that the governor was willing to meet with the inmates, but only after all the hostages were released, the inmates were back in their cells, and control of the prison had been passed back into the hands of officials. Within these limits, Kirby and the other negotiators were allowed to iron out an agreement as best they could. Kirby told the inmates, "You *are* going to sit down with the governor, so you have won. You don't have any officers dead yet."

The inmates insisted on a meeting with the governor before releasing the hostages. They also wanted additional time to clean up the prison and restore it to its pre-riot condition, to the extent possible. Eventually the inmates agreed to turn over some of the hostages immediately, and the remainder the following day when the governor would meet with the inmates' committee. Kirby suggested that all but one of the hostages be released immediately, since "one is as good as thirteen." The inmates counter-offered with a split more favorable to them. After some haggling, it was finally agreed that six guards would be released that afternoon and the remainder on Friday, the third.

Finally, the inmate committee typed out an agreement with six provisions:

1. The return of the institution will be done with West Virginia Penitentiary employees only, and with no assistance from the Department of Public Safety.

2. Media coverage is to be handled by residents Danny Lehman and Alvin Gregory.

3. Inmate population will have time to police or clean their respective areas before the entry of West Virginia Penitentiary personnel.

4. The Governor's representative and the Commissioner agree to the meeting with inmate committee personnel. *(Governor will meet with inmate committee at noon,* January 3, 1986.)

5. There will be no retaliation as a result of resident takeover of the institution nor in the normal clean up of operation. In consideration for the above statements there will be an immediate release of six (6) unharmed hostages and the remaining seven (7) unharmed hostages at 12:00 noon on January 3, 1986.

6. The allowable time limits for return of the institution will be at 12:00 noon on January 3, 1986. If the above criteria are defaulted in any way, this agreement will be null and void. (emphasis in original)

The first provision stemmed from the inmates' fear that the state police would again brutalize inmates as they allegedly had in the 1979 Joint Operation. Point three may be unique in the history of U.S. prison riots: the opportunity to clean up the prison before turning it over to state officials.

The critical issue of whether the hostages would be released before or after the meeting with the governor was left, in effect, unresolved. When points four and five are considered together, they suggest that the release and the meeting would occur simultaneously at noon on January 3.

Finally, the reader is invited to study point five and consider what the phrase "no retaliation as a result of resident takeover of the institution" might mean. Inmates did not take it as an amnesty from criminal charges, but they believed it guaranteed against physical retaliation and also against internal punishment such as segregation and loss of privileges. But this was not spelled out. We will see later how Governor Moore interpreted the phrase.

It was agreed that the signing of the document would be televised, and that Lehman and Gregory could hold a press conference afterwards. About 2:00 p.m., Lehman and Gregory met Commissioner Dodrill and Press Secretary

Price in the lobby of the penitentiary. On live local television, Dodrill and Price signed the document.[62] The national media were excluded because Price feared they might provoke an incident to get a better story. Immediately after the signing, Gregory asked Dodrill:

> We would like to know if you signed under duress or if you signed of your own free will?
> *Dodrill:* I'm not sure what you mean by that. Certainly if we did not have the disturbance we would not have had an agreement to sign.
> *Gregory:* Let me put it like this: is this going to be a valid agreement?
> *Dodrill:* We signed this in front of an awful lot of witnesses. We have no intention of backing out.
> *Gregory:* That's what we want to know.[63]

Gregory's seemingly peculiar question—peculiar at least to Dodrill—was the result of an earlier meeting of the inmate negotiating committee. An inmate on the committee had remembered that a federal court had once overturned an agreement between rioting inmates and prison officials on the grounds that it had been signed under duress. (If this occurred, we are unaware of it.) Gregory wanted to make sure that the same thing would not happen to their agreement.

After the exchange, Lehman and Gregory answered questions from the press. When asked about the takeover, Lehman responded, "Nobody wanted this thing. We tried to avoid it for a long time. . . . This thing was not done by the Avengers. It was done by the whole population." Gregory stated that the prison had not been improved, despite repeated promises that it would be. He added, "All we want is to be treated like human beings. We are tired of being treated like juveniles. Why can't we grow our hair long or grow a beard or mustache?"

Both Gregory and Lehman stated that they "regretted" the death of an inmate. Gregory said that the hostages were safe and "in just as good of health as when they came in there." Lehman added that the hostages would remain in their custody for another 24 hours, but would be protected, cared for, and allowed to talk to their families regularly.[64]

At 3:00 p.m., six hostages were released, as the agreement had called for. They were taken by ambulance to a nearby hospital and held overnight for observation.

Before the prison was returned, two more inmates were killed. Robert Dean, a small, 35-year-old white man, had been convicted of armed robbery and kidnapping. While in prison, he gave state authorities information which helped in the arrest and conviction of a number of drug dealers. On the morning of January 2, several inmates gave Dean a severe beating in P & R and then dropped him from the third tier with a telephone cord tied around his neck. The cord broke, but Dean died from the impact after a few hours. His body was taken to the basement. Lehman called the administration negotiators with the location of Dean's body. Three of the four negotiators, along with Lehman and Gregory, entered the dark (and potentially menacing) basement to bring out the body without incident.

The last inmate killed, Jeff Atkinson, had been convicted of the stabbing murder of a woman eight months pregnant and of the fetus. The state supreme court had overturned the latter conviction. Many inmates were disgusted by Atkinson's "sick" crime. Furthermore, Atkinson had twice been taken out of the prison to go to court, and had refused to say why; it was thought he was informing on those charged with the murder of his girlfriend's mother during a robbery attempt. On the evening of the second, an inmate stuck a screwdriver through his throat. Atkinson's body was put in a locker in the main hallway, and then turned over to authorities the next morning.

## Termination

At 9:00 a.m. Friday, the inmate leaders began to prepare to return the prison to the authorities. The committee members told the inmates to return to their own cells, and then went through the blocks with garbage cans to collect weapons:

> We told 'em, "They gonna shake down. If you got weapons, you can either throw 'em in or you can keep it. It's up to you. You'll have to take that risk." We got all the keys that we could get, brought them up the hall, and laid all the keys on the law library desk.

Around noon, the committee was told that the governor had arrived. Kirby remembered:

> Right at the last minute, there was a big to-do. The governor said, "I will not speak with the inmates until the institution is mine." He meant "mine" was that our [Department of Corrections] people were to be inside, locking doors.

In Jeff Fromhart's view, it was the administration that was reneging: "The top administration wanted the officers to go in and secure before the governor will speak to them. Which wasn't the deal. They [the inmates] wanted to police it themselves. It worked out ok, but I didn't like the last minute change."

Exhausted, tired of rioting, and feeling they had no realistic choice, the inmates gave in. "Everybody's tired. We wanted the s––t to be over with," one inmate described the mood.

An elaborate formal procedure had been developed for the release of the hostages. Lehman, Gregory, and Kirby would escort them one by one from the prison across the South Yard; the Fromharts and Wood would take each to the South Wagon Gate, and the governor would greet each hostage and take him to a waiting ambulance. The last stage would be carried live by the local television station.

The first three hostages were escorted to the South Gate as planned. But the governor was late; the hostages queued up inside the South Gate, waiting for Moore's ceremonial greeting; and the inmates, who were watching the TV and hadn't seen the guards come *out* of the South Gate, became afraid they were being set up for an assault. When Kirby returned to the prison for the fourth hostage, the inmates told him that there were going to be no more hostages released. Furious, Kirby stormed back to the South Gate and bluntly demanded, "You get them officers out that gate now. This guy's [i.e., Moore] holding up the whole show."

A few minutes later, the governor arrived and began to escort the hostages one at a time from the South Gate to the ambulances. The process went ahead. After the last hostage was taken out, Lehman and Gregory returned to the housing units to lock the other committee members in their cells. The two of them then returned to the South Gate, told officials about the weapons they had confiscated, and turned over what keys they had. But the governor wanted to meet with all eight of the committee; so Lehman and Gregory were given back some keys and told to fetch the other six to the administration building. After that, 110 uniformed correctional officers entered the prison, ending 42 hours of inmate control.[65]

At about 3:30 p.m., after two strip-searches, the eight inmates were taken to meet with Governor Moore around a large table in the prison lobby. Also in attendance were Commissioner Dodrill and Press Secretary Price.[66]

Moore asked the inmates to speak frankly; Commissioner Dodrill took notes. Gregory complained that privileges had been taken from the inmates recently: "They keep taking away from us. Every time it gets calm in here they want to initiate shakedowns, changes in recreation procedures and visitation." He added, "We can't understand why we must get shaves and haircuts." Another inmate told Moore that he had been at Moundsville for five years and had not "learned anything." He suggested that there be more programs to better prepare inmates for their release. Lehman expressed concern over the quality of the food, but then told the governor that the medical treatment he had received for his phlebitis could not have been better.

Moore responded that he would discuss the matters brought up with the warden, but that complaints against individual officers would have to be taken up elsewhere. He added, "Any action to be taken against any particular correction officer must be submitted by a written complaint to the civil service commission which is completely out of my bailiwick." The meeting concluded after about an hour of mostly amicable conversation.[67]

Moore then held a news conference, packed with a 100 reporters. Moore thanked the inmate negotiators for the safe release of the hostages and took issue with a reporter who suggested that negotiating with rioting convicts might set an unwise precedent, adding, "I felt compelled to keep my end of the bargain." He pledged that inmates would not be beaten. In 1979, he said, "there was wanton, physical violence wreaked upon every individual prisoner in this institution. Now, I've said that's not going to happen."[68] This, it developed, was the *full* meaning of provision five of the accord. He later commented in a newspaper interview, "There is no way we can talk about amnesty. Amnesty was never mentioned in the negotiations. . . . The 'no retaliation' meant that there wouldn't be a repeat of what happened in 1979," when inmates were "badly beaten and it was after the state had already had the place under control."[69]

## Aftermath

Damage to the institution was not extensive. A fire had gutted the captain's office, but one in the inmate store had been extinguished before it could spread. Inmates had hammered through some interior walls, broken windows, and overturned tables and other furniture. The plumbing and wiring had been left intact. Most costly was the failure to return all of the keys, requiring much of the locking system to be rekeyed. In assessing the damage, Commissioner Dodrill remarked that it "is very, very light when you consider what could have been done. They were kind to us."[70]

The 1980 New Mexico riot had, by 1985, resulted in significant improvements in the Santa Fe Penitentiary; the Michigan riots had not. While we are writing too soon after the West Virginia riot to close the books, the developments in the first post-riot year have given no reason for optimism.

Several months after the riot, inmates won another major legal victory, although its effects are yet to be observed. The state supreme court ruled that the department's plan of compliance, which had been accepted in September 1984 by Judge Bronson, did not meet the requirements set forth by Judge Recht's original ruling. The court found that "health care at West Virginia Penitentiary, even assuming full implementation of the compliance plan as approved, constitutes deliberate indifference to the serious medical needs of the prisoners." The justices also concluded that "we cannot envision how it would be economically feasible to increase the cell size with the confines of the existing structure. It is apparent that the compliance plan must be revised by the Department of Corrections to include the development of new facilities." The court ordered the Department of Corrections to draft a new plan in 120 days.[71]

But neither the riot nor the latest court decision has moved the state legislature to increase funding for the state's prisons. Even liberal state delegate Thomas Knight, a committed reformer on prison matters, admitted:

> The problem is that you have a dollar choice between providing assistance to good and decent people who had their lives destroyed by the flood or good and decent people who live in an area of high unemployment or good and decent children who need an education or people who have so violated society that they are sent to prison. When it comes to that you make the choice of people who are good and decent.[72]

On the one-year anniversary of the riot, the speaker of the house stated that, because the state continued to face severe financial woes in 1987, the money for corrections and the penitentiary will remain a "stepchild" to other state concerns.[73] The state's fiscal crisis turned sharply worse in the first quarter of 1987; in response, Governor Moore issued an executive order requiring a 20 percent spending cut on all state agencies, including the Department of Corrections. Special Master Poffenberger concluded that these cuts would not only halt further progress toward compliance with the court's rulings, but would "engulf what efforts have been made thus far."[74]

As Moore had promised, physical retaliation against the inmates did not occur. Two weeks after the riot, though, on Moore's direct orders, 86 inmates were transferred to segregation for their suspected roles in the riot.[75] This included all but one of the inmates who had attended the negotiation session with the governor, and many more whose roles in the riot were (according to the inmates transferred) primarily to maintain order and restrain the more violent prisoners. One of those who had negotiated with the governor, and was later transferred to segregation, commented sarcastically:

> They locked up the people who took the officers. That is understandable. You don't want people running around that snatch up your officers. Then you lock up the guys who stood with the officers to prevent them from being hurt by anyone else. Then you lock up the guys who are there to help out with non-riot stuff [such as first aid]. I'd characterize my own participation this way. You wonder what the administration is trying to teach you. Is it "Don't participate"? Or is it "We can't catch everyone, so we catch the ones we can identify"?

Many inmates believed that subsequent disciplinary hearings for riot participants violated principles of due process. In a quarterly report, Special Master Poffenberger concurred: "Prison officials disregarded the rules designed to safeguard the individual's due process guarantees and the efficacy of the penitentiary's disciplinary process."[76] Furious, inmates saw the state's actions as a blatant and dishonorable violation of the "no retaliation" pledge. The governor saw it differently; in his view, the promise meant only that the inmates "would be secure in their body and person."

Over a period of several months, attacks and counter-attacks between inmates and guards in the segregation unit spiraled out of control. Inmates threw urine, feces, and boiling water on the guards and on several occasions attacked them with broom handles and other makeshift weapons. The guards, in turn, turned off the electricity for long periods and refused to enter the tiers unless absolutely necessary. On a visit to the unit in March, the special master observed on the floor "approximately two inches of water, urine and garbage— just floating."[77] Because of the escalating hostilities, the unit's guards were required to wear flak-jackets and helmets with face shields. In one especially violent incident, 12 inmates refused to return to their cells after taking showers. A riot squad arrived and opened fire on the inmates after one allegedly doused a guard with a flammable liquid and several other inmates pulled prison-made knives. (Inmates claim that the shootings were unprovoked.) Bullets injured 5 inmates, one seriously.[78]

In Michigan, guard union activism sparked an inmate riot; at Moundsville, it was the other way around. A majority of guards belonged to the Communication Workers of America (CWA), but under state law it could not act as a collective bargaining agent, and the union was relatively inactive. After the riot, the union mobilized the public in an effort to increase security and "safety" at the institution. In February, the CWA staged a five-hour protest in front of the penitentiary. Two guards, one of them a former hostage, carried a mock coffin, with a third guard trailing them with a sign, "Let's keep this empty." In March, the CWA collected signatures throughout the state on a petition to Governor Moore. At an October, 1986 press conference, a CWA spokesman said that guards would refrain from striking, but that they would retaliate against state legislators at the ballot box who failed to support their demands.[79]

Also, in June 1986, the CWA filed in court a mandamus petition, demanding that the Department of Corrections implement 23 safety measures.[80] Although the state contested the CWA's right to file the petition, the department did meet some of the key demands.[81] Gun cages were installed in each block, manned by guards equipped with a shotgun and a rifle—highly unusual for American prisons. The captain's office was moved to a more secure location and the eight door was removed to give free sight down the South Hall corridor. In addition, the correctional officers were given a one-time raise of $1,500.

Still, by the end of 1986, the CWA leaders were publicly demanding Warden Hedrick's replacement. Rick Swiger, president of the CWA, told a Charleston reporter:

> The inmates asked for their [Hedrick's and his deputies'] removal, and I understand that you can't give in to prisoners on something like that. But when your guard force comes and starts asking for them to be removed, you'd better take some notice.[82]

As of 1987, though, Governor Moore and Commissioner Dodrill remained unwavering in their support for Hedrick.

The state indicted 23 inmates: 10 on murder charges, 7 on kidnapping charges, and the remainder on charges of aggravated robbery or conspiracy to resist authority. As we write, one of the defendants is dead (Danny Lehman), one was granted immunity, two pled guilty, and the remainder are awaiting trial.

# III

# CONCLUSIONS

# 9

# The Nature and Course of Prison Riots

## The Nature of Riots

At the beginning of this book, we pointed out that most people commonly believe "riots" to be chaotic and somewhat irrational events, while prisoners expect prison riots to be purposeful and organized. Actually, this difference is reflected throughout the scholarly study of collective action.[1] Some treat riots as merely "expressive" acts, purposeless emotional outpourings. Those who are more prepared to view the masses as rational look for evidence of plan and strategy, interpreting riots as "instrumental," not merely expressive, and designed to relieve their suffering.

Within the latter framework, it is most common to see riots as a form of *protest*. By definition, a protest must be directed at an audience, whether it be the public at large or the upper reaches of government.

However, even still assuming that riots are "about" grievances, they are not necessarily attempts to persuade elites. They may, indeed, be actions designed to punish those thought responsible for oppression—whether to deter them from future injustice or simply to inflict just retribution on them for their past moral crimes. The rioter may be no more interested, while burning a module, in "persuading" the state to provide better conditions than the state was, when imprisoning the rioter, in "persuading" him not to be criminal.

Clearly, much riot activity, and some riots, are not "about" grievances at all in the sense that the participants are intentionally acting against the state. Prisoners taking food and soap from the canteens at Jackson and Moundsville were not saying to themselves, "This is how we punish the state!"; they were obtaining consumer goods which were normally unavailable to them. Such activity may be interpreted as "caused by" poverty, even as a "response to" poverty; this is not the same as saying it was a protest against poverty. Where interpersonal, racial, or gang-related violence takes place, the administration may not even be an (obvious) party to the conflict. In the case of New Mexico, the killings of inmates may have been largely occasioned by the snitch system, but the participants were not (at least at first glance) acting against the state at all—they were eliminating a perceived internal menace, or exacting retribution against treacherous inmates. Prisoners raping other inmates, or stealing their property, in the Ionia riot were flouting the laws of the state, but not in the spirit of protest against the state.

The understanding that not all riot activity is intended as protest should help us take a new look at the question of whether prison riots are "instrumental" or "expressive." If one supposes that the instrumental content of riots is limited to their role in bargaining with the state or dramatizing grievances to the outside world, and one notes that many riot participants do things poorly suited to those ends, like looting, raping, killing, and burning, one is tempted to conclude that those persons' actions were "expressive." But it is not "irrational" to lack collective spirit. Nothing is so individualistically instrumental as theft and rape. Bearing this in mind, we conclude that there was little activity in the riots we studied which could not be called rational or instrumental.

The best candidates for exceptions to this generalization are the torture-killings in New Mexico and the arsons there and in Michigan. Readers who encounter descriptions of the killings in Cell Block 4 are certain to be horrified, and likely to say that it is implausible on its face to categorize them as rational, instrumental activity. But "rational" is not a synonym for "humane." Torture is the policy of many governments, and public torture-killings were commonplace in England until the days of King George III, and in the American South within living memory. One has to examine how and why such policies are pursued before concluding that they are "irrational."

If one considers "snitching" an offense against inmates, one can apply to it the "economic" analysis which is applied by the state to crime. This involves manipulating the cost to the offender of his or her offense, calculated on the basis of certainty of apprehension, certainty of conviction, and severity of punishment. When certainty of apprehension and conviction are low, punishment must be severe in order to significantly deter offenders.

Inmates are seldom able to apprehend and punish "snitches." They are under surveillance; the "snitches" are not known with certainty; when they are, they are often segregated from the general population of inmates just as they were at New Mexico. Punishment can be inflicted only under special circumstances, such as those of a prison riot. From this point of view, punishing "snitches" by burning out their eyes and privates with a torch may make sense; with certainty of punishment that low, only a punishment more severe and memorable than mere death will have significant deterrent effect.

Indeed, the inmate interviews suggest that some may have decided on torture-killings as a calculated policy of deterrence. But a far stronger motive appears to have been hatred and desire for vengeance. They wanted the victims to suffer in order to pay manyfold for their past offenses.

Still, how "irrational" is this? In Plato's *Protagoras,* retribution is characterized as the action of a "reasonless brute." Contemporary scholars are divided. Conservatives, like van den Haag, believe the desire for retribution to be a thoroughly moral one, which society must satisfy through law to forestall the upsurge of private vengeance. Liberal thinkers, such as Skolnick, sharply disagree with this position.[2] Whether retribution is in the final analysis "rational" we leave to the judgment of the reader.

There is evidence, though, that some of the victims at New Mexico were killed simply so that the perpetrators could enjoy the victims' suffering and the novelty of the experience, regardless of the victims' past actions. Some of the perpetrators were heavily intoxicated with drugs. We will not quarrel at this point with those who wish to call such action "irrational." The overwhelming bulk of the deaths were not of this type; none of them at Attica, Joliet, or Moundsville were.

As for arson, some of it is understandable as retributive, like the burning of the counselors' offices at Jackson–Central Complex and the modular units at Jackson–North Complex. Some of the heavy destruction was the result of fires getting out of hand; the burning of the gym at New Mexico may be an example. A fire in the commissary at Moundsville could have spread, but it was put out by an organized team of inmates.

Finally, we would point out that retributive and instrumental violence against the state or other inmates may be reinterpreted as, or have the effect of, protest. Violence grabs the attention of the outside elites and convinces them that conditions must have been horrible and inmates must have been desperate. Indeed, the more general and less comprehensible the violence, the greater the likelihood of its being attributed to prison conditions rather than to the deviant intentions of individual inmates. This was how it worked at New Mexico.

Of course, one cannot reason back from the consequences of action (improved prison conditions) to its intention. Prison violence may bring about prison reform without its perpetrators intending it. On the other hand, inmates cannot foresee all the consequences of riots which begin in an instrumental spirit; if the results are bloodbaths such as at Attica or New Mexico, this is not necessarily evidence that the riots were nothing but mindless mania at their core. One must look at the actual intentions of the actors, as we have done.

Scholars arguing over the nature of the urban disorders of the 1960s sometimes adopted a certain shorthand usage: they claimed that one or another event was or was not "political." To claim that an event was "political" was to say that the actors were rational, that there were real grievances at stake, that it was not "mere" crime or deviance, and so on. To deny it was to label the event as trivial or inconsequential.

We suggest that this misleading usage be abandoned, or at any rate sharpened. Actually there are three separate questions: whether the cause of an event is "political" (in that it somehow flows from perceived group interests, needs, inequities, or injustices); whether the course of an event is "political" (typified by intentional group conflict, debate, demands, ideology); and whether it has a political effect (alters the balance of power or rewards in society). The Russian Revolution was political in all three senses; a wild street rumpus after a Super Bowl win may be political in no sense; but prison riots are often mixed cases.

## Grievances and Ideology

Once a riot has begun, many inmates use it as an occasion for purely individualistic predation. But such motives will not initiate a riot. Inmates do not band together, even momentarily, to seize hostages or expel the guards from an area merely in order to steal food from the canteen or to steal from other inmates' cells. In some riots the initiators are motivated by racial or gang-related hostility; but no riot we studied was of this type. In the cases we studied, the initiators were motivated by grievances against the state or the guard force.

We believe that deprivation does have to do with prison riots. It is not the physical condition of the inmates which matters, but their mental state; not their "objective" deprivation (at least not directly), but their subjective experience of deprivation and grievance. Subjective deprivation cannot be inferred with confidence from measures of income, caloric consumption, square feet per inmate, or the like. Between the objective stimuli and the subjective response there is a mediating linkage of cognitive processes. Subjective deprivation is hard to isolate and study. This is not a reason to suppose that it is of negligible importance.

Subjective deprivation is not a constant. There is great variation in the sense of injustice felt by prisoners. Some seethe with repressed fury, others gripe, others would much rather be outside but exhibit stoic resignation, and still others go to school, learn trades, and optimistically, contentedly, prepare for their release. There is variation among prisoners and among prisons. In some minimum-security facilities hardly anyone is inclined to riot, with or without organization.

In general, information, change and instability, and ideology can intensify the feelings of deprivation and destroy the presumption of legitimacy. One telling sort of information is evidence that other persons, similar in the relevant aspects, have better lives; for instance, prisoners in other prisons, with similar records, in the same or different states. If conditions actually are better elsewhere or have been better here in the past, it must be shown that these comparisons are irrelevant because circumstances now and here create a special situation, universally judged to be qualitatively different from those others. In particular, since the prisoner (unlike the Russian serf, the born slave, e.g.) has actually lived in better conditions of life, those of freedom, the authorities must impress upon him the universality of society's judgment that he is no longer the same sort of being that he was when he was a free man, a citizen, and that he is no longer entitled to the same privileges of life.

Uniformity and stability also contribute to the presumption of legitimacy; change and disorder weaken it; and arbitrariness and chaos shatter it. Fluctuating and unpredictable standards, a multiplicity of competing rules, give the lie to the legitimacy of an order. When every shift commander has a different set of rules, the odds are that they are all wrong; when the administration says something different every day, all its pronouncements are certainly lies; when corrections officials bicker and fight among themselves, they all must be scoundrels: this is how the inmate reasons. If none of the authorities' statements about what is possible need be believed, then the measure of what is "possible" becomes, for the inmate, a matter of rumor, speculation, wishful thinking, and study. When things are made worse, there had better be a cause—a decline in resources, a mass escape, or a noticeable change in the balance of political force; otherwise, the new level of deprivation will be taken as illegitimate. Even when things are made better, there had better be a cause—otherwise, yesterday's rule was illegitimate; and if the rule was illegitimate yesterday, mightn't it be so again today?

## Ideology and Prison Sub-Culture

Ideology, by its very nature, has the potential to undercut the presumption of legitimacy. In his book *Delinquency and Drift,* David Matza argues that the principal role of the "youth gang" subculture in facilitating crime is to provide a set of rationalizing frameworks wherein delinquency can be seen as justifiable.[3] He goes on to point out that these frameworks are not self-created but are borrowed (though altered) from the norms of the larger society. Much the same thing happens in prisons. Ideas are taken from the larger culture, remolded in prison, and then become the frameworks for collective action by inmates.

The four ideologies which we observed inmates use to justify their rebellious impulses we call Rationalism, Constitutionalism, Rehabilitationism, and Revolutionism.

Rationalism is the belief that things are bad in the prison because people do not do their jobs. Guards are seen as lazy, corrupt, ill-trained, and incompetent. Management is often imagined to be engaged in widespread embezzlement and graft; they line their pockets, while the inmates suffer. One of the strengths of this ideology is that the public at large in modern capitalist society is known to accept the norms of organizational rationality according to which the prison is condemned. Therefore, all that is necessary is to make known what is going on, either to some official who is seen as honest (the warden, the secretary of corrections, the governor) or to the aroused electorate. The rascals will be thrown out and conditions will improve.

Constitutionalism is the belief that things will improve if the prison or state authorities can be forced to conform to the U.S. Constitution. This ideology has a strong base in the fact that many abuses in the state prison systems have been struck down by federal courts and that the federal government has the power to impose its will on the states. Furthermore, most members of the public are thought to support the notion that prisons should be administered in accordance with the Constitution. Within the prison, a sort of "folk-constitutional law" develops, in which terms like "freedom of speech," "cruel and unusual," and "jury of one's peers" are imbued with expanded meaning and used in contexts that might not be actually supported by real court decisions. Inmates believe they know what their constitutional rights are and when they are being violated.

The basic constitutionalist remedy is the class action suit, and great faith is often put in the power and willingness of federal judges to change things if they are not deceived by legal maneuvering and manufactured evidence. However, the revolutionary connotations of the term "constitution" give some substance to the idea that force may legitimately be used to recover one's "constitutional" rights; authorities who deny such rights are illegitimate and may be rightfully defied. Insofar as racial discrimination by state authorities is prohibited by the Constitution, much of the ideology uniting black and Latin inmates in opposing discrimination by guards and administrators can be considered as "constitutionalist."

Rehabilitationism is the ideology, held by many persons outside prisons and nearly all prisoners, which maintains that a prison is "legitimately" a place for rehabilitation, but not for punishment or "vengeance." Rehabilitationists claim that prisons should offer job training, education, psychological and psychiatric help, and substance abuse therapy, in order to "cure" or "repair" those defects in the inmate which caused him to commit crime. If a prison is seen as analogous to other rehabilitative environments, like the convalescent wards of hospitals, then the inmate is analogous to a patient and may claim that measure of privilege and dignity appropriate to the "sick" role. "Purposeless, vindictive" incarceration, denial of privilege, enforced idleness, and guard hostility are the chief targets of criticism. It is often pointed out by those taking this view that the brutality of prison existence aggravates, rather than ameliorates, inmates' aggressive and criminal tendencies. Wise public officials are exhorted to reorder prison policies so that inmates will depart better, not worse, than when they arrived. The actual level of commitment on the part of the public and of correctional officials to rehabilitation has varied greatly over time; it is much lower today than it was a decade ago. Inmates often overestimate its appeal.

These three are reformist ideologies in that they do not challenge the existence of prisons or the criteria used to fill them. Most inmates are reformists in this sense, at least today. Many, indeed, do claim to be innocent themselves; but, at the same time, they generally believe that all the other inmates they see did the things they were charged with, "legitimately" deserve to be there, and ought not to be let out en masse. Further, they know that there is little public support for mass amnesty, and, knowing it to be politically impossible, they do not insist upon it as a condition of legitimacy.

Revolutionism, in contrast, conceptualizes the prison as an instrument of repression and stresses the fundamental similarity of the inmate population to the community outside the walls. The prisoners are there not for what they have done, but primarily because they are poor, powerless, and (in the United States) black and Latin. The implication is that inmates deserve not merely benign imprisonment, but freedom; and that their degree of deprivation must be measured not against better prison conditions, but life on the outside. Thus, revolutionary ideology promotes an especially intense consciousness of deprivation and injustice. Such a critique can probably only arise when there is a climate of revolutionary consciousness and agitation on the outside, at least in the communities from which the prisoners come.

These four ideologies varied in strength among the prisons studied. Revolutionism was strongest at Attica, present at Joliet, but almost non-existent at Michigan, West Virginia, and New Mexico. Few Joliet inmates criticized their facility for its failure to rehabilitate (even though the prison had few programs), but inmates at West Virginia and Marquette did. Many inmates at Jackson believed that the programs there lived up to rehabilitative standards. Constitutionalism was strongest at New Mexico and West Virginia. The courts had declared these two prisons in violation of constitutional and statutory law, but the mandated reforms had not been made. Criticism based on Rationalism was especially intense at Attica, Ionia, New Mexico, and West Virginia. At Attica and Ionia, inmates had been told by authorities that their facility did not live up to rational standards, but the necessary changes had not been made. At New Mexico and West Virginia, earlier wardens had lived up to the standards of rationalism, but they had been replaced by ones inmates said did not.

## Riot Stages and Riot Variation

While riots are born in the spirit of indignation against the state, they may live in any number of forms. This depends upon other predisposing factors and the current situation. Attica, New Mexico, and the Michigan riots were virtually indistinguishable at their inception: a fight between inmates and guards. What happens after that depends not only on the capabilities of the state but also on the inmates' pre-existing organizations, their patterns of ethnic and "inmate" identification, and the level of their hostility to the state, guards, and informers; and, more directly, on the events of crucial phases of the riot. What happens in one stage may depend on the outcome of the previous ones.

### Pre-Riot Stage: Orientation, Planning, and Organization

As we have defined it, the pre-riot stage is the period before the riot during which inmates and authorities develop dispositions to act during the riot situation. The pre-riot conditions we examined varied along these lines:

## SOLIDARITY AND HOSTILITY AMONG INMATES

Hard to quantify, but obvious, was a broad scope of variation in strength of inmates' feelings of solidarity and hostility toward each other, racial and ethnic groups, and "snitches." This variation depended both on the conditions of imprisonment and on broader trends of the time and place.

Mutual identification among prisoners as prisoners varied both in the clarity of its articulation (from vague sentiment to formal ideology) and in its sway (the proportion disposed to it). Clarity was greatest at Attica, due largely to the fact that the picture of inmates as an oppressed group was widely disseminated at that time both inside and outside the walls. At Moundsville and New Mexico some inmates did talk about "inmate unity." Clarity was quite low in all the Michigan disturbances, and nonexistent at Joliet (where all loyalty was to the individual gang). Sway is harder to gauge. In general, honor blocks, inmates with "good" jobs, and inmates in protective custody (who fear other inmates) do not support inmate unity.

Racial sentiment can be subdivided into intraracial cohesion (solidarity within the racial group) and interracial attitudes (positive or negative identification with other racial groups). Cohesion comes either from conflict with the administration (with support from prevailing ideology) or from minority status in the prison. An example of the former is black solidarity at Attica; examples of the latter were the defecting blacks at New Mexico and the anti-riot whites at Ionia. Interracial attitudes vary from explicit support of interracial unity (as at Attica) through unconcern (as at Jackson and Moundsville) to outright mistrust or hostility (as at New Mexico and Ionia).

Few inmates approve of "snitches," but the hatred is greater where snitching is fostered by the administration—as at New Mexico. In Michigan, "snitching" was discouraged by the administration. At Joliet, inmates did "gang-time," which all but precluded a snitch system.

## HOSTILITY TOWARD GUARD FORCE

Inmates in all prisons express some measure of hostility toward their keepers; still, there is variation in its intensity. New Mexico stood at one extreme, where the hostility was deep and unrelieved. Inmates at West Virginia did not feel deeply maligned by the guard force. At Joliet, inmates had thoroughly intimidated the staff and were more contemptuous of the staff than hateful toward them.

## INMATE ORGANIZATION

Inmate organizations stand in varying levels of opposition to authorities. Some of these organizations, such as religious groups or drug and alcohol rehabilitation groups, are tolerated or even sponsored by the administration. Participation in these organizations may improve the lives of inmates, making them less disposed to riot; or these organizations may instill a belief that rioting and violence is wrong. For these reasons, born-again Christians at Moundsville and Muslim inmates at Michigan were not disposed toward riot-ous behavior.

Other inmate groups may stand in opposition to the administration, which (if not suppressed) may reinforce and clarify inmates' identification with each other and their opposition to the regime and demonstrate to themselves and to other inmates that the regime can be resisted. Just as important, if these groups are connected (through actual ties or subjectively) with groups outside the prison, the standards for behavior of these external groups may be adopted by inmates. This was most visible at Attica, where inmates identified with various left-wing political groups.

## "PREPARATION"

After analyzing gang subculture, Matza argues that, once morally released to commit delinquent acts by rationalizing frameworks, potential delinquents are most likely to do so under conditions of "preparation." This refers to having committed similar acts previously, learning how to perform them, and reassuring oneself that it is possible to get away with them. In prison, preparation may be found in the pattern of events preceding the riot, which illustrate the ability of the inmates to outwit the administration, while showing up the guards as "paper tigers." Escapes, demonstrations, stabbings, and the like alert inmates to their own potential power and ready them mentally for the next opportunity. On the other hand, Matza also points out that a delinquent who sees himself as failing or making a fool of himself the first time he commits a delinquent act of a certain type is less likely to try again. An act of resistance in prison that fails may teach inmates that the prison is secure, the guards really are alert, and that future, more serious action would be foolish.

Common to nearly all of the pre-riot prisons we studied was a period during which the tempo of conflict escalated and the rebellious side won some sort of battle demonstrating the vulnerability of its opponents. At Attica there was a series of collective actions and a round of physical skirmishes in the 24 hours preceding the riot. At New Mexico there was the escape. At Jackson a guard was stabbed despite a shakedown intended to clear the prison of weapons. The mutinous guards, moreover, had won a victory in pressuring the SPSM administration into holding the shakedown in the first place and were about to put other plans for collective action into place at the time of the stabbing incident. The Jackson riot itself played the same "instructive" role for inmates at Ionia and Marquette (the latter of whom had already organized a food boycott). Looting incidents and illicit meetings preceded the Northside II outbreak. Such incidents encourage inmates to speculate about the vulnerability of the security forces and the tactics and strategies of riot.

## EXISTENCE OF A RIOT PLAN

The extent to which inmates have planned for a riot, individually or collectively, is a variable. There can be a detailed conspiracy to riot among most inmates with well-defined demands. On the other hand, inmates can find themselves in a riot at a moment's notice, never having considered what they might do in such an event. The latter was pretty much the case in the first disturbance at SPSM. The New Mexico, West Virginia, and Northside II cases fall nearer the "planned" end of the scale. At New Mexico and West Virginia rumors and possible plans for riots circulated through the institutions in the weeks preceding the takeover, giving inmates plenty of opportunity to speculate on what they would do in a riot. The takeover at New Mexico actually was the product of a conscious plan by inmates in E-2; at West Virginia, a small group carefully planned the takeover; and the details of the second Northside riot were well known among inmates a day in advance. At Joliet, inmates had been organizing against the administration for days, but the actual plan for the riot was laid in a single morning. The initiation of the Ionia riot was apparently planned on short notice, and most inmates were not aware of it. Marquette and Attica showed little evidence of planning.

In the pre-riot stage, the state also establishes its material, organizational, and cognitive resources. Prison authorities at Attica, Joliet, West Virginia, and New Mexico were largely unprepared for the riots in their institutions. The worst of the organizational problems included the primitive communication system at Attica, the failure to lock gates at New Mexico, and the unmanned posts at West Virginia. The worst of the material deficiencies included the cracked gate at Times Square at Attica, the control center glass at New Mexico, and the absence of a clear sight down the South Hall at West Virginia. Authorities were apparently better prepared at the three Michigan prisons, though they faced less severe challenges by inmates. On other hand, the "severity" of the challenge posed by inmates depends (in part) on how far inmates can get. Luck also has a role. Inmates at Ionia may have been able to seize the control center had they moved only a little faster.

Of course, the other thing the state can do in the pre-riot stage is to improve the conditions of imprisonment, to the extent that they have fallen below legitimate standards. Inmates will then be less disposed to riot.

## Initiation

The biggest problem facing inmates desiring to start a riot is to get fellow inmates to act in concert. There are three solutions to the problem of coordination—exclusive of SPSM, which may be unique in that guards allegedly provided the keys themselves.

Overt leadership is one. At Moundsville, New Mexico, and Joliet the rebellion began as a planned seizure of hostages. Once a plan is hatched, this is probably the hardest type of event to contain. It is particularly difficult if, as at Moundsville, inmates can seize more than one unit at the same time (mess hall and New Wall) and time the takeover for when the guard force is weak (guards "sick" on New Year's Day).

The difficulty of a pre-set plan is the costs it imposes on its planners. If identified in the pre-riot stage, they can be locked up in solitary confinement, transferred to another prison, or criminally prosecuted. Also, this type of seizure is the easiest to prosecute, which serves as a deterrent. Even if the specific conspirators are not detected, rumors of a planned disturbance may leak to authorities and the plan thwarted. Sometimes, however, authorities will fail to take the appropriate steps. At Northside II, the rebellion was initiated with the destruction of state property according to a pre-set plan. The administration had ample warning that a disturbance was brewing, but it mistakenly disregarded it.

The problem of coordination can also be solved through an escalating and snowballing set of events. Brawls can grow and grow and then spill over into full-scale riots. The decisive event of the spillover is when guards are forced to retreat. At Attica the initiating event was a brawl between guards and inmates, with little or no planning for subsequent actions. In such cases the administration has rather good chances to contain the riot. Officials are usually on the scene and (because brawls usually happen during the day) state forces can be summoned quickly. Another question, though, is where the brawl takes place. Guards can usually escape from yards, but are more easily taken hostage indoors. Still, even the Attica riot (which began in an indoor "tunnel") could have been contained if it hadn't been for the prison's abysmal organization and communication system.

A third solution is an event which signals all inmates that if they act, they can count on the actions of others. At Ionia and Marquette, riots at other prisons played this signaling role. Such events, though, may be insufficient to tell inmates precisely when and how to act in concert. The news of a riot elsewhere does not arrive all at once, but takes time to spread—leaving undetermined the precise moment to act. Thus, this third solution may be combined with the second. At both Ionia and Marquette, the disturbances were primed by the news of other riots, but then finally set off by brawls in the exercise yard.

Obviously, the state's initial response to the outbreak of rebellion is critical. Will it be quick and effective or sluggish and inept? Many of the crucial decisions will be made not by top administrators, in accordance with a "riot plan," but by individual correctional officers: to stay? to go? to fight? to hand over the keys? to stop to lock a grill? Poor tactical judgment and response in these matters appears to be coupled with poor training, laxity in routine, and lack of material readiness. The riots at Attica and New Mexico spread because of the poor preparation and facilities. At West Virginia, a questionable initial response also contributed to the broad expansion of the riot, though less decisively. In contrast, at SPSM (first riot), gun squads were quickly mobilized and able to contain the disturbance to two large blocks.

## Expansion: Recruitment, Hostage-taking, Seizure of Territory and Resources

Expansion is critical in the development of a riot. The rebellious inmates, unless they are in the most unprepared or disorganized state, free as many other inmates as possible and try to recruit them to the work of the riot; they seize as many blocks, units, buildings, facilities as possible; and, in short, they try to subject as much of what was under the administration's power to their own, as quickly as they can. However, hostages are not taken in every case—

even when it is clearly possible to do so. Inmates could have taken guards hostage in Michigan, but didn't; apparently they simply did not hate the guards as much as their New Mexico counterparts did. In addition, Michigan inmates had less time to "rehearse."

The logical limit of the process of expansion is to "expand" right out the door of the place, that is, to escape en masse. In fact, this was attempted much more often in prison riots around the turn of the century, but it is infrequent now. Even under the most favorable conditions, the rioters stop at the prison walls. Why this has changed is a matter for study. It may be that improved technology, such as more effective fences and sensing devices, have made mass escape more difficult; improved transportation and communication among law enforcement agencies may also have made re-capture easier. There is some indication, however, that inmates now do not try very hard to escape en masse, do not even consider it; this may be because they think re-capture and additional time would be likely, or it may be that (although they do not articulate it) they consider their incarceration "legitimate," but want only to alter its conditions or achieve other personal goals.

The stage of expansion may last as long as several hours. At the Penitentiary of New Mexico, the inmates methodically occupied the entire institution, block by block, over a five-hour period, cutting their way through the obstructing grills with acetylene torches (themselves seized in the process of expansion). It is unusual for this stage to last as long as five hours. The Moundsville riot expanded to its limit in about a half an hour, Attica took about one and a half hours, and Joliet just a few minutes.

Much of the subsequent activity will depend on what is taken, and in particular on whether the solitary confinement and protective custody units are taken. Certainly, if either one falls, the likelihood of violence increases. If both fall, as at New Mexico, the chances for deadly conflict are greatest.

## State of Siege—Inmate Power

As the society of captives becomes an actual polity, a new set of rules must be established—but what kind? The Michigan riots, Attica, and New Mexico demarcate the range of solutions to the problem of internal order. At Attica, despite pre-existing tendencies to dissension and intergroup conflict, the inmates established a democratic government—due heavily to the ideological connection of many of the inmates with externally developed standards and models for conduct. At Jackson (Central), no internal order was created, but inmates were not particularly hostile toward each other either; the result was a sort of benign anarchy. At Santa Fe, inmates' hostility toward each other was grave, due in significant part to administration policy. The inmates who initiated the riot had no strategy for dealing with the problem and were unable to establish themselves as legitimate authorities.

Another aspect of the problem of internal order is the ability of the inmates to prevent defection. In general, the higher the level of inter-inmate violence, the greater the proportion who will defect. At Santa Fe, over 80 percent of the prisoners left the institution before the prison was re-captured. The possibilities of defection may also depend on the location of the riot, the architecture of the prison, and the existence of an inmate security force. Defection from D Yard was most difficult; an inmate security force could spot any potential defectors in the open-air, walled-in yard. Many inmates, though, defected from the outer buildings and blocks in the first hours of the riot before D Yard was established. At New Mexico, some inmates welded shut exits to prevent inmates from leaving. But their forces were so poorly organized, and the desire to defect was so great, that people cut new exits until, by the second day, the building leaked like a sieve.

There is also variation in the treatment of hostages, in those riots where they are taken. At Attica, the Muslim inmates formed a security force which protected them from assaults by other inmates or recapture by the state. New Mexico inmates brutalized their hostages, causing permanent psychological damage in some of them. At West Virginia, inmates kept the hostages well fed, released those hostages requiring medical treatment, and allowed them to communicate with their families. At Joliet, black inmates held both guards and white inmates as hostages; except for one guard roughed up in the take-over, neither group was seriously harmed.

The pre-existing racial or ethnic sentiments may become important. At Jackson, there was little racial conflict; at Ionia, numerically superior blacks attacked some whites, who banded together for self-protection; at New Mexico, fear of racial assault caused all blacks to escape as a group. At Moundsville, there was some racial tension at the beginning of the riot, but it quickly dissipated.

The prison's layout and condition may also be important for the state of siege. At New Mexico, because of the telephone pole–style layout, there was no open area, such as an exercise yard, under the inmates' control. The gymnasium and mess hall, where inmates might have gathered, were unusable due to fire and smoke. The resulting dispersion of inmates throughout the prison further reduced the already slim chance that inmate unity would emerge in the course of the riot. In contrast, as occupants of D Yard, the Attica inmates were in constant contact with each other and a sense of common fate did emerge, though time, failed negotiations, and rain lessened its salience. A prison's layout may also determine whether authorities can observe the activities of inmates. At SPSM (Central) authorities observed, and video-taped, the inmates from cell-block roofs. Inmate violence would have been met with immediate restraint and certain prosecution; for this reason (in part) none occurred. Inmates at Ionia and New Mexico could not be directly observed, allowing for greater predatory violence.

Also important, as already noted, is access to the protective custody unit. The Moundsville and Attica inmates did not control the PC unit, whereas those at New Mexico did. Therein lays some of the explanation for the extraordinary brutality at New Mexico. But the importance of this should not be exaggerated. Only a third of the inmates who died at Santa Fe resided in PC.

Further, rumors were circulating among inmates *before* the riot that the "snitches" were to be attacked; similar rumors did not occur before the disturbances at Moundsville or Attica. At Moundsville, inmates may have been able to break into the PC unit in North Hall in the early stages of the riot, but they didn't try. Apparently, it wasn't a high priority.

Akin to the problem of internal order is the problem of conducting negotiations—who shall negotiate, and for what. Depending on the legacy of the pre-riot stage, there may or may not be people willing and able to negotiate, or a clear idea of what demands to make. In the initial Michigan disturbances, there were no negotiators and no demands. Neither had the inmates in these disturbances taken the hostages which are traditionally assumed to be necessary for bargaining power with the administration. At Northside II, guards were chased and might have been taken hostage; but their capture was not central to the participants' strategy. If there are hostages, then the negotiator must have sufficient control over their custody to be able to bargain effectively with the state. This was achieved by the Attica and West Virginia inmates, but not by those at New Mexico.

An additional variable important to this process is the ease of communication among inmates. Factors such as smoke, darkness, the layout of the prison (as noted above), the danger of assault, the general level of distrust among inmates, and the use of drugs may impede communication among inmates, dull the reactions of the leaders, delay the onset of negotiations, and isolate all inmates from each other and the negotiators from the rest. All these factors worked against the inmates at New Mexico.

Organization established before the riot may carry over into the riot. Obvious examples are the role of the Blackstone Rangers in the Joliet riot and the the Avengers in the West Virginia riot. In both cases, gang leaders kept the riots relatively orderly and restrained the more violent of their number. At Attica, the Black Muslim inmates formed the backbone of the security force, and some played key roles in the leadership. Islamic groups stayed aloof from the Michigan riots. The difference had to do with the increased conservatism of the Muslim movement, both inside and outside prisons, in the intervening decade. By 1981, many prison authorities considered Muslims "model inmates," disinclined to rebellion.

Also during this stage of siege, when inmates are "free" to act as they choose, inmates occupy themselves with a range of activities for recreation and sustenance. At Michigan, inmates looted the store in a more or less orderly fashion and later shared and traded their booty with one another. At West Virginia, inmates cooked for themselves and for each other. Where violence occurs, inmates may play the part of a volunteer medical corps, as happened at Attica, New Mexico, West Virginia, and Ionia. For some inmates, the riot situation is an occasion for predation or retribution, casting others into the role of potential victim. For the latter, the state of siege is a nightmare, as they must defend themselves and their possessions, unprotected by the authority of the state.

## Termination or Recapture

Riots end in three ways. The state may forcibly retake the prison (Attica, Ionia, Northside II); the riot may end through negotiations (Joliet, West Virginia); or the riot may die because inmates are exhausted or simply don't want to riot any further (Northside I, New Mexico).

Although prison authorities invariably have the power to retake a prison held by inmates at any time, they differ in their ability to retake the prison effectively, depending on the danger of loss of life and injury to the assault force and to the inmates and their hostages. Perhaps most important is the ability to maintain discipline among the assault. At one extreme stands Attica, where, according to the official state investigation, the disorganization among the assault team resulted in unnecessary shooting and deaths of numerous hostages and inmates. At Michigan Reformatory, the assault force was much better organized, although they did not have to be concerned about the lives of hostages.

The problem with discussing negotiation is that it often has different meanings for the inmates and the state. When inmates want to negotiate, they believe that they have put themselves in a position to bargain with the state. They may have acquired hostages as "chips;" they want to trade these chips for publicity, amnesty, or improved conditions, in a mixture that varies from riot to riot. Sometimes they are willing to settle for a news conference; hostages were traded away for such coin at West Virginia. At Attica, much more was desired, including federal intervention and "transportation" to a "non-imperialist" country. (In 1987 riots at two federal penitentiaries, Cuban detainees demanded *not* to be transported to a "non-imperialist" country.)

The state may or may not accept that this is what negotiation is. It may take the view that "the strategy of negotiations in hostage situations is a strategy of stalling for time." In this scenario, the state has no intention of bargaining seriously with its opponent; it merely wants to stall while collecting intelligence and optimizing its military position, and to "cool out" and tire the opponent. In Austria this is called "the salami game"—" 'promise him everything, but give him nothing.' "[4] Negotiations at New Mexico had some salami character to them. Hostages were released in return for access to the media; meanwhile, time was bought while the riot succumbed to massive defection.

Joliet, Attica, and West Virginia were cases of genuine negotiation. Attica shows that serious negotiation about serious matters must be undertaken seriously or not at all. Joliet shows that it is possible to bargain with criminal gangs, but most readers will not be persuaded that such bargains are good. Negotiations at West Virginia succeeded in ending the disturbance and freeing the hostages unharmed, although it is unclear if anything was actually solved (other than the end of the riot itself). There are a number of factors that make such agreements more likely.

## SCOPE OF DEMANDS

At first glance, it might seem that the broader the scope of the inmates' demands, the less chance of attaining a negotiated settlement. Our data do not support this idea. Inmates and authorities are usually able to agree, at least "in principle," on the big demand of prison reform, if that means improved facilities and services. This was the case at Attica and West Virginia.

Authorities are most reluctant to agree to demands that legitimate the rebellion itself. Examples include "amnesty" and the firing of a certain prison official. Both inherently imply a broadening of the scope of permissible behavior for inmates, and a corresponding diminution of the scope of the authority of prison officials. At Attica, authorities refused to grant the inmate demands to fire Mancusi and for amnesty, even though this was precisely what was to happen. (At West Virginia, a pledge of "no retaliation" was made, but this was never intended to mean full amnesty.)

## BARGAINING GROUP AND SECRECY.

The general inmate population may be more or less informed of the ongoing negotiations, be participants in them, and have an opportunity to ratify them. At Attica, bargaining occurred on the yard in open view of all the inmates and required a voice vote to ratify an agreement; at West Virginia, two inmates conducted the negotiations over the phone and in an enclosed room, but the negotiations were supervised by a larger inmate committee and closely followed by the rest of the inmates. At New Mexico, a small group of inmates negotiated with the administration, but were detached from the central activities of the riot.

Some of the difficulty in reaching a settlement at Attica was probably due to the openness of the negotiations. Inmates shouted down proposals as they were put forward, and did not have a chance to consider a package of concessions as a totality. Moderates who favored a compromise risked being branded as traitors. This does not necessarily mean that open negotiations are impossible, but it does mean that once they are begun serious consideration must be given to conducting them in such a way as to maintain or win the trust of the inmate body. At Attica, the inmates were generally left to stew and wonder on D Yard for hours between "sessions," saving up their frustrations and anger to be shouted out at a pre-packaged set of proposals.

At New Mexico, inmates were suspicious of the negotiating group to begin with, and the private negotiations did nothing to allay their fears that the negotiating team was engaging in treachery and would sell them out. At West Virginia, the negotiating group had the advantage of greater legitimacy among the inmates, and the negotiations in private did lead to a settlement.

## ORGANIZATION AND STRATEGY OF THE STATE

The chances for successful resolution depend on the skill and organization of the state. Oswald's vacillation, personal despondency, and failure to define the role for the observers all contributed to the breakdown of the negotiations. Governor Moore established his negotiating strategy during the first hours of the disturbance and was able to coordinate efforts to ensure its success. Of equal importance were the skill and intelligence of the four prison employee negotiators, though their selection occurred on the spot. Two of the negotiators were picked by the inmates and one joined the team due to a chance family connection. New Mexico demonstrates that the "lessons of history" cannot be mechanically applied. Authorities let the riot burn itself out because they feared an assault would produce another Attica. Meanwhile, guards were tortured and inmates were killed.

# 10

# Causes and Effects of Prison Riots

## A Theory of Prison Riot Causation

The commission that investigated the Attica riot declared that "Attica is every prison; and every prison is Attica." It is indeed true that many of the sources of tension that existed at Attica (perceived racism, poor conditions, e.g.) exist in many, if not most, other American prisons. However, if the commission's declaration is taken to mean that riots like the one which took place at Attica in 1971 can be taken as impending at all times at all other prisons, the statement was false then and is false now. It is neither true that a riot can break out in any prison, nor that a serious riot can take place at any time, nor that riots which do take place must resemble that at Attica, that at New Mexico, or any other model.

Several years ago we suspected that there was probably not much hope that riots could be predicted. We suspected that a riot could be sparked by a random event at pretty much any maximum security prison, at pretty much any time. We were prepared to settle for explaining variation in the type of riot which such random events touch off. But we were mistaken. Our data suggest that major riots in recent decades have taken place not in just any old prisons, and not even in any old "bad" prisons, but in prisons with a particular sort of pathology. The key factor has not been organization of the inmates but the disorganization of the state. The riot-prone system is characterized by certain ailments which, on the one hand, sap the ability of the state to contain disturbances and, on the other hand, convince the inmates that the imprisoning conditions are unjust.

## Breakdown in Prisons

Prior to all the riots under study, there was a breakdown in administrative control and operation of the prison. Prison riots are a product of that breakdown and should be thought of as such. Constituent elements of this break-down included scandals; escapes; inconsistent and incoherent rules for inmates and guards; fragmentation, multiplication of levels, and instability within the correctional chain of command; weak administrators, often "outsiders" to the system; conflict between administration and guards, often resulting from strong guards organized in a union or otherwise cohesive and with good bargaining position relative to the state; public dissent among correctional actors; and the disruption of everyday routines for eating, work, and recreation.

One symptom of disorganization we stumbled across by accident: the quality of the annual reports issued by the departments of corrections became far worse in the years immediately leading up to a riot. The reports issued by the New Mexico Department of Corrections in the period 1975–1980 are ragged compared to those issued in the first half of the decade. The shift corresponds to the disorganization within the department that began after Rodriguez's departure. The same thing happened in the Michigan system: a graphically sophisticated annual report was replaced after 1978 by a leaner statistical summary. This was probably due to budget cutbacks.

Of course, we only have detailed information on prisons where there *were* riots, not on those that avoided them, so our comparison is mainly a matter of inference. It is possible that all prison systems, even those without riots, had problems as severe as the ones we have recorded here; but we doubt it. The political tensions at Attica, the role of gangs at Joliet, the chaos in the New Mexico system, the guard rebelliousness in Michigan, and the poverty-driven noncompliance in West Virginia seem to us to be special things, beyond the pressures faced by the average underfunded and overcrowded system.

The effects of this breakdown are twofold. First, the deprivations of imprisonment surpass legitimate bounds. Inmates are not propelled to riot merely because they are deprived of the amenities available outside of prison—for punishment is the purpose of prison—but because the prison violates the standards subscribed to concurrently or previously by the state or by significant groups outside of the prison. Well-managed prisons, with adequate staffing and physical resources, perpetuate a feeling among inmates that the system conforms to reasonable standards of imprisonment. When stability and uniformity are not present, inmates look to other standards to judge their conditions.

At Attica, inmates judged their conditions according to standards advanced by radical groups on the outside, which held that inmates are the victims of a racist, oppressive system and therefore deserve a standard of living far above the existing one. Inmates at New Mexico, Michigan, and West Virginia turned to the courts and were able to demonstrate that their facilities fell below the standards set forth by the Constitution as currently interpreted by the courts.

Perhaps most important, where administrators and guards are powerful, unified, and competent, the conditions of imprisonment themselves seem more legitimate; the captors are seen as authoritative rather than merely powerful. On the other hand, where various actors in the prison structure are, or view each other as, fools, incompetents, or rascals, the appearance of legitimacy and of competence (and the two always go together) dissipates. Albert Salomon has pointed out the importance in the preparation of great revolutions of scandals destroying the people's faith in their rulers, and Peter Berger's comment on this is relevant here: "Long before social systems are brought down in violence, they are deprived of their ideological sustenance by contempt."[1] The prison is not rehabilitative, say inmates; it is not constitutional; it is not even rational.

## Vulnerability and Preparation

The second effect of a generalized systemic breakdown is the erosion of the security system. Poorly organized prisons are prone to appalling lapses in security, both in the indiscipline or inadequacies of the guard force and in the failures of the physical structure. This is the other necessary element of a pre-riot situation. In addition to the perception of their privation as illegitimate, the inmates must also perceive the system as physically vulnerable, and it must *be* vulnerable.

As security erodes, the acts of resistance we call "preparation" are more and more apt to succeed. Resistance snowballs; plans for a riot are widely discussed; they become realistic.

Erosion of security not only makes it more likely that inmates will initiate a disturbance; it makes it more likely that the disturbance will mushroom into a full-scale riot. Its spread to the rest of the institution is not inevitable, but depends on the organization and responsiveness of the guard force and on the adequacy of the architectural and human factors of security. Locked and maintained security grills or a quickly mobilized show of force can prevent a riot's spread and shorten its duration. Although the prison may still have experienced a "riot," the magnitude of the disturbance will put it in a different class from the disturbances we have studied. Recent riots at Iowa State Penitentiary and South Carolina's Kirkland Correctional Institution began the same way the New Mexico riot had begun; the former was crushed in two hours and the latter in four, in each case by practiced action of a riot control team.[2]

Prison administrators who want, above all, not to have the name of their facility known as we know of Attica and New Mexico may think on this: in each case, the riot could have been confined to a single housing unit. At Attica, steel gates broke and there were no radios; at New Mexico, guards left the doors open and "unbreakable" glass wasn't. Therein was the difference. Such failings arise in the context of systemic crisis we describe above.

A prison whose deprivations are considered no longer legitimate by prisoners can maintain stability through a well-maintained, disciplined security system. A security system which breaks down may not lead to a riot if the deprivations do not fall below what inmates believe is fair. But the two failings are likely to occur in tandem. First, they can share a common cause in administrative breakdown. Furthermore, they reinforce each other. A failure in security erodes the legitimacy of the deprivations and may make the conditions of life worse, as it did at New Mexico. Inmates preyed on each other, making the war of all against all intolerable for everyone, and certainly far worse than what it had been under Rodriguez. On the other hand, disgruntled inmates put a greater strain on the security system. For example, they can make the guards' lives miserable, inducing them to transfer (as at Attica), quit (as at New Mexico), or rebel (as at Jackson).

The case of Joliet is a partial exception to the particular scheme outlined above, but an instructive one. Joliet was not an offensive riot, sparked by the failure of the facility to keep promises made from above. It was a defensive, conservative riot, organized explicitly for the purpose of maintaining the status quo. At Joliet, it was the state that was trying to upset the previously bargained order, and the schism was between the gangs, as joint operators of the facility under the old order, and the new administration, which was no longer willing to permit that arrangement.

One advantage of the approach we outline is that it accounts for the Michigan riot wave even though the first rebellion was initiated by the guard force at SPSM. What is most striking is how similar the spiral of preparation among the SPSM guards was to the pre-riot activities of inmates in prisons like Attica and PNM. This suggests that it is not necessary to develop a special theory to deal with prison inmates—that they may react much as anyone else—and that insights based on their actions are more widely generalizable.

The question, then, is, When will guards recognize the limits on their control as illegitimate? The factors are the same as with inmates. Are constitutional standards universally accepted in the system? In Michigan they were not. In the original F Block incident, the warden at Marquette and ultimately the governor of the state upheld their position against a federal judge. Warden Mintzes' own subordinates at Jackson opposed his efforts to make the discipline system work. The success of Proposition B not only worsened the lot of inmates, but told guards that voters in the state did not trust the authority of the Department of Corrections. The widely publicized anti-inmate activities of L. Brooks Patterson made him seem a powerful ally of guards. The guards at SPSM became convinced that their situation was illegitimately dangerous, and they became convinced by their own victories that they could change it.

Aside from the validity of the theory we propose, our data also suggest that the Sykesian theory cannot be relied upon.

First, the Sykesian model predicts riots in the events under study when none occurred. The clearest example is the events surrounding the 1979 mass escape at Moundsville. Before the break, inmates "ran" the prison; a crisis (the mass escape) led to a public outcry demanding the tightening up of the prison; and a new regime (Bordenkircher's) was brought in to regain the power which had fallen into the hands of inmates. This fits the Sykes's scenario all but perfectly—but no riot occurred. In fact, the Bordenkircher period was marked by the absence of collective action and escapes.

Second, in all but one of the riots studied, the pre-riot events were not the ones Sykes says must be present if a riot is to happen. The Attica rebellion occurred in a period of liberalization, or at least attempted liberalization, of New York's prisons, not a crackdown. The precipitating events at Marquette were the riots at Jackson and Ionia and a peaceful strike against cutbacks in food portions. The latter had a unifying effect, and there is no evidence of a dethroning of a previously stable inmate leadership. Neither in our interviews at PNM nor in those conducted by the state Attorney General's Office did we find any evidence that inmate leaders had kept order in the prison in the past, or that they had been recently supplanted.

Third, the exception, Joliet, did follow a crackdown to regain control of the prison. But the riot's leaders were not young punks taking advantage of a power vacuum. They were the established gang members, whose privileges had been threatened.

## Center and Periphery

We can take the analysis a step further and ask what brought about administrative breakdown in the historic period under consideration. Again, there were two important factors: the imposition of ameliorative standards from the outside, and fiscal pressures making these standards difficult or impossible to meet.

Central to the period of U.S. history under consideration was the effort by "center" elites to incorporate and integrate excluded groups into the mainstream of American life. These peripheral groups included blacks, the aged and disabled, the poor, and (for some) prisoners. With regard to prisoners, it was believed that their living conditions should be improved, their constitutional rights should be expanded, and they should be accorded respect and dignity. One expression of the movement toward incorporation was the emphasis on rehabilitation in the 1950s and early 1960s. In the 1970s, a citizenship model became the dominant mode of incorporationist thought.

Partly as a result of the new social programs called into being on incorporationist principles, and partly because of independent economic problems, many states faced a fiscal crisis. Severe fiscal pressure forced legislatures to cut back rather than increase the funds that incorporationist strategy required. This made it impossible, for example, to build new prisons to relieve unconstitutional overcrowding or renovate old ones. Adding to these pressures, the incorporationist approach sought to empower local communities; some of these communities, such as those in and around Detroit, blocked the construction of new prisons in or near them.

As a consequence, the prison systems at Attica, Michigan, New Mexico, and Moundsville were suffering from a form of internal conflict in which the superior and more remote actors promoted constitutionalist prison reform while their supposed subordinates developed a will of their own and frustrated those policies. Even where subordinates were not willfully insubordinate, fiscal difficulties made these standards difficult, if not impossible, to meet.

These schisms were most acute when "pro-inmate" forces won the battle above but not below; when courts ordered reform, but the state did not implement it; or when department heads or wardens desired reform but their subordinates successfully resisted it.

Fiscal pressure is relative to the living standards enforced by the federal courts and to the number of inmates who must be housed. The worst possible case is one in which revenues decline, courts impose new, higher standards, and changes in the criminal law, enforcement patterns, and/or the crime rate cause more people to be sent to prison and/or to stay there longer—all simultaneously. This conjuncture of events approximates the situation in Michigan in 1981, New Mexico in 1980, and West Virginia in 1985.

In sum, conditions in pathological prison systems in this period were not necessarily worse than they were in earlier decades; but these conditions were declared to be *unconstitutionally* bad. The state was always in court, continually dipping below the constitutional line, continually being ordered back by a judge. The limit on prison capacity became not what the prison was designed for but what the most recent judge failed to forbid. There was no slack. Continually deviant, prisons were, to say the least, hard pressed to establish legitimacy.

## Riot "Success"

Except in unusual cases, inmates must expect that the return to control by authorities will mean, at least in the short run, a return to much worse conditions of life than before the rebellion: a lockdown, angry guards, less freedom, damaged facilities, lost and destroyed personal property, and possible administrative or criminal prosecutions and penalties.* Whether there are long-term improvements is another matter.

A riot can be said to have failed if these penalties are severe and benefits are few, and to have succeeded if penalties are mild and benefits are great. (Of course, "success" means something quite different to those inmates for whom a riot is primarily an opportunity for retribution, predation, or recreation.) In the riots under study, the legal penalties (as opposed to the casualties of the riot and its termination) were mildest at Attica and at New Mexico. In both cases, riot prosecutions mostly collapsed. In part, this was a product of the intensity of the riots. Evidence was destroyed in the course of the riots and recaptures; the state did not have the resources or competence to collect it all, and at Attica the crimes committed by the forces of the state irretrievably contaminated the prosecutions. Moreover, public attention was focused on the cases, particularly on the Attica defendants, and legal talent was attracted. There may also have been less willingness by inmate witnesses to cooperate with the state in New Mexico than in Michigan, after the lesson in

---

*Although inmates at Santa Fe praised the treatment and food they received from the National Guard as better than usual.

what can happen to "snitches." It is easier to get the goods on publicly identified leaders of more orderly riots, such as that at Moundsville.

It is tempting to suppose that riots will be most successful when inmates
are well organized, resourceful, rational, in control of themselves and, because of these attributes, can force officials to agree to their demands. This
would follow logically from the resource mobilization perspective, which em-
phasizes the importance of resources and skill for both the initiation and
success of collective action. However, it does not follow that the greater an
adversary's skill, resources, capacity for rational thought, the stronger its
bargaining position. It is the paradox of the bargaining situation, as Schelling
has pointed out, that the very lack of rationality and organization can give a
party power to compel concessions.[3] The weak can credibly threaten, "Improve our conditions, or we will injure ourselves, our surroundings, and our
blood will be on your hands." Groups more in control of themselves, less
disposed to "irrational" self-injury, do not pose the same threat. Prison officials fear most of all another New Mexico–type bloodbath. The officials in
West Virginia, with "better organized," more "rational" inmates, had less to
fear. Officials will do a lot to avoid a New Mexico; they are less inclined to
respond deeply to a West Virginia.

Of course, there is variation in the extent to which legislators, governors,
and other state officials will and can shoulder the responsibility for a blowout
in their prisons. They vary in their indifference or concern, access to resources, and degrees of freedom as limited by political forces and other encum-
brances and commitments. The very conditions of disorganization which
brought on the riot may make it impossible for prison authorities to bring
reform even if they desire it. Funds may be even tighter after the expenses of
the riot are settled.

Thus, we should not expect a one-to-one correspondence between a riot
type and riot success. While the riots at Attica and New Mexico did effect
profound changes, these same riots, in more conservative or leaner times or
states, may have unleashed a backlash of anti-inmate sentiment. It seems
unlikely that the West Virginia riot would have brought about deeper changes
had there been more New Mexico- or Attica-style killings.

On the other hand, there is some (unmeasurable) chance that additional
death and destruction would have created a consciousness of emergency in the
court system or even in federal agencies, resulting in the allocation of more
funds to the West Virginia system.

Another factor may be as simple as the belief by the public and officials
that riot organizers and hostage-takers should be punished, not rewarded, for
their actions. If identifiable, rational inmates negotiate a riot settlement without getting themselves killed, then prison improvements may be seen as
impermissibly rewarding their riot, even legitimating it. But if the rioters are
"punished" enough, as at Attica, in the course of the recapture, then perhaps
the state can move on to deal with the prison's problems. Or, if the rioters are
seen as a faceless, irrational mass, as at New Mexico, it is mentally easier to

see prison improvements as "solving a problem" rather than caving into inmate demands.

From a different perspective, "effectiveness" can be thought to involve not only concrete concessions (e.g., better prison conditions), but how the activity transforms the participants themselves and those who model their behavior after the participants. Even if one agrees with Piven and Cloward,[4] and with Schelling, that the most successful riots are the least organized, one can still suspect that a "success" like New Mexico teaches no useful lessons. The notion is that this sort of violence and disorder are debasing to the individual and the (inmate) collectivity.[5]

To draw a parallel, extensive research has confirmed Piven's and Cloward's point that the urban riots of the 1960s produced higher welfare payments and other government benefits.[6] Other studies conducted soon after the disturbances found that they contributed to black pride.[7] But little is known about the long term impact of these disturbances on the communities in which they occurred. Since the riots, inner-city black communities have become increasingly isolated from the rest of society and ravaged by high crime rates.[8] The climb in crime rate began abruptly in about 1964—the same year as the first serious black riot in the North. Whether, or in what measure, the riots contributed to this steep rise is not known. Still, even if riots did not have the mixed results of higher welfare benefits and higher crime rates and isolation, they may have been less than an unalloyed blessing. A different strategy of protest (e.g, community organization) might have obtained the same material benefits yet reinforced solidarity both internally and with the rest of society. This was the great achievement of the civil rights movement, though the beneficiaries were primarily middle-class blacks.

On the other hand, groups—prisoners, the urban poor—sometimes have little other recourse. Organization does require resources, not the least of these being traditions, trust, information, and community ties. A group deprived of these is not "free" to take collective action in its best organized forms. Perhaps this is the true paradox of collective action.

## Back to Collective Action Theory: The "Normalization" of Protest

Over the past couple of decades, a consensus has emerged among resource mobilization theorists that protest, rebellions, and even riots are "fundamentally" the same as conventional means of political participation. "Rebellion," Gamson states, "is simply politics by other means."[9] Aminzade refers to "revolutionary violence as an extension or continuation, in a particular form, of everyday, non-violent political activity."[10] In part, this represents a praiseworthy rejection of the assumption, long held by breakdown theorists, that people in motion are irrational.

But, in our view, there *is* something extraordinary about collective violence. There is a fundamental difference between, say, voting and violent rioting: one affirms the political institutions as legitimate, the other challenges them; one follows the established procedures, the other disrupts them; one is non-coercive, the other is coercive; one is lawful, the other can be prosecuted by the state; and one is relatively easy, the other takes daring, courage, or foolhardiness.

Probably it is not so much that the participants hurt, kill, or restrain people—after all, soldiers, police, and hockey players commit physically similar actions—but that to do so they must free themselves from the internal and external restraints which the society is most concerned with and makes the strongest. We believe that these differences are what makes collective violence a phenomenon apart from routine politics. Further, while any society can survive a certain level of collective violence, and this collective violence might even become routinized and "normal," there are limits. Social orders can, and do, crumble when violence becomes the dominant way to carry out politics.

These considerations, in turn, again raise the issue of the relationship between crime and collective action. Resource mobilization theorists emphasize the differences between violence/collective action and ordinary criminal activity. The two phenomena, they argue, spring from different causes and have different consequences.

Few are tempted to confuse ritualized, peaceful, elite-supported protests with individual street crime. But the argument is less persuasive when one considers the more defiant forms of collective action, such as the urban riots of the 1960s or the street demonstrations in Chicago in the summer of 1968. In the first place, crime waves (like rioting) disrupt the social order and may pressure government officials to ameliorate the conditions thought to cause them. Indeed, Alexander Hicks and Duane Swank found that, in the post–World War II period, both the urban rioting *and* increased crime contributed to an increase in welfare benefits. Put in cold statistical form, "a one-unit increase in crime rate (robberies per 100,000) is associated with a 2,000-family increase in AFDC rolls."[11]

Further, both crime (by definition) and defiant collective action (in varying degrees) violates the constraints imposed by authorities and convention. And for this reason, like crime, the more radical forms of defiance require a rationalizing framework that "neutralizes" the laws and moral constraints which govern everyday life.

Finally, civil disorders may, themselves, contribute to crime. It may be that the rationalizing frameworks for political defiance are sometimes later put in the service of crime. For example, we can speculate that the turmoil and political disobedience of the 1960s, and their rationalizing frameworks, contributed to the lawlessness of the next decade. We know as a fact that contemporaneous with this period of political defiance was a sharp increase in violent crime in the inner city and tax fraud in the suburbs.[12] Although we know of no direct evidence to test the hypothesis, it may well be that this increased lawlessness was (in part) a product of a spiraling erosion of generalized obedience to authority. Americans in the the 1970s, compared to their

1950s counterparts, found it easier to break the law, in part because of the political turmoil of the intervening decade.

We hasten to add, however, we are not suggesting that all forms of collective action inevitably "breed crime." For example, as moral leader of the civil rights movement, Martin Luther King was at pains to point out the ethical basis of breaking unjust laws, and that his defiance was meant to affirm, not deny, his duty as a citizen. But this moral reconstruction is more difficult to establish in riots and other sorts of highly disorderly collective action, however "effective" they are in the short run. This makes the presence of social movement ideology and organization critical factors, to the extent that they oppose nihilistic and individualistic justifications of violence and offer an explicitly moral basis of conduct.

## Policy Conclusions

This work has thus far presented a set of factual conclusions about what prison riots are like. More tentative are the conclusions we offer about how best to run prisons. This is because any policy recommendation, made by anybody, having to do with prisons rests on some set of evaluative preferences, and on some other set of empirical beliefs, having to do with crime, criminals, prisons, and the state. Sociology can boast of a reigning consensus on neither score. Informed judgments, though, are preferable to the misinformed type.

If one accepts our thesis that the cause of prison riots is the disorganization of the state, then it follows that maintaining a strong, coherent prison administration is the crucial ingredient in avoiding disturbances. New Mexico and the other prison systems under study "blew," not because they chose the wrong style of management, but because their efforts were so thoroughly disorganized and incoherent. In short, good administration is the key. This may be an obvious point, but if so it has been missed by other students of prison riots, such as Sykes.

The generalizability and usefulness of this finding, however, require some qualifying notes. First, maintaining a "coherent prison administration" is not a trivially simple task. Prisons are impinged upon by the political upheavals of the outside world. If the laws and the government enjoy broad social support outside the walls; if state finances remain sound; if the economy is healthy, racial discrimination is curbed, and crime cannot be convincingly portrayed as the last resort of the unemployed and outcast; then the task of prison administration is eased. If these assumptions fail, so, to that measure, will the task of maintaining a coherent prison system be made more difficult. On the other hand, even in the worst of times, good administration can overcome great difficulties.

It must be stressed that "good administration" means much more here than military discipline. It also refers to the provision of programming, work, cell space, and the amenities of life, to a reasonably legitimate standard. Any administrator who takes our finding as warrant for the belief that firm enough discipline in a given prison can prevent a riot, regardless of how flagrantly unconstitutional the conditions are, is taking a chance. Of course, the resources of the state can limit rebellion. But it is equally true that offenses by the state promote it.

A related concern is the relationship between inmate organization, inmate freedom, and collective violence under existing and possible administrative regimes. Many in the correctional system believe that when inmates' rights are expanded, violence and riot ensue. Is this indeed the case? In principle, this question is somewhat independent of the related, evaluative question of whether inmates' rights *ought* to be expanded. A committed liberal may believe that inmates' rights ought to be expanded *even though* there is a greater danger of riot. Conversely, a correctional conservative might believe that inmates' rights should be kept to a minimum, even if this makes riots more likely, in order to fulfill the penal system's functions of deterrence and retribution.

Still, there is a problem in reducing the question to "pure" investigation: there is no such thing as the "pure" increase in rights which holds all other factors constant and enables the investigator to reach an easy conclusion. "Rights" are composed of many dimensions: their formulation by publics and interest groups, their enactment by legislative bodies, their recognition by courts, their implementation by administrators, their respect by guards, the allocation of funds for their enforcement, and the context in which they are exercised. Liberal reformers want all of these; traditionalists want none of these; but what prison systems usually display is some of these, the quantity varying for different rights.

The traditionalist can make a plausible case blaming liberal court decisions and legislation for prison riots. Rights give inmates something to demand and take away from the state instruments of and efficiency in control. This case works best if the traditionalist is allowed to treat other factors of the system, such as warden attitude and funding levels, as constants. Then even the liberal can echo: "When courts say that prisoners have rights, and the state continues to deny them, the likelihood of riot increases."

The problem is that it does not necessarily make any sense to put the liberalization of inmate rights in a causal model as if it were something that could be *varied at will.* These court decisions did not come out of nowhere. They came out of a period of formalization and clarification of constitutional liberties which benefited the great majority of Americans. No matter how much a judge dislikes prison inmates, it is not as easy today as it was before to ignore the inmates' claims to protection under the Bill of Rights. And how many of us would prefer to live in a society where it would be easier for the state to ignore the Bill of Rights?

Some of us would. Recently some black parents in Detroit demonstrated with signs saying "ACLU Get Out" (of the schools). The ACLU had intervened to enjoin searches of students' lockers for drugs. The parents in question took the position that their children's rights to be protected from unreasonable search and seizure were of little value compared to the need to apprehend drug users and traffickers. Other people, using a similar balancing test, believe that constitutional rights ought to stop at the prison gate. It is possible that this may become the majority position; the public consensuses regarding inmate rights are historically unstable. Whether the courts would follow such a consensus is another question.

The strain between promulgated rights and practice produces conflict. Liberals want to reduce that strain by bringing practice in line with the promise. They believe that societies that want to have the luxury of imprisoning people must pay the price of adequate cell size, programming, and competent and humane supervision; there's no shortcut, no free lunch. Systems which can't afford to house their present population of inmates constitutionally must let some of them go; they can't have cheaper, half-constitutional prisons any more than they could have shorter, half-constitutional trials. Many states have done just this. Not only Michigan, but Arizona, Connecticut, Florida, Iowa, New Jersey, South Carolina, and Washington have established procedures for releasing inmates when their prisons are above capacity.[13]

Traditionalists see incarceration, and not inmates' rights, as the overriding imperative. Their solution is to trim rights, not because they are necessarily anti-inmate, but that they value the other goals of imprisonment more.

There are a host of rights to be bargained over, including "rights" to medical care, conjugal visitation, rehabilitation, one prisoner per cell, nutritious food, and so on. There is, though, one right that is particularly important, because this right more than others directly bears on the stability of the prison. This is the "right" to form and join organizations. In 1976, the Supreme Court ruled that prisoners need not be granted the right to organize.[14] They made this decision on the basis of uncontested testimony in the trial court that such organizations would make riots more likely and imperil the security function of the prison. But why should this be so? Is it feared that organizations dedicated to peaceful protest and negotiation would transform themselves into riot organizing centers? Neither at Attica nor in the Michigan system did this happen. The people who want to discuss remedies with the administration or to organize a peaceful work stoppage are usually not the ones who will slug a guard and take the keys. Often they are the ones who are most aware of the hazards and costs of riots. None of the riots we studied was the product of actions by prisoner unions or prisoners' rights groups. At least in one case (Northside II), an inmate reform organization tried to prevent the disturbance.

Furthermore, the prohibition of such organizations does not seem to prevent riots where the conditions of breakdown and deprivation are such as to summon them forth. To repeat our earlier conclusion, it is the disorganization of the state, not the organization of inmates, that is crucial. Tolerated organizations of other types—such as at Joliet and Moundsville—or mere ad hoc collections of inmates take the role of riot organizers.

Still, it might be that prisoner organization can promote unity and show inmates that they can trust each other and overwhelm the guard force. There is some evidence for this. Through organization and common struggle, inmates at Attica, Marquette, and West Virginia had become more united before each disturbance. However, disunity among inmates is no guarantee against a riot. Jackson, Ionia, and New Mexico prove this. Organization has more to do with how a riot will be made than if it will be made. Riots with organization are not necessarily worse than riots without organization. Who would prefer New Mexico to West Virginia or Marquette?

Joliet might be seen as strong evidence that inmate organization increases the chances of riots and violence. Prior to the 1975 disturbance, criminal gangs were recognized as religious and political representatives of inmates and given free rein to intimidate and exploit other inmates. Violence came when the administration tried to curtail their power. But, it would seem, competent administrators with adequate resources should be able to distinguish and prohibit criminal enterprises.

This point is further illuminated by the experience of the Washington State Penitentiary at Walla Walla, site of an experiment in inmate power from 1970 to 1974. An elected Resident Governing Council (RGC) was established which had the right to call news conferences and campaign for reforms over the head of the prison administration. The experiment turned into a disaster, as the prison became violent and bloody for inmates and guards alike.[15]

The multiple causes are not easy to untangle. In addition to the problems inherent in sharing power with inmates, the unwillingness of the guards and superintendent to go along with the plan are also cited, as are the lack of work and programs for inmates, an ill-trained staff, a poor physical plant, and overcrowding.[16] One episode in the decline of the RGC came when the RGC called a work stoppage in 1973 in support of 11 demands for reform. These included the firing of an unpopular physician and reforms in disciplinary hearings. The superintendent locked down the prison, increased the security classification from minimum to maximum of 60 RGC "leaders," and negotiated with the leaders of various inmate "clubs," including (motorcycle) "bikers." After this the warden came to rely on the bikers as unofficial trustees. A violent hostage seizure in 1974 was blamed by the superintendent on elements in the RGC which were trying to regain power, but this was disputed. In any case, the RGC was disbanded forthwith.

Whether any form, or any degree, of "inmate democracy" can ever succeed is a matter of current debate.[17] This issue aside, administrative tolerance of and reliance on violent groups helped nail shut the coffin at Walla Walla. In justifying his reliance on biker groups, the warden claimed that these inmates were ignorant of the meaning of the swastika which they used to decorate themselves from head to foot.[18] Such a claim is not very credible. Certainly prison rules cannot be *more* lenient and tolerant of violent, racist groups than the ones established by constitutional regimes on the outside.

What one believes might come of prison organization depends a lot on who one believes convicts to be. Some scholars argue that they are very different from other people, in heredity, constitution, upbringing, temperament, intelligence, and capacity to act like civilized human beings.[19] If this is fundamentally true, then inmates may be unable to organize peacefully. Perhaps any reform organization, no matter how well supported, must be perverted toward criminal and exploitative purposes.

On the other hand, in the mainstream sociological tradition is the notion that behavior is the product of the situations in which people find themselves. This implies the possibility of rehabilitation and of managed institutional conflict within prisons; all that is necessary is to create the right situation. It does not imply that the situation is easy to define, politically feasible, or cheap to create. Nobody doubts that the influences of temperament and upbringing are resistant to planned change. Nobody knows for certain that the task is impossible or exactly how the degree of change varies with the amount of resources expended.

Some of the inmates we met in the course of our interviews were pretty disturbing people. One retarded youth rattled on and on in a contented monotone about the violence and rapes that had taken place at his institution. Another affable psychopath spun interesting tales about the robbery schemes that had gotten him there—not his fault, one of the victims had died of fright. A third explained matter-of-factly how he had to kill and injure those who "bothered" him. He was easily bothered, too—by loud footsteps, for example. Fortunately, we weren't bothersome, in his view. Another old fellow told exciting stories about his holdups and escapes from prisons in five or six states. We were grateful to this lot for their all-too-revealing confidences, but it was pretty clear to us that these people thought and acted differently from most people most of the time, and in dangerous ways.

But those people were the exceptions. Most of prisoners we talked with carried on normal, rational conversations with us about the prisons, the riots, and life in general. Whatever led them to commit their crimes—greed, passion, drugs—they are not visitors from a different moral universe. They do not argue that crime is good; they accept, at least in words, our understanding that crime is bad. But they also take seriously our understanding that the Constitution should be enforced, that filthy and unhealthy prisons should be corrected, that guards should not be abusive or punishment arbitrary, that court decisions should be obeyed. When we violate these understandings, proffering rationalizations about expense and practicality, they are as indignant and impatient as we expect judges to be with the rationalizations of the criminal. When they break our rules, we punish them. When we break our rules, they punish us.

# Appendix A

# The Context of Breakdown/ Deprivation Theory of Protest

Sociologists have developed two basic explanations of why people riot or revolt. One is that people revolt because conditions are bad. The other is that they revolt because some mechanism of social control has broken down.[1] In explaining prison riots, we have drawn on both.

The position that people revolt when there is tyranny, poverty, and oppression is known in sociological circles as the "deprivation" approach.[2] People are assumed to be orderly, peaceable, and rational by nature. Thus, when they pour into the streets with rocks and sticks in hand they must have a reason: they were "forced" by bad conditions. This view is generally consistent with democratic sympathies, and it is echoed in the works of the philosopher's of the bourgeois and democratic revolutions, such as Jefferson. Marxists are also in this camp.

The other position is that rioting is the work of disoriented or unthinking mobs. Ordinary social life is the product of controls which check people's natural impulse to act aggressively and selfishly. These controls include religion, community ties, and shared ideology. Riots happen when these mechanisms fail to operate as they should. The problem then is not how to meet the mob's just demands, but how to fix the mechanisms. This view was given expression by conservative critics of the French Revolution, such as Burke and LeBon. In sociology, this is known as the "breakdown" approach, and it was the classic sociological line represented by the mainstream of the discipline from Comte through Durkheim to Talcott Parsons and to his student Neil Smelser.[3] Furthermore, there is a tendency (as old as sociology) to look for links between rebellion and other signs of "breakdown" in mechanisms of social control, such as crime and suicide.[4]

Both lines had developed over the years, but starting in the early 1970s, a number of researchers began to consider whether the breakdown theory had any value whatsoever. Charles Tilly believed his inquiry into European history might turn up the evidence for a "decisive refutation of the Durkheimian line."[5] Others objected to the model's premise that participation in social movements is irrational.[6] By decade's end, the breakdown model was pretty much discredited. Writing in 1984, Mark Traugott wondered not whether breakdown theory is valid ("When subjected to empirical test, [breakdown theory's] principal conclusions have been consistently been shown to be at variance with reality"[7]), but whether Durkheim really was a breakdown theorist or if his reputation had been unfairly sullied. If breakdown theory could not be saved, perhaps the founder of modern sociology could.

Meanwhile, researchers began to test whether bad conditions, indeed, breed revolt. An early effort was James Davies' explanation of revolution. Davies developed the notion of the "level of expectations," sort of a shadow standard of living which went up when things improved, but which continued to go up when things got worse.[8] When the gap between the level of expectations and reality got wide enough, people would revolt and make revolutions.

Although the theory seemed plausible, Davies had a hard time proving it. He graphed the economic and social conditions over time in a number of pre-revolutionary societies. Although he claimed the curves fit his theory, there was a great deal of impressionistic guessing as to where the lines went up and where they went down. Further, as computers became increasingly available, many sociologists began to demand that hypotheses be backed up with numbers. If one's theory says that people revolt when times are getting bad, then one develops some measures of "badness of times," such as prices, unemployment, or wages, and tests whether revolts happen when these measures change for the worse. Davies didn't do this, and ended up convincing few.

A political scientist picked up where Davies left off. Like Davies, Ted Gurr believed that men rebel when their hopes are raised for a better life but then find those hopes dashed.[9] But Gurr tested his version with state-of-the-art statistics and data he had collected on over 100 countries. Computer results in hand, Gurr reported that he had been able to "explain" over two-thirds of the variation of collective violence—powerful stuff by social science standards. Although the publication of *Why Men Rebel* in 1970 was met with a burst of enthusiasm, there was a problem: Gurr could not directly measure many of the variables, including "deprivation." Again, as the dust settled, few ended up convinced. Others followed suit, testing the deprivation model on phenomena ranging from the urban riots of the 1960s to protest movements against school busing and nuclear energy.[10] The weight of the evidence, though, didn't seem to fall on one side or the other.

Contemporaneous with these developments, other approaches began to emerge, all sharing the assumption underlying deprivation theory that people are rational. Some, however, had new slants quite at odds with the original formulation. One line of research began to study movements led or conducted by well-formed organizations like labor unions or "single-issue" organizations. These were groups with constitutions, treasuries, policy statements, and even lobbyists. However, researchers in this "resource mobilization" school had traveled a long way from the study of revolts and riots. The organizations they studied were in business in good years and bad and did not depend on anger, but rather on dues and pledges, to keep them going or bring them success. The resource mobilization theorists began to argue that money and other resources are essentially all that matter in accounting for the course and success of the movements they study. Deprivation didn't matter, because it was present everywhere.[11]

Others tried to save the rationality assumption by methodological individualism. Instead of looking at the interests of "groups," the researcher looks at what is in the interests of the individual. If joining some collective activity, as opposed to just watching, is likely to bring increased benefits which outweigh the costs, then the individual joins. Otherwise, he or she stands on the sidelines. This "economic" analysis of collective action was most notably represented in sociology by Mancur Olson, but similar accounts had existed in political science for 30 years or so.[12]

However, this theory ran into immediate difficulties. Take a protest group of 10,000 members—what are the chances that 10,001 would win its demands *and* that a mere 10,000 would fail? Trivial, of course. Why then doesn't everyone stand on the sideline, since each individual's contribution is unlikely to make or break the effort? This put Olson on the spot: obviously people participate in all kinds of collective action, but the model seemed to predict they wouldn't. Olson had to pull a pretty big rabbit out of the hat, and fast, to save his theory. Its name was "selective incentives." People join organizations and movements when and if the organization or movement can give them something for themselves: interesting meetings, social companionship, a monthly magazine, or group insurance. This fit in nicely with resource mobilization theory: groups with resources can keep and recruit members by providing selective incentives. But it still didn't account very well for most protest unless more ghostly currency, like "self-respect" or "reputation," is thrown into the kitty.

In explaining prison riots, we have tried to fuse deprivation theory with breakdown theory. Given the assumptions underlying the two theories, this may seem like a paradox. It is true that classical breakdown theory rests both on the idea that the impulse to revolt is irrational and on the idea that in normal times the impulse to revolt is kept under control by the system. But the first assumption can be discarded and the second one kept. One may, without contradiction, believe both that the masses are rational and that their impulse to revolt usually does not arise, or is kept in check, thanks to the operation of some social mechanism. When the functioning of the mechanism goes haywire, it might actually make things worse for people; it might make them more conscious of their deprivation; it might provide better opportunities for revolt on account of pre-existing grievances; it might do all three.

Somewhere halfway down the road toward this position, we discovered that two other researchers had also seen the value of combining deprivation and breakdown theory. Frances Piven and Richard Cloward rejected the breakdown theorist's view of protest as an irrational outburst; at the same time, they embraced the idea that grievances, and the freedom to act on them, increased when the mechanisms of social control weakened.[13] They argued that the same breakdown forces that produce protest also cause crime rates to rise, but they cautioned that they did "not consider the issue yet settled."[14] Piven and Cloward supported their argument with a detailed study of four social movements: the movements of unemployed workers and industrial workers in the 1930s, and the civil rights and welfare rights movements of the 1960s.

Finally, breakdown/deprivation theory can be formulated several ways, depending on the social control mechanism postulated, and how it breaks down:

—A liberal deprivation/breakdown theory, in which the system normally keeps people well fed, employed, fulfilled, and happy. When the system fails to do so, through greed on the part of the elite or because of stupid policy choices or because of other "strains" in the social order, the masses revolt.

—A praetorian-military deprivation/breakdown theory, in which the malevolent elite normally stifles the impulse to revolt through constant brainwashing and/or naked force (threatened or real). But if they make a mistake, or even if they don't, the forces of rebellion may yet have a chance, due to their craft, originality, or the power of the human spirit.

—A Marxist deprivation/breakdown theory, in which the (capitalist) system is booby-trapped from the start due to the contradictions inherent in that particular mode of production. In periods of boom, more workers may become employed and enjoy a better standard of living. Then comes the bust. Try as it might to buy, divide, or brainwash the masses, the system is beset by deeper and deeper crises, both increasing the deprivation of the masses and fatally impairing the ability of the system to respond.

—A (neo)conservative deprivation/breakdown theory, in which government transfer payments and other giveaways corrode the work ethic, elevate expectations, and absorb resources needed for economic investment. This kills the goose that lays the golden egg. Productivity and, with it, the standard of living go down; government increasingly cannot afford to meet the demands put on it; and eventually the entire system becomes unworkable, leading to additional strife.

In sum, deprivation theory can be wed with a breakdown theory shorn of its assumption of irrationality. The full value of this marriage is yet to be explored.

# Appendix B

# Immediate Demands*
## (Attica)

### To the people of America

The incident that has erupted here at Attica is not a result of the dastardly bushwacking of the two prisoners Sept. 8, 1971 but of the unmitigated oppression wrought by the racist administration network of the prison, throughout the year.

WE are MEN! We are not beasts and do not intend to be beaten or driven as such. The entire prison populace has set forth to change forever the ruthless brutalization and disregard for the lives of the prisoners here and throughout the United States. What has happened here is but the sound before the fury of those who are oppressed.

We will not compromise on any terms except those that are agreeable to us. We call upon all the conscientious citizens of America to assist us in putting an end to this situation that threatens the lives of not only us, but each and everyone of us as well.

We have set forth demands that will bring closer to reality the demise of these prisons institutions that serve no useful purpose to the People of America, but to those who would enslave and exploit the people of America.

OUR DEMANDS ARE SUCH:
  1. We want Complete Amnesty. Meaning freedom for all and from all physical, mental and legal reprisals.

*This appendix is drawn from two versions of the "Immediate Demands," one presented by the McKay Commission and the other by Tom Wicker. The numbered demands are from McKay, which presented them verbatim. McKay omitted the introductory paragraphs, the last two sentences of demand 5, and the signature. These are from Wicker, who cleaned up the grammar and spelling.

2. We want now speedy and safe transportation out of confinement, to a Non-Imperialistic country.

3. We demand that Fed. Government intervine, so that we will be under direct Fed. Jurisdiction.

4. We demand the reconstruction of Attica Prison to be done by Inmates and/or inmates supervision.

5. We urgently demand immediate negotiation thru Wm. M. Kunstler, Attorney at Law—588 Ninth Ave., New York City, Assemblyman Arthur O. Eve, of Buffalo, New York. The Solidarity Prison Committee, Minister Farrekhan of M.S. Palante, the Young Lords Party Paper, the Black Panther Party. [Clarence Jones, of Amster News.] Tom Wicker, of the New York Times, Richard Roth from the Courier Express, The Fortune Society, Dave Anderson of the Urban League of Rochester, New York, Blond Eva-Bond Nicap., and Jim Ingram of Democratic Chronicle of Detroit, Mic. We guarantee the safe passage of all people to and from this institution. We invite *all the people* to come here and witness this degradation, so that they can better know how to bring this degradation to an end.

6. We intensely demand that all Communication will be conducted in "OUR" Doman "GUARANTEE ING SAFE TRANSPORTATION TO AND FROM."

## THE INMATES OF ATTICA PRISON

# Appendix C

# Practical Proposals
# (Attica)

## Practical Proposals

1. Apply the New York State minimum wage law to all state institutions. STOP SLAVE LABOR.

2. Allow all New York State prisoners to be politically active, without intimidation of reprisals.

3. Give us true religious freedom.

4. End all censorship of newspapers, magazines, letters and other publications coming from the publisher.

5. Allow all inmates, at their own expense, to communicate with anyone they please.

6. When an inmate reaches conditional release date, give him a full release without parole.

7. Cease administrative resentencing of inmates returned for parole violations.

8. Institute realistic rehabilitation programs for all inmates according to their offense and personal needs.

9. Educate all correctional officers to the needs of the inmates, i.e., understanding rather than punishment.

10. Give us a healthy diet, stop feeding us so much pork, and give us some fresh fruit daily.

11. Modernize the inmate education system.

12. Give us a doctor that will examine and treat all inmates that request treatment.

13. Have an institutional delegation comprised of one inmate from each company authorized to speak to the institution administration concerning grievances (QUARTERLY).

14. Give us less cell time and more recreation with better recreational equipment and facilities.

15. Remove inside walls, making one open yard, and no more segregation or punishment.

# Appendix D

# Proposals Collected Friday Night (Attica)

1. Provide adequate food and water and shelter for this group.
2. Replace Superintendent Mancusi immediately.
3. Grant complete administrative and legal amnesty to all persons associated with this matter.
4. Place this institution under federal jurisdiction.
5. Apply the New York State minimum wage law to all work done by inmates. STOP SLAVE LABOR.
6. Allow all New York State prisoners to be politically active, without intimidation or reprisal.
7. Allow true religious freedom.
8. End all censorship of newspaper, magazines, letters, and other publications from publishers.
9. Allow all inmates on their own to communicate with anyone they please.
10. When an inmate reaches conditional release, give him a full release without parole.
11. Institute realistic, effective rehabilitation programs for all inmates according to their offense and personal needs.
12. Modernize the education system.
13. Provide a narcotics treatment program that is effective.
14. Provide adequate legal assistance to all inmates requesting it.
15. Provide a healthy diet; reduce the number of pork dishes; serve fresh fruit daily.
16. Reduce cell time, increase recreation time, and provide better recreation facilities and equipment.
17. Provide adequate medical treatment for every inmate, engage either a Spanish-speaking doctor or interpreters who will accompany Spanish-speaking inmates to medical interviews.
18. Provide a complete Spanish library.

19. Educate all correction officers in the needs of inmates.

20. Institute a program for the employment of significant number of black and Spanish-speaking officers.

21. Establish an inmate grievance delegation comprised of one elected inmate from each company which is authorized to speak to the administration concerning grievances, and develop other procedures for community control of the institution.

22. Conduct a grand-jury investigation of the expropriation of inmate funds and the use of profits from the metal and other shops.

23. Cease administrative resentencing of inmates returned for parole violation.

24. Conduct Menechino hearings in a fair manner.

25. Permit other inmates in C block and the box to join this group.

26. Arrange flights out of this country to nonimperialist nations for those inmates desiring to leave this country.

27. Remove inside walls, making one open yard and no more segregation or punishment.

28. Expansion of work-release program.

29. End approved lists for visiting and correspondence.

30. Remove screens in visitation rooms as soon as possible.

31. Institute parole violation changes—revocation of parole shall not be for vehicle and traffic violation.

32. Due process hearing for all disciplinary proceedings with 30-day maximum.

33. Access to facility for outside dentists and doctors at inmates' expense.

# Appendix E

# The James Letter
# (Attica)

I have been asked by Messrs. Clarence Jones, Tom Wicker and Julian Tepper, representing the Committee of Observers at Attica Correctional Facility, to express my views as to the possible prosecutions that might arise from recent events at the Facility.

First, I deem it to be my duty as a prosecuting attorney to prosecute without fear or favor ALL substantial crimes committed within this county, if sufficient evidence exists to warrant prosecution.

Second, in prosecuting any crime, I do and would endeavor to prosecute fully and impartially and for the sole purpose of attempting to see that justice is done.

Third, under the circumstances of the present situation at Attica, I deem it to be my obligation to prosecute only when in my judgment there is substantial evidence to link a specific individual with the commission of a specific crime.

Fourth, in this particular instance at Attica, I am unalterably opposed to the commencement of indiscriminate mass prosecutions of any and all persons who may have been present, and to prosecutions brought solely for the sake of vindictive reprisals.

Fifth, in the prosecution of any crime, in this as in every other situation, I would endeavor to prosecute honorably, fairly and impartially, with full regard for the rights of the defendants.

Finally, as a prosecuting attorney, I regard it as my paramount duty to attempt to assure justice, both in the trial itself, the outcome of the trial, and in the possible sentence.

Louis R. James
Wyoming County District Attorney

# Appendix F

# The 28 Points
# (Attica)

## Proposals Acceptable to Commissioner Oswald

1. Provide adequate food, water, and shelter for all inmates.

2. Inmates shall be permitted to return to their cells or to other suitable accommodations or shelter under their own power. The observers' committee shall monitor the implementation of this operation.

3. Grant complete administrative amnesty to all persons associated with this matter. By administrative amnesty, the state agrees:

   a. Not to take any adverse parole actions, administrative proceedings, physical punishment, or other type of harassment such as holding inmates incommunicado, segregating any inmates, or keeping them in isolation or in 24-hour lockup.

   b. The state will grant legal amnesty in regard to all civil actions which could arise from this matter.

   c. It is agreed that the State of New York and all its departments, division, and subdivisions, including the State Department of Corrections and the Attica Correctional Facility, and its employees and agents shall not file or initiate any criminal complaint or act on complaints in any criminal action of any kind or nature relating to property, property damage, or property-related crimes arising out of the incidents at the Attica Correctional Facility during September 9, 10, 11, 1971.

   d. The District Attorney of Wyoming County, New York, has issued and signed the attached letter as of this date.

4. Establish by October 1, 1971, a permanent ombudsman service for this facility staffed by appropriate persons from the neighboring communities.

5. Recommend the application of the New York State minimum wage law

standards to all work done by inmates. Every effort will be made to make the records of payments available to inmates.

6. Allow all New York State prisoners to be politically active, without intimidation or reprisal.

7. Allow true religious freedom.

8. End all censorship of newspaper, magazines, and other publications from publishers, unless there is determined by qualified authority which includes the ombudsman that the literature in question presents a clear and present danger to the safety and security of the institution. Institution spot censoring only of letters.

9. Allow all inmates at their own expense, to communicate with anyone they please.

10. Institute realistic, effective rehabilitation programs for all inmates, according to their offense and personal needs.

11. Modernize the inmate education system, including the establishment of a Latin library.

12. Provide an effective narcotics treatment program for all prisoners requesting such treatment.

13. Provide or allow adequate legal assistance to all inmates requesting it or permit them to use inmate legal assistance of their choice in any proceeding whatsoever. In all such proceedings, inmates shall be entitled to appropriate due process of law.

14. Provide a healthy diet; reduce the number of pork dishes; increase fresh fruit daily.

15. Reduce cell time, increase recreation facilities and equipment, hopefully by November 1, 1971.

16. Provide adequate medical treatment for every inmate; engage either a Spanish-speaking doctor or inmate interpreters who will accompany Spanish-speaking inmates to medical interviews.

17. Institute a program for the recruitment and employment of a significant number of black and Spanish-speaking officers.

18. Establish an inmate grievance commission comprised of one elected inmate from each company which is authorized to speak to the administration concerning grievances, and develop other procedures for inmate participation in the operation and decision-making processes of the institution.

19. Investigate the alleged expropriation of inmate funds and the use of profits from the metal and other shops.

20. The State Commissioner of Correctional Services will recommend that the penal law be changed to cease administrative resentencing of inmates returned for parole violation.

21. Recommend that Menechino hearings be held promptly and fairly.

22. Recommend necessary legislation and more adequate funds to expand work-release program.

23. End approved lists for correspondence and visitors.

24. Remove visitation screens as soon as possible.

25. Paroled inmates shall not be charged with parole violations for moving traffic violations or driving without a license, unconnected with any other crime.

26. Institute a 30-day maximum for segregation arising out of any one offense. Every effort should be geared toward restoring the individual to regular housing as soon as possible, consistent with safety regulations.

27. Permit access to outside dentists and doctors at the inmates' own expense within the institution, where possible, and consistent with scheduling problems, medical diagnosis, and health needs.

28. It is expressly understood that members of the observers' committee will be permitted into the institution on a reasonable basis to determine whether all of the above provisions are being effectively carried out. If questions of adequacy are raised, the matter will be brought to the attention of the Commissioner of Correctional Services for clearance.

# Appendix G

# Sunday Afternoon Ultimatum
# (Attica)

As Commissioner of Correctional Services, I have personally met with you several times in areas under your control for the purposes of ensuring the immediate safety of employee hostages, and the safety of all others concerned during the current difficult situation. As you all know, food, clothing, bedding, and water and medical care have been available to you. You have been able to meet with outside observers of your choice and representatives of the news media. A Federal court order was obtained promptly to guarantee that there would be no administrative reprisals; your representatives have been able to ascertain that no mistreatment of inmates has occurred.

I urgently request you to release the hostages unharmed, now, and to accept the recommendations of the committee of outside observers which recommendations were approved by me, and join with me in restoring order to this institution.

Only after these steps are taken am I willing to meet with a five-member committee chosen by you to discuss any grievances you may have and to create a mechanism by which you can be assured that the recommendations I have agreed to are implemented.

All possible efforts have been made to deal fairly with your problems and grievances to resolve the present situation.

All good faith is embodied in the proposed agreement I signed which is in your hands.

It is in the interest of all concerned that you now respond affirmatively to this request.

# Appendix H

# Monday Morning Ultimatum
## (Attica)

For four days I have been using every resource available to me to settle peacefully the tragic situation here at Attica. We have met with you. We have granted your requests for food, clothing, bedding, and water, for medical aid, for an immediate court order against administrative reprisals. We have worked with the special citizens' committee which you have requested. We have acceded to 28 major demands which you have made and which the citizens' committee has recommended. In spite of these efforts you continue to hold hostages. I am anxious to achieve a peaceful resolution to the situation which now prevails here. I urgently request you to seriously reconsider my earlier appeal that, one, all hostages be released immediately, unharmed, and two, you join with me in restoring order to the facility. I must have your reply to this urgent appeal within the hour. I hope and pray your answer will be in the affirmative.

# Appendix I

# Public Appeal by Observers
# (Attica)

The committee of observers in Attica Prison is now convinced a massacre of prisoners and guards may take place in this institution. For the sake of our common humanity, we call on every person who hears these words to implore the Governor of this state to come to Attica to consult with the observer committee, so we can spend time and not lives in an attempt to resolve the issues before us. Send the following telegram immediately to Gov. Nelson Rockefeller in New York City: "Please go to Attica Prison to meet with the observers committee."

# Appendix J

# Inmate Grievances [Abridged] (West Virginia Penitentiary)

1. ADMINISTRATION—Suspend, transfer, replace J. C. Hedrick [warden] G. Gillespie [deputy warden], D. Eisenhauer [deputy warden], R. Lohr [chief correctional officer], and B. Moore—Their insensitivity and lack of communication cause widespread distrust and frustrations.

2. SEGREGATION—Placement in administration segregation is abused: no programs; handcuffs and shackles for everyone punitive and unwarranted.

3. HOBBIES AND CRAFTS—The only practical outlet—music room—must be permitted in cell so leisure time can be constructively employed.

4. VISITATION—Maximum physical contact with visitors for all visits every day of the week. Anyone should be allowed to visit Family and Friends—It encourages contact with the larger community.

5. PHYSICAL ENVIRONMENT—Cells are too small; allow personal preference as to arrangement of possession.

6. PERSONAL EXPRESSION—Hair and beards; street clothes; adequate laundry equipment and materials to insure clean clothes.

7. FOOD—Money being wasted on food service contract. Adequate food and preparation for all meals. Hot, nourishing meals to all prisoners.

8. MEDICAL CARE—Dr. needs to be present 40 hours each week. Unimpeded access to physician.

9. CORRESPONDENCE AND TELEPHONE—Assign two prisoners to mailroom to guarantee mail is not read, delayed or monitored without due process.

10. ACCESS TO COURTS—Pro se petitioners are not receiving fair hearing of legitimate complaints. Need trained personnel to help draft reasonable legal documents. Assignment of review committee of magistrate to scrutinize complaints.

11. RECREATION PACKAGES—Reasonable packages on a regular basis.

12. PAROLE—No program provided to equip prisoners for life after release. No reasonable criteria provided to advance prisoner's release.

13. INMATE BENEFIT FUND—Public accounting of funds received by inmate benefit fund. Co-op exchange needs to be opened daily.

14. RECREATION—Access to the exercise yard in all weather conditions; need adequate equipment.

15. HEATING AND COOLING—Reasonable efforts to provide sufficient warmth to all cells must be provided immediately. Circulation of air needed to safeguard prisoner and guard's health.

# Notes

## Chapter 1

1. A quite similar framework was developed independently by Vernon Fox in "The Enigma of Prison Riots," Paper delivered at the Southern Conference on Corrections, Tallahassee, Florida, February 28, 1986.

2. James C. Davies, "Toward A Theory of Revolution," *American Sociological Review* 27 (February 1962):5–19; Ted Robert Gurr, *Why Men Rebel* (Princeton: Princeton University Press, 1970).

3. John D. McCarthy and Mayer N. Zald, "Resource Mobilization and Social Movements," *American Journal of Sociology* 82 (May 1977):1212–41; J. Craig Jenkins, "Resource Mobilization Theory and the Study of Social Movements," in *Annual Review of Sociology,* ed. Alex Inkeles and James Short (Palo Alto: Annual Reviews, 1983), 527–33.

4. Samuel P. Huntington, *Political Order in Changing Societies* (New Haven: Yale University Press, 1968); William Kornhauser, *The Politics of Mass Society* (New York: Free Press, 1959); Neil Smelser, *Theory of Collective Behavior* (New York: Free Press, 1962); Hannah Arendt, *Origins of Totalitarianism* (New York: Harcourt, Brace, and Company, 1951).

5. Norris Johnson, "Collective Behavior as Group-Induced Shift," in *Collective Behavior: A Source Book,* ed. Meredith D. Pugh (St. Paul, MN: West Publishing, 1980); Kurt Lang and Gladys Engel Lang, *Collective Dynamics* (New York: Thomas Y. Crowell, 1961); Ralph S. Turner and Lewis M. Killian, *Collective Behavior,* 3rd ed. (Englewood Cliffs: Prentice-Hall, 1987). Note: some of these works draw on a number of traditions and are not "pure" examples of the collective behavior approach (e.g., the second half of *Collective Behavior*).

6. Gresham Sykes, *The Society of Captives: A Study of a Maximum Security Prison* (Princeton: Princeton University Press, 1958).

7. Mark Colvin, "The 1980 New Mexico Riot," *Social Problems* 29 (1982):449–63.

## Chapter 2

1. Daniel Bell, *The End of Ideology* (New York: Free Press, 1960), 151.

2. James Q. Wilson, *Thinking About Crime,* rev. ed. (New York: Basic Books, 1983), 15.

3. Department of Justice, Bureau of Justice Statistics, *Sourcebook of Criminal Justice Statistics—1984* (Washington, D.C.: Government Printing Office, 1984), 649.

4. The Edna McConnell Clark Foundation, *Overcrowded Time: Why Prisons Are So Crowded and What Can Be Done* (New York: The Edna McConnell Clark Foundation, 1982).

5. More precisely, an "indeterminate sentence" is a prison term with a wide gap between the minimum and the maximum (e.g., one year to life). In effect, this gives the parole board the authority to determine the length of sentence an inmate actually serves.

6. Blake McKelvey, *American Prisons: A History of Good Intentions* (Montclair, NJ: Patterson Smith, 1973), 327.

7. South Carolina Department of Corrections, *Collective Violence in Correctional Institutions: A Search for Causes,* (Columbia, SC: South Carolina Department of Corrections, 1973), Appendix B.

8. Richard A. McGee, *Riots and Disturbances in Correctional Institutions* (Washington, D.C.: American Prison Association, 1953).

9. Austin H. MacCormick, "Behind the Prison Riots," *The Annals of the American Academy of Political and Social Science* 293 (1954):18–19.

10. Observation based on authors' examination of the archives of the State of Michigan.

11. McKelvey, *American Prisons,* 352.

12. American Correctional Association, *Proceedings of the Ninety-Second Annual Congress of Correction of the American Correctional Association* (New York: American Correctional Association, 1962), 352.

13. McKelvey, *American Prisons,* 351; see also Keith Butler, "The Muslims Are No Longer an Unknown Quantity" *Corrections Magazine* 4, no. 2 (June 1978):55.

14. James B. Jacobs, *New Perspectives on Prisons and Imprisonment* (Ithaca: Cornell University Press, 1983), 36.

15. Daniel Bell, *The Cultural Contradictions of Capitalism* (New York: Basic Books, 1976), 232–36.

16. Prior to these rulings, the courts had considered welfare benefits a "privilege," akin to charity. Accordingly, government welfare agencies could provide or withhold welfare payments at their discretion and without judicial scrutiny. Eventually, the courts took the position that welfare benefits are a form of property which, like other forms of property, is protected by the due process clause of the Constitution. Rand E. Rosenblatt, "Legal Entitlement and Welfare Benefits," in *The Politics of Law,* ed. David Kairys (New York: Pantheon Books, 1982), 268–86.

17. Bureau of the Census, *Statistical Abstract of the United States, 1986* (Washington, D.C.: Government Printing Office), 331, 356.

18. Citations to, and discussion of, the cases mentioned can be found in: David Rudovsky, Alvin Bronstein, and Edward Koren, *The Rights of Prisoners,* rev. ed. (Washington, D.C.: American Civil Liberties Union, 1983); and Sheldon Krantz, "Legal Rights of Prisoners," in *Encyclopedia of Crime and Justice,* ed. Sanford H. Kadish (New York: Free Press, 1983), 1192; Alvin J. Bronstein, "Prisoners and Their Endangered Rights," *Prison Journal,* 65, no. 1 (1985):4–5; Stephen Gettinger, " 'Cruel and Unusual' Prisons," *Corrections Magazine,* 3, no. 4 (December 1977):3–10.

19. *Wolff v. McDonnell,* 418 U.S. 539 (1974).

20. National Advisory Commission on Civil Disorders, *Report of the National Advisory Commission on Civil Disorders* (Washington, D.C.: Government Printing Office, 1968).

21. Max Frankel, "Introduction," in Daniel Walker, *Rights in Conflict* (New York: Bantam Books, 1968), vii.

22. Wilson, *Thinking About Crime,* 15.

23. Carolyn R. Block and Richard L. Block, *Patterns of Change in Chicago Homicide: The Twenties, the Sixties, and the Seventies* (Chicago: Illinois Criminal Justice Information Authority, 1980), 2.

24. Frances Fox Piven and Richard A. Cloward, *Regulating the Poor: The Functions of Public Welfare* (New York: Random House, 1971), 226

25. Ibid., 227.

26. Reported in Thomas E. Cronin, Tania Z. Cronin, and Michael E. Milakovich, *U.S. v. Crime in the Streets* (Bloomington: Indiana University Press), 60, 69.

27. James Q. Wilson, "The Urban Unease," *The Public Interest* 12 (Summer 1968):26–27.

28. Cronin and associates provide an excellent history of the controversy over the establishment of LEAA and the crime control issue. Cronin et al., *U.S. v. Crime.*

29. Seymour Martin Lipset and William Schneider, *The Confidence Gap: Business, Labor, and Government in the Public Mind* (New York: Free Press, 1983), 16.

30. Ibid., 48, Table 2.1.

31. Francis A. Allen, *The Decline of the Rehabilitative Ideal* (New Haven: Yale University Press, 1981), 11

32. American Friends Service Committee, *Struggle for Justice: A Report on Crime and Punishment in America* (New York: Hill and Wang, 1971); David F. Greenberg and Drew Humphries, "The Cooptation of Fixed Sentencing Reform," *Crime and Delinquency,* 76, no. 2 (April 1980):206–25.

33. Recent statements of this position include Charles Murray, *Losing Ground: American Social Policy, 1950–1980* (New York: Basic Books, 1984), 168–72; and Ernest van den Haag, *Punishing Criminals: Concerning a Very Old and Painful Question,* (New York: Basic Books, 1975), 184–91.

34. Robert Martison, "What Works?—Questions and Answers About Prison Reform," *The Public Interest,* 35 (Spring 1974):22–54.

35. John Irwin, *Prisons in Turmoil* (Boston: Little Brown, 1980), 162.

36. Gabrielle Tyrnauer, "What Went Wrong at Walla Walla?" *Corrections Magazine* 7, no. 3 (June 1981):37–41; Charles Stastny and Gabrielle Tyrnauer, *Who Rules the Joint? The Changing Political Culture of Maximum-Security Prisons in America* (Lexington, MA: D.C. Heath and Company, 1982).

37. Alan Dershowitz, "Let the Punishment Fit the Crime," *New York Times Magazine,* 28 December 1975, 26.

38. In the early 1960s, the NAACP Legal Defense Fund was alone in its effort to bring about social change through litigation. A decade later, public interest law firms were active in numerous areas, including auto-safety, housing, education, bi-lingual education, welfare, environment, mental health, and prisons. Nathan Glazer, "Toward an Imperial Judiciary?" *The Public Interest* 41 (Fall 1975):104–23.

39. Interview with Jeffrey Haas, a founding member of Peoples Law Office; also "After 15 Years, the Peoples Law Office Still Hangs Tough," *Chicago Lawyer* (November 1984).

40. Jacobs, *New Perspectives,* 38.

41. Data on contributions in the 1980s are not available. The data reported here are from work by Craig Jenkins on the funding of social movement organizations by foundations. We thank Professor Jenkins for making them available to us. The broader project is described in Craig Jenkins, "Foundation Funding of Progressive Movements," in *The Grant-Seekers Guide,* 2nd edition, ed. Jill Shellow (New York: Kampmann and Co., 1985).

42. James B. Jacobs, *Stateville: The Penitentiary in Mass Society* (Chicago: University of Chicago Press, 1977), 28–51.

## Chapter 3

1. New York State Special Commission on Attica (hereafter cited as NYSSCOA), *Attica: The Official Report of the New York State Special Commission on Attica* (New York: Bantam Books, 1972),13–15. The media referred to the investigative group as the "McKay Commission" and the report the "McKay Report," after its chairman (Robert B. McKay), a convention we adopt.

2. A note on sources. We rely most heavily on the McKay Report. We do this not because it was commissioned by the state and is "official;" an uncritical reliance on state sources should be discouraged. Neither do we suggest that the commission had "no viewpoint." It clearly had a liberal viewpoint, critical of harsh penal practices on the one hand but refusing, on the other, to identify with or condone the inmates' rebellion. As William Wilbanks, a member of the commission, said, "I do not believe that a single member of the McKay Commission would suggest that the inmates were 'heroic brothers laying down their lives for human dignity.' " William Wilbanks, review of *Attica—My Story*, by Russell Oswald, *Criminal Law Bulletin* 9, no. 2 (1973):124–39. On the basis of the evidence, we believe that the commission collected and presented its data in good faith, without falsification. The inmates most active in the rebellion, who were locked in segregation at the time of the interviews, and who were awaiting indictment and trial, for the most part declined to be interviewed. Still, there is no comparable source.

Oswald's book, *Attica—My Story* (New York: Doubleday and Company, 1972), is a self-exculpatory work of little value. We rely on it mainly for information about Oswald's own attitudes and beliefs, such as his attribution of the riot to international revolutionary conspiracy. But even this is not necessarily trustworthy, as he did not present this theory in his earlier testimony before the McKay Commission and may have concocted it later on. Any attempt to treat Oswald's book as a trustworthy source has to get over the considerations raised in Wilbanks' review cited above.

Richard X Clark's *The Brothers of Attica*, ed. Leonard Levitt (New York: Links, 1973), is the testimony of an inmate leader. When we take McKay's word over Clark's, it is because the book gives the impression of having been written in a hurry and of having few resources behind it. Certainly, Clark could not have been able to check his recollections with other inmate leaders (still in lockup) while writing it.

Tom Wicker's book, *A Time to Die* (New York: New York Times, 1975), is an engrossing account. Those interested in the dynamics of the Observers' Committee must read it. Most of his description of the riot is taken from McKay or from articles we also cite.

The virtues of Herman Badillo's book, *A Bill of No Rights: Attica and the American Prison System* (New York: Outerbridge and Lazard, 1972), are mainly as a polemic on behalf of prisoners. It contains little information not found elsewhere.

3. NYSSCOA, *Attica*, 22–23.

4. Ibid., 28–29.

5. Ibid., 24–28.

6. Ibid., 126.

7. Ibid., 31–102.

8. Ibid., xii.

9. Ibid., xii.

10. James B. Jacobs, *New Perspectives on Prisons and Imprisonment* (Ithaca: Cornell University Press, 1983), 33–60

11. NYSSCOA, *Attica,* 35.

12. Ibid., 79–82.

13. Robert Harsh, "Inside Attica" (interview), *Christianity and Crisis* 29 May 1972, 130.

14. *Fortune v. McGinnis,* 319 F Supp 901 (S.D. NY 1970).

15. NYSSCOA, *Attica,* 46, 49, 74–75.

16. *Sostre v. Rockefeller,* 312 F Supp 863 (S.D. NY 1970), modified sub nom *Sostre v. McGinnis,* 442 F 2d 178 (2d Cir. 1971).

17. NYSSCOA, *Attica,* 131–32, 137; "State's Corrections Aides Split Anew by Attica Riot: Rehabilitate or Get Tough?" *Buffalo Evening News,* 10 September 1971.

18. Ibid., 137.

19. Ibid., 128–29.

20. Ibid., 129–30.

21. Wicker, *Time to Die,* 237.

22. NYSSCOA, *Attica,* 134–35.

23. Ibid., 139.

24. Ibid., 139, 140.

25. Ibid., 140, 141.

26. Ibid., 145, 146.

27. Ibid., 147; Wicker, *Time to Die,* 10; Clark, *Brothers,* 5.

28. This point is made by Wilbanks, review of Oswald, *Attica—My Story, 136–37.*

29. NYSSCOA, *Attica,* 155–58.

30. Ibid., 155.

31. Clark, *Brothers,* 21–22.

32. NYSSCOA, *Attica,* 157.

33. Ibid., 159.

34. Ibid., 162–63.

35. Ibid., 164–65.

36. Ibid., 159.

37. Ibid., 165.

38. Ibid., 161.

39. Ibid., 160–61.

40. Ibid., 167.

41. Ibid., 172.

42. Ibid., 181.

43. Ibid., 175.

44. Ibid., 170.

45. Ibid., 184.

46. Ibid., 183.

47. Ibid., 178.

48. Ibid., 175.

49. Ibid., 170. We can only speculate on how the riot would have been affected if inmates had had access to the stores of drugs at the hospital and if inmates in punitive segregation had been released into the population. This speculation should be informed, on the one hand, by the experience of the New Mexico riot of 1980 (see ch. 5), in which both occurred, and, on the other hand, by the superior inmate organization at Attica.

50. NYSSCOA, *Attica,* 190.

51. Ibid., 191.

52. Ibid., 195–203.

53. Tony Fitch and Julian Tepper, "No Time to Talk: Hour by Hour at Attica," *Christianity and Crisis,* 18 October 1971, 211.

54. Wicker, *Time to Die,* 53.

55. Clark, *Brothers,* 56–59; Oswald, *Attica,* 20–27.

56. Oswald, *Attica,* 27–28.

57. Wicker, *Time to Die,* 55.

58. NYSSCOA, *Attica,* 238–40.

59. Ibid., 288.

60. Ibid., 200.

61. Ibid., 287.

62. Clark, *Brothers,* 41.

63. NYSSCOA, *Attica,* 299.

64. Ibid., 299–313.

65. Ibid., 318.

66. Ibid., 219.

67. In justifying his visiting the yard to the McKay Commission, Oswald stressed the "iconoclastic" nature of his action in talking with the rebellious inmates, believing that it "defied tradition." NYSSCOA, *Attica,* 219n. This was not strictly true. Negotiation with rioting prisoners was standard practice from the 1920s through the 1950s.

68. NYSSCOA, *Attica,* 220–21.

69. Ibid., 224.

70. Ibid., 221.

71. Ibid., 222, 223.

72. Ibid., 223.

73. Oswald, *Attica,* 93.

74. Ibid., 91.

75. Ibid., 85.

76. NYSSCOA, *Attica,* 223.

77. Ibid., 223.

78. Ibid., 223–25.

79. Ibid., 226

80 Ibid., 227–28

81. Ibid., 230–32. In accounts of the riot, the injunction disappears from the story here. But of course the destruction of the piece of paper on which the injunction was written had no legal effect; the injunction took effect once Oswald had notice that it was signed, and was still in full force three days later, on September 13. It obviously had no practical effect, at least under the circumstances that were later to obtain.

82. Ibid., 233–35.

83. Wicker, *Time to Die,* 40.

84. NYSCCOA, *Attica,* 316–17, 326–28.

85. Ibid., 315.

86. Ibid., 277.

87. Ibid., 320.

88. Oswald, *Attica,* 237; NYSSCOA, *Attica,* 320.

89. NYSSCOA, *Attica,* 280.

90. Ibid., 280.

91. Ibid., 289.

92. Harsh, "Inside Attica," 134.

93. Fitch and Tepper, "No Time to Talk," 214.
94. Wicker, *Time to Die*, 231.
95. NYSSCOA, *Attica*, 287–88.
96. Oswald, *Attica*, 264.
97. NYSSCOA, *Attica*, 286.
98. Oswald, *Attica*, 245.
99. NYSSCOA, *Attica*, 284.
100. Ibid., 200.
101. Ibid., 282.
102. Oswald, *Attica*, 251–52.
103. NYSSCOA, *Attica*, 329.
104. Ibid., 344.
105. This consideration is raised by James Carney, review of *A Time to Die*, by Tom Wicker *Yale Law Journal*, 85, no. 1 (November 1975):150–58.
106. NYSSCOA, *Attica*, 343.
107. Ibid., 371.
108. Ibid., 377–78.
109. Ibid., 355.
110. Ibid., 403 ff.; Malcolm Bell, *The Turkey Shoot* (New York: Grove Press, 1985).
111. Wilbanks, review of Oswald, *Attica—My Story*.
112. NYSSCOA, *Attica*, 426–52; Bell, *Turkey Shoot,* in its entirety.
113. Wicker, *Time to Die*, 309; Bell, *Turkey Shoot,* 364, 370.
114. Bell, *Turkey Shoot*, 364, 370, 389.
115. Susan Sheehan, *A Prison and a Prisoner* (Boston: Houghton Mifflin, 1978).
116. Ibid., 131.
117. Ibid., 131–37, 144–45, 157–58.
118. Wicker, *Time to Die*, 307; NYSSCOA, *Attica*, 466–69.
119. Sheehan, *A Prison*, 157.

## Chapter 4

1. The labor violence of the 1870s and 1930s was less widespread; the Civil War did not involve internal dissent but rather was a conflict between two organized polities. This point is made by Daniel P. Moynihan in *Maximum Feasible Misunderstanding: Community Action in the War on Poverty* (New York: Free Press, 1969), xi.

2. Daniel P. Moynihan, *The Politics of a Guaranteed Income: The Nixon Administration and the Family Assistance Plan* (New York: Vantage Books, 1973), 103.

3. A note on sources. Several months after the riot, the Illinois House of Representatives directed a commission to investigate the riot. Like the McKay Commission, this one took seriously the task of writing a factual report, and it is a key source of our information. State of Illinois Legislative Investigating Commission (hereafter cited as SILIC), *The Joliet Correctional Center Riot of April 22, 1975* (Chicago: State of Illinois Legislative Investigating Commission, 1975).

Another important source is James Jacobs' *Stateville: The Penitentiary in Mass Society*. (Chicago: University of Chicago Press, 1977). Perhaps the best study ever done of an American prison, *Stateville* is based on research conducted between 1972 and 1975, including eight months of participant observation and interviewing.

Further, we obtained the detailed reports of the Citizens Visitation Committee, a Chicago-based prison reform group which visited Joliet prisons monthly from June

1974 to May 1976. The committee was given access to all areas of the prison and was allowed to talk freely with inmates and personnel on duty. We also obtained the files of an attorney who worked with Joliet inmate groups in this period, which included transcripts of interviews with inmates. We also drew on other published material, including documents of the Department of Corrections, histories of Chicago politics in this period, and other government documents. Finally, we conducted interviews of several of the hostages, a Joliet warden from the period under study, and another official who was at the center of the riot.

4. Quoted in Blake McKelvey, *American Prisons: A History of Good Intentions* (Montclair, NJ: Patterson Smith, 1973), 179 ; also Linda Pahl, "Joliet State Prison," *Illinois History* 31 (1978):152–54.

5. Department of Corrections, State of Illinois, *1973–1974 Annual Report, Department of Corrections* (Springfield: Illinois Department of Corrections, 1975), 6; idem, *Statistical Presentation, 1979* (Springfield: Illinois Department of Corrections, 1980), 72.

6. Illinois Department of Corrections, *Illinois Corrections Master Plan, Adult Division* (Springfield: Illinois Department of Corrections, 1977); Citizens Visiting Committee, "Report No.3 on Joliet Correctional Center" (Illinois Prisons and Jails Project, 14 August 1975, Mimeographed); *Hanrahan v. Lane,* "Memorandum of Findings and Conclusions," U.S. District Court of Northern Illinois, Eastern Division, No. 80 C 2982.

7. Citizens Visiting Committee, "CVC Visit to Joliet" (Illinois Prisons and Jails Project, 21 February 1975, Mimeographed).

8. Citizens Visiting Committee, "Report No.2 on Joliet Correctional Complex" (Illinois Prisons and Jails Project, 16 July 1974, Mimeographed).

9. James B. Jacobs, *New Perspectives on Prisons and Imprisonment* (Ithaca: Cornell University Press, 1983), 163.

10. James B. Jacobs, *Stateville,* 146.

11. Ibid., 153

12. SILIC, *Joliet Riot,* 24.

13. Jacobs, *Stateville,* 166, 177; Kevin Krajick, "At Stateville, the Calm Is Tense," *Corrections Magazine* (June 1980):10.

14. Jacobs, *Stateville,* p. 163.

15. Citizens Visiting Committee, "CVC Visit to Joliet" (Illinois Prisons and Jails Project, 18 October 1974, Mimeographed).

16. Citizens Visiting Committee, "CVC Visit to Joliet" (Illinois Prisons and Jails Project, 17 January 1975, Mimeographed).

17. Citizens Visiting Committee, "Memo To Allyn R. Sielaff" (Illinois Prisons and Jails Project, 12 June 1974, Mimeographed); Illinois Department of Corrections, *Master Plan,* 194.

18. Citizens Visiting Committee, "CVC Visit to Joliet' (Illinois Prisons and Jails Project, 21 March 1975, Mimeographed).

19. Illinois Department of Corrections, *Annual Report, 1976* (Springfield: Illinois Department of Corrections, 1977), 11.

20. Jacobs, *Stateville,* 163; SILIC, *Joliet Riot,* 35; Kevin Krajick, "The Menace of the Supergangs," *Corrections Magazine* (June 1980):11; "Assaults, Drug Traffic, and Powerful Gangs Plague a Penitentiary," *Wall Street Journal,* 20 August 1981.

21. Krajick, "Menace," 12.

22. Jacobs, *Stateville,* 152, 153. Although Jacobs was primarily concerned with the Stateville facility of the Joliet-Stateville complex, he mentions both facilities through-

out his monograph. There is no suggestion that the two populations differed in any relevant way.

23. Jacobs, *Stateville,* 150; Krajick, "Menace," 12; U.S. District Court, "Memorandum of Findings," 22.

24. Quoted in Jacobs, *Stateville,* 150.

25. Jacobs, *Stateville,* 157.

26. In its 25-year history up to today, the gang changed its names several times. The "Blackstones" became the "Blackstone Rangers," and then "Blackstone Nation," and finally, after claiming to be a religious group, the "El Rukns." Sources for the history of the Rangers are: Irving Spergel, "Youth Manpower Project: What Happened in Woodlawn," (University of Chicago, School of Social Service Administration 1969, Mimeographed), 52; John R. Fry, *Fire and Blackstone,* (Philadelphia: J.P. Lippincott, 1969); idem, *Locked-Out Americans: A Memoir* (New York: Harper and Row, 1973); John Hall Fish, *Black Power/White Control: The Struggle of the Woodlawn Organization in Chicago* (Princeton: Princeton University Press, 1973); James A. McPherson, "Almighty Black P Stone and What Does that Mean," *Atlantic Monthly* (May 1969); *Science News,* 27 July 1968; Robert A. Levin, "South Side Story," *New Republic,* 1 July 1968, 16.

27. Quoted in Spergel, "Youth Manpower," 242.

28. Fry, *Locked-Out,* 15.

29. Ibid., 80.

30. Fry, *Fire,* 7; Testimony of John R. Fry, Senate Permanent Subcommittee on Investigations of the Committee on Government Operations, *Hearings on Riots, Civil and Criminal Disorders,* 90th Congress, 2d session, Part 10, 1968, 2016; Spergel, "Youth Manpower," 54, 55.

31. Permanent Subcommittee, *Riots,* 2702.

32. Fry, *Fire,* 13.

33. Michael Killian, Connie Fletcher, and F. Richard Ciccone, *Who Runs Chicago?* (New York: St. Martin's Press, 1979), 150.

34. Jerome H. Skolnick, *The Politics of Protest: A Task Force Report Submitted to the National Commission on the Causes and Prevention of Violence* (New York: Simon and Schuster, 1969), 168.

35. Fish, *Black Power,* 121; James F. Short, "Youth, Gangs, and Society: Micro- and Macro-sociological Processes," *The Sociological Quarterly* 15 (Winter 1974):12.

36. Gad J. Bensinger, "Chicago Youth Gangs: A New Old Problem," *Journal of Crime and Justice* 7 (1984):4.

37. Spergel, "Youth Manpower," 165, 166.

38. Virgil W. Peterson, *Report on Chicago Crime for 1968* (Chicago: Chicago Crime Commission, 1969), 27; also "Jeff Fort: 'Criminal Genius' or a Punk?" *Chicago Tribune,* 18 October 1981.

39. Krajick, "Menace," 11; Jacobs, *Stateville,* 143.

40. Jacobs, *Stateville,* 28–51; Gladys A. Erickson, *Warden Ragen of Joliet* (New York: E.P. Dutton, 1957); "Prison Reform Set for February, *Chicago Tribune,* 10 January 1972.

41. Jacobs, *Stateville,* 74–79; Department of Corrections, State of Illinois, *Dimensions in Corrections,* 1, no. 2 (Springfield: Illinois Department of Corrections, 1970), 15. "Prison Reform Set for February," *Chicago Tribune,* 10 January 1972;

42. Jacobs, *Stateville,* 267, n. 35; Jeanette Musengo, "Statement to the Illinois Legislative Investigating Commission" (John Howard Association, 26 February 1982, Mimeographed), 9; authors' interview with John Twomey.

43. Jacobs, *Stateville,* 80.

44. "An Avenue of Communication: Open Letter to the Community: To So-Called Gangs and/or Trouble Makers at Stateville Prison and the Relationship of this Prison to the Community" (Stateville Penitentiary, n.d., Mimeographed..).

45. "Tentative Recommendations to Hon. Peter B. Bensinger, Director of the Department of Corrections, Mr. A.M. Monohan, Asst. Director of Corrections, Hon. John J. Twomey, Warden, and Mr. Terrence E. Bergin, Superintendent of Education, et al., For the Purpose of Establishing a Realistic and Meaningful Constructive Program(s) and Rapport Between the Inmate Body and Institutional Officials" (Internal ABLE document, March, 1972).

46. ABLE existed at Stateville but not Joliet. We describe it here because our current focus is on the administration's response to gangs, and the two prisons were governed by the same administration in this period. The following account of ABLE is based on Jacobs' *Stateville,* 121–22, 169–71, and the files of an attorney for ABLE.

47. "Open Letter to the Community: To So-Called Gangs and/or Trouble Makers at Stateville Prison and the Relationship of this Prison to the Community," (ABLE memorandum, 1973, Mimeographed).

48. Inmate interview, May 6, 1973, conducted by an assistant to an ABLE attorney.

49. "Open Letter," (1973), 4.

50. SILIC, *Joliet Riot,* 26.

51. Ibid., 3, 27.

52. Ibid., 30.

53. Department of Corrections, State of Illinois, *1970 Annual Report, Department of Corrections* (Springfield: Illinois Department of Corrections, 1971), 50.

54. SILIC, *Joliet Riot,* 19.

55. Jacobs, *Stateville,* 86–87.

56. Department of Corrections, *1973–1974 Annual Report,* 1.

57. SILIC, *Joliet Riot,* 17.

58. Author's interview with John Twomey; also "Stateville Prison Warden Quits," *Chicago Tribune,* 21 July 1973.

59. "Major Prison Overhaul Pledged," *Chicago Tribune,* 20 August 1973.

60. "Ex-Joliet Prison Warden Explains Resignation," *Chicago Tribune,* 28 March 1974.

61. SILIC, *Joliet Riot,* 17.

62. Ibid., 19.

63. Ibid., 20.

64. Ibid., 12.

65. Ibid., 9, 24.

66. "Joliet Guard Tells Terror of Kill Order," *Chicago Tribune,* 24 April 24 1975; "Joliet Prison Riot Quelled; Inmate Slain," *Chicago Sun Times,* 23 April 1975.

67. The $5,000 figure was the Department of Correction's estimate. One eyewitness was convinced that the damage was much greater. We have no independent evidence on this.

68. "Hostage Freed as Cops Quell Joliet Prison Riot," *Chicago Tribune,* 25 April 1975.

69. "Sielaff: Cook Prisoners Will Not Transfer to State," *Joliet Herald-News,* 27 April 1975; "Gangs Tested Us at Joliet and They Lost, Sielaff Says," *Chicago Tribune,* 24 April 1975.

70. U.S. Department of Justice, Office of Legal Policy, Federal Justice Research Program, *Prison Gangs: Their Extent, Nature and Impact on Prisons* (Washington, D.C.: U.S. Department of Justice, 1985), 19.

71. "Gang's Religion Label Rejected," *Chicago Tribune,* 2 June 1986.

72. "Pontiac Warden Met with Gangs in Past," *Chicago Tribune,* 22 November 1987; "Inmates Suing Over Gangs Lose Case," *Chicago Tribune,* 8 March 1988.

73. "Fort, Rukn Followers Convicted of Conspiracy," *Chicago Tribune,* 25 November 1987.


# Chapter 5

1. W. Allen Spivey, "Problems and Paradoxes in Economic and Social Policies of Modern Welfare States," *The Annals of the American Academy of Political and Social Science,* 479 (1985):14–19; "The Average Guy Takes It on the Chin," *New York Times,* 13 July 1986, Business Sec., 1.

2. Clarence Lo, "Mobilizing the Tax Revolt: The Emergent Alliance Between Homeowners and Local Elites," in *Research in Social Movements, Conflicts and Change,* Vol. 6, ed., Richard E. Ratcliff (Greenwich, CT: JAI Press, 1984), 293–328.

3. Anthony Oberschall, "The Decline of the 1960's Social Movements," in *Research in Social Movements, Conflict and Change,* Vol. 1, ed. Louis Kriesberg (Greenwich, CT: JAI Press, 1977), 257–89.

4. Samuel P. Huntington, *American Politics: The Promise of Disharmony* (Cambridge: Harvard University Press, 1981).

5. Bureau of Justice Statistics, *Statistics—1984,* 649.

6. The Edna McConnell Clark Foundation, *Overcrowded Time: Why Prisons Are So Crowded and What Can Be Done.* (New York: The Edna McConnell Clark Foundation, 1982), 22.

7. Ibid., 5.

8. Reported in Peter Finn, "Judicial Response to Prison Crowding," *Judicature* 67, no. 7 (February 1984):320.

9. "Complex Enforcement: Unconstitutional Prison Conditions," *Harvard Law Review* 94 (1981):626–46; Stephen Gettinger, " 'Cruel and Unusual' Prisons," *Corrections Magazine,* 3, no. 4 (December 1977):3–10.

10. Alvin J. Bronstein, "Prisoners and Their Endangered Rights," *Prison Journal,* 65, no. 1 (1985):3.

11. Keith Butler, "The Muslims Are No Longer an Unknown Quantity," *Corrections Magazine* 4, no. 2 (June 1978):55–63.


# Chapter 6

1. A note on sources. In recounting and interpreting the events, we rely on the transcripts of interviews conducted by the Attorney General's Office in the course of its investigation, and on its report (though we differ with some of the report's conclusions): Office of the Attorney General, State of New Mexico (hereafter cited as OAGSNM), *Report of the Attorney General on the February 2 and 3, Riot at the Penitentiary of New Mexico: Part I: The Penitentiary, the Riot, the Aftermath* (Santa Fe: Office of the Attorney General of the State of New Mexico, 1980); idem, *Report of the Attorney General on the February 2 and 3, Riot at the Penitentiary of New Mexico, Part II: The Last Ten Years, Conditions Leading to the Riot Conclusions and Recommendations* (Santa Fe: Office of the Attorney General of the State of New Mexico, 1980); on material collected by Santa Fe journalist Roger Morris for his book, *The Devil's Butcher Shop: The New Mexico Prison Uprising* (New York:

Franklin Watts, 1983), and the book itself; and on interviews we conducted in 1985 with inmates of PNM who had been there at the time of the riot. Other sources are noted below.

2. "Santa Fe Convicts End Revolt, Free Eight," *New York Times,* 9 December 1953; "Two Convicts Killed in Riot at Prison," *New York Times,* 16 June 1953.

3. The following five paragraphs are based on these sources: New Mexico Department of Corrections, *Annual Report, 1976* (Santa Fe: New Mexico Department of Corrections, 1977), 6; OAGSNM, *Part I;* idem, *Part II.*

4. Morris, *Butcher Shop,* 38–39.

5. Transcript of interviews conducted by the Attorney General's Office in preparation of OAGSNM, *Part I* and *Part II* (hereafter cited as OAGSNM interview). Interviews not noted were conducted by the authors in 1985.

6. One account suggests that Rodriguez possessed information concerning illegal actions by Anaya involving traffic in paroles while Anaya was an aide to Governor King. Morris, *Butcher Shop,* 153–59.

7. OAGSNM interview.

8. Ibid.

9. Ibid.

10. Ibid.

11. OAGSNM, *Part II,* 12, 23.

12. OAGSNM, *Part I,* 24.

13. Ibid.,12, 23.

14. OAGSNM interview.

15. Ibid.

16. Ibid.

17. Morris, *Butcher Shop,* 47.

18. *Albuquerque Journal,* 3 February 1985.

19. *Albuquerque Journal,* September 24, 1980, quoted in Morris, *Butcher Shop,* p. 111.

20. W. G. Stone, *The Hate Factory* (Agoura, CA: Paisan, 1982), 90.

21. New Mexico Department of Corrections, *Annual Report, 1979* (Santa Fe: New Mexico Department of Corrections, 1980).

22. Morris, *Butcher Shop,* 46.

23. OAGSNM, *Part II,* 31.

24. Ibid., 22.

25. Ibid., 8.

26. Morris, *Butcher Shop,* 14.

27. Ibid., 22.

28. Interview by the New Mexico State Police.

29. Ibid.

30. Confidential inmate essay; also OAGSNM *Part I,* 41.

31. Interview by New Mexico State Police.

32. Morris, *Butcher Shop,* 100; Michael S. Serrill and Peter Katel, "New Mexico: The Anatomy of a Riot," *Corrections Magazine* (April 1980):12.

33. Confidential inmate essay.

34. Morris, *Butcher Shop,* 100.

35. Confidential inmate essay.

36. OAGSNM interview.

37. Personal communication, confidential source.

38. Interview by the New Mexico State Police.

39. Stone, *Hate Factory,* 194.

40. *New Mexican,* February 3, 1985.

41. OAGSNM, *Part I,* 34.

42. Ibid.,33.

43. Morris, *Butcher Shop.* 166.

44. OAGSNM *Part I* 36,47,48; Morris, *Butcher Shop,* 81, 82, 136, 138, 167, 169, 173.

45. Morris, *Butcher Shop,* 75.

46. Interviews by New Mexico State Police; Morris, *Butcher Shop,* 78.

47. Confidential inmate essay.

48. Morris, *Butcher Shop,* 96; OAGSNM, *Part I,* 38.

49. Interview by New Mexico State Police.

50. OAGSNM, *Part I,* 38.

51. Interviews by New Mexico State Police and authors.

52. OAGSNM *Part I,* 49; Morris, *Butcher Shop,* 169–70.

53. Morris, *Butcher Shop,* 171; OAGSNM, *Part I,* 50.

54. OAGSNM, *Part I,* 35–50.

55. Of course, the riot was not the only force for change. Under a consent decree signed in July 1980, the U.S. district judge appointed a "special master" to oversee the changes specified in the decree.

56. *Albuquerque Journal,* February 3, 1985.

57. Ibid., February 3, 1985.

58. The 1985 figures are from George M. Camp and Camille G. Camp, *The Corrections Yearbook, 1986* (South Salem, NY: Criminal Justice Institute, 1986), 22.

Figures for the 1979 comparison were computed by us, based on data reported in the American Correctional Association's publication, *Juvenile and Adult Correctional Departments, Institutions, Agencies and Paroling Authorities* (College Park, MD: American Correctional Association, 1980, vii–xi.) Expenditure per inmate was derived by dividing the operational budget of each department of corrections by the number of inmates in institutions and community homes. This yields only a rough estimate, since most (although not all) corrections departments are responsible for the operation of probation, parole, and work release programs. We were unable to disaggregate these various expenditures.

59. Robert G. Hillman, "The Psychopathology of Being Held Hostage," *American Journal of Psychiatry* 138, no. 9 (September 1981):1193–97.

## Chapter 7

1. Joint Committee to Study the Prison Disturbances, Michigan State Legislature (hereafter cited as JCIPD—this is the Padden Commission), *Report of the Joint Committee to Investigate the Prison Disturbances* (Lansing: State of Michigan, 1981), 3.

2. One source of information for this chapter is the documentation used to produce the JCIPD report, which we were able to obtain. This in turn includes a collection of MCO material assembled by Fred Parks and submitted to the commission. Furthermore, we conducted an extensive series of interviews with inmates in all three prisons affected. Newspaper and other miscellaneous sources are noted below. All quotes from inmates are from our interviews, unless it is stated otherwise.

3. This and later discussions of population trends in the Michigan system are taken from: Michigan Department of Corrections, *Dimensions, 1975–1976* (Lansing: State of Michigan, 1977); idem, *Dimensions, 1976–1977* (Lansing: State of Michigan,

1978); idem, *Dimensions, 1977–1978* (Lansing: State of Michigan, 1979); idem, *Statistical Presentation, 1979* (Lansing: State of Michigan, 1980); idem, *Statistical Presentation, 1981* (Lansing: State of Michigan, 1982); idem, *Statistical Presentation, 1984* (Lansing: State of Michigan, 1985); "At crisis point" quote: "Prison Overcrowding at Crisis Point, with No Solution in Sight," *Detroit News,* 13 February 1977.

4. "Our Crowded Prisons," *Detroit News,* 21 April 1980.

5. "State Woos Locals in Prison Plan," *Detroit News,* 27 June 1979.

6 "Inside Jackson Prison: Crowding Puts Squeeze on Discipline," *Detroit News,* 17 June 1979;

7. "Old Insane Asylum Ranks as State's Rankest Prison," *Detroit News,* 17 June 1979;

8. "Milliken, Top Officials Tour Prison," *Detroit News,* 9 October 1980; *Detroit News,* 17 June 1979.

9. "Prison Crowding Getting Worse," *Detroit News,* 7 April 1978.

10. "The Candidates of '78: L. Brooks Patterson," *Detroit News,* 6 August 1978.

11. "Fake Nurse Aids Hospital Escape; Pontiac Cop Dies," *Detroit News,* 7 December 1976; "Daring Raid Cost Officer His Life," *Detroit News,* 8 December 1976.

12. "Police Killing Tied to Parole Reform," *Detroit News,* 8 December 1976.

13. "Slaying Revives Demand for Tightening of Parole," *Detroit News,* 10 December 1976.

14. Fred Girard, " 'Good Time' Parole Law—Why It Should Be Changed," *Detroit News,* 16 December 1976; Joel Smith, "Patterson Forming 'Army' To Fight for Parole Reform," *Detroit News,* 14 January 1977.

15. Don Ball, "Violence-Prone Cons to Find That Paroles Aren't So Easy to Get," *Detroit News,* 18 January, 1978. Michigan Department of Corrections, *Dimensions 1977–1978.*

16. "Judge To Force State To Ease Prison Crowding," *Detroit News,* 11 October 1980.

17. Ibid.; "Proposal E Makes Bid to Ease Inmate Overcrowding," *Detroit News,* 13 October 1980; "State Has Until Jan. 1 to Ease Prison Crowding," *Detroit News,* 28 October 1980; "Voters Reject Drink-at-19 Proposal; New-Prison Measure Also Fails," *Detroit News,* 5 November 1980.

18. "Come on Brooks. . . . Once is Enough!" *Ionia Hill Top News,* May 1981.

19. "Marquette State Prison: It's the Place All Inmates Fear the Most," *Detroit News,* 18 June 1979.

20. "Guards' Unions: The Search For Solidarity," *Corrections Magazine* 5, no. 3 (September 1979):25–35.

21. "Guards May Strike to Protest Abuse," *Detroit News,* 16 August 1979.

22. 'State Workers Pick Union," *Detroit News,* 23 June 1979.

23. "Guards May Strike to Protest Abuse," *Detroit News,* 16 August 1979; "Guards Drop Threat to Strike," *Detroit News,* 22 August 1979; "Unruly Inmates Face Curbs," *Detroit News,* 23 August 1979.

24. *Wolff v. McDonnell,* 418 U.S. 539 (1974); Penelope Clute, *The Legal Aspects of Prisons and Jails* (Springfield, IL: Charles Thomas, 1980), 113–14; Marjorie VanOchten, "Report on Major Misconduct Hearings Process" (Lansing, MI, 1981, Mimeographed).

25. VanOchten, "Report," 4.

26. Israel Barak-Glantz, "The Anatomy of Another Prison Riot," in *Prison Violence in America,* ed. Michael Braswell, Steven Dillingham, and Reid Montgomery, Jr. (Cincinnati: Anderson, 1983); Adrienne Eaton, John Knox, Frank Sudia, Mari-

anne Carduner, Roy Doppelt, Judy George, Ellen Leopold, and Charles Bright,"A History of Jackson Prison, 1920–1975" (Ann Arbor, MI: Residential College/Social Science Research Community, Winter 1979, Mimeographed), 133; Norman Sinclair, "Inside Jackson Prison: Crowding Puts Squeeze on Discipline," *Detroit News,* 17 June 1979; "Inquiry Sought on Inmate Abuse," *Detroit News,* 21 August 1979.

27. Charles Anderson, "Memo to Perry M. Johnson, Director of the Department of Corrections," June 7, 1980; VanOchten, "Report," 14.

28. "Prison Warden's Nightmare Comes True—Again," *Detroit Free Press,* 27 May 1981.

29. VanOchten, "Report," 10, 16.

30. Inmate interview summarized in Norma Keefer, "Memo to Rep. Jeffrey D. Padden," June 19, 1981.

31. VanOchten, "Report," 13, 16

32. Ibid., 12, 19; Fred Parks, "Michigan Corrections Organization Report on Disturbances in the Michigan Corrections System (Lansing, MI, June 5, 1981, Mimeographed).

33. Parks, "Report."

34. Testimony of Leonard Esquina, Ombudsman, before the Legislative Council, June 8, 1981.

35. *Instead of Prisons: A Newsletter of the Michigan Coalition for Prison Alternatives* (Published by the American Friends Service Committee, June 1981), 3.

36. JCIPD, *Report,* 27.

37. "Memo to MCO Vice-President Mittney," December 11, 1980.

38. Barry Mintzes, "Memo to All Shift Commanders," March 2, 1981; Fred Parks, "Memo to MCO Chapters," May 21, 1981.

39. *Jackson Citizen Patriot,* 11 March, 1981; Leaflet, Attachment 6 to Fred Parks, MCO Report.

40. Letters: Fred Parks to Perry Johnson, April 22, 1981, and Perry Johnson to Fred Parks, May 6, 1981; Attachments #9 and #10 to Fred Parks, MCO Report.

41. Scott's Memo: "Memo to All Concerned," as Attachment #11 to Fred Parks, MCO Report; DOC Statistics: Robert Brown, "Memo to Perry Johnson," May 27, 1981; Perry Johnson, "Memo to William Kime," June 4, 1981.

42. Fred Parks, "Letter to Jeffrey D. Padden, Chairman, Joint Legislative Committee on Corrections," June 22, 1981; reprinted in the Appendix to JCIPD.

43. Staffing had improved: William Kime, "Memo to John Kerekes," July 20, 1981. Resolution: "Resolution on Understaffing," attached to Fred Parks, "Memo to MCO Chapters," May 21, 1981.

44. Fred Parks, "Memo to MCO Chapters," May 21, 1981.

45. On Fryt's actions on May 20 to May 22, we have the "Brief of the Union," "Award and Opinion of Arbitrator," and "Post-Arbitration Brief" from Fryt's unsuccessful appeal of his dismissal before the American Arbitration Association, Case #54 39 1286 81. Two guard sources: Jeffrey D. Padden, "Preliminary Report of the Joint Committee to Investigate the Prison Disturbances," July 7, 1981 (Published in Appendix to JCIPD), 1.

46. This account is pieced together from stories in the *Detroit News* and *Detroit Free Press;* a memo from Leonard Esquina, Corrections Ombudsman, to the Legislative Council, dated June 8, 1981; copies of incident reports by guards on the scene furnished to the Padden Commission; and testimony in the Fryt arbitration.

47. See note 45.

48. The takeover: this account, and the subsequent account of the riot events at SPSM, is assembled from the arbitration material at note 45; from newspaper ac-

counts; from the MCO Report; and from "Friday, May 22. Uprising at SPSM," an unsigned chronology of events prepared by a staff member of the DOC for the use of the Padden Commission.

49. "Guards Gave Rioters Keys, Lie Tests Show," *Detroit News*, 14 June 1981; "Uprising Leaves Chief of Prison Troubled," *Detroit Free Press*, 23 June, 1981.

50 Lombardo, *Guards Imprisoned: Correctional Officers at Work*, (New York: Elsevier North Holland, 1981), 165–68.

51. "Michigan Prison Riots: Why Did They Happen?," *Instead of Prisons* June 1981.

52. Elton Scott, "Factual Summary," 1981.

53. Mintzes' talk: Verbatim transcript supplied to JCIPD.

54. MCO claim: Parks, MCO Report, 7–8. DOC official: Robert Brown, "Memo to Perry Johnson," May 27, 1981, 2.

55. William Hart, "In Michigan, Officers Rebel, Then Inmates Riot," *Corrections Magazine* 7, no. 4 (August 1981), 52–57, 54.

56. "Jackson Problem: 'It's Just Too Big,' " *Detroit News*, 27 May 1981.

57. "2 Inmates Fear for Their Lives," *Detroit News*, 25 May 1981.

58. "How a Twin Rebellion Lashed Jackson Prison," *Detroit Free Press*, 31 May 1981.

59. "1000 Riot Again at Jackson Prison," *Detroit Free Press*, 27 May 1981.

60. Our account of the May 26 Northside riot relies on authors' interviews, newspaper accounts, and "Northside—May 25 [*sic*], 1981," a mimeographed chronology prepared for JCIPD by DOC staff.

61. Population figures: Michigan Department of Corrections, *1982 Statistical Presentation*.

62. The fall of aggregate inmate industrial earnings in the preceding two years is documented in Michigan Department of Corrections, *1981 Statistical Presentation*.

63. "100 Police Storm Inmate-Held Ionia," *Detroit Free Press*, 23 May 1981. The following events are described in Dale Foltz, "Memo to Robert Brown, Jr.," May 25,1981, and in "Michigan Reformatory," an unsigned summary prepared by DOC staff for use of the JCIPD.

64. Time sequence: "Michigan Reformatory."

65. Henry quote: Paul B. Henry, "Letter to Hon. William G. Milliken," May 26, 1981.

66. Mary Kay Scullion, "Memo to Representative Jeffrey D. Padden and Joint Committee Members," June 30, 1981.

67. Ibid.

68. William Hart, "In Michigan, Officers Rebel, Then Inmates Riot." Activities of the forces of the administration after this point in the termination of the riot are covered by Lt. Bruce Forstrom, "Memo to Deputy's Office," June 1, 1981.

69. Press Release, June 15, 1981.

70. "Prisoners Locked in Cells," *Detroit News*, 28 May 1981.

71. "Marquette Riot Planned, Officials Say," *Detroit Free Press*, 29 May 1981; cf. Scullion, "Memo to Padden," June 30, 1981.

72. "Poll Blames Riots on Crowding," *Detroit Free Press*, 1 June 1981.

## Chapter 8

1. Note on sources. Ten days after the riot's end, the state senate announced the formation of a five-member committee to investigate the riot; but the inquiry never got off the ground. "Committee Formed to Probe Penitentiary Riot," *Charleston Gazette*,

14 January 1986. No other investigative or scholarly study was conducted. To gather the necessary information, we interviewed inmates, guards, all four of the negotiators for the administration, the penitentiary's warden and deputy wardens, an ex-warden, several state legislators and their staff, the court-appointed special master, journalists who had covered the Penitentiary or state politics, the superintendent of the state police, the governor's press secretary, and the governor. These interviews are the primary source for this chapter. Other sources are noted below.

2. The following description of West Virginia's economy is based on these sources: John Alexander Williams, *West Virginia: A Bicentennial History* (New York: W.W. Norton, 1976); "Acid Rain Reality Dampens Glow of Illinois Coal," *Chicago Tribune,* 16 March 1987; Bureau of Census, *Statistical Abstract Supplement: State and Metropolitan Area Data Book, 1986.* (Washington D.C.: Government Printing Office), 29, 30; "Moore Stresses West Virginia's Troubles as He Resumes Post," *New York Times,* 15 January 1985; "West Virginia's 'Almost Heaven' Becomes a Nightmare," *Washington Post,* 16 May 1983; "West Virginia's Latest Attempts to Mine New Industry Are Hurt by Its Poor Image," *Wall Street Journal,* 29 December 1982.

3. "West Virginia School Funding Is Declared Unconstitutional," *Washington Post,* 15 May 1982; Helen M. Hazi, "Co-Rechting West Virginia's Schools," *Educational Leadership: Journal of the Association for Supervision and Curriculum Development,* 42, no. 6. (March 1985):75–78; Otis K. Rice, *West Virginia, A History* (Lexington: University Press of Kentucky, 1985), 252, 286;

4. "Arthur Recht: Circuit Judge and Author of the Controversial Lincoln County School Decision Is the Sunday Gazette-Mail's West Virginian of the Year," *Charleston Sunday Gazette-Mail,* 2 January 1983.

5. William P. Cheshire, "West Virginia's Rocky Road," *Policy Review* 27 (Winter 1984):65; "Legislature To Focus on Flood First, Leaders Say," *Charleston Sunday Gazette-Mail,* 2 February 1986.

6. An "index crime" is one of seven serious crimes on which statistics are kept by the FBI (murder, forcible rape, robbery, aggravated assault, burglary, larceny-theft, and motor vehicle theft).

7. Federal Bureau of Investigation, *Uniform Crime Reports for the United States, 1986* (Washington, D.C.: Government Printing Office, 1986), 44–51.

8. U.S. Department of Justice, Bureau of Justice Statistics, *Justice Expenditure and Employment, 1983* (Washington, D.C.: Government Printing Office), 6.

9. The FBI considers a crime "solved or cleared" when one or more people are arrested, charged with the crime, and turned over to the court.

10. These data were prepared for this chapter by Mr. J. Harper Wilson, of the Uniform Crime Reporting Program, Federal Bureau of Investigation. We thank him for his assistance.

11. Bureau of Census, *Abstract Supplement, 1986,* 27.

12. George Camp and Camille Camp, *Corrections Yearbook* (Pound Ridge, NY: Criminal Justice Institute, 1983), 27–28.

13. Justice Statistics, *Expenditure and Employment, 1983,* 6.

14. *Souvenir of the West Virginia Penitentiary,* compiled by Work and Hope, The Prison Magazine (Moundsville: West Virginia Penitentiary, n.d. [circa 1925]); "Marshall Memories: The Prison (1866–1929)," *Wheeling News Register,* 20 August 1980.

15. "Moundsville—It's a Mixed Bag," *Charleston Daily Mail,* 19 May 1978.

16. "Warden Describes Prison Conditions," *Wheeling News Register,* 23 February 1982.

17. "Inmates Learn How to Cope," *Pittsburg Post Gazette,* 31 January 1986.

18. "Picnic at Penitentiary," *Keyser News-Tribune,* 16 October 1974.

19. "No Better Neighbor on Jefferson Avenue: Across the Street from the Prison, Residents Say They Feel Safe," *Washington Post,* 4 January 1986.

20. "Question & Answer: Warden Bordenkircher on the W. Va. Penitentiary," *Wheeling Intelligencer,* 26 April 1981.

21. West Virginia Department of Corrections, *Cumulative Annual Report, Fiscal Years 1981–1984,* (Charleston, WV: State of West Virginia), Appendix.

22. Governor John D. Rockefeller, "Executive Order No. 3–79" (Executive Department, State of West Virginia, 20 November 1979), 2.

23. "Warden Feels 'A Little Bit Like MacArthur,' " *Wheeling Intelligencer* 28 January 1982.

24. "Corrupt, Incompetent Staff Prison Problem," *Wheeling Intelligencer,* 27 January 1982.

25. "Warden Outlines 'Simple' Hostages Policy," *Charleston Gazette,* 29 January 1980.

26. "New Pen Programs Ceased Due to a Lack of Funding," *Wheeling Intelligencer,* 1 July 1981.

27. "Legislators Tour 'Deplorable Pen,' " *Wheeling News Register,* 23 July 1981.

28. Ibid.

29. "Inmate Civil Suits Cost W. Va. $500,000 a Year," *Wheeling Intelligencer,* 24 October 1981.

30. *Crain v. Bordenkircher,* "Memorandum of Opinion, Finding of Fact, Conclusions of Law and Order," Civil Action No. 81-C-320 R, Circuit Court of Marshall County, West Virginia.

31. Ibid., 24, 52.

32. "Warden Describes Prison Conditions," *Wheeling News Register* 23 February 1982.

33. *Cooper v. Gwinn,* W.Va., 298 S.E.2d 781.

34. *Newman v. Alabama,* 559 F. 2d at 291 (5th Cir. 1977). Quoted in "Complex Enforcement: Unconstitutional Prison Conditions," *Harvard Law Review,* 94 (1981):644.

35. *Cooper v. Gwinn,* W.Va., 298 S.E.2d 781, 790.

36. Ibid., 790.

37. "Senate Education Chief To Fight Recht Decision," *Charleston Daily Mail,* 11 January 1985.

38. "Economic Weight of Recht's Prison Decision Cited," *Charleston Gazette,* 22 June 1983.

39. "Riot Won't Improve Prison," *Wheeling Intelligencer,* 4 January 1986.

40. Donald Poffenberger, "Quarterly Report: October 9, 1984, to January 9, 1985," filed in the Circuit Court of Marshall County, West Virginia, in the case of *Crain v. Bordenkircher.*

41. "Report Says Corrections Makes Progress," *Charleston Daily Mail,* 31 January 1985.

42. Donald Poffenberger, "Quarterly Report: July 9, 1985, to October 9, 1985," filed in the Circuit Court of Marshall County, West Virginia, in the case of *Crain v. Bordenkircher,* 1

43. "West Virginia Prisons Not Complying with Standards, New Chief Says," *Charleston Daily Mail,* 8 July 1985.

44. Quoted in Poffenberger, "Report: July 9, 1985, to October 9, 1985," 8–9.

45. *Crain,* "Memorandum," 20.

46. "Testimony Concludes in Inmates' Hearings," *Wheeling News Register,* 28 February 1982.

47. In using Lehman's name, we are not following our practice of maintaining the anonymity of our interviewees. We feel at liberty to mention Lehman's name, and later Alvin Gregory's, because their names and pictures appeared in newspapers throughout the country. Also, Danny Lehman was killed several weeks after we interviewed him.

48. "Inmates Learn How to Cope," *Pittsburg Post Gazette,* 31 January 1986.

49. "Inmates Level Abuse Charges After Transfer," *Charleston Gazette,* 20 July 1984.

50. "Deputy Warden Appointed to Replace Bordenkircher," *Charleston Daily Mail,* 14 September 1983.

51. Our interviews were conducted, and this text was written, while inmates were facing felony charges for the riot. A full set of details concerning the initial plot were not available to us, nor could we have reported them had they been.

52. Interview by West Virginia State Police and authors' interview.

53. "Guards Recount Narrow Escape from Violence," *Charleston Daily Mail,* 4 January 1986.

54. "Inmates Hold 13 Hostages at State Prison," *Charleston Gazette,* 2 January 1986.

55. "Five Hostages Free Unharmed as 'Spontaneous' Riot Ends," *Charleston Gazette,* 22 March 1973.

56. " 'They Treated Us Very Well,' Hostages Say," *Charleston Gazette,* 4 January 1986.

57. "Riot at Prison Ends in a Relief and a Dispute," *New York Times,* 5 January 1986.

58. West Virginia State Police interview.

59. "No Better Neighbor on Jefferson Avenue," *Washington Post,* 4 January 1986.

60. "News Coverage of Prison Crisis Could Have Gone Smoother," *Charleston Gazette,* 5 January 1986.

61. West Virginia State Police interview.

62. "Inmates Free Six Hostages," *Wheeling Intelligencer,* 3 January 1986.

63. We thank Mark Erste of WEIF radio station (Moundsville) for the tape of the press conference.

64. "Inmates Free 6 Hostages," *Wheeling Intelligencer,* 3 January 1986.

65. "Governor Meets Rebellious Inmates," *Charleston Gazette,* 4 January 1986; "Standoff; Hostages Freed," *Wheeling News Register,* 3 January 1986.

66. "Moore-Inmate Talks Have Easy Air," *Wheeling Intelligencer,* 4 January 1986.

67. Ibid., "Taking of Few Key Guards Led to Takeover," *Charleston Daily Mail,* 4 January 1986.

68. "Transcript from a Portion of a News Briefing by Governor Moore in Moundsville, Friday, January 3, 1986" (Charleston: Governor's Office, Mimeographed). Moore's public statements suggest that he credited the inmates' allegation that the state police had treated inmates brutally during the Joint Operation. In our private conversation with the governor, however, he stated that he had no direct knowledge of the Joint Operation and could neither confirm nor deny the inmates' allegations.

69. "Moore Says 'No Retaliation' Pledge Not Same as Amnesty," *Charleston Daily Mail,* 3 January 1986.

70. "Damage to Penitentiary Estimated at $600,000," *Charleston Gazette,* 9 January 1986.

71. *Crain v. Bordenkircher,* W.Va., 342 S.E.2d 422.

72. "Legislators Aware of Powder Keg Conditions at Prison," *Charleston Gazette,* 3 January 1986.

73. "Prison Security an Issue," *Charleston Gazette,* 4 January 1987.

74. Donald Poffenberger, "Quarterly Report: January 9, 1987, to April 9, 1987," filed in the Circuit Court of Marshall County, West Virginia, in the case of *Crain v. Bordenkircher,* 1.

75. "Eight-Six Convicts Are Moved," *Charleston Gazette,* 20 February 1986.

76. Poffenberger, "Report, January 9, 1986, to April 9, 1986," filed in the Circuit Court of Marshall County, West Virginia, in the case of *Crain v. Bordenkircher,* 15.

77. "Beatings, Restrictions at Prison Described," *Charleston Gazette,* 7 March 1986.

78. "Tension Continues in Penitentiary's North Hall Area," *Charleston Daily Mail,* 28 June 1986.

79. "Union Sponsors Protest at State Penitentiary," *Charleston Gazette,* 2 February 1986; "Guard Union's Petitions Urge Prison Problems to Be Corrected," *Charleston Gazette,* 15 March 1986.

80. *Smith v. Dodrill,* "Petition for Writ of Mandamus," Pending before Circuit Court of Kanawha County, West Virginia, 18 June 1986. Civil Action No. 86–325.

81. This issue is before the court as we write. We thank Mr. Vincent King, attorney for the correctional officers, for providing us with a full set of documents related to the case.

82. "Frustrations, Tension Fill Prison Atmosphere," *Charleston Daily Mail,* 2 January 1987.

# Chapter 9

1. The descriptions of events in the previous chapters have been factual accounts. The two authors have different political views, but these differences did not lead us to disagree as to how many people were in a group, what they did, when they did it, or other, similar findings of fact. This means that we never felt forced to choose between a Useem version and a Kimball version of the events of a riot, or to develop some sort of hybrid version.

But our political differences are relevant to the interpretation of these events. If it had been entirely up to Kimball, a Marxist, a different set of conclusions would have been drawn. They would have shown how imprisonment and prison riots are pieces of a global economic and political pattern, a design, which Marxist theory makes visible and comprehensible. Further, the writing method would have differed. Kimball prefers the term "rebellions" rather than "riots," as the former term implies political struggle. He concedes that there are plenty of violent episodes with scant political content; but he is ready to find political content in just about every anti-administration action by inmates. He would capitalize the word "Black" everywhere it is used for persons, and claims that a correct understanding of the "national question" necessitates this.

Finally, Kimball would have written from a partisan point of view. He believes that the conflict between prisoners and the state is inevitable, and he is on the side of the prisoners. He believes this to be part and parcel of the solidarity Marxists feel for the poor, the downtrodden, and the exploited, and the hostility they must feel for the state as an institution of capitalist domination. The reader may wonder whether Kimball has never heard that criminals prey on the poor. Kimball has. He regrets that space is lacking here to flesh out his position, which, in brief, is that poor and working people ought not to support the monopoly on violence of the capitalist state as a presumed sole alternative to being preyed on by killers and thieves, but should seek paths to independent action and power.

Useem doubts that the global patterns that Marxists claim to identify really exist. Accordingly, he is happier to let this work stand as it currently does.

2. Ernest van den Haag, *Punishing Criminals: Concerning a Very Old and Painful Question* (New York: Basic Books, 1975); Jerome Skolnick, review of *Punishing Criminals,* by Van den Haag, *Contemporary Sociology* 5, no. 6 (1976):747.

3. David Matza, *Delinquency and Drift* (New York: Wiley, 1964).

4. James P. Needham, *Neutralization of Prison Hostage Situations,* Criminal Justice Monograph, Institute of Contemporary Corrections and the Behavioral Sciences, vol. 8, no. 1 (Huntsville, TX: Sam Houston State University, 1977), 7.

## Chapter 10

1. Peter L. Berger, *Invitation to Sociology* (New York: Anchor Books, 1963), 130. Similarly, Aleksander Solzhenitsyn writes about the Russian Revolution:

The defeat of Tsarism came not when Kolchak was routed, not when the February Revolution was raging, but much earlier! It was overthrown without hope of restoration once Russian literature adopted the convention that anyone who depicted a gendarme or policeman with any hint of sympathy was a lickspittle and a reactionary thug; when you didn't have to shake a policeman's hand, cultivate his acquaintance, nod to him in the street, but merely brush sleeves with him in passing to consider yourself disgraced.

*The Gulag Archipelago, 1918–1956* (New York: Harper and Row, 1985 [1973]), 352.

2. "Interoffice Memorandum: Chronology of the Disturbance in Cellhouse 319, January 6, 1986" (Iowa State Penitentiary, n.d., Mimeographed). "A Review of the Kirkland Correctional Institution Disturbance of April 1, 1986. A Report for the Board of Corrections and the Commissioner of the South Carolina Department of Corrections" (South Carolina Department of Corrections, May 20, 1986, Mimeographed).

3. See Thomas Schelling *The Strategy of Conflict* (Cambridge: Harvard University Press, 1960), 21–52; also Kenneth Boulding, *Conflict and Defense: A General Theory* (New York: Harper and Row, 1962), 90.

4. Frances Fox Piven and Richard A. Cloward, *Poor People's Movements: Why They Succeed, How They Fail* (New York: Pantheon, 1977).

5. See, for example, Hannah Arendt, *On Violence* (New York: Harcourt, Brace and World, 1969); Lewis Coser, *Continuities in the Study of Social Conflict* (New York: Free Press, 1967), 213–22; cf. Franz Fanon, *The Wretched of the Earth* (New York: Grove Press, 1965).

6. Frances Fox Piven and Richard A. Cloward, *Regulating the Poor: The Functions of Public Welfare* (New York: Pantheon, 1977). Efforts to test Piven's and Cloward's thesis include Sanford Schram and J. Patrick Turbett, "Civil Disorder and the Welfare Explosion: A Two-Step Process," *American Sociological Review,* 48, no. 3 (June 1983):408–14; and a half-dozen articles by Alexander Hicks and Duane Swank. For the latter, see, for example, Alexander Hicks and Duane Swank, "Civil Disorder, Relief Mobilization, and AFDC Caseloads: A Reexamination of the Piven and Cloward Thesis," *American Journal of Political Science* 27, no. 4 (November 1983):695–716; Alexander Hicks and Duane Swank, "On the Political Economy of Welfare Expansion: A Comparative Analysis of 18 Advanced Capi-

talists Democracies, 1960–1971," *Comparative Political Studies,* 17, no. 1 (April 1984):81–119.

7. For a thoughtful review, see Jack Bloom, *Class, Race, and the Civil Rights Movement* (Bloomington: Indiana University Press, 1987), 204–13.

8. William J. Wilson *The Truly Disadvantaged: The Inner City, the Underclass, and Public Policy* (Chicago: University of Chicago Press, 1987); Christopher Jencks, "Deadly Neighborhoods," *The New Republic* (June 13, 1988):23–32.

9. William A. Gamson, *The Strategy of Social Protest* (Homewood, IL: Dorsey), 139.

10. Ronald Aminzade, "Revolution and Collective Political Violence: The Case of the Working Class of Marseille, France 1830–1871," Working Paper No. 86 (Center for Research on Social Organization, University of Michigan, October, 1973), quoted in Gamson, *Strategy,* 139.

11. Hicks and Swank, "Civil Disorder," 708.

12. Lester C. Thurow, *The Zero-Sum Solution: Building a World-Class American Economy* (New York: Simon and Schuster, 1985), 234–36.

13. Edna McConnell Clark Foundation, *Time to Build? The Realities of Prison Construction* (New York: Edna McConnell Clark Foundation, 1984), 36.

14. *Jones v. North Carolina Prisoners' Labor Union, Inc.,* 433 US 119 (1977). Also discussed by Penelope Clute, *The Legal Aspects of Prisons and Jails* (Springfield, IL: Thomas, 1980), 35–38.

15. George M. Camp, "Managing the Sources of Disruption" (Paper delivered at the Southern Conference on Corrections, Tallahassee, Florida, February 28, 1986), and table distributed by Camp at presentation, "Homicide Victims at Walla Walla."

16. Gabrielle Tyrnauer, "What Went Wrong at Walla Walla?" *Corrections Magazine* (June 1981):37–41; Charles Stastny and Gabrielle Tyrnauer, *Who Rules the Joint? The Changing Political Culture of Maximum-Security Prisons in America* (Lexington, MA: D.C. Heath and Company, 1982), 151–88; Ethan Hoffman and John McCoy, *Concrete Mama: Prison Profiles from Walla Walla* (Columbia: University of Missouri Press, 1981), 6.

17. The case for (some measure of) "inmate self-government" is made by Statsny and Tyrnauer, *Who Rules;* David Fogel, *." . . We Are Living Proof:" The Justice Model for Corrections* (Cincinatti: W.H. Anderson, 1979); and John Irwin, *Prisons in Turmoil.* (Boston: Little, Brown, 1980). A strong case against is made by John J. DiIulio, Jr., *Governing Prisons: A Comparative Study of Correctional Management* (New York: Free Press, 1987), 37–38.

18. Tyrnauer, "Walla Walla?," 40.

19. The best presentation of this view is by James Q. Wilson and Richard J. Hernstein, in *Crime and Human Nature* (New York: Simon and Schuster, 1985)

## Appendix A

1. More comprehensive reviews can be found in Gary T. Marx and James L. Wood, "Strands of Theory and Research in Collective Behavior," in *Annual Review of Sociology,* ed. Alex Inkeles and James Short (Palo Alto: Annual Reviews, 1975); Anthony Oberschall, "Theories of Social Conflict," in *Annual Review of Sociology,* ed. Ralph Turner, James Coleman, and Renee C. Fox (Palo Alto: Annual Reviews, 1978); J. Craig Jenkins, "Sociopolitical Movements," in *Handbook of Political Science,* ed. Samuel Long (New York: Plenum, 1981).

2. Citations to the sociological literature include Ted Robert Gurr, *Why Men*

*Rebel* (Princeton: Princeton University Press, 1970); Anthony Oberschall, *Social Conflict and Social Movements* (Englewood Cliffs, NJ: Prentice-Hall, 1973); Maurice Pinard, *The Rise of a Third Party: A Study in Crisis Politics* (Englewood Cliffs, NJ: Prentice-Hall, 1971), Ralph Turner and Lewis Killian, *Collective Behavior,* 3rd ed. (Englewood Cliffs, NJ: Prentice-Hall, 1987), esp. ch. 14.

3. Emile Durkheim, *Suicide* (New York: Free Press, 1966); Talcott Parsons, *Structure and Process in Modern Society* (New York: Free Press, 1960); Neil Smelser, *Theory of Collective Behavior* (New York: Free Press, 1962).

4. This theme runs from Durkheim to Smelser. Smelser concludes his study of collective behavior with the observation that his framework, when "relaxed" in appropriate ways, can explain suicide. This is because "suicide . . . arises from some of the same kinds of social malintegration that underlie many collective outbursts." *Collective Behavior,* 387.

5. Charles Tilly, *As Sociology Meets History* (New York: Academic Press, 1981), 107.

6. See, e.g., Michael Schwartz, *Radical Protest and Social Structure* (New York: Academic Press, 1976), 135.

7. Mark Traugott, "Durkheim and Social Movements," *European Journal of Sociology* 25 (1984):320. Similarly, Craig Jenkins refers to the breakdown model as an "erroneous line of argument, one at odds with readily ample evidence" (review of Frances Piven and Richard Cloward, *Poor People's Movements: Why the Succeed, How They Fail,* in *Contemporary Sociology,* 8, no. 2 [1979]:224). If the evidence is readily available, we don't see it. For example, we know of only two efforts to test the proposition that crime and collective action vary together over time. The Tillys found that crime varied independently of collective violence in France, Italy, and Germany from 1830 to 1930. Ted Gurr found the opposite in his study of London, Stockholm, New South Wales, and Calcutta from 1840 to 1960. Charles Tilly, Louis Tilly, and Richard Tilly, *The Rebellious Century: 1830–1930* (Cambridge: Harvard University Press, 1975); Ted Robert Gurr, *Rogues, Rebels, and Reformers: A Political History of Urban Crime and Conflict* (Beverly Hills: Sage, 1976).

8. James C. Davies, "Toward A Theory of Revolution," *American Sociological Review* 27 (February 1962):5–19.

9. Ted Robert Gurr, *Why Men Rebel;* Ted Gurr, "A Causal Model of Civil Strife: A Comparative Analysis Using New Indicies," *American Political Science Review* 27 (1968):1104–24.

10. Nathan S. Caplan and Jeffrey M. Paige, "A Study of Ghetto Rioters," *Scientific American* 219 (1968):15–20; Bert Useem, "Solidarity Model, Breakdown Model, and the Boston Anti-Busing Movement," *American Sociological Review* 45 (June 1980):357–69; Edward J. Walsh, "Resource Mobilization and Citizen Protest in Communities Around Three Mile Island," *Social Problems* 26 (1981):1–21.

11. See, e.g., J. Craig Jenkins, "Resource Mobilization Theory and the Study of Social Movements," in *Annual Review of Sociology,* ed. Alex Inkeles and James Short (Palo Alto: Annual Reviews, 1983), 530.

12. Mancur Olson, *The Logic of Collective Action* (Cambridge: Harvard University Press, 1971). An ancestral work in political science is Anthony Downs, *An Economic Theory of Democracy* (New York: Harper and Brothers, 1957).

13. Frances Fox Piven and Richard A. Cloward, *Poor People's Movements: Why They Succeed, How They Fail* (New York: Pantheon, 1977).

14. Ibid., 11, n. 9.

# Index